Lecture Notes in Computer Science   16365

Founding Editors

Gerhard Goos
Juris Hartmanis

The series Lecture Notes in Computer Science (LNCS), including its subseries Lecture Notes in Artificial Intelligence (LNAI) and Lecture Notes in Bioinformatics (LNBI), has established itself as a medium for the publication of new developments in computer science and information technology research, teaching, and education.

LNCS enjoys close cooperation with the computer science R & D community, the series counts many renowned academics among its volume editors and paper authors, and collaborates with prestigious societies. Its mission is to serve this international community by providing an invaluable service, mainly focused on the publication of conference and workshop proceedings and postproceedings. LNCS commenced publication in 1973.

Barbara Fila · Hugo Jonker · Saša Radomirovič
Editors

Juggling Formal Methods and Security

Essays Dedicated to Sjouke Mauw
on the Occasion of His 65th Birthday

 Springer

Editors
Barbara Fila [iD]
IRISA, INSA Rennes
Rennes, France

Hugo Jonker [iD]
Open University of the Netherlands
Heerlen, Limburg, The Netherlands

Saša Radomirovič [iD]
Heriot-Watt University
Edinburgh, UK

ISSN 0302-9743   ISSN 1611-3349 (electronic)
Lecture Notes in Computer Science
ISBN 978-3-032-20683-1   ISBN 978-3-032-20684-8 (eBook)
https://doi.org/10.1007/978-3-032-20684-8

Preface

This Festschrift is dedicated to Sjouke Mauw on the occasion of his 65th birthday. Its title, *"Juggling Formal Methods and Security,"* reflects not only two of Sjouke's central academic pursuits, but also hints at his hobby and his playful nature.

Sjouke's academic career started with a focus on formal specifications which expanded to encompass the field of digital security. His œuvre is marked by a rigorously formal approach to problems. This allowed him not only to reveal technical subtleties that even experts often overlooked, but also to anticipate important conceptual shifts.

A powerful example is his inaugural lecture *"A window of vulnerability: the virtual world eyeing the physical world"*, given at the University of Luxembourg on the 29th of April, 2008. At the time, the prevalent attitude to security was to consider the impact of security breaches on the digital realm. Sjouke discussed how security breaches in the virtual world could also impact the real world. Back then, this was an interesting and novel viewpoint. Today, we regularly witness how virtual-world weaknesses can lead to tangible real-world problems: failed software updates grounding thousands of flights world-wide, coordinated troll campaigns attempting to influence elections, or state-sponsored actors leveraging AI-generated disinformation to destabilize the world's geopolitical order.

In addition to his research, Sjouke has always been deeply committed to teaching and mentoring. He has consistently taken great care in nurturing and challenging students and mentees to grow beyond their expectations.

We invited Sjouke's current and former colleagues, collaborators and group members to contribute to this volume. Each submission was carefully reviewed by at least two independent referees, resulting in thirteen scientific accepted papers. A more personal perspective on Sjouke's academic career by two of his former mentees complements the book.

We are grateful to the Faculty of Science of the University of Luxembourg for their support in organizing *The Symposium on Formal Methods for Security, Privacy, and Trust*, where contributions from this volume were presented. We thank the IRISA laboratory in Rennes, France for its financial contribution, and acknowledge the EasyChair platform which greatly helped us in this Festschrift preparation.

Sjouke has always managed to combine his academic pursuits with a positive attitude, not shying away from occasionally coauthoring a more playful paper. Yet even in these, Sjouke's formal background shines through, and such papers tend to make the reader smile, and then think. We hope the works contained in this volume will similarly make the reader both think and smile.

January 2026

Barbara Fila
Hugo Jonker
Saša Radomirovič

Organization

Program Committee

Jos Baeten	Centrum Wiskunde & Informatica, The Netherlands
Jan A. Bergstra	University of Amsterdam, The Netherlands
Michèle Feltz	Independent Researcher, Luxembourg
Barbara Fila	IRISA, INSA Rennes, France
Reynaldo Gil-Pons	NEAR One, Luxembourg
Jan Friso Groote	Eindhoven University of Technology, The Netherlands
Bart Jacobs	Radboud University, The Netherlands
Hugo Jonker	Open University of the Netherlands, The Netherlands
Bas Luttik	Eindhoven University of Technology, The Netherlands
Jan J. M. Martens	Leiden University, The Netherlands
Tim Muller	University of Nottingham, UK
Erik Poll	Radboud University, The Netherlands
Saša Radomirović	Heriot-Watt University, UK
Zach Smith	Independent Researcher, UK
Felix Stutz	University of Luxembourg, Luxembourg
Rolando Trujillo-Rasua	Universitat Rovira i Virgili, Spain
Michiel van Osch	Fontys University of Applied Sciences, The Netherlands
Tim Willemse	Eindhoven University of Technology, The Netherlands
Chenyi Zhang	University of Canterbury, New Zealand

Contents

Sjouke Mauw: Conqueror of Ambiguities, Inconsistencies, and Incompleteness

Jun Pang[1] and Saša Radomirović[2]([✉])

[1] University of Luxembourg, Esch-sur-Alzette, Luxembourg
`jun.pang@uni.lu`
[2] Heriot–Watt University, Edinburgh, UK
`sasa.radomirovic@hw.ac.uk`

1 Sjouke's Origins and Journey to Luxembourg

Sjouke Mauw [ˈʃaukɛ ˈmau] was born in Amsterdam, the Netherlands, in 1961. He studied Mathematics at the University of Amsterdam (UvA) specializing in Mathematical Logic, with minors in Computer Science and the Didactics of Mathematics Education, and obtained his Master's degree in 1985. He continued at UvA to write his doctoral dissertation "PSF – A Process Specification Formalism" under the enviable supervision of Jan Bergstra and Jos Baeten. Sjouke received his PhD degree in Computer Science in 1991.

Near the end of his doctoral studies, Sjouke became an assistant professor in the Programming Research Group at UvA. In 1992, he joined Eindhoven University of Technology (TU/e) as an assistant professor in the Formal Methods group and was promoted to associate professor in 1999. Beginning in 1997, Sjouke also held a secondment as senior researcher at the Centrum Wiskunde & Informatica (CWI) in Amsterdam, the national research institute for mathematics and computer science in the Netherlands.

Sjouke developed an interest in formal methods for information security in the early 2000s. By 2005, he was working and publishing exclusively in this domain. That year, he took a sabbatical, which included (1) a research visit to the Norwegian University of Science and Technology (NTNU) in Trondheim and (2) leaving a fresh postdoc very much impressed with his inimitable research style.

In 2007, Sjouke was appointed full professor in Security and Trust of Software Systems (SaToSS) at the University of Luxembourg. Starting with a PhD student who joined him from Eindhoven and the postdoc from Trondheim, his SaToSS research group grew to over a dozen members within its first three years. To date, the group has hosted more than 40 early-career researchers and has supported 20 PhD students through to the completion of their degrees.

2 Sjouke's Research

Sjouke's research journey began in the domain of process algebra, with a focus on algebraic techniques for software specification. During his PhD, he designed and

B. Fila et al. (Eds.): Sjouke Mauw Festschrift, LNCS 16365, pp. 1–7, 2026.
https://doi.org/10.1007/978-3-032-20684-8_1

co-developed the process specification formalism PSF with Gert Veltink [26]. In the introduction to his dissertation [29], Sjouke wrote: *"The main problem with informal specification techniques is that they allow ambiguities, inconsistencies and incompleteness, while [...] a formal approach enables formal verification."* Ever since, whatever system he came to, he saw problems due to ambiguities, inconsistencies or incompleteness, and he conquered them with a formal semantics and a formal verification. We highlight here three areas where Sjouke's work was particularly impactful: message sequence charts, security protocols, and threat modeling with attack trees.

2.1   Message Sequence Charts

Message Sequence Chart (MSC) is a graphical language widely used in systems engineering and protocol design to describe interactions between system components. Its first version, MSC'92, was standardized by the International Telecommunication Union (ITU) in 1993 as ITU-T Z.120 [20] and, *"according to popular belief, [had] largely been written in a Spanish pub in Geneva"* [37]. MSC'92 lacked a formal semantics.

After the release of MSC'92, Sjouke made significant contributions to the language by proposing key features, such as High-level Message Sequence Charts, and—of course—a formal semantics for MSC. These proposals were adopted and integrated into the MSC'96 standard. Sjouke's contributions to the MSC standard arose out of his prior work on the syntax and semantics of a related language *Interworking* [27,28] and the subsequent work with his PhD students André Engels and Michel Reniers, e.g., [16,31,32]. Sjouke has also made significant contributions to the development of the MSC standard as *associate rapporteur* for the ITU-T Z.120 standard committee.

A further notable contribution is the widely used MSC LaTeX package [6], initially developed by Sjouke and his PhD student Victor Bos, which has become a standard tool for specifying communication protocols.

2.2   Security Protocols

Following on from his work on communicating processes and message sequence charts, Sjouke became interested in the formal specification and verification of security protocols—a domain where ensuring correctness against powerful adversaries is notoriously challenging.

Sjouke and his PhD student Cas Cremers observed that while many tools and formalisms had been developed to verify security protocols, the tools lacked formal definitions of the protocol model and security properties, and the formalisms lacked tools with a formal semantics[1]. And thus began the development of their operational semantics for security protocols and associated verification

---

[1] An obvious candidate, the MSC semantics, is quickly seen to be insufficient for security protocols. We leave this as an exercise for the reader.

framework [9], which was implemented in the Scyther tool [11] and applied, for example, to analyze protocols in the IEEE-WiMAX standard [1].

At the University of Luxembourg, Sjouke's work on security protocols expanded into two prominent directions: electronic voting protocols [2–4,21] and RFID protocols [12,14,33–35]. In the area of electronic voting, he supervised two PhD theses on privacy and election verifiability [5,22], and exposed and fixed with his team critical flaws in deployed electronic voting systems [2–4].

In RFID security, some members of Sjouke's group identified security vulnerabilities that got themselves into trouble with the local transport authority, and others identified privacy vulnerabilities in the international e-passport standard [17]. The latter members' findings attracted media attention and parliamentary scrutiny [8] in Luxembourg. The former proposed a data carving technique that allowed them to reverse engineer whether and where a particular type of data is stored on an RFID tag [13]. Sjouke and his group have also made contributions to the definition and formal verification of privacy [12], secure ownership [14], and distance bounding properties [33–35].

Sjouke co-authored two textbooks on the formal verification of security protocols aimed at graduate students. *Operational Semantics and Verification of Security Protocols* [10] teaches a methodology of formal security protocol verification, while his more recent book, *Security Protocols and Threat Models* [36], focuses on the design and analysis of security protocols.

2.3 Attack Trees

Attack trees are a graphical modeling technique to represent how an attacker could compromise a system. Today, they are one of the most common techniques used in industry and academia to systematically guide the elicitation of and reason about security threats to complex systems. Sjouke played a pivotal role in transforming attack trees from a simple illustrative concept into a rigorous methodology for security risk analysis. Originally introduced by Bruce Schneier [38], attack trees lacked formal underpinnings until Sjouke's seminal 2005 paper [30], which provided a formalization of the language and established its use as a systematic approach to threat modeling and security risk assessment. This work had a profound impact on the international research community, inspiring numerous follow-up studies and applications.

At the University of Luxembourg, Sjouke has led the further development of attack trees into a well-established formal threat modeling methodology as (co-)principal investigator of several national and international research projects involving both academic and industrial partners. This work resulted in the development of attack–defense trees [25]—and his second most influential publication [24] after the attack trees paper [30]—as well as a suite of tools and methodologies that advanced attack tree-based analysis, e.g., [7,18,19,23]. His contributions have firmly positioned attack(–defense) trees as a cornerstone technique in security engineering and risk management.

3 Sjouke's PhD Students (TU/e and UL)

For those unfamiliar with Dutch law, we note that until 2017 only full professors had the right to be a *promotor*, i.e., the principal supervisor of a PhD candidate at a Dutch university with the right to confer the doctorate. Associate and assistant professors had the right to be *co-promotors* and carried out the daily supervision. With the legal fine-print out of the way, we can state that Sjouke has been the co-promotor of seven PhD students at TU/e and the supervisor of fifteen PhD students at the University of Luxembourg, hereafter listed with the year of their successful completion:

PhDs from TU/e:

- Vereijken, Jan Joris, 1997
- Reniers, Michel, 1999
- Engels, Andreas (André), 2001
- Bos, Victor, 2002
- Goga, Nicolae, 2004
- van Beek, Henricus (Harm), 2005
- Cremers, Cas, 2006

PhD from TU/e and University of Luxembourg:

- Jonker, Hugo, 2009

PhDs from the University of Luxembourg:

- van Deursen, Ton, 2011
- Dong, Naipeng, 2013
- Melissen, Matthijs, 2013
- Muller, Tim, 2013
- Schweitzer, Patrick, 2013
- Chen, Xihui, 2014
- Zhang, Yang, 2016
- Yuan, Qixia, 2017
- Toro Pozo, Jorge, 2019
- Smith, Zachary Daniel, 2020
- Pilgun, Aleksandr, 2020
- Yurkov, Semen, 2023
- Baloglu, Sevdenur, 2023
- Gil Pons, Reynaldo, 2024

We are convinced that all 22 of these talented individuals were fortunate to have Sjouke as their supervisor and mentor. And since Hugo is the only person to have been Sjouke's PhD student both in Eindhoven and in Luxembourg, we have chosen the following quote from his PhD thesis [22] as a representative testimonial:

"A special mention goes to Sjouke. He has supported me throughout my PhD career, has given me the room to explore, provided advice and feedback, often shared a cup of tea with me, and believed in me. I am lucky to have worked with him, and I look forward to doing so again."

4   Sjouke

We have highlighted some of Sjouke's many achievements and omitted all services to his universities, such as being Chair of the University of Luxembourg's Ethical Review Panel, Head of the Laboratory of Algorithmics, Cryptology and Security (LACS), and Vice-head as well as Head of the Department of Computer Science at the University of Luxembourg, all of which Sjouke has been, too. Yet none of these achievements and roles are the first things that come to mind when we think of Sjouke.

The qualities that immediately impressed the postdoc from Trondheim (and many other future team members) are Sjouke's enthusiasm for thinking and brainstorming at the white board and his very, very clever questions. Sjouke is also open to—even fond of—quirky puzzles. So the first paper that comes to mind when we think of a quintessential Sjouke paper, is not *Foundations of Attack Trees*, but rather *Why men (and octopuses) cannot juggle a four ball cascade* [15].

Looking back on the years spent in Sjouke's group, what stand out are his calm, smiling nature, his thoughtfulness, and his sense of responsibility for his group members. He gave us clear expectations, structure, inspiration, motivation, courage, self-confidence, . . .—whatever was needed at that moment to complete the current career step and launch into the next one. To quote from Patrick Schweitzer's PhD thesis [39]: *"His enthusiasm for and capability to inspire individuals to perform theoretical research continues to fascinate me."*

Disclosure of Interests. The authors declare that Sjouke is their friend.

References

1. Andova, S., Cremers, C., Gjøsteen, K., Mauw, S., Mjølsnes, S.F., Radomirovic, S.: A framework for compositional verification of security protocols. Inf. Comput. **206**(2–4), 425–459 (2008). https://doi.org/10.1016/J.IC.2007.07.002
2. Baloglu, S., Bursuc, S., Mauw, S., Pang, J.: Election verifiability revisited: automated security proofs and attacks on Helios and Belenios. In: Proceedings of the 34th IEEE Computer Security Foundations Symposium, pp. 1–15. IEEE Computer Society (2021)
3. Baloglu, S., Bursuc, S., Mauw, S., Pang, J.: Election Verifiability in receipt-free voting protocols. In: Proceedings of the 36th IEEE Computer Security Foundations Symposium, pp. 63–78. IEEE Computer Society (2023)
4. Baloglu, S., Bursuc, S., Mauw, S., Pang, J.: Formal verification and solutions for Estonian e-voting. In: Proceedings of the 19th ACM Asia Conference on Computer and Communications Security, pp. 728–742. ACM Press (2024)

5. Baloglu, S.: Formal verification of verifiability in E-Voting Protocols. Ph.D. thesis, University of Luxembourg, Luxembourg City, Luxembourg (2023). http://orbilu. uni.lu/handle/10993/55700
6. Bos, V., van Deursen, T., Kordy, P., Mauw, S.: A LaTeX macro package for Message Sequence Charts (2022). https://ctan.org/ctan-ann/pkg/msc
7. Buldas, A., Gadyatskaya, O., Lenin, A., Mauw, S., Trujillo-Rasua, R.: Attribute evaluation on attack trees with incomplete information. Comput. Secur. **88** (2020)
8. Clement, S.: Question parlementaire n° 1254 – Sécurité du passeport biométrique. https://www.chd.lu/en/question/17991
9. Cremers, C., Mauw, S.: Operational semantics of security protocols. In: Scenarios: Models, Transformations and Tools, International Workshop. Lecture Notes in Computer Science, vol. 3466, pp. 66–89. Springer (2003). https://doi.org/10.1007/11495628_4
10. Cremers, C., Mauw, S.: Operational Semantics and Verification of Security Protocols. Information Security and Cryptography, Springer (2012). https://doi.org/10.1007/978-3-540-78636-8
11. Cremers, C.J.F.: The ScyTher tool: verification, falsification, and analysis of security protocols. In: Gupta, A., Malik, S. (eds.) CAV 2008. LNCS, vol. 5123, pp. 414–418. Springer, Heidelberg (2008). https://doi.org/10.1007/978-3-540-70545-1_38
12. van Deursen, T., Mauw, S., Radomirović, S.: Untraceability of RFID protocols. In: Onieva, J.A., Sauveron, D., Chaumette, S., Gollmann, D., Markantonakis, K. (eds.) WISTP 2008. LNCS, vol. 5019, pp. 1–15. Springer, Heidelberg (2008). https://doi.org/10.1007/978-3-540-79966-5_1
13. van Deursen, T., Mauw, S., Radomirovic, S.: mcarve: carving attributed dump sets. In: 20th USENIX Security Symposium, San Francisco, CA, USA, August 8-12, 2011, Proceedings. USENIX Association (2011). http://static.usenix.org/events/sec11/tech/full_papers/Deursen.pdf
14. van Deursen, T., Mauw, S., Radomirović, S., Vullers, P.: Secure ownership and ownership transfer in RFID systems. In: Backes, M., Ning, P. (eds.) ESORICS 2009. LNCS, vol. 5789, pp. 637–654. Springer, Heidelberg (2009). https://doi.org/10.1007/978-3-642-04444-1_39
15. Engels, A., Mauw, S.: Why men (and octopuses) cannot juggle a four ball cascade. Comput. Sci. Reports **9914**, 10 (1999)
16. Engels, A., Mauw, S., Reniers, M.A.: A hierarchy of communication models for message sequence charts. In: Proceedings of Joint International Conference on Formal Description Techniques for Distributed Systems and Communication Protocols (FORTE X) and Protocol Specification, Testing and Verification (PSTV XVII). IFIP Conference Proceedings, vol. 107, pp. 75–90. Chapman & Hall (1997)
17. Filimonov, I., Horne, R., Mauw, S., Smith, Z.: Breaking unlinkability of the ICAO 9303 standard for e-passports using bisimilarity. In: Sako, K., Schneider, S., Ryan, P.Y.A. (eds.) ESORICS 2019. LNCS, vol. 11735, pp. 577–594. Springer, Cham (2019). https://doi.org/10.1007/978-3-030-29959-0_28
18. Gadyatskaya, O., Jhawar, R., Kordy, P., Lounis, K., Mauw, S., Trujillo-Rasua, R.: Attack trees for practical security assessment: ranking of attack scenarios with ADTool 2.0. In: Agha, G., Van Houdt, B. (eds.) QEST 2016. LNCS, vol. 9826, pp. 159–162. Springer, Cham (2016). https://doi.org/10.1007/978-3-319-43425-4_10
19. Horne, R., Mauw, S., Tiu, A.: Semantics for specialising attack trees based on linear logic. Fund. Inform. **153**(1–2), 57–86 (2017)
20. ITU-T: Recommendation Z.120: Message Sequence Chart (MSC). Tech. rep., International Telecommunication Union, Geneva (1993)

21. Jonker, H.L., Mauw, S., Pang, J.: Privacy and verifiability in voting systems: methods, developments and trends. Comput. Sci. Rev. **10**, 1–30 (2013)
22. Jonker, H.L.: Security Matters: Privacy in Voting and Fairness in Digital Exchange. Ph.D. thesis, University of Eindhoven and University of Luxembourg (2009)
23. Kordy, B., Kordy, P., Mauw, S., Schweitzer, P.: ADTool: security analysis with attack–defense trees. In: Joshi, K., Siegle, M., Stoelinga, M., D'Argenio, P.R. (eds.) QEST 2013. LNCS, vol. 8054, pp. 173–176. Springer, Heidelberg (2013). https://doi.org/10.1007/978-3-642-40196-1_15
24. Kordy, B., Mauw, S., Radomirović, S., Schweitzer, P.: Foundations of attack–defense trees. In: Degano, P., Etalle, S., Guttman, J. (eds.) FAST 2010. LNCS, vol. 6561, pp. 80–95. Springer, Heidelberg (2011). https://doi.org/10.1007/978-3-642-19751-2_6
25. Kordy, B., Mauw, S., Radomirovic, S., Schweitzer, P.: Attack-defense trees. J. Log. Comput. **24**(1), 55–87 (2014). https://doi.org/10.1093/LOGCOM/EXS029
26. Mauw, S., Veltink, G.J.: A process specification formalism. Fund. Inform. **13**(2), 85–139 (1990)
27. Mauw, S., van Wijk, M., Winter, T.: A formal semantics of synchronous Interworkings. In: Færgemand, O., Sarma, A. (eds.) SDL'93 - Using Objects, Proceedings of the Sixth SDL Forum, pp. 167–178. Amsterdam, North-Holland (1993)
28. Mauw, S., Winter, T.: A prototype toolset for Interworkings. Philips Telecommun. Rev. **51**(3), 41–45 (1993)
29. Mauw, S.: PSF - A Process Specification Formalistm. Ph.D. thesis, University of Amsterdam (1991)
30. Mauw, S., Oostdijk, M.: Foundations of attack trees. In: Won, D.H., Kim, S. (eds.) ICISC 2005. LNCS, vol. 3935, pp. 186–198. Springer, Heidelberg (2006). https://doi.org/10.1007/11734727_17
31. Mauw, S., Reniers, M.A.: An algebraic semantics of basic message sequence charts. Comput. J. **37**(4), 269–278 (1994). https://doi.org/10.1093/COMJNL/37.4.269
32. Mauw, S., Reniers, M.A.: Operational semantics for MSC'96. Comput. Netw. **31**(17), 1785–1799 (1999). https://doi.org/10.1016/S1389-1286(99)00060-2
33. Mauw, S., Smith, Z., Toro-Pozo, J., Trujillo-Rasua, R.: Distance-bounding protocols: verification without time and location. In: Proceedings of the IEEE Symposium on Security and Privacy, pp. 549–566. IEEE Computer Society (2018). https://doi.org/10.1109/SP.2018.00001
34. Mauw, S., Smith, Z., Toro-Pozo, J., Trujillo-Rasua, R.: Post-collusion security and distance bounding. In: Proceedings of the ACM SIGSAC Conference on Computer and Communications Security, pp. 941–958. ACM (2019). https://doi.org/10.1145/3319535.3345651
35. Mauw, S., Toro-Pozo, J., Trujillo-Rasua, R.: A class of precomputation-based distance-bounding protocols. In: Proceedings of the IEEE European Symposium on Security and Privacy, pp. 97–111. IEEE (2016). https://doi.org/10.1109/EUROSP.2016.19
36. Pons, R.G., Horne, R., Mauw, S., Stutz, F., Yurkov, S.: Security protocols and threat models - security and privacy via the applied π-calculus. Information Security and Cryptography, Springer (2026). https://doi.org/10.1007/978-3-032-08249-7
37. Reniers, M.A.: Message sequence chart: Syntax and semantics. Ph.D. thesis, Eindhoven University of Technology (Jun 1999). https://doi.org/10.6100/IR524323
38. Schneier, B.: Attack Trees. Dr. Dobb's Journal (1999)
39. Schweitzer, P.: Attack-defense trees. Ph.D. thesis, University of Luxembourg (2013). http://eprints.eemcs.utwente.nl/27479/

The Queue Automaton Revisited

Jos C. M. Baeten[1](✉) ⓘ and Bas Luttik[2] ⓘ

[1] CWI, Amsterdam, The Netherlands
`Jos.Baeten@cwi.nl`
[2] Eindhoven University of Technology, Eindhoven, The Netherlands
`s.p.luttik@tue.nl`

Abstract. We consider the computational model of the Queue Automaton. An old result is that the deterministic queue automaton is equally expressive as the Turing machine. In a previous paper, we introduced the Reactive Turing Machine, enhancing the Turing machine with a notion of interaction. The Reactive Turing Machine defines all executable processes. In this paper, we prove that the non-deterministic queue automaton is equally expressive as the Reactive Turing Machine. Together with finite automata, pushdown automata and parallel pushdown automata, queue automata form a nice hierarchy of executable processes, with stacks, bags and queues as central elements.

1 Introduction

Replacing, in a pushdown automaton, the (last-in first-out) stack memory by a (first-in first-out) queue memory yields the computational model of the queue automaton. This computational model, sometimes also called a Post machine or a pullup automaton, has not raised a lot of attention in the literature, but it is a known result that the deterministic queue automaton is equally expressive as the Turing machine of [24], so that it defines all computable languages and all computable functions. Implicitly, this result is already mentioned in [21], and further given in [18,25].

In this paper, we investigate the (non-deterministic) queue automaton. We do not define the language of a queue automaton directly, but instead, we define its process graph or transition system. A state of this process graph is given by the state of the queue automaton together with the contents of the queue and a transition is given by the label of the transition of the queue automaton. By considering the language equivalence class of the process graph, we obtain again the language, but we can also divide out other equivalence relations. Notable among these is branching bisimilarity (see [14]). By dividing out branching bisimilarity, we obtain the *process* of the queue automaton, incorporating a notion of interaction or communication. These notions of process and communication come from process theory or concurrency theory [1,20]. We prove that several variants of the queue automaton yield the same set of languages and the same set of processes, and prove that a queue automaton with two queues also yields the same set of languages and the same set of processes.

Also the Turing machine can be extended to incorporate processes and communication, but this is not so straightforward as we just sketched for the queue automaton. We

B. Fila et al. (Eds.): Sjouke Mauw Festschrift, LNCS 16365, pp. 8–28, 2026.
https://doi.org/10.1007/978-3-032-20684-8_2

achieved this, nonetheless, in [8], where we introduced the Reactive Turing Machine. Whereas the classical Turing machine defines the class of computable languages and computable functions, the reactive Turing machine also yields a process graph that can be used to define the class of executable processes. In this paper, we prove that the non-deterministic queue automaton is equally expressive as the reactive Turing machine. This shows again that the notion of executability we introduced is robust: it is given by different computational models and also by the π-calculus, see [17].

The queue automaton has certain advantages over the reactive Turing machine: it is mathematically simpler, the extension with interaction is easier, and we get a better process hierarchy, as we explain now. In the queue automaton, we can make the interaction between the finite control and the queue memory explicit, by proving that every executable process is branching bisimilar to a regular process communicating with a queue. In earlier papers [5,6], we proved that every pushdown process is branching bisimilar to a regular process communicating with a stack, and every parallel pushdown process is branching bisimilar to a regular process communicating with a bag. Thus, the queue, stack and bag are the central elements in this Chomsky-Turing hierarchy.

This paper contributes to our ongoing project to integrate the theory of automata and formal languages on the one hand and concurrency theory on the other hand. The integration requires a more refined view on the semantics of automata, grammars and expressions. Instead of treating automata as language acceptors, and grammars and expressions as syntactic means to specify languages, we propose to view them both as defining process graphs. The great benefit of this approach is that process graphs can be considered modulo a plethora of behavioural equivalences [11]. One can still consider language equivalence and recover the classical theory of automata and formal languages. But one can also consider finer notions such as bisimilarity, which is better suited for interacting processes.

Note 1. This paper is dedicated to Sjouke Mauw, our friend and colleague, on the occasion of his 65th birthday. Sjouke was one of the first to see that information security would become an important area, in practice and research, and that formal methods can play an important role in this area. Sjouke does not stop at borders in order to realise his ambition.

As we said, this paper is part of our ongoing project to integrate automata theory and concurrency theory. In this project, we looked at context-free processes in, e.g., [4,5]. Here, we considered the place of context-free processes in the Chomsky-Turing hierarchy. Sjouke already considered context-free processes in [19].

2   Preliminaries

As a common semantic framework we use the notion of a *labelled transition system.*

Definition 1. *A labelled transition system is a quadruple* $(\mathcal{S}, \mathcal{A}, \rightarrow, \downarrow)$*, where*

1. *$\mathcal{S}$ is a set of* states;
2. *$\mathcal{A}$ is a set of* actions, *$\tau \notin \mathcal{A}$ is the* unobservable *or* silent *action;*
3. *$\rightarrow \subseteq \mathcal{S} \times (\mathcal{A} \cup \{\tau\}) \times \mathcal{S}$ is an* $\mathcal{A} \cup \{\tau\}$*-labelled* transition relation; *and*

4. $\downarrow \subseteq \mathcal{S}$ is the set of final, accepting *or* terminating *states.*

A process graph *is a labelled transition system with a special designated* root state *or* initial state $\uparrow$, *i.e., it is a quintuple* $(\mathcal{S}, \mathcal{A}, \rightarrow, \uparrow, \downarrow)$ *such that* $(\mathcal{S}, \mathcal{A}, \rightarrow, \downarrow)$ *is a labelled transition system, and* $\uparrow \in \mathcal{S}$. *We write* $s \xrightarrow{a} s'$ *for* $(s, a, s') \in \rightarrow$ *and* $s\downarrow$ *for* $s \in \downarrow$. *We write* $\mathcal{A}_\tau$ *for* $\mathcal{A} \cup \{\tau\}$.

For $w \in \mathcal{A}^*$ we define $s \xrightarrow{w} t$ inductively, for all states s, t, u: first, $s \xrightarrow{\varepsilon} s$, and then, for $a \in \mathcal{A}$, if $s \xrightarrow{a} t$ and $t \xrightarrow{w} u$, then $s \xrightarrow{aw} u$, and if $s \xrightarrow{\tau} t$ and $t \xrightarrow{w} u$, then $s \xrightarrow{w} u$. We see that τ-steps do not contribute to the string w. We write $s \longrightarrow t$ for there exists $a \in \mathcal{A}_\tau$ such that $s \xrightarrow{a} t$. Similarly, we write $s \longrightarrow\!\!\!\!\!\rightarrow t$ for "there exists $w \in \mathcal{A}^*$ such that $s \xrightarrow{w} t$" and say that t is *reachable* from s. Finally, we write $s \xrightarrow{(a)} t$ for "$s \xrightarrow{a} t$ or $a = \tau$ and $s = t$".

By considering language equivalence classes of process graphs, we recover language equivalence as a semantics, but we can also consider other equivalence relations. Notable among these is *bisimilarity*.

Definition 2. *Let* $(\mathcal{S}, \mathcal{A}, \rightarrow, \downarrow)$ *be a labelled transition system. A binary relation R on $\mathcal{S}$ is a* strong bisimulation *iff it is symmetric and satisfies the following conditions for every $s, t \in \mathcal{S}$ such that $s\,R\,t$ and for all $a \in \mathcal{A}_\tau$:*

1. if $s \xrightarrow{a} s'$ for some $s' \in \mathcal{S}$, then there is a $t' \in \mathcal{S}$ such that $t \xrightarrow{a} t'$ and $s'\,R\,t'$; and
2. if $s\downarrow$, then $t\downarrow$.

If there is a strong bisimulation relating s and t we write $s \leftrightarrow t$.

Sometimes we can use the *strong* version of bisimilarity defined above, which does not give special treatment to τ-labelled transitions. In general, when we do give special treatment to τ-labeled transitions, we use (some form of) *branching bisimulation* [14].

Definition 3. *Let* $(\mathcal{S}, \mathcal{A}, \rightarrow, \downarrow)$ *be a labelled transition system. A binary relation R on $\mathcal{S}$ is a* branching bisimulation *iff it is symmetric and satisfies the following conditions for every $s, t \in \mathcal{S}$ such that $s\,R\,t$ and for all $a \in \mathcal{A}_\tau$:*

1. if $s \xrightarrow{a} s'$ for some $s' \in \mathcal{S}$, then there are states $t', t'' \in \mathcal{S}$ such that $t \xrightarrow{\varepsilon} t'' \xrightarrow{(a)} t'$, $s\,R\,t''$ and $s'\,R\,t'$; and
2. if $s\downarrow$, then there is a state $t' \in \mathcal{S}$ such that $t \xrightarrow{\varepsilon} t'$ and $t'\downarrow$.

If there is a branching bisimulation relating s and t, we write $s \leftrightarrow_b t$. If $s \xrightarrow{\tau} t$ and $s \leftrightarrow_b t$, we say this τ-step is inert.

Again, a non-symmetric relation is never a branching bisimulation.

Theorem 1. *Strong bisimilarity and branching bisimilarity are equivalence relations on labeled transition systems.*

Proof. See [9] and [12].

Now suppose we are given a labelled transition system and two states s, t in this labelled transition system. These states give rise to two process graphs with the given states as initial states. We say the two process graphs are strongly bisimilar or branching bisimilar if there is a strong bisimulation or a branching bisimulation on the labelled transition system that relates s and t.

A *process* is a branching bisimilarity equivalence class of process graphs. We say a process is *regular* if its branching bisimilarity equivalence class contains an element with finitely many states and finitely many transitions.

Finally, we define when a labelled transition system is *deterministic*.

Definition 4. *A labelled transition system* $(\mathcal{S}, \mathcal{A}, \rightarrow, \downarrow)$ *is deterministic iff for all* $s \in \mathcal{S}$ *and for all* $a \in \mathcal{A}_\tau$ *there is at most one* $t \in \mathcal{S}$ *with* $s \xrightarrow{a} t$. *Moreover, whenever* $s \xrightarrow{\tau} t$, *there is no* $a \in \mathcal{A}$ *and* $u \in \mathcal{S}$ *with* $s \xrightarrow{a} u$.

A process graph $(\mathcal{S}, \mathcal{A}, \rightarrow, \uparrow, \downarrow)$ *is deterministic if the labelled transition system* $(\mathcal{S}, \mathcal{A}, \rightarrow, \downarrow)$ *is deterministic.*

3   Queue Automata

We define queue automata, prove that their type of transitions can be restricted without losing expressiveness, and prove that having two queues instead of one does not increase their expressiveness.

Definition 5 (Queue automaton). *A queue automaton* Q *is a sixtuple* $(\mathcal{S}, \mathcal{A}, \mathcal{D}, \rightarrow, \uparrow, \downarrow)$ *where:*

1. $\mathcal{S}$ *is a non-empty finite set of states,*
2. $\mathcal{A}$ *is a non-empty finite action alphabet,*
3. $\mathcal{D}$ *is a non-empty finite data alphabet,*
4. $\rightarrow \subseteq \mathcal{S} \times \mathcal{A}_\tau \times (\mathcal{D} \cup \{\varepsilon, *\}) \times \mathcal{D}^* \times \mathcal{S}$ *is a finite set of* transitions *or* steps,
5. $\uparrow \in \mathcal{S}$ *is the root state or initial state,*
6. $\downarrow \subseteq \mathcal{S}$ *is the set of final, accepting or terminating states.*

If $(s, a, d, \delta, t) \in \rightarrow$ *with* $d \in \mathcal{D}$, *we write* $s \xrightarrow{a[d/\delta]} t$, *and this means that the machine, when it is in state s and d is the head element of the queue, can execute action a, dequeue this d and enqueue the string δ and thereby move to state t. Likewise, writing* $s \xrightarrow{a[\varepsilon/\delta]} t$ *means that the machine, when it is in state s and the queue is empty, can execute action a, enqueue the string δ and thereby move to state t. Writing* $s \xrightarrow{a[*/\delta]} t$ *means that the machine, when it is in state s, can execute action a, enqueue δ and thereby move to state t, irrespective of the contents of the queue and without dequeueing anything. In steps* $s \xrightarrow{\tau[d/\delta]} t$, $s \xrightarrow{\tau[\varepsilon/\delta]} t$ *and* $s \xrightarrow{\tau[*/\delta]} t$, *no action is executed, only the queue is modified. The semantic interpretation of the elements of the action alphabet can be left unspecified, but often they stand for some kind of interaction with the automaton.*

In definitions of queue automata appearing in the literature, the set of transitions is sometimes defined a little differently, but all of them are equally expressive, in the sense that they all give rise to the same set of languages and the same set of processes. For instance, in [16], the $a[*/\delta]$-labeled transitions do not occur, but there are two variants of the $a[d/\delta]$-labeled transitions: one where d is dequeued, and one where d is not dequeued. Moreover, instead of using general sequences δ, only singleton sequences or empty sequences are used. We show some of these expressiveness results in the sequel.

We believe the present definition fits in best with the definitions of a pushdown automaton (in [5]) and parallel pushdown automaton (in [6]).

The notion of queue automaton is very similar to the classical notion of a pushdown automaton (see, e.g., [15]), only there, a stack is used instead of a queue, and in a stack, push and pop (as enqueue and dequeue are called) occur according to the last-in first-out principle. Therefore, in a pushdown automaton, we do not need the separate $s \xrightarrow{a[*/\delta]} t$ transitions, as they can be replaced by a $s \xrightarrow{a[\varepsilon/\delta]} t$ transition in combination with $s \xrightarrow{a[d/\delta d]} t$ transitions for all $d \in \mathcal{D}$. Further on, we will see that the expressivity of the queue automaton does not change when we omit these transitions, using a recycle operation and working modulo branching bisimulation.

Now we could proceed to define the language of a queue automaton, but instead, we take an intermediate step and first define the process graph of a queue automaton. By considering the language of this process graph, we find the language of the queue automaton again, and by considering its branching bisimulation equivalence class, we obtain the process of the queue automaton.

Definition 6. *Let* $Q = (\mathcal{S}, \mathcal{A}, \mathcal{D}, \rightarrow, \uparrow, \downarrow)$ *be a queue automaton. The* process graph *of* Q *is defined as follows, for all* $\delta \in \mathcal{D}^*$:

1. *the set of states is* $\{(s, \delta) \mid s \in \mathcal{S}, \delta \in \mathcal{D}^*\}$;
2. *the set of actions is* $\mathcal{A}$;
3. *the transition relation is generated by the following clauses:*
    - *if* $s \xrightarrow{a[\varepsilon/\delta]} t$ *then* $(s, \varepsilon) \xrightarrow{a} (t, \delta)$;
    - *if* $s \xrightarrow{a[d/\delta]} t$ *then* $(s, \zeta d) \xrightarrow{a} (t, \delta\zeta)$, *for all* $\zeta \in \mathcal{D}^*$;
    - *if* $s \xrightarrow{a[*/\delta]} t$ *then* $(s, \zeta) \xrightarrow{a} (t, \delta\zeta)$, *for all* $\zeta \in \mathcal{D}^*$;
4. *the initial state is* $(\uparrow, \varepsilon)$; *and*
5. $(s, \delta) \downarrow$ *if* $s \downarrow$.

Usually, we consider only those states (s, δ) that are reachable from the initial state. According to this definition, a state (s, δ) can be final also when the queue contents δ is non-empty. Defining that only states (s, ε) can be final is more limiting, and yields a smaller set of processes that are the process of a queue automaton. We can still code in a queue automaton that only states of the form (s, ε) can be final, by only allowing to enter such a state by means of a transition labeled by $a[\varepsilon/\varepsilon]$. This is illustrated in Examples 1 and 3. For an extensive treatment of termination conditions for pushdown automata and parallel pushdown automata, see [23].

Definition 7. *Let* $Q = (\mathcal{S}, \mathcal{A}, \mathcal{D}, \rightarrow, \uparrow, \downarrow)$ *be a queue automaton. The* language *accepted by* Q, $\mathcal{L}(Q)$, *is the language of its transition system, i.e.*

$$\mathcal{L}(Q) = \{w \in \mathcal{A}^* \mid \exists s \in \mathcal{S} \quad \exists \delta \in \mathcal{D}^* \text{ such that } s \downarrow \text{ and } (\uparrow, \varepsilon) \xrightarrow{w} (s, \delta)\}.$$

The process *of Q, P(Q), is the branching bisimulation equivalence class of its transition system, often represented by its minimal element (identifying all branching bisimilar states).*

Example 1. Let us construct a queue automaton for the language $\{ww \mid w \in \{a,b\}^*\}$. This language is not a pushdown language and also not a parallel pushdown language. We use a, b also as data symbols, so $\mathcal{D} = \{a, b\}$. In the initial state, a string can be read and enqueued. At some point (non-deterministically) it will switch to dequeue elements of the string again by moving to the second state, using the same order (the queue is first-in-first-out). Acceptance or termination takes place when the queue is empty again. See Fig. 1. In the figure, we represent the states by circles, the initial state by a small incoming arrow and a final state by a double circle. An arrow that is labeled with multiple labels means that there is such a transition for each of these labels.

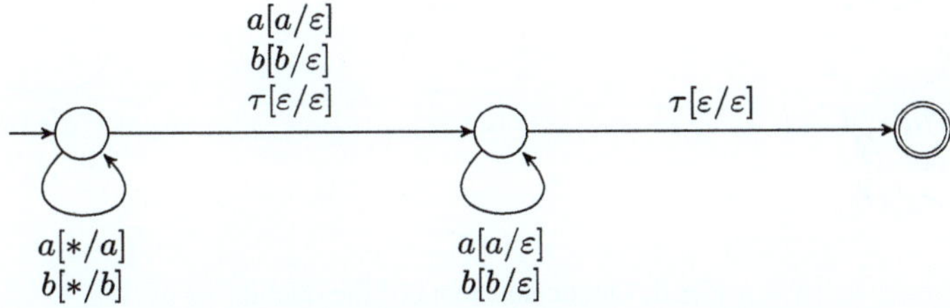

Fig. 1. Queue automaton for the language $\{ww \mid w \in \{a,b\}^*\}$.

Example 2. Figure 2 shows a queue automaton for the language $\{a^n b^n c^n \mid n > 0\}$; it uses data symbols $1, 2$. The language is not a pushdown language and also not a parallel pushdown language.

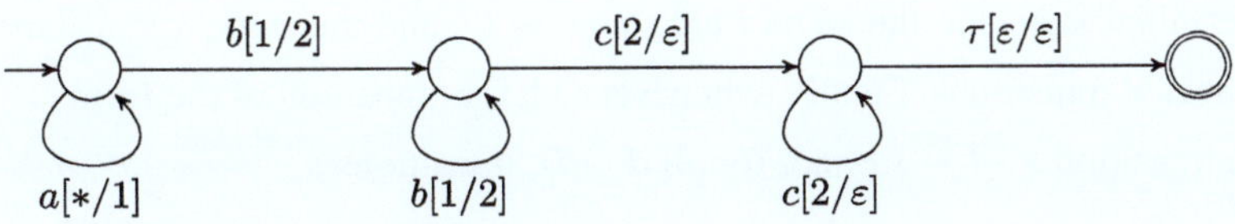

Fig. 2. Queue automaton for the language $\{a^n b^n c^n \mid n > 0\}$.

Example 3. We can define the behaviour of the (first-in first-out) queue itself. Given a finite data set $\mathcal{D}$, the queue process can execute the following actions:

- $i?d$, **enqueue** data element d (input at port i);
- $o!d$, **dequeue** data element d, if this is the element at the head of the queue (output at port o);

– $o!\varepsilon$, show that the queue is empty.

We consider two variants: either the queue can always terminate, or it can terminate only when empty. We can define queue automata for these two queues, see Fig. 3: for all $d \in \mathcal{D}$, there are the edges shown. The queue automaton on the left has only one state and can always terminate, irrespective of the contents of the queue the behaviour of which it represents. The queue automaton on the right has an additional τ-transition, that can only be executed when the queue the behaviour of which it represents has become empty: for this queue automaton, termination can only take place when the queue is empty.

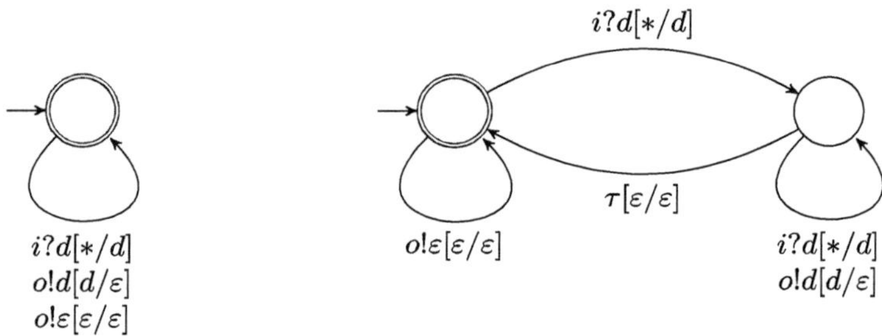

Fig. 3. Queue automata of the queue.

We stated before that the $a[*/\delta]$-labeled transitions are not really needed in the definition of queue automata. We prove this in the following lemma.

Lemma 1. *Let $Q = (\mathcal{S}, \mathcal{A}, \mathcal{D}, \rightarrow, \uparrow, \downarrow)$ be a queue automaton. Then there is a queue automaton Q' that does not have any $a[*/\delta]$-labeled transitions and has the same process as Q.*

Proof. We construct the queue automaton Q' as follows. The data set is $\mathcal{D}$ plus an extra data element $\$ \notin \mathcal{D}$. The state set is $\mathcal{S}$ plus fresh states s^* for each $s \in \mathcal{S}$. Q' has the same initial state and the same final states as Q, and the same $a[\varepsilon/\delta]$-labeled and $a[d/\delta]$-labeled transitions. Finally, whenever Q has a transition of the form $s \xrightarrow{a[*/\delta]} t$, Q' has a transition $s \xrightarrow{a[\varepsilon/\delta]} t$ and, for all $d \in \mathcal{D}$, transitions $s \xrightarrow{a[d/d\$]} s^* \xrightarrow{\tau[\$/\delta]} t$ and $s^* \xrightarrow{\tau[d/d]} s^*$.

Now we show that the process graphs of Q and Q' are branching bisimilar. We start out from the identity relation on all common states. Note that, whenever $s \xrightarrow{a[*/\delta]} t$ in Q, then we have $(s, \varepsilon) \xrightarrow{a} (t, \delta)$ in the process graph of Q but also in the process graph of Q'. For nonempty memory contents, say of the form ζd for some $\zeta \in \mathcal{D}^*, d \in \mathcal{D}$, we have $(s, \zeta d) \xrightarrow{a} (t, \delta \zeta d)$ in the process graph of Q, and $(s, \zeta d) \xrightarrow{a} (s^*, d\$\zeta) \xrightarrow{\varepsilon} (s^*, \zeta d\$) \xrightarrow{\tau} (t, \delta \zeta d)$ in the process graph of Q', so it is enough to relate s^* to t. Note that all of the added τ-steps are inert because whenever some state in the process graph has an outgoing τ-transition, then this τ-transition is the unique outgoing transition. Therefore, the source and target states of the τ-transition are branching bisimilar.

We use the $a[*/\delta]$-labeled transitions, nonetheless, because they allow for concise descriptions of interesting processes such as the queue of Example 3. In the following proofs, it will be useful on occasion to restrict the transitions in a queue automaton to only singleton enqueues, and to separate enqueues and dequeues.

Definition 8. *A transition in a queue automaton is a* singleton enqueue *iff it has a label of the form* $a[*/d]$ *for some* $d \in \mathcal{D}$*; it is a* separate dequeue *iff it has a label of the form* $a[\varepsilon/\varepsilon]$ *or* $a[d/\varepsilon]$ *for some* $d \in \mathcal{D}$.

Notice that the queue automata of the queue of Example 3 have only singleton enqueues and separate dequeues.

Lemma 2. *Let* $Q = (\mathcal{S}, \mathcal{A}, \mathcal{D}, \rightarrow, \uparrow, \downarrow)$ *be a queue automaton. Then, there is a queue automaton* Q' *with only singleton enqueues and separate dequeues with the same process and language.*

Proof. Let N be the maximum length of a data sequence occurring in any transition of Q, and enumerate the transitions of Q in a sequence $u_1, \ldots, u_K$. The queue automaton Q' uses an extra data element $\$ \notin \mathcal{D}$ and has the set of states of Q plus new states $\{s_{ik} \mid i \leq N, k \leq K\} \cup \{s_{1k}^d \mid d \in \mathcal{D}, k \leq K\}$. Q' has the same action set, initial state and final states as Q. The transitions of Q' are defined as follows:

1. For each transition in Q of the form $s \xrightarrow{a[*/\varepsilon]} t$, if this is transition u_k, then Q' has transitions $s \xrightarrow{a[*/\$]} s_{1k} \xrightarrow{\tau[\$/\varepsilon]} t$, and transitions $s_{1k} \xrightarrow{\tau[d/\varepsilon]} s_{1k}^d \xrightarrow{\tau[*/d]} s_{1k}$ for all $d \in \mathcal{D}$;

2. For each transition in Q of the form $s \xrightarrow{a[*/\delta]} t$ with $\delta \neq \varepsilon$, if this is transition u_k and $\delta = d_1 \ldots d_n$ with $n > 1$, then Q' has transitions $s \xrightarrow{a[*/d_n]} s_{1k} \xrightarrow{\tau[*/d_{n-1}]}$ $\cdots s_{(n-1)k} \xrightarrow{\tau[*/d_1]} t$;

3. For each transition in Q of the form $s \xrightarrow{a[\varepsilon/\delta]} t$ with $\delta \neq \varepsilon$, if this is transition u_k and $\delta = d_1 \ldots d_n$ with $n \geq 1$, then Q' has transitions $s \xrightarrow{a[\varepsilon/\varepsilon]} s_{1k} \xrightarrow{\tau[*/d_n]}$ $\cdots s_{nk} \xrightarrow{\tau[*/d_1]} t$;

4. For each transition in Q of the form $s \xrightarrow{a[d/\delta]} t$ with $\delta \neq \varepsilon$, if this is transition u_k and $\delta = d_1 \ldots d_n$ with $n \geq 1$, then Q' has transitions $s \xrightarrow{a[d/\varepsilon]} s_{1k} \xrightarrow{\tau[*/d_n]}$ $\cdots s_{nk} \xrightarrow{\tau[*/d_1]} t$.

In the process graph of Q', all the added τ-steps are inert, so it is branching bisimilar to the process graph of Q.

We see that the notion of the queue automaton is quite robust, as different variants of the queue automaton yield the same set of processes and the same set of languages. As a final illustration of the robustness of the notion of a queue automaton, we show that we can code a memory of two queues into one queue. In order to show this, we first define what a queue automaton with two queues is, and then show that its behaviour can also be obtained by a queue automaton with one queue.

Definition 9 (Queue automaton, two queues). *A queue automaton with two queues Q is a sixtuple $(\mathcal{S}, \mathcal{A}, \mathcal{D}, \rightarrow, \uparrow, \downarrow)$ that is just like a queue automaton, only the transition relation $\rightarrow$ is now a subset of $\mathcal{S} \times \mathcal{A}_\tau \times (\mathcal{D} \cup \{\varepsilon, *\})^2 \times (\mathcal{D}^*)^2 \times \mathcal{S}$, i.e. a pair of elements of $\mathcal{D} \cup \{\varepsilon, *\}$ and a pair of sequences from $\mathcal{D}^*$ is considered. We write $s \xrightarrow{a[(d,e)/(\delta,\zeta)]} t$ for $(s, a, d, e, \delta, \zeta, t) \in \rightarrow$ (here, $s, t \in \mathcal{S}, a \in \mathcal{A}_\tau, d, e \in \mathcal{D} \cup \{\varepsilon, *\}, \delta, \zeta \in \mathcal{D}^*$).*

From this definition, we get a process graph as expected: the states of the process graph are the triples (s, δ, ζ) reachable from initial state $(\uparrow, \varepsilon, \varepsilon)$ by means of the transition relation generated from the following clauses:

1. if $s \xrightarrow{a[(\varepsilon,\varepsilon)/(\delta,\delta')]} t$ then $(s, \varepsilon, \varepsilon) \xrightarrow{a} (t, \delta, \delta')$;
2. if $s \xrightarrow{a[(\varepsilon,*)/(\delta,\delta')]} t$ then $(s, \varepsilon, \zeta) \xrightarrow{a} (t, \delta, \delta'\zeta)$ for all $\zeta \in \mathcal{D}^*$;
3. if $s \xrightarrow{a[(*,\varepsilon)/(\delta,\delta')]} t$ then $(s, \zeta, \varepsilon) \xrightarrow{a} (t, \delta\zeta, \delta')$ for all $\zeta \in \mathcal{D}^*$;
4. if $s \xrightarrow{a[(*,*)/(\delta,\delta')]} t$ then $(s, \zeta, \zeta') \xrightarrow{a} (t, \delta\zeta, \delta'\zeta')$ for all $\zeta, \zeta' \in \mathcal{D}^*$;
5. if $s \xrightarrow{a[(d,\varepsilon)/(\delta,\delta')]} t$ then $(s, \zeta d, \varepsilon) \xrightarrow{a} (t, \delta\zeta, \delta')$ for all $\zeta \in \mathcal{D}^*$;
6. if $s \xrightarrow{a[(\varepsilon,d)/(\delta,\delta')]} t$ then $(s, \varepsilon, \zeta d) \xrightarrow{a} (t, \delta, \delta'\zeta)$ for all $\zeta \in \mathcal{D}^*$;
7. if $s \xrightarrow{a[(d,*)/(\delta,\delta')]} t$ then $(s, \zeta d, \zeta') \xrightarrow{a} (t, \delta\zeta, \delta'\zeta')$ for all $\zeta, \zeta' \in \mathcal{D}^*$;
8. if $s \xrightarrow{a[(*,d)/(\delta,\delta')]} t$ then $(s, \zeta, \zeta' d) \xrightarrow{a} (t, \delta\zeta, \delta'\zeta')$ for all $\zeta, \zeta' \in \mathcal{D}^*$;
9. if $s \xrightarrow{a[(d,e)/(\delta,\delta')]} t$ then $(s, \zeta d, \zeta' e) \xrightarrow{a} (t, \delta\zeta, \delta'\zeta')$ for all $\zeta, \zeta' \in \mathcal{D}^*$.

Theorem 2. *Let Q be a queue automaton with two queues. Then there is a queue automaton with one queue M such that the process graphs of Q and M are branching bisimilar.*

Proof. Let Q be a queue automaton with two queues. We define the queue automaton with one queue M in the following. As in the proof of Lemma 1, we use an extra data element \$ to be able to traverse the contents of a queue. A state in Q will contain the contents of two queues, two sequences δ and ζ. In M, this will be encoded as the contents of one queue: $\delta \lozenge \zeta$, where extra data element $\lozenge$ is the separator between the two sequences. A state (s, δ, ζ) in Q will correspond to the state $(s, \delta \lozenge \zeta)$ in M. Enumerate all transitions of Q in a sequence $u_1, \ldots, u_K$. For each transition u_k we add four new states $s_k^1, s_k^2, s_k^3, s_k^4$ in M, moreover, there is a new initial state $\uparrow'$ in M. The further elements are as follows.

1. M has the same action set and the same final states as Q;
2. M has the data set $\mathcal{D}$ of Q and in addition the symbols $\lozenge, \$$;
3. M has initial state $\uparrow'$ and a transition labelled $\tau[\varepsilon/\lozenge]$ to the initial state of Q;
4. if transition $s \xrightarrow{a[(*,*)/(\delta,\zeta)]} t$ is transition u_k in Q, then in M there are transitions $s \xrightarrow{a[*/\$]} s_k^1 \xrightarrow{\tau[\lozenge/\lozenge\zeta]} s_k^2 \xrightarrow{\tau[\$/\delta]} t$, and for all $d \in \mathcal{D}$ transitions $s_k^1 \xrightarrow{\tau[d/d]} s_k^1$ and $s_k^2 \xrightarrow{\tau[d/d]} s_k^2$; note that in this case, in the process graph of M, there is always an a-step possible, irrespective of the contents of the queues in the state;

5. if transition $s \xrightarrow{a[(*,\varepsilon)/(\delta,\zeta)]} t$ is transition u_k in Q, then in M there are transitions $s \xrightarrow{a[\lozenge/\lozenge\zeta\$]} s_k^1 \xrightarrow{\tau[\$/\delta]} t$ and for all $d \in \mathcal{D}$ transitions $s_k^1 \xrightarrow{\tau[d/d]} s_k^1$; in this case, in the process graph of M, there is only an a-step possible if the second queue is empty, which can be checked by seeing $\lozenge$ at the head of the queue;

6. if transition $s \xrightarrow{a[(\varepsilon,\varepsilon)/(\delta,\zeta)]} t$ is transition u_k in Q, then in M, there is only an a-labeled transition if both queues are empty. We can check whether the second queue is empty by seeing $\lozenge$ at the head of the queue, for the first queue we have to traverse the queue. The succeeding transitions in M (i.e., the transitions that correspond to the situation that the checks that both queues are empty are successful) are $s \xrightarrow{\tau[\lozenge/\lozenge\$]} s_k^1 \xrightarrow{\tau[\$/\varepsilon]} s_k^2 \xrightarrow{a[\lozenge/\delta\lozenge\zeta]} t$ and the failing transitions (i.e., the transitions that correspond to the situation that the check revealed that one of the queues is not empty) are, for all $d \in \mathcal{D}$, $s_k^1 \xrightarrow{\tau[d/d]} s_k^3$ and $s_k^3 \xrightarrow{\tau[d/d]} s_k^3$ and, finally, $s_k^3 \xrightarrow{\tau[\$/\varepsilon]} s$;

7. if transition $s \xrightarrow{a[(\varepsilon,*)/(\delta,\zeta)]} t$ is transition u_k in Q, then again, we need to check whether the first queue is empty. In M, we add the succeeding transitions $s \xrightarrow{\tau[*/\$]} s_k^1 \xrightarrow{\tau[\lozenge/\varepsilon]} s_k^2 \xrightarrow{a[\$/\delta\lozenge\zeta]} t$ and for all $d \in \mathcal{D}$ transitions $s_k^1 \xrightarrow{\tau[d/d]} s_k^1$; moreover, we add in M the failing transitions $s_k^3 \xrightarrow{\tau[\$/\varepsilon]} s$ and for all $d \in \mathcal{D}$ transitions $s_k^2 \xrightarrow{\tau[d/d\lozenge]} s_k^3$ and $s_k^3 \xrightarrow{\tau[d/d]} s_k^3$;

8. if transition $s \xrightarrow{a[(*,d)/(\delta,\zeta)]} t$ is transition u_k in Q, then in M there are transitions $s \xrightarrow{a[d/\$]} s_k^1 \xrightarrow{\tau[\lozenge/\lozenge\zeta]} s_k^2 \xrightarrow{\tau[\$/\delta]} t$ and for all $f \in \mathcal{D}$ transitions $s_k^1 \xrightarrow{\tau[f/f]} s_k^1$ and $s_k^2 \xrightarrow{\tau[f/f]} s_k^2$;

9. if transition $s \xrightarrow{a[(\varepsilon,d)/(\delta,\zeta)]} t$ is transition u_k in Q, then in M there are succeeding transitions $s \xrightarrow{\tau[d/\$]} s_k^1 \xrightarrow{\tau[\lozenge/\varepsilon]} s_k^2 \xrightarrow{a[\$/\delta\lozenge\zeta]} t$ and for all $f \in \mathcal{D}$ transitions $s_k^1 \xrightarrow{\tau[f/f]} s_k^1$; moreover, there are failing transitions $s_k^3 \xrightarrow{\tau[\$/\varepsilon]} s$ and, for all $f \in \mathcal{D}$, $s_k^2 \xrightarrow{\tau[f/f\lozenge]} s_k^3$ and $s_k^3 \xrightarrow{\tau[f/f]} s_k^3$;

10. if transition $s \xrightarrow{a[(d,\varepsilon)/(\delta,\zeta)]} t$ is transition u_k in Q, then in M there are succeeding transitions $s \xrightarrow{\tau[\lozenge/\$]} s_k^1 \xrightarrow{a[d/\lozenge\zeta]} s_k^2 \xrightarrow{\tau[\$/\delta]} t$ and for all $f \in \mathcal{D}$ transitions $s_k^2 \xrightarrow{\tau[f/f]} s_k^2$; moreover, there are failing transitions $s_k^1 \xrightarrow{\tau[\$/\varepsilon]} s$ and $s_k^3 \xrightarrow{\tau[\$/\varepsilon]} s$ and, for all $e \in \mathcal{D}, e \neq d, s_k^1 \xrightarrow{\tau[e/e\lozenge]} s_k^3$ and, for all $f \in \mathcal{D}, s_k^3 \xrightarrow{\tau[f/f]} s_k^3$;

11. if transition $s \xrightarrow{a[(d,*)/(\delta,\zeta)]} t$ is transition u_k in Q, then in M there are succeeding transitions $s \xrightarrow{\tau[*/\$]} s_k^1 \xrightarrow{\tau[\lozenge/\varepsilon]} s_k^2 \xrightarrow{a[d/\lozenge\zeta]} s_k^3 \xrightarrow{\tau[\$/\delta]} t$ and for all $f \in \mathcal{D}$ transitions $s_k^1 \xrightarrow{\tau[f/f]} s_k^1$ and $s_k^3 \xrightarrow{\tau[f/f]} s_k^3$; moreover, there are failing transitions $s_k^1 \xrightarrow{\tau[\$/\varepsilon]} s$ and $s_k^4 \xrightarrow{\tau[\$/\varepsilon]} s$ and, for all $e \in \mathcal{D}, e \neq d, s_k^2 \xrightarrow{\tau[e/e\lozenge]} s_k^4$ and, for all $f \in \mathcal{D}, s_k^4 \xrightarrow{\tau[f/f]} s_k^4$;

12. if transition $s \xrightarrow{a[(d,e)/(\delta,\zeta)]} t$ is transition u_k in Q, then in M there are succeeding transitions $s \xrightarrow{\tau[e/\$]} s_k^1 \xrightarrow{\tau[\lozenge/\varepsilon]} s_k^2 \xrightarrow{a[d/\lozenge\zeta]} s_k^3 \xrightarrow{\tau[\$/\delta]} t$ and for all $f \in \mathcal{D}$ transitions $s_k^1 \xrightarrow{\tau[f/f]} s_k^1$ and $s_k^3 \xrightarrow{\tau[f/f]} s_k^3$; moreover, there are failing transitions $s_k^2 \xrightarrow{\tau[\$/\varepsilon]} s$

and $s_k^4 \xrightarrow{\tau[\$/\varepsilon]} s$ and, for all $g \in \mathcal{D}, g \neq d$, $s_k^2 \xrightarrow{\tau[g/g\check{0}]} s_k^4$ and, for all $f \in \mathcal{D}$, $s_k^4 \xrightarrow{\tau[f/f]} s_k^4$.

Finally, it is straightforward to check that in the process graph of M, all the extra τ-steps are inert.

We see that the set of processes and the set of languages given by a queue automaton is not enlarged by adding another queue memory. Further on, we use this to show that the the composition of two interacting processes both given by queue automata is again given by a queue automaton.

4   Comparison with Reactive Turing Machines

We use the definition of the Reactive Turing Machine (RTM) from [8].

Definition 10 (Reactive Turing machine). *A reactive Turing machine M is a sixtuple $(\mathcal{S}, \mathcal{A}, \mathcal{D}, \rightarrow, \uparrow, \downarrow)$ where:*

1. *$\mathcal{S}$ is a non-empty finite set of states;*
2. *$\mathcal{A}$ is a non-empty finite action alphabet;*
3. *$\mathcal{D}$ is a non-empty finite data alphabet;*
4. *$\rightarrow \subseteq \mathcal{S} \times \mathcal{A}_\tau \times (\mathcal{D} \cup \{\square\}) \times (\mathcal{D} \cup \{\square\}) \times \{L, R\} \times \mathcal{S}$ is a finite set of* transitions *or* steps*;*
5. *$\uparrow \in \mathcal{S}$ is the initial state;*
6. *$\downarrow \subseteq \mathcal{S}$ is the set of final states.*

The blank $\square$ represents an empty tape cell. Henceforth, we will write $\mathcal{D}_\square$ instead of $\mathcal{D} \cup \{\square\}$. If $(s, a, d, e, T, t) \in \rightarrow$, we write $s \xrightarrow{a[d/e]T} t$, and this means that the machine, when it is in state s and d is the data element read by the tape head, can execute action a, replace d by e, can move one position left (L) or right (R) and end up in state t.

It requires quite some notational overhead to define the transition relation and the process graph associated to an RTM. The states of the process graph are the configurations of the RTM, consisting of a state of the RTM, the contents of the tape, and the position of the read/write head on the tape. We represent the tape contents by an element of $(\mathcal{D}_\square)^*$, replacing exactly one occurrence of a tape symbol d by a *marked* symbol $\check{d}$, indicating that the read/write head is on this symbol. We denote by $\check{\mathcal{D}}_\square = \{\check{d} \mid d \in \mathcal{D}_\square\}$ the set of marked tape symbols; a *tape instance* is a sequence $\delta \in (\mathcal{D}_\square \cup \check{\mathcal{D}}_\square)^*$ containing exactly one element of $\check{\mathcal{D}}_\square$. Note that we do not use δ exclusively for tape instances; we also use δ for sequences over $\mathcal{D}$. A tape instance thus is a finite sequence of symbols that represents the contents of a two-way infinite tape. Henceforth, we do not distinguish between tape instances that are equal modulo the addition or removal of extra occurrences of the blank symbol $\square$ at the left or right extremes of the sequence. That is, we do not distinguish tape instances δ and ζ if $\square^\omega \delta \square^\omega = \square^\omega \zeta \square^\omega$.

A *configuration* of an RTM M is a pair (s, δ) where $s \in \mathcal{S}$ is a state of the RTM and δ is a tape instance.

We define an $\mathcal{A}_\tau$-labelled transition system for each RTM such that a transition $s \xrightarrow{a[d/e]T} t$ corresponds to a transition $(s,\delta) \xrightarrow{a} (t,\zeta)$, where in δ some occurrence of d is marked, and in ζ this marked d is replaced by e, and the symbol to the left in ζ is marked (if $T = L$) or the symbol to the right in ζ is marked (if $T = R$). If necessary, a blank $\square$ is added. For this, we use the following notation: if $\delta \in \mathcal{D}_\square^*$, then $\delta^< = \check{\square}$ if $\delta = \varepsilon$ and $\delta^< = \zeta\check{d}$ if $\delta = \zeta d$ for some $d \in \mathcal{D}_\square, \zeta \in \mathcal{D}_\square^*$. Likewise, if $\delta \in \mathcal{D}_\square^*$, then $^>\delta = \check{\square}$ if $\delta = \varepsilon$ and $^>\delta = \check{d}\zeta$ if $\delta = d\zeta$ for some $d \in \mathcal{D}_\square, \zeta \in \mathcal{D}_\square^*$.

Definition 11. *Let $M = (\mathcal{S}, \mathcal{A}, \mathcal{D}, \rightarrow, \uparrow, \downarrow)$ be an RTM. The* process graph associated with M *is defined as follows:*

1. *the set of states is the set of configurations (s,δ) of M;*
2. *the set of actions is $\mathcal{A}$;*
3. *the transition relation $\rightarrow$ is the least relation satisfying, for all $a \in \mathcal{A}_\tau, d, e \in \mathcal{D}_\square, \delta, \zeta \in \mathcal{D}_\square^*$:*

$$(s, \delta\check{d}\zeta) \xrightarrow{a} (t, \delta^< e\zeta) \iff s \xrightarrow{a[d/e]L} t$$

and

$$(s, \delta\check{d}\zeta) \xrightarrow{a} (t, \delta e^> \zeta) \iff s \xrightarrow{a[d/e]R} t$$

4. *the initial state is $(\uparrow, \check{\square})$;*
5. *the set of final states is $\{(s,\delta) \mid s \downarrow\}$.*

A process is executable iff *its branching bisimulation equivalence class of process graphs contains a process graph associated with an RTM. A language is computable* iff *it is the language of a process graph associated with an RTM.*

Theorem 3. *A process is executable if and only if it is the process of a queue automaton.*

Proof. Let $M = (\mathcal{S}, \mathcal{A}, \mathcal{D}, \rightarrow, \uparrow, \downarrow)$ be an RTM, and suppose M has n transitions $T_1, \dots, T_n$. For each transition T_i, we have 5 new states $s_i^1, s_i^2, s_i^3, s_i^4, s_i^5$. In addition, we have an extra state $\uparrow'$. A configuration $(s, \delta\check{d}\zeta)$ of the RTM will correspond to the state $(s, \zeta^R \lozenge \delta d)$ of the queue automaton to be constructed, where the symbol $\lozenge$ is a separator and ζ^R is the reverse of the string ζ. Note that we have to treat $\square$ as an extra data element, because the RTM uses blanks in this way. Now we define the queue automaton Q as follows:

1. the set of states is $\mathcal{S}$, extended with new states $\{s_i^1, s_i^2, s_i^3, s_i^4, s_i^5 \mid i \leq n\} \cup \{\uparrow'\}$;
2. the set of actions is $\mathcal{A}$;
3. the set of data is $\mathcal{D} \cup \{\square, \lozenge, \$\}$ ($\$$ is a new data element used as a bookmark);
4. if $s \xrightarrow{a[d/e]L} t$ is the transition T_i in M, then in Q there are transitions $s \xrightarrow{a[d/\$]} s_i^1 \xrightarrow{\tau[\lozenge/e\lozenge\square]} s_i^2 \xrightarrow{\tau[\$/\varepsilon]} t$ and, for each $f \in \mathcal{D}_\square$, transitions $s_i^1 \xrightarrow{\tau[f/f]} s_i^1$ and $s_i^2 \xrightarrow{\tau[f/f]} s_i^2$; moreover, if $s \xrightarrow{a[d/e]R} t$ is transition T_j in M, then there are transitions $s \xrightarrow{a[d/\$e]} s_j^1 \xrightarrow{\tau[\lozenge/\lozenge]} s_j^2 \xrightarrow{\tau[\$/\square\$]} s_j^4 \xrightarrow{\tau[\$/\varepsilon]} t$ and, for each $f, g \in \mathcal{D}_\square$, transitions $s_j^2 \xrightarrow{\tau[g/\varepsilon]} s_j^3 \xrightarrow{\tau[\$/g\$]} s_j^4, s_j^1 \xrightarrow{\tau[f/f]} s_j^1, s_i^3 \xrightarrow{\tau[f/f]} s_i^3$ and $s_j^4 \xrightarrow{\tau[f/f]} s_j^4$ in Q.

5. the initial state is $\uparrow$ and add a transition $\uparrow \xrightarrow{\tau[\varepsilon/\lozenge\square]} \uparrow'$ in Q.
6. the set of final states is $\downarrow$.

Then, we can establish that the process graph of Q is branching bisimilar to the process graph associated with M.

For the other direction, suppose a process has a process graph given by a queue automaton $Q = (\mathcal{S}, \mathcal{A}, \mathcal{D}, \rightarrow, \uparrow, \downarrow)$. Without loss of generality, we can suppose Q has only singleton enqueues and separate dequeues. Suppose Q has n transitions $T_1, \ldots, T_n$. For each transition T_i, we have a new state s'_i. A state $(s, \delta d)$ of the queue automaton will correspond to the configuration $(s, \square \delta \check{d} \square)$ of the RTM to be constructed, and state (s, ε) to configuration $(s, \check{\square})$. Now define an RTM M as follows:

1. the set of states is $\mathcal{S}$, extended with new states $\{s'_i, s''_i \mid i \leq n\}$;
2. the set of actions is $\mathcal{A}$, the set of data is $\mathcal{D}$;
3. if $s \xrightarrow{a[d/\varepsilon]} t$ is a transition in Q, then $s \xrightarrow{a[d/\square]L} t$ is a transition in M; further, if $s \xrightarrow{a[\varepsilon/\varepsilon]} t$ is a transition in Q, then $s \xrightarrow{a[\square/\square]L} t$ is a transition in M; lastly, if $s \xrightarrow{a[*/d]} t$ is the transition T_i in Q, then $s \xrightarrow{a[\square/d]R} s'_i \xrightarrow{\tau[\square/\square]L} t$ are transitions in M and, for each $e \in \mathcal{D}$, $s \xrightarrow{a[e/e]L} s''_i$ and $s''_i \xrightarrow{\tau[e/e]L} s''_i$ and $s'_i \xrightarrow{\tau[e/e]R} s'_i$ are also transitions in M; finally, also $s''_i \xrightarrow{\tau[\square/d]R} s'_i$ is a transition in M;
4. the initial state is $\uparrow$, and the set of final states is $\downarrow$.

Again, we can establish that the process graph of M is branching bisimilar to the process graph of Q.

Corollary 1. *A language is computable if and only if it is the language of a queue automaton.*

A Turing machine can also be used to define when a function is computable. In [8], we defined this also for the Reactive Turing Machine. Here, we do this for the queue automaton, and give a couple of examples. We designate an input port i and an output port o.

Definition 12. *We say a queue automaton performs a* computation *if*

1. *the process graph of the queue automaton is deterministic;*
2. *every string in the language of the queue automaton consists of a sequence of inputs $i?d_1 \cdots i?d_n$ and a sequence of outputs $o!e_1 \cdots o!e_m$ interleaved (so not necessarily all outputs after all inputs) for some $n, m \geq 0$, $d_i, e_j \in \mathcal{D}$. Note that the length of input and output may differ.*

In this case, we say the queue automaton computes the function f on a domain of data strings D ($D \subseteq \mathcal{D}^*$) *if for all input $w \in D$ it has output $f(w) \in \mathcal{D}^*$.*

Example 4. By an adaptation of Example 1, we can define the function $f(w) = ww$ on $\mathcal{D}^*$. See Fig. 4.

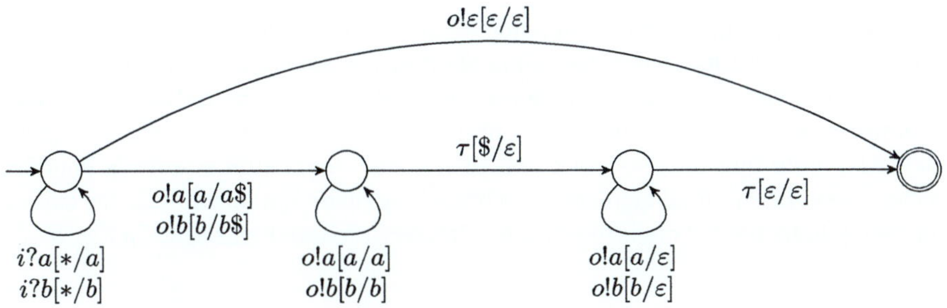

Fig. 4. Queue automaton for the function $f(w) = ww$ on $\{a, b\}^*$.

Example 5. There is a queue automaton that compares quantities. Suppose we have two numbers in binary notation and we want to know whether the first number is larger than the second. For simplicity, we assume the numbers have an equal number of digits, adding leading zeroes if necessary. The input consists of the two numbers separated by a $>$-sign, and $\mathcal{D} = \{0, 1, >, yes, no\}$. Figure 5 explains the rest. Note that no τ-steps are needed.

Thus, a queue automaton can be used to program a conditional branching in a program. In the same way, we can find queue automata for other program constructs, and other mathematical functions. Notice that there is a clear separation between input and output on the one hand, and memory use on the other hand. In this case, we only need to store the first number in memory, not the second one. Also notice that as soon as we have a difference between the two numbers, we can determine the output, and there is no need for the rest of the input.

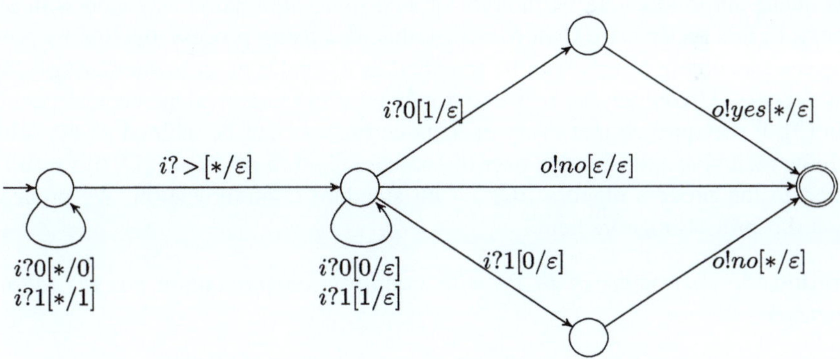

Fig. 5. Queue automaton comparing quantities.

In the following, we use some basic recursion theory. The reader is refered to, e.g., [22]. In [8], we characterised the set of executable processes as follows. We call a process graph *effective* if its transition relation and its set of final states are recursively enumerable (with some suitable encoding of these into natural numbers), see [10]. A process is effective if its branching bisimulation equivalence class contains an effective process graph. We proved in [8] that a process is effective if and only it is executable. In this result, it is needed to abstract from divergencies (infinite sequences of inert τ-steps). Also note that the process graph of a queue automaton is always boundedly branching, but the minimal element of its branching bisimulation equivalence class can be infinitely branching. This is the case for the queue automaton shown in Fig. 6.

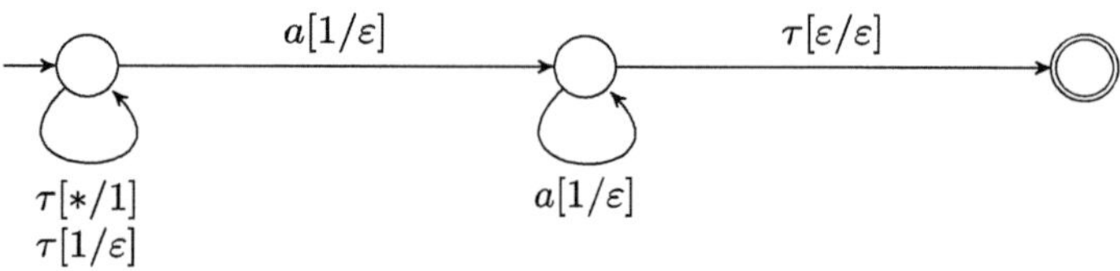

Fig. 6. Queue automaton, of which the process graph is branching bisimilar to an infinitely branching process graph.

5   Process Algebra

In this section, we express the executable processes in a mathematical formalism. In the theory of automata and formal languages, such a notation is often called a *grammar*. In concurrency theory or process theory, such a notation is often called a *process algebra*. In this process algebra, we can concisely express communication between executable processes.

A queue automaton can be thought of as a finite automaton extended with queue memory. In this section, we shall formalise this idea using process algebra, by proving that every executable process can be specified as a regular process interacting with the queue process. Thereafter, we will also briefly consider universal queue automata.

In [3], it was proven that every executable process can be defined as the solution of a finite recursive specification over the process algebra ACP_τ; in [1], this result was updated to the process algebra BCP_τ with standard communication. We proceed to present this process algebra here.

Definition 13. *The syntax of BCP_τ with standard communication has the following ingredients:*

1. *there is a constant* **0** *denoting inaction or deadlock: it denotes the finite automaton with a single state that is initial but not final and that has no transitions;*
2. *there is a constant* **1** *denoting termination or acceptance: it denotes the finite automaton with a single state that is initial and final and that has no transitions;*
3. *there is a finite set of constants $\mathcal{X}$ of process identifiers or process variables; we use capital letters $X, Y, \ldots$ to range over $\mathcal{X}$;*

4. *there is a set $\mathcal{A}$ of actions, a finite set $\mathcal{D}$ of data and a finite set $\mathcal{C}$ of communication ports: for each $d \in \mathcal{D}, c \in \mathcal{C}$ there are actions $c!d$ (send or output d at c), $c?d$ (receive or input d at c) and $c(d)$ (communicate d at c); in addition, there is the unobservable action τ; for each action $a \in \mathcal{A}_\tau$, there is the unary action prefix $a.\_$;*
5. *there is the binary operator $+$ denoting choice or alternative composition;*
6. *there is the binary operator $\|$ denoting merge or parallel composition;*
7. *for each communication port c, there is the unary operator $\partial_c(\_)$ denoting restriction or encapsulation of all actions $c?d, c!d$ for $d \in \mathcal{D}$;*
8. *there is the unary operator $\tau_C(\_)$ denoting hiding or abstraction of all actions $c(d)$ for $d \in \mathcal{D}, c \in \mathcal{C}$.*

A recursive specification over BCP_τ is a mapping Γ from $\mathcal{X}$ to the set of BCP_τ expressions. The idea is that the process expression p associated with a process identifier $X \in \mathcal{X}$ by Γ defines the behaviour of X. We prefer to think of Γ as a collection of defining equations $X \stackrel{\text{def}}{=} p$, exactly one for every $X \in \mathcal{X}$. We shall, in the sequel, presuppose a recursive specification Γ defining the process identifiers in $\mathcal{X}$, and we shall usually simply write $X \stackrel{\text{def}}{=} p$ for $\Gamma(X) = p$. Note that, by our assumption that $\mathcal{X}$ is finite, Γ is finite too.

$$\frac{}{1 \downarrow} \qquad \frac{}{a.p \xrightarrow{a} p}$$

$$\frac{p \downarrow}{(p+q) \downarrow} \qquad \frac{q \downarrow}{(p+q) \downarrow} \qquad \frac{p \xrightarrow{a} p'}{p+q \xrightarrow{a} p'} \qquad \frac{q \xrightarrow{a} q'}{p+q \xrightarrow{a} q'}$$

$$\frac{p \downarrow \quad q \downarrow}{p \| q \downarrow} \qquad \frac{p \xrightarrow{a} p'}{p \| q \xrightarrow{a} p' \| q} \qquad \frac{q \xrightarrow{a} q'}{p \| q \xrightarrow{a} p \| q'}$$

$$\frac{p \xrightarrow{c!d} p' \quad q \xrightarrow{c?d} q'}{p \| q \xrightarrow{c(d)} p' \| q'} \qquad \frac{p \xrightarrow{c?d} p' \quad q \xrightarrow{c!d} q'}{p \| q \xrightarrow{c(d)} p' \| q'}$$

$$\frac{p \downarrow}{\partial_c(p) \downarrow} \qquad \frac{p \xrightarrow{a} p' \quad a \neq c!d, c?d}{\partial_c(p) \xrightarrow{a} \partial_c(p')}$$

$$\frac{p \downarrow}{\tau_C(p) \downarrow} \qquad \frac{p \xrightarrow{c(d)} p'}{\tau_C(p) \xrightarrow{\tau} \tau_C(p')} \qquad \frac{p \xrightarrow{a} p' \quad a \neq c(d)}{\tau_C(p) \xrightarrow{a} \tau_C(p')}$$

$$\frac{p\downarrow \quad X \stackrel{\text{def}}{=} p}{X \downarrow} \qquad \frac{p \xrightarrow{a} p' \quad X \stackrel{\text{def}}{=} p}{X \xrightarrow{a} p'}$$

Fig. 7. Operational semantics for BCP_τ with standard communication ($a \in \mathcal{A}_\tau, c \in \mathcal{C}, d \in \mathcal{D}, X \in \mathcal{X}$).

We associate behaviour with process expressions by defining, on the set of process expressions, a unary acceptance predicate $\downarrow$ (written postfix) and, for every $a \in \mathcal{A}_\tau$, a binary transition relation $\xrightarrow{a}$ (written infix), by means of the transition system specification presented in Fig. 7.

By means of these rules, the set of process expressions turns into a labelled transition system, so we have strong bisimilarity and branching bisimilarity on process expressions. Suppose p is a BCP_τ expression (possibly containing variables from $\mathcal{X}$). Then the *process* of p is the branching bisimulation equivalence class of the process graph generated by the operational rules.

We explicitly state the result in [1]:

Theorem 4. *The process of every BCP_τ expression is executable. For every executable process, there is a BCP_τ expression with this process.*

Corollary 2. *Let p, q be two BCP_τ expressions, and $c \in \mathcal{C}$ a communication port. Then $p \parallel q$, $\partial_c(p \parallel q)$ and $\tau_{\mathcal{C}}(\partial_c(p \parallel q))$ denote executable processes.*

In this way, we can express the communication of two processes. Using Theorem 2, we can also obtain this result directly for queue automata.

Example 6. We give the following finite specification of the queue process of Example 3, adapted from [13]:

$$Q^{io} \stackrel{\text{def}}{=} 1 + o!\varepsilon.Q^{io} + \sum_{d \in \mathcal{D}} i?d.\tau_{\mathcal{C}}(\partial_\ell(Q^{i\ell} \parallel (1 + o!d.Q^{\ell o})))$$

$$Q^{i\ell} \stackrel{\text{def}}{=} 1 + \ell!\varepsilon.Q^{i\ell} + \sum_{d \in \mathcal{D}} i?d.\tau_{\mathcal{C}}(\partial_o(Q^{io} \parallel (1 + \ell!d.Q^{oi})))$$

$$Q^{\ell o} \stackrel{\text{def}}{=} 1 + o!\varepsilon.Q^{\ell o} + \sum_{d \in \mathcal{D}} \ell?d.\tau_{\mathcal{C}}(\partial_i(Q^{\ell i} \parallel (1 + o!d.Q^{io})))$$

$$Q^{o\ell} \stackrel{\text{def}}{=} 1 + \ell!\varepsilon.Q^{o\ell} + \sum_{d \in \mathcal{D}} o?d.\tau_{\mathcal{C}}(\partial_i(Q^{oi} \parallel (1 + \ell!d.Q^{i\ell})))$$

$$Q^{\ell i} \stackrel{\text{def}}{=} 1 + i!\varepsilon.Q^{\ell i} + \sum_{d \in \mathcal{D}} \ell?d.\tau_{\mathcal{C}}(\partial_o(Q^{\ell o} \parallel (1 + o!d.Q^{oi})))$$

$$Q^{oi} \stackrel{\text{def}}{=} 1 + i!\varepsilon.Q^{oi} + \sum_{d \in \mathcal{D}} o?d.\tau_{\mathcal{C}}(\partial_\ell(Q^{o\ell} \parallel (1 + i!d.Q^{\ell i})))$$

This specification uses data set $\mathcal{D} \cup \{\varepsilon\}$.

Recall that a regular process has a process graph with finitely many states and transitions.

Theorem 5. *Let p be an executable process. Then there is a regular process q such that $p \leftrightarrow_b \tau_{\mathcal{C}}(\partial_{io}(q \parallel Q^{io}))$.*

Proof. Let p be an executable process. Then by Theorem 3 there is a queue automaton $Q = (\mathcal{S}, \mathcal{A}, \mathcal{D}, \rightarrow, \uparrow, \downarrow)$ that defines p. By Lemma 2, we can assume without loss of generality that Q has singleton enqueues and separate dequeues. In order to define q, we have to remember the head of the queue or remember that the queue is empty, in order to be able to know which following step is possible.

1. for each state $s \in \mathcal{S}$ and $d \in \mathcal{D} \cup \{\varepsilon\}$, q has states s_d, s_d^1, s_d^2, s_d^3;
2. the queue Q^{io} uses data set $\mathcal{D} \cup \{\$\}$;
3. the initial state of q is $\uparrow_\varepsilon$, and state s_d is final whenever s is final in Q;
4. whenever Q has $s \xrightarrow{a[\varepsilon/\varepsilon]} t$, then q has $s_\varepsilon \xrightarrow{a} t_\varepsilon$;
5. whenever Q has $s \xrightarrow{a[*/d]} t$ for some $d \in \mathcal{D}$, then q has $s_e \xrightarrow{a} t_e^1 \xrightarrow{i!d} t_e$ for all $e \in \mathcal{D}$ and $s_\varepsilon \xrightarrow{a} t_d^1 \xrightarrow{i!d} t_d$;
6. whenever Q has $s \xrightarrow{a[d/\varepsilon]} t$ for some $d \in \mathcal{D}$, then q has $s_d \xrightarrow{a} s_d^1 \xrightarrow{o?d} s_d^2 \xrightarrow{o?\varepsilon} t_\varepsilon$; moreover, for all $e \in \mathcal{D}$ q has steps $s_d^2 \xrightarrow{o?e} t_e^3 \xrightarrow{i!\$} t_e^2 \xrightarrow{i!e} t_e^1 \xrightarrow{o?\$} t_e$ and for all $f \in \mathcal{D}$ steps $t_e^1 \xrightarrow{o?f} t_e^1$.

All input and output steps in q will successfully communicate with the queue, and be turned into τ-steps by the abstraction operator. All will turn out to be inert.

Note that the converse of this theorem is also true, as every process defined by a finite specification over BCP_τ with standard communication is executable.

Just like we did in [8], we can prove a universal queue automaton U exists. For an arbitrary queue automaton M, let $\overline{M}$ be the deterministic queue automaton that outputs the Gödel number of M (in some appropriate representation) along a special communication port u, then terminates with empty queue, and has no other behaviour. Then a *universal* queue automaton U is such that $\tau_C(\partial_u(\overline{M} \parallel U))$ has the same process as M for all queue automata M (here, we use the BCP_τ-expressions of these queue automata to define this process).

6 A Hierarchy

A computer shows interaction between the finite control and the memory. The finite control can be represented by a regular process (a finite automaton). In this article, we considered a memory in the form of a queue.

In [5], we considered a memory in the form of a stack, and we established that a pushdown process can be characterised as a regular process communicating with a stack. This work was continued in [4] and [7] to find the process algebra $\mathrm{TSP};_{sc}$ that is associated with pushdown automata. $\mathrm{TSP};_{sc}$ is obtained from the process algebra BCP_τ of the previous section by leaving out parallel composition, encapsulation and abstraction, and adding sequencing with sequential value passing.

In [6], we considered a memory in the form of a bag, and we established that a parallel pushdown process can be characterised as a regular process communicating with a bag. We found the process algebra associated with parallel pushdown automata. This process algebra is obtained from the process algebra BCP_τ of the previous section by leaving out the abstraction operator and adding the priority operator of [2].

We see that the queue is the prototypical executable process, as all executable processes can be realised as a regular process communicating with a queue. Likewise, the bag is the prototypical parallel pushdown process. A bag is an executable process, but not a pushdown process. Further, the stack is the prototypical pushdown process, but not a parallel pushdown process.

A counter can be realised as a stack with a singleton data set, and also as a bag with a singleton data set. Thus, it is in the intersection of pushdown processes and parallel pushdown processes. It is not a regular process, as it has infinitely many different states that are not bisimilar. We conjecture that every process in the intersection of pushdown processes and parallel pushdown processes can be realised as a regular process communicating with a counter, but have no proof of this yet. Figure 8 provides a complete picture.

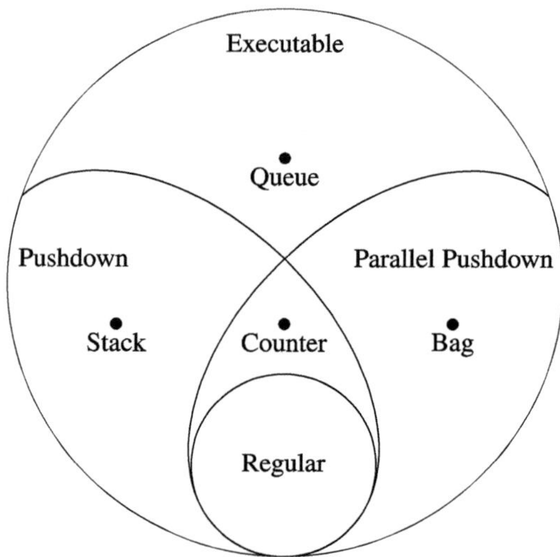

Fig. 8. Classification of Executable, Pushdown, Parallel Pushdown, and Regular processes and the prototypical processes Queue, Bag, Stack and Counter.

7   Conclusion

We considered the computational model of the Queue Automaton, and have proved that it is equally expressive as the Reactive Turing Machine of [8]. Thus, a process is executable if and only if it is the process of a queue automaton, and a language or function is computable if and only if it is the language or function of a queue automaton. Every executable process can be defined as a regular process communicating with a queue. This fits in very well with earlier results, that every pushdown process can be defined as a regular process communicating with a stack, and a parallel pushdown process can be defined as a regular process communicating with a bag. We think that a pushdown automaton can be better called a stack automaton, and a parallel pushdown automaton a bag automaton, in order to emphasise the relation to the queue automaton. As grammar for executable processes we use the process algebra BCP_τ, Basic Communicating Processes with abstraction and standard communication.

Disclosure of Interests. The authors have no competing interests to declare that are relevant to the content of this article.

References

1. Baeten, J.C.M., Basten, T., Reniers, M.: Process Algebra: Equational Theories of Communicating Processes, vol. 50. Cambridge University Press (2010)
2. Baeten, J.C.M., Bergstra, J.A., Klop, J.W.: Syntax and defining equations for an interrupt mechanism in process algebra. Fund. Inform. **9**, 127–168 (1986)
3. Baeten, J.C.M., Bergstra, J.A., Klop, J.W.: On the consistency of Koomen's fair abstraction rule. Theoret. Comput. Sci. **51**(1–2), 129–176 (1987)
4. Baeten, J.C.M., Carissimo, C., Luttik, B.: Pushdown automata and context-free grammars in bisimulation semantics. Logical Meth. Comput. Sci. **19**, 15:1-15:32 (2023). https://doi.org/10.46298/LMCS-19(1:15)2023
5. Baeten, J.C.M., Cuijpers, P.J.L., van Tilburg, P.J.A.: A context-free process as a pushdown automaton. In: van Breugel, F., Chechik, M. (eds.) CONCUR 2008. LNCS, vol. 5201, pp. 98–113. Springer, Heidelberg (2008). https://doi.org/10.1007/978-3-540-85361-9_11
6. Baeten, J.C.M., Luttik, B.: Parallel pushdown automata and commutative context-free grammars in bisimulation semantics (extended abstract). In: Mezzina, C.A., Caltais, G. (eds.) Proceedings Combined 30th International Workshop on Expressiveness in Concurrency and 20th Workshop on Structural Operational Semantics, EXPRESS/SOS 2023, Antwerp, Belgium, 18th September 2023. EPTCS, vol. 387, pp. 114–131 (2023). https://doi.org/10.4204/EPTCS.387.9
7. Baeten, J.C.M., Luttik, B.: Sequential value passing yields a Kleene theorem for processes. In: Capretta, V., Krebbers, R., Wiedijk, F. (eds.) Logics and Type Systems in Theory and Practice. LNCS, vol. 14560, pp. 1–16. Springer, Cham (2024). https://doi.org/10.1007/978-3-031-61716-4_1
8. Baeten, J.C.M., Luttik, B., van Tilburg, P.: Reactive Turing machines. Inf. Comput. **231**, 143–166 (2013). https://doi.org/10.1016/j.ic.2013.08.010. fundamentals of Computation Theory
9. Basten, T.: Branching bisimulation is an equivalence indeed! Inf. Process. Lett. **58**, 141–147 (1996)
10. Boudol, G.: Notes on algebraic calculi of processes. In: Apt, K.R. (ed.) Logics and Models of Concurrent Systems, pp. 261–303. Springer, Heidelberg (1985). https://doi.org/10.1007/978-3-642-82453-1_9
11. Glabbeek, R.J.: The linear time — branching time spectrum II. In: Best, E. (ed.) CONCUR 1993. LNCS, vol. 715, pp. 66–81. Springer, Heidelberg (1993). https://doi.org/10.1007/3-540-57208-2_6
12. van Glabbeek, R.J., Luttik, B., Trčka, N.: Branching bisimilarity with explicit divergence. Fund. Inform. **93**(4), 371–392 (2009). https://doi.org/10.3233/FI-2009-109
13. van Glabbeek, R.J., Vaandrager, F.W.: Modular specification of process algebras. Theor. Comput. Sci. **113**(2), 293–348 (1993). https://doi.org/10.1016/0304-3975(93)90006-F
14. van Glabbeek, R.J., Weijland, P.: Branching time and abstraction in bisimulation semantics. J. ACM **43**(3), 555–600 (1996). https://doi.org/10.1145/233551.233556
15. Hopcroft, J.E., Motwani, R., Ullman, J.D.: Introduction to Automata Theory, Languages, and Computation. Pearson Education (2007)
16. Kutrib, M., Malcher, A., Wendlandt, M.: Queue automata: foundations and developments. In: Adamatzky, A. (ed.) Reversibility and Universality. ECC, vol. 30, pp. 385–431. Springer, Cham (2018). https://doi.org/10.1007/978-3-319-73216-9_19

17. Luttik, B., Yang, F.: The π-calculus is behaviourally complete and orbit-finitely executable. Log. Methods Comput. Sci. **17**(1) (2021). https://lmcs.episciences.org/7165
18. Manna, Z.: Mathematical Theory of Computation. McGraw-Hill (1974)
19. Mauw, S., Mulder, H.: Regularity of BPA-systems is decidable. In: Jonsson, B., Parrow, J. (eds.) CONCUR 1994. LNCS, vol. 836, pp. 34–47. Springer, Heidelberg (1994). https://doi.org/10.1007/978-3-540-48654-1_4
20. Milner, R.: Communication and Concurrency. Prentice Hall, Englewood Cliffs (1989)
21. Post, E.L.: Formal reductions of the classical combinatorial decision problem. Am. J. Math. **65**, 197–215 (1943)
22. Rogers, Jr., H.: Theory of Recursive Functions and Effective Computability. McGraw-Hill (1967)
23. van Tilburg, P.: From Computability to Executability. Ph.D. thesis, Eindhoven University of Technology (2011)
24. Turing, A.M.: On computable numbers, with an application to the Entscheidungsproblem. Proc. Lond. Math. Soc. **2**(42), 230–265 (1936)
25. Vollmar, R.: Über einen automaten mit pufferspeicherung. Computing **5**, 57–70 (1970)

Fracterm Calculus for Partial Meadows

Jan A. Bergstra and Alban Ponse[(✉)]

Informatics Institute, University of Amsterdam, Science Park 900, 1098 XH
Amsterdam, The Netherlands
`J.A.Bergstra@uva.nl`, `A.Ponse@uva.nl`

Abstract. Partial algebras and partial data types are discussed with
the use of signatures that allow partial functions, and a three-valued
short-circuit (sequential) first order logic with a Tarski semantics. The
propositional part of this logic is also known as McCarthy calculus and
has been studied extensively.

Axioms for the fracterm calculus of partial meadows are given. The
case is made that in this way a rather natural formalisation of fields with
division operator is obtained. It is noticed that the logic thus obtained
cannot express that division by zero must be undefined.

An interpretation of the three-valued sequential logic into $\perp$-enlarge-
ments of partial algebras is given, for which it is concluded that the
consequence relation of the former logic is semi-computable, and that
the $\perp$-enlargement of a partial meadow is a common meadow.

Keywords: fracterm calculus · partial meadow · common meadow ·
abstract data type

1   Introduction

Following [10], we use *meadow* for fields equipped with an inverse or a division
function. A *partial* meadow is a field equipped with a partial division function,
here written $\frac{x}{y}$ in fractional notation. A partial meadow is a partial algebra
because division is partial as $\frac{x}{0}$ is undefined. A *fracterm* is an expression of the
form $\frac{p}{q}$, where p and q are terms over the signature under consideration.

Fracterm calculus for partial meadows (FTCpm) fully accepts $\frac{1}{0}$ as a fracterm, in spite of it having no value. At the same time a three valued logic is
adopted. For instance in FTCpm it is not the case that $\frac{1}{0} = \frac{1}{0}$ and neither is it
the case that $\frac{1}{0} \neq \frac{1}{0}$. Both assertions are considered syntactically valid, however.
We will use *partial equality*, written $=_\mathsf{p}$ for the equality sign for partial data
types. If either t or r has no value then $t =_\mathsf{p} r$ has no classical truth value, i.e.
true or false. The assertion $\phi(x)$ with

$$\phi(x) \equiv x \neq_\mathsf{p} 0 \rightarrow \frac{x}{x} =_\mathsf{p} 1$$

This paper is dedicated to Sjouke Mauw, a full version including all longer proofs
appeared as [7].

B. Fila et al. (Eds.): Sjouke Mauw Festschrift, LNCS 16365, pp. 29–53, 2026.
https://doi.org/10.1007/978-3-032-20684-8_3

is taken for a fundamental fact about partial meadows which holds for all x. Contemplating the substitution $x = 0$ suggests that the most plausible reading of the implication in $\phi(x)$ is a short-circuit implication (also referred to as sequential implication, or as the implication of McCarthy's logic), a state of affairs which we wish to make explicit in the symbolic notation. Following [2] we will denote short-circuit implication with the connective $\circ\!\!\rightarrow$, thereby changing ϕ to ϕ':

$$\phi'(x) \equiv x \neq_\mathsf{p} 0 \circ\!\!\rightarrow \frac{x}{x} =_\mathsf{p} 1.$$

We notice that evaluation of $\phi'(0)$ will not involve an attempt to evaluate the fracterm $\frac{0}{0}$, because $0 \neq_\mathsf{p} 0$ evaluates to false, thereby rendering the implication at hand true without further inspection of its consequent. Moreover, once division is modelled as a partial function, assigning a Boolean truth value to $\frac{0}{0} =_\mathsf{p} \frac{0}{0}$ becomes artificial and the use of a non-classical logic with three or more truth values becomes plausible if not unavoidable. One may object that $\frac{0}{0} =_\mathsf{p} \frac{0}{0}$ is an assertion that "asks" for division by 0 which for that reason must be excluded. The reasons for understanding logical connectives in a short-circuited manner (i.e. McCarthy logic) are these: the most plausible alternatives are versions of strong Kleene logic which allow $\mathsf{T} \vee x = x \vee \mathsf{T} = \mathsf{T}$ for all truth values x including non-Boolean ones and T a constant for truth. The use of such logics is plausible in computer science, for instance in [19] the equality relation $=_\mathsf{p}$ (in [19] simply denoted with $=$) is combined with a strong Kleene logic. The preference of [19] for that logic is based on the symmetry of conjunction and disjunction, symmetries which are lost in the short-circuit case. By consequence one finds that $\psi(x) \equiv \frac{x}{0} = 2 \vee x = 3$ would be true for $x = 3$. Evaluating $\psi(3)$, however, seems to call for an attempt to evaluate $\frac{3}{0}$ which is impossible for elementary arithmetic. For these reasons we deviate from [19] by adopting short-circuit logic as preferable in the case of rational numbers with a partial division function. Some general background on short-circuit logic is given in Sect. 6.

We are unaware of any existing work which investigates the details of the above view of partial meadows, or stated differently of formalising arithmetics involving a partial division function.

1.1   Survey of the Paper

The contents of this paper corresponds to [7], only some explanation of *Prover9* and *Mace4* results has been omitted, as well as the proofs of Propositions 1 and 2, and Theorems 2 and 3(see [7, Prop.2.2.1 & 3.3.1, Thm.3.3.3 & 5.2.1]).

We consider the following results of this paper to be new:

(i) The claim that short-circuit logic is the most natural logic for use in the context of partial meadows, plus a listing of reasons, together constituting a rationale, for that claim (see below).

(ii) A complete axiomatisation of the fracterm calculus of partial meadows. Here we notice that two variants of completeness must be distinguished:

 – Axiomatisation completeness: complete axiomatisation of a class of (partial) algebras using a logic with given semantics.

- Logical completeness: completeness of a proof system for a logic with given semantics.

Axiomatisation completeness is the focus of our paper. Axiomatisation completeness (with fracterm calculus for partial meadows as the intended application) can be understood and appreciated without any regard to logical completeness. We intend this paper to be fully self-contained, both mathematically and in terms of motivation, and to be independent from any proof theoretic considerations.

(iii) A result on fracterm flattening in the context of the fracterm calculus of partial meadows.

(iv) An interpretation of the short-circuit logic for partial algebras into the first order logic of algebras enlarged with an element $\perp$ which serves as an absorptive element. The interpretation demonstrates that the consequence relation for short-circuit logic on partial algebras is semi-computable. Moreover, said interpretation indirectly provides a proof system, or rather a formal proof method for short-circuit logic over partial algebras, thereby demonstrating that a proof theory can be developed in principle. As a proof of concept, it is shown that the $\perp$-enlargement of a partial meadow is a *common* meadow, see e.g. [4,5,12] for common meadows.

1.2   On the Rationale of Fracterm Calculus for Partial Meadows

Fracterm calculus for partial meadows aims at formalising elementary arithmetic including division. Modelling division as a partial function is motivated by the idea that this is the most conventional viewpoint on division. All views where division has been made total are, however useful these views may be in the context of certain specific objectives, somehow unconventional.

Even if formalisation of elementary arithmetic can be simplified by having division total (which may be achieved in different ways), then it is still the case that using a partial function for modelling division provides a very relevant alternative which merits systematic investigation. At this stage it is unclear whether or not, and if so to which extent, totalisation of division is helpful for the formalisation and understanding of elementary arithmetic. Once the notion that division is modelled as a partial function, undefined when the denominator equals zero, has been adopted, it is plausible to require (i.e. as a design constraint for texts) that texts are to be written in such a manner and ordering that a reader, when reading in the order of presentation, will never be asked or invited to contemplate what happens when dividing by 0.

Dedication. We wrote this paper in honour of Sjouke Mauw. Sjouke was a very enthusiastic and effective member of the process algebra group in the late 1980s. His contribution ranged from theory (see, e.g., [21]) to the design and, in joint work with Gert Veltink and Bob Diertens the implementation, of the specification language PSF where process algebra and ASF-style algebraic specifications of abstract data types were combined into a language and the PSF Toolkit that were used for many years in educational practice, see, e.g., [17,22]. PSF uses total functions for data types, here we depart from that path and look at partial functions for abstract data types with a tailor-made logic for these.

Table 1. The set EqCL of axioms of CℓSCL with T, F and the connective $\mathbin{\circ\!\!\!\rightarrow}$

$$F = \neg T \tag{e1}$$

$$\phi \mathbin{\vee\!\!\!{}^{\circ}} \psi = \neg(\neg\phi \mathbin{\wedge\!\!\!{}_{\cdot}} \neg\psi) \tag{e2}$$

$$T \mathbin{\wedge\!\!\!{}_{\cdot}} \phi = \phi \tag{e3}$$

$$\phi \mathbin{\wedge\!\!\!{}_{\cdot}} (\phi \mathbin{\vee\!\!\!{}^{\circ}} \psi) = \phi \tag{e4}$$

$$(\phi \mathbin{\vee\!\!\!{}^{\circ}} \psi) \mathbin{\wedge\!\!\!{}_{\cdot}} \xi = (\neg\phi \mathbin{\wedge\!\!\!{}_{\cdot}} (\psi \mathbin{\wedge\!\!\!{}_{\cdot}} \xi)) \mathbin{\vee\!\!\!{}^{\circ}} (\phi \mathbin{\wedge\!\!\!{}_{\cdot}} \xi) \tag{e5}$$

$$(\phi \mathbin{\wedge\!\!\!{}_{\cdot}} \psi) \mathbin{\vee\!\!\!{}^{\circ}} (\psi \mathbin{\wedge\!\!\!{}_{\cdot}} \phi) = (\psi \mathbin{\wedge\!\!\!{}_{\cdot}} \phi) \mathbin{\vee\!\!\!{}^{\circ}} (\phi \mathbin{\wedge\!\!\!{}_{\cdot}} \psi) \tag{e6}$$

$$\phi \mathbin{\circ\!\!\!\rightarrow} \psi = \neg\phi \mathbin{\vee\!\!\!{}^{\circ}} \psi \tag{e7}$$

2 Partial Algebras with 3-Valued Sequential Logic

In Sect. 2.1 we define a three-valued sequential first order logic for partial algebras, and in Sect. 2.2 we discuss its semantics.

2.1 Sequential First Order Logic for Partial Algebras

We start by recalling an equational logic that defines the sequential, short-circuited connectives $\mathbin{\wedge\!\!\!{}_{\cdot}}$ and $\mathbin{\vee\!\!\!{}^{\circ}}$, called *short-circuit* (or *sequential*) disjunction and conjunction. In [6] we introduced so-called CℓSCL, Conditional Short-Circuit Logic, together with a relatively simple semantics based on evaluation trees for the sequential evaluation of atoms (propositional variables). In this paper, atoms will be partial equalities.

CℓSCL is equivalent with three-valued Conditional Logic, as introduced by Guzmán and Squier in [18], but is distinguished by the use of the specific notation for the short-circuit connectives mentioned above. In [6] we provided several complete, independent equational axiomatisations of CℓSCL, based on whether or not to include the constants T, F and U for the three truth values true, false and undefined, respectively.

In Table 1, we define the set EqCL of axioms of CℓSCL with constants T and F and and with the addition of the connective $\mathbin{\circ\!\!\!\rightarrow}$ that defines short-circuit implication. The axioms of EqCL imply double negation elimination, i.e.

$$\neg\neg\phi = \phi, \tag{DNE}$$

and therewith a sequential version of the duality principle: in equations without occurrences of $\mathbin{\circ\!\!\!\rightarrow}$, the connectives $\mathbin{\wedge\!\!\!{}_{\cdot}}$ and $\mathbin{\vee\!\!\!{}^{\circ}}$ and occurrences of T and F can be swapped. Axiom (e4) is a sequential version of the absorption law. Axioms (e5) and (e6) imply some other properties of these connectives and (e7) defines $\circ\!\!\rightarrow$. Next to (DNE), other useful consequences of EqCL are the following:

(a) $\phi \curlywedge \mathsf{T} = \phi$ and $\mathsf{T} \curlyvee \phi = \mathsf{T}$,
(b) $(\phi \curlywedge \psi) \curlywedge \xi = \phi \curlywedge (\psi \curlywedge \xi)$, so the connective $\curlywedge$ is associative,
(c) $\phi \curlywedge (\psi \curlywedge \phi) = \phi \curlywedge \psi$, so, with $\psi = \mathsf{T}$, $\curlywedge$ is idempotent, i.e. $\phi \curlywedge \phi = \phi$,
(d) $\phi \curlywedge (\psi \curlyvee \xi) = (\phi \curlywedge \psi) \curlyvee (\phi \curlywedge \xi)$, so $\curlywedge$ is left-distributive,
(e) $\phi \curlywedge \neg\phi = \neg\phi \curlywedge \phi$,
(f) $(\phi \curlywedge \psi) \circ\!\!\rightarrow \xi = \phi \circ\!\!\rightarrow (\psi \circ\!\!\rightarrow \xi)$.

Of course, the duals of (a)–(e), say (a)′–(e)′, are also consequences of EqCL. Consequences (DNE) and (a)–(f) follow quickly with help of the theorem prover *Prover9* [23]. Simple short proofs of (DNE) and (a)–(e) from (only) (e1)–(e5) are included in [9, App.A.3 & A.4]. At the end of Sect. 2.2 we discuss an example that refutes the commutativity of $\curlyvee$ and give a completeness result for EqCL.

Based on EqCL, we define a sequential first order logic for partial algebras, and in Sect. 3 we wil refine this logic to the specific case of partial meadows. Let Σ be a signature that contains one or more partial functions and a constant symbol c. Consider a partial Σ-algebra A with non-empty domain $|A|$. There is an equality relation called *partial equality* and written $=_{\mathsf{p}}$ which behaves on all domains as usual, i.e. as a normal equality relation. This means that for $a, b \in |A|$, $a =_{\mathsf{p}} b$ if, and only if, $a = b$, where $=$ is the normal equality relation on $|A|$. For clarification, we will illustrate further axioms and rules of inference with informal use of the semantics defined in Sect. 2.2.

With $\mathsf{L}_{\mathsf{sfol}}(\Sigma)$ we denote the collection of formulae inductively defined as follows, assuming a set V_{var} of variables:

− $\mathsf{T}, \mathsf{F} \in \mathsf{L}_{\mathsf{sfol}}(\Sigma)$,
− for Σ-terms t and r the *atomic* formulae $(t =_{\mathsf{p}} r) \in \mathsf{L}_{\mathsf{sfol}}(\Sigma)$,
− if $\phi \in \mathsf{L}_{\mathsf{sfol}}(\Sigma)$ then $\neg\phi \in \mathsf{L}_{\mathsf{sfol}}(\Sigma)$,
− if $\phi, \psi \in \mathsf{L}_{\mathsf{sfol}}(\Sigma)$, then $\phi \curlyvee \psi$, $\phi \curlywedge \psi$, and $\phi \circ\!\!\rightarrow \psi$ are in $\mathsf{L}_{\mathsf{sfol}}(\Sigma)$,
− if $\phi \in \mathsf{L}_{\mathsf{sfol}}(\Sigma)$ and $x \in V_{var}$, then $\exists_{\mathsf{p}}x.\phi$ and $\forall_{\mathsf{p}}x.\phi$ are in $\mathsf{L}_{\mathsf{sfol}}(\Sigma)$.

So, in $\mathsf{L}_{\mathsf{sfol}}(\Sigma)$, there is explicit quantification over variables that occur in atomic formulae. For example, we will see that a partial meadow satisfies

$$(\forall_{\mathsf{p}}x.x \neq_{\mathsf{p}} 0 \circ\!\!\rightarrow \frac{x}{x} =_{\mathsf{p}} 1) = \mathsf{T}.$$

We extend EqCL by adding the following axiom:

$$\exists_{\mathsf{p}}x.\phi = \neg\forall_{\mathsf{p}}x.\neg\phi. \tag{e8}$$

Next, we define $\mathsf{UL}_{\mathsf{sfol}}(\Sigma)$, the universal quantifier-free fragment of $\mathsf{L}_{\mathsf{sfol}}(\Sigma)$, and $\mathsf{Eq}(\mathsf{L}_{\mathsf{sfol}}(\Sigma))$, the collection of equations over $\mathsf{L}_{\mathsf{sfol}}(\Sigma)$ and the largest language we consider:

− If $\phi \in \mathsf{L}_{\mathsf{sfol}}(\Sigma)$ is quantifier-free, then $\phi \in \mathsf{UL}_{\mathsf{sfol}}(\Sigma)$,

– If $\phi, \psi \in \mathsf{L}_{\mathsf{sfol}}(\Sigma)$ then $(\phi = \psi) \in \mathsf{Eq}(\mathsf{L}_{\mathsf{sfol}}(\Sigma))$.

Hence, in both $\mathsf{UL}_{\mathsf{sfol}}(\Sigma)$ and $\mathsf{Eq}(\mathsf{L}_{\mathsf{sfol}}(\Sigma))$, variables can occur free. We give an example of a valid $\mathsf{Eq}(\mathsf{L}_{\mathsf{sfol}}(\Sigma))$-formula: a partial meadow A satisfies both $(x \neq_{\mathsf{p}} 0 \circ\!\!\rightarrow \frac{x}{x} =_{\mathsf{p}} 1) = \mathsf{T}$ and $(\forall_{\mathsf{p}} x.x \neq_{\mathsf{p}} 0 \circ\!\!\rightarrow \frac{x}{x} =_{\mathsf{p}} 1) = \mathsf{T}$, which is characterised by the equivalence

$$A \models (x \neq_{\mathsf{p}} 0 \circ\!\!\rightarrow \tfrac{x}{x} =_{\mathsf{p}} 1) = \mathsf{T} \iff A \models (\forall_{\mathsf{p}} x.\ x \neq_{\mathsf{p}} 0 \circ\!\!\rightarrow \tfrac{x}{x} =_{\mathsf{p}} 1) = \mathsf{T}.$$

More generally, for a partial Σ-algebra A, the following equivalences hold true for $\phi \in \mathsf{UL}_{\mathsf{sfol}}(\Sigma)$:

$$A \models \phi = \mathsf{T} \iff A \models (\forall_{\mathsf{p}} x.\phi) = \mathsf{T} \iff A \models (\neg \exists_{\mathsf{p}} x.\neg\phi) = \mathsf{T}, \qquad \text{(qF)}$$

where the second equivalence is a consequence of axiom (e8). The related equivalence $A \models (\exists_{\mathsf{p}} x.\phi) = \mathsf{T} \iff A \models (\neg\forall_{\mathsf{p}} x.\neg\phi) = \mathsf{T}$ is more complex, see Sect. 2.2.

We are especially interested in $\mathsf{Eq}(\mathsf{L}_{\mathsf{sfol}}(\Sigma))$-formulae of the form

$$\phi = \mathsf{T},$$

and give below axioms and rules for deriving such equations, accompanied by examples for partial meadows (which will be formally defined in Sect. 3). When proving results, and in some cases when writing axiom systems or designing operations on the syntax, we assume for simplification that all formulas can be written with a subset of the sequential connectives, for example, with connectives $\neg$ and $\,^{\vee}\!\!\wedge$ and with the universal quantifier $\forall_{\mathsf{p}}$ only (by axiom (e8)). Alternatively one may assume that connectives $\,^{\wedge}\!\!\wedge$ and $\circ\!\!\rightarrow$ are used as well as both quantifiers $\exists_{\mathsf{p}}$ and $\forall_{\mathsf{p}}$, on top of equations and denial inequations, that is negated equations written in the form $t \neq_{\mathsf{p}} r$.

Axioms for the Relation $=_{\mathsf{p}}$. This relation is not a congruence relation because it is not reflexive on expressions, for example, in a partial meadow it is not the case that $\frac{1}{0} =_{\mathsf{p}} \frac{1}{0}$ and neither is it the case that $\frac{1}{0} \neq_{\mathsf{p}} \frac{1}{0}$. Equations of the form $t =_{\mathsf{p}} t$ are used to express that t is defined and occur in the 'weak substitution property' (p6) and (p7) (cf. [3]). We write $\,^{\wedge}\!\!\wedge_{i=1}^{1} \phi_i = \phi_1$ and for $k > 0$, $\,^{\wedge}\!\!\wedge_{i=1}^{k+1} \phi_i = \phi_1 \,^{\wedge}\!\!\wedge (\,^{\wedge}\!\!\wedge_{i=2}^{k+1} \phi_i)$.

Axioms (and axiom schemes) for the relation $=_{\mathsf{p}}$ are the following, for any constant $c \in \Sigma$ and $x \in V_{var}$ and (open) Σ-terms t_i:

(p1) $(c =_{\mathsf{p}} c) = \mathsf{T}$,   (reflexivity for constants)

(p2) $(x =_{\mathsf{p}} x) = \mathsf{T}$,   (reflexivity for variables)

(p3) $((\,^{\wedge}\!\!\wedge_{i=1}^{2} t_i =_{\mathsf{p}} t_i) \circ\!\!\rightarrow (t_1 =_{\mathsf{p}} t_2 \circ\!\!\rightarrow t_2 =_{\mathsf{p}} t_1)) = \mathsf{T}$,   (symmetry)

(p4) $((\,^{\wedge}\!\!\wedge_{i=1}^{3} t_i =_{\mathsf{p}} t_i) \circ\!\!\rightarrow ((t_1 =_{\mathsf{p}} t_2 \,^{\wedge}\!\!\wedge t_2 =_{\mathsf{p}} t_3) \circ\!\!\rightarrow t_1 =_{\mathsf{p}} t_3)) = \mathsf{T}$.   (transitivity)

For each k-ary $f \in \Sigma$ that is total and all (open) Σ-terms $t_1, ..., t_k$:

(p5) $((\,^{\wedge}\!\!\wedge_{i=1}^{k} t_i =_{\mathsf{p}} t_i) \circ\!\!\rightarrow f(t_1, ..., t_k) =_{\mathsf{p}} f(t_1, ..., t_k)) = \mathsf{T}$.   (definedness)

For all k-ary $f \in \Sigma$ and all (open) Σ-terms $t_1, ..., t_k$, $r_1, ..., r_k$, the *weak substitution property*:

(p6) $(f(t_1, ..., t_k) =_{\mathsf{p}} f(t_1, ..., t_k) \multimap (\bigwedge_{i=1}^{k} t_i =_{\mathsf{p}} t_i)) = \mathsf{T}$,

(p7) $(((f(t_1, ..., t_k) =_{\mathsf{p}} f(t_1, ..., t_k) \wedge (\bigwedge_{i=1}^{k} t_i =_{\mathsf{p}} r_i))) \multimap$
$$f(t_1, ..., t_k) =_{\mathsf{p}} f(r_1, ..., r_k)) = \mathsf{T}.$$

For example, if in a partial meadow $\frac{t}{t}$ is defined then so is t by (p6), and if $\frac{t}{t}$ is defined and $t =_{\mathsf{p}} r$, then $\frac{t}{t} =_{\mathsf{p}} \frac{r}{r}$ by (p7).

More Axioms for $\mathsf{Eq}(\mathsf{L_{sfol}}(\Sigma))$. For t a Σ-term, $x \in V_{var}$, $\phi \in \mathsf{L_{sfol}}(\Sigma)$, and constant $c \in \Sigma$:

(a1) $((t =_{\mathsf{p}} t \wedge \forall_{\mathsf{p}} x.\phi) \multimap \phi[t/x]) = \mathsf{T}$ if no variables in t occur bounded in ϕ,

(a2) $(\forall_{\mathsf{p}} x.\ x =_{\mathsf{p}} c \vee x \neq_{\mathsf{p}} c) = \mathsf{T}$.

For example, with respect to a partial meadow, axiom (a1) excludes the substitution $x \mapsto \frac{y}{0}$ (because that would introduce undefinedness). A more extensive example using (a2) is the derivation of (Ex.1) on page 8. Note that by consequence (f) of EqCL, (a1) can also be written as

$$(t =_{\mathsf{p}} t \multimap (\forall_{\mathsf{p}} x.\phi \multimap \phi[t/x])) = \mathsf{T}.$$

Below we define two replacement rules (i1) and (i2) with help of the notion of a 'context': if a formula ϕ in $\mathsf{L_{sfol}}(\Sigma)$ has a subformula ψ, then ϕ is a *context* for ψ, notation $\phi \equiv C[\psi]$, where ψ can be written in boldface to indicate a single occurrence. For example, if $\phi \equiv (\psi \wedge \xi) \vee (\neg\psi)$, then

$$\phi \equiv C_1[\boldsymbol{\psi}] \equiv (\boldsymbol{\psi} \wedge \xi) \vee (\neg\psi) \quad \text{and} \quad \phi \equiv C_2[\boldsymbol{\psi}] \equiv (\psi \wedge \xi) \vee (\neg\boldsymbol{\psi}).$$

Rules of Inference for $\mathsf{Eq}(\mathsf{L_{sfol}}(\Sigma))$. We write $\vdash \phi = \psi$ for the derivability of $\phi = \psi$ from the above axioms, in particular including those of EqCL (Table 1) extended with axiom (e8):

(i1) If $\vdash C[\boldsymbol{t =_{\mathsf{p}} r}] = \mathsf{T}$ and $\vdash (r =_{\mathsf{p}} s) = \mathsf{T}$ then $\vdash C[\boldsymbol{t =_{\mathsf{p}} s}] = \mathsf{T}$,
$$\text{(replacement rule 1)}$$

(i2) If $\vdash C[\boldsymbol{\phi}] = \mathsf{T}$ and $\vdash \phi = \psi$ then $\vdash C[\boldsymbol{\psi}] = \mathsf{T}$,   (replacement rule 2)

(i3) If $\vdash \phi = \mathsf{T}$ and $\vdash (\phi \multimap \psi) = \mathsf{T}$ then $\vdash \psi = \mathsf{T}$,   (modus ponens for $\multimap$)

(i4) If $\vdash \phi = \mathsf{T}$ and $\vdash \psi = \mathsf{T}$, then $\vdash (\phi \wedge \psi) = \mathsf{T}$,   ($\wedge$-introduction)

(i5) If $\vdash (\phi \multimap \psi) = \mathsf{T}$ and $\vdash (\psi \vee \neg\psi) = \mathsf{T}$ and $\vdash (\xi \vee \neg\xi) = \mathsf{T}$,
then $\vdash ((\phi \vee \xi) \multimap (\psi \vee \xi)) = \mathsf{T}$.   ($\vee$-introduction)

Inference rule (i1) is a replacement rule that captures some properties of $=_{\mathsf{p}}$. For example, a partial meadow has the properties that $\vdash (1 =_{\mathsf{p}} 1 + 0) = \mathsf{T}$ and $\vdash (0 \neq_{\mathsf{p}} 1) = \mathsf{T}$. So, with $C[0 =_{\mathsf{p}} 1] = \neg(0 =_{\mathsf{p}} 1)$ it follows by (i1) that $\vdash (0 \neq_{\mathsf{p}} 1 + 0) = \mathsf{T}$.

As for (i2), we first note that this rule expresses the common congruence rule for EqCL-expressions. Furthermore, ϕ is a subformula of itself ($\phi \equiv C[\phi]$), so if

$\vdash \phi = \psi$ and $\vdash \phi = \mathsf{T}$, then $\psi \equiv C[\psi]$ and $\psi = \mathsf{T}$ is derived by (i2). Below, we give an example that uses (i2).

For an example of (i3), instantiate ϕ with $\forall_p x.\ x =_p c \mathbin{{}^{\circ}\!\!\vee} x \neq_p c$, i.e. the left-hand side of (a2): $\vdash (x =_p x \rightarrowtail ((\forall_p x. x =_p c \mathbin{{}^{\circ}\!\!\vee} x \neq_p c) \rightarrowtail (x =_p c \mathbin{{}^{\circ}\!\!\vee} x \neq_p c))) = \mathsf{T}$. By (p1), $\vdash (x =_p x) = \mathsf{T}$, so by (i3),

$$\vdash ((\forall_p x.\ x =_p c \mathbin{{}^{\circ}\!\!\vee} x \neq_p c) \rightarrowtail (x =_p c \mathbin{{}^{\circ}\!\!\vee} x \neq_p c)) = \mathsf{T}.$$

With (a2) and (i3), the leftmost consequence of (Ex.1) below is obtained, and hence, with consequence (e)$'$ (i.e. $\vdash \phi_1 \mathbin{{}^{\circ}\!\!\vee} \neg\phi_1 = \neg\phi_1 \mathbin{{}^{\circ}\!\!\vee} \phi_1$), say $\vdash \phi = \psi$) and (i2) with $\phi \equiv C[\phi]$, also the second consequence of (Ex.1), i.e. $C[\psi] = \mathsf{T}$:

$$\vdash (x =_p c \mathbin{{}^{\circ}\!\!\vee} x \neq_p c) = \mathsf{T}, \quad \text{and thus} \quad \vdash (x \neq_p c \mathbin{{}^{\circ}\!\!\vee} x =_p c) = \mathsf{T}. \qquad \text{(Ex.1)}$$

As for rule (i5), we note that the conditions $\vdash (\psi \mathbin{{}^{\circ}\!\!\vee} \neg\psi) = \mathsf{T}$ and $\vdash (\xi \mathbin{{}^{\circ}\!\!\vee} \neg\xi) = \mathsf{T}$ exclude undefinedness of ψ and ξ; for an application of (i5), see the proof of Theorem 2 in [7, Thm.3.3.3]. Inference rules (i2)–(i5) are derivable from EqCL, this follows easily with *Prover9* [23].

Lemma 1. *The relation $\{(t,r) \mid t, r\ \Sigma\text{-terms such that } \vdash (t =_p t) = \mathsf{T},$ $\vdash (r =_p r) = \mathsf{T} \text{ and } \vdash (t =_p r) = \mathsf{T}\}$ is a congruence.*

Proof. The combination of (p5) and (p7) implies with (i4) that for each total k-ary function f and for all defined Σ-terms $t_1, ..., t_k$ and $r_1, ..., r_k$ that satisfy $\vdash (t_i =_p r_i) = \mathsf{T}$, $(f(t_1, ..., t_k) =_p f(r_1, ..., r_k)) = \mathsf{T}$. So, with (p1)–(p4) we are done. $\qquad \square$

2.2 Inductively Defined Tarski Semantics of $\mathsf{Eq}(\mathsf{L}_{\mathsf{sfol}}(\Sigma))$

Assume A is a partial Σ-algebra and σ is a valuation that assigns values from $|A|$ to the variables in V_{var}. We write $\sigma[a/x]$ with $a \in |A|$ for the valuation that assigns a to x and is otherwise defined as σ. A valuation σ extends to Σ-terms provided their constituents are defined: if $f(\sigma(t_1), ..., \sigma(t_k))$ is defined, then $\sigma(f(t_1, ..., t_k)) = f(\sigma(t_1), ..., \sigma(t_k))$.

We first consider formulae of the form $\phi = \mathsf{T}$ (and their universal quantifications) and define $A, \sigma \models \phi = \mathsf{T}$ if, and only if, $A, \sigma \models \phi$. A key role is played by the negation of partial equality $A, \sigma \models t \neq_p r$, also called denial inequality. For denial inequality we will have three notations:

$$A, \sigma \models \neg(t =_p r),\ A, \sigma \models t \neq_p r,\ \text{and}\ A, \sigma \mathbin{!}\models t =_p r.$$

We notice that when working with total algebras, $=_p$ coincides with $=$ and denial inequality coincides with dissatisfaction: $A, \sigma \models t \neq_p r \iff A, \sigma \not\models t =_p r$.

For $\phi \in \mathsf{L}_{\mathsf{sfol}}(\Sigma)$, satisfaction $A, \sigma \models \phi$ complemented with denial satisfaction $A, \sigma \mathbin{!}\models \phi$ is inductively defined as follows:

(1) $A, \sigma \models \mathsf{T}$,

(2) $A, \sigma \,!\models \mathsf{F}$,

(3) $A, \sigma \models t =_{\mathsf{p}} r$ if, and only if, both evaluation results $\sigma(t)$ and $\sigma(r)$ are defined (exist) and are equal: $\sigma(t) = \sigma(r)$,

(4) $A, \sigma \,!\models t =_{\mathsf{p}} r$ if, and only if, both evaluation results $\sigma(t)$ and $\sigma(r)$ are defined (exist) and are different elements of $|A|$: $\sigma(t) \neq \sigma(r)$,

(5) $A, \sigma \models \neg\phi$ if $A, \sigma \,!\models \phi$,

(6) $A, \sigma \,!\models \neg\phi$ if $A, \sigma \models \phi$,

(7) $A, \sigma \models \phi_1 \mathbin{\vee} \phi_2$ if either (i) $A, \sigma \models \phi_1$ or (ii) $A, \sigma \,!\models \phi_1$ and $A, \sigma \models \phi_2$,

(8) $A, \sigma \,!\models \phi_1 \mathbin{\vee} \phi_2$ if $A, \sigma \,!\models \phi_1$ and $A, \sigma \,!\models \phi_2$,

(9) $A, \sigma \models \forall_{\mathsf{p}} x.\phi$ if for all $a \in |A|$, it is the case that $A, \sigma[a/x] \models \phi$,

(10) $A, \sigma \,!\models \forall_{\mathsf{p}} x.\phi$ if for some $a \in |A|$, it is the case that $A, \sigma[a/x] \,!\models \phi$ and for all $b \in |A|$, it is the case that $A, \sigma[b/x] \models \phi \mathbin{\vee} \neg\phi$ (i.e. ϕ is not undefined).

It follows that $A, \sigma \models \phi \circ\!\!\rightarrow \psi$ if either (i) $A, \sigma \,!\models \phi$ or (ii) $A, \sigma \models \phi$ and $A, \sigma \models \psi$. By duality and inference rule (i2), it follows that $A, \sigma \models \phi \mathbin{\wedge} \psi$ if $A, \sigma \models \phi$ and $A, \sigma \models \psi$. This does not contradict the fact that $\mathbin{\wedge}$ and $\mathbin{\vee}$ are *not* commutative, as is demonstrated at the end of this section. Furthermore, it follows that

$$A, \sigma \models \exists_{\mathsf{p}} x.\phi \text{ if for some } a \in |A|, \text{ it is the case that } A, \sigma[a/x] \models \phi$$
$$\text{and for all } b \in |A|, \text{ it is the case that } A, \sigma[b/x] \models \phi \mathbin{\vee} \neg\phi. \qquad \text{(qE)}$$
$$A, \sigma \,!\models \exists_{\mathsf{p}} x.\phi \text{ if for all } a \in |A|, \text{ it is the case that } A, \sigma[a/x] \,!\models \phi.$$

Note that in a quantification $\forall_{\mathsf{p}} x.\phi$ or $\exists_{\mathsf{p}} x.\phi$ the free variable x ranges over $|A|$ and not over Σ-terms. So a term t may only be substituted for the variable x when the definedness of t is valid.

As usual, with

$$A \models \phi$$

it is denoted that for all valuations σ it is the case that $A, \sigma \models \phi$. With $A \,!\models \phi$ it is denoted that for all valuations σ, $A, \sigma \,!\models \phi$. In [7, Prop.2.2.1], we prove:

Proposition 1. *The axioms and inference rules for* $\mathsf{Eq}(\mathsf{L}_{\mathsf{sfol}}(\Sigma))$ *given in Sect. 2.1 are valid in all partial Σ-algebras.*

A partial equality $t =_{\mathsf{p}} r$ is undefined if at least one of t and r is undefined. In the following we generalise 'undefinedness' to $\mathsf{L}_{\mathsf{sfol}}(\Sigma)$-formulae and $\mathsf{Eq}(\mathsf{L}_{\mathsf{sfol}}(\Sigma))$-formulae using an adaptation of the notation for satisfiability. For a partial Σ-algebra A and a valuation σ, we write

$$A, \sigma \uparrow\!\models \phi$$

to express that ϕ is undefined in A according to σ, and we define this notion inductively:

(1) $A, \sigma \uparrow\!\models t =_{\mathsf{p}} r$ if, and only if, at least one of both evaluation results $\sigma(t)$ and $\sigma(r)$ is undefined,

(2) $A, \sigma \uparrow\!\models \neg\phi$ if $A, \sigma \uparrow\!\models \phi$,

(3) $A, \sigma \uparrow\!\models \phi_1 \veebar \phi_2$ if either (i) $A, \sigma \uparrow\!\models \phi_1$ or (ii) $A, \sigma \,!\!\models \phi_1$ and $A, \sigma \uparrow\!\models \phi_2$,
(4) $A, \sigma \uparrow\!\models \forall_\mathsf{p} x.\phi$ if for some $a \in |A|$, it is the case that $A, \sigma[a/x] \uparrow\!\models \phi$.

Some consequences that follow from clause (2) and axiom (e8) (i.e. $\forall_\mathsf{p} x.\phi = \neg\exists_\mathsf{p} x.\neg\phi$):

$$A, \sigma \uparrow\!\models \phi_1 \wedge \phi_2 \qquad \text{iff either (i) } A, \sigma \uparrow\!\models \phi_1 \text{ or (ii)} A, \sigma \models \phi_1 \text{ and } A, \sigma \uparrow\!\models \phi_2,$$
$$A, \sigma \uparrow\!\models \forall_\mathsf{p} x.\neg\phi \qquad \text{iff } A, \sigma \uparrow\!\models \forall_\mathsf{p} x.\phi,$$
$$A, \sigma \uparrow\!\models \exists_\mathsf{p} x.\phi \qquad \text{iff } A, \sigma \uparrow\!\models \forall_\mathsf{p} x.\phi.$$

It easily follows that for any formula $\phi \in \mathsf{UL_{sfol}}(\Sigma)$ (thus ϕ quantifier-free) and any σ, either $A, \sigma \models \phi$, or $A, \sigma \,!\!\models \phi$, or $A, \sigma \uparrow\!\models \phi$.

We write $A \uparrow\!\models \phi$ if for all valuations σ, $A, \sigma \uparrow\!\models \phi$. Some examples where we take A to satisfy $0, 1 \in |A|$, $A \models 0 \neq_\mathsf{p} 1$, $A \uparrow\!\models \frac{1}{0} =_\mathsf{p} t$ for any term t and $A \models \frac{1}{1} =_\mathsf{p} 1$ (properties of a partial meadow):

(i) $A \uparrow\!\models \frac{1}{0} =_\mathsf{p} 1$, so $A \uparrow\!\models \frac{1}{0} =_\mathsf{p} 1 \veebar 0 \neq_\mathsf{p} 1$, while $A \models 0 \neq_\mathsf{p} 1 \veebar \frac{1}{0} =_\mathsf{p} 1$, so $\veebar$ is not commutative.

(ii) $A \uparrow\!\models \forall_\mathsf{p} x.\frac{x}{x} =_\mathsf{p} 1$ because $A \uparrow\!\models \frac{0}{0} =_\mathsf{p} 1$, and thus also $A \uparrow\!\models \exists_\mathsf{p} x.\frac{x}{x} =_\mathsf{p} 1$.

More generally, if $A, \sigma \uparrow\!\models \forall_\mathsf{p} x.\phi$ then neither $A, \sigma \models \forall_\mathsf{p} x.\phi$ nor $A, \sigma \models \forall_\mathsf{p} x.\neg\phi$. This follows by choosing $a \in |A|$ that witnesses $A, \sigma[a/x] \uparrow\!\models \phi$ (and hence also $A, \sigma[a/x] \uparrow\!\models \neg\phi$).

For $\mathsf{Eq}(\mathsf{L_{sfol}}(\Sigma))$-formulae and a partial Σ-algebra A we define $A, \sigma \models \phi = \psi$ by the following three clauses:

(1) either $A, \sigma \models \phi$ and $A, \sigma \models \psi$,
(2) or $A, \sigma \,!\!\models \phi$ and $A, \sigma \,!\!\models \psi$,
(3) or $A, \sigma \uparrow\!\models \phi$ and $A, \sigma \uparrow\!\models \psi$.

We write $A \models \phi = \psi$ if $A, \sigma \models \phi = \psi$ for all σ. For example, if A is a partial meadow (like in (i)–(ii) above), we find $A \models (\frac{1}{0} =_\mathsf{p} 1) = (\frac{1}{0} =_\mathsf{p} 0)$. For another example, see Proposition 3.

The following theorem concerns the axiomatisation EqCL in Table 1 and is a minor generalisation of the result cited in [6, Thm.5.2.(ii)] because short-circuit implication $\circ\!\!\rightarrow$ has been added as a definable connective. It immediately follows that this addition preserves that result.

Theorem (Cf. Thm.5.2 in [6]). *Conditional logic with* T *and* F *distinguished is completely axiomatised by the seven axioms (e1)–(e7) of* EqCL *in Table 1. Moreover, these axioms are independent.*

3   Fracterm Calculus for Partial Meadows

In Sect. 3.1 we define 'fracterm calculus for partial meadows', FTCpm in short, and prove a completeness result for FTCpm. In Sect. 3.2, we introduce a convention for concise notation for FTCpm for the sake of readability of axioms and proofs. In Sect. 3.3 we derive some properties of partial meadows and prove some results, among which "conditional flattening", and pay attention to some $\mathsf{Eq}(\mathsf{L_{sfol}}(\Sigma))$-identities.

3.1   FTCpm: a Specification

The signature of partial meadows with divisive notation Σ_m^{pd} is obtained by extending the signature of unital rings with a two place division operator (denoted $\frac{x}{y}$), where it is indicated in the signature description that division is a partial function. The sort of numbers involved is named Number.

Table 2. Specification of the signature Σ_m^{pd} of fracterm calculus of partial meadows and a set AxFTCpm of axioms in the format of $\mathsf{Eq}(\mathsf{L}_{\mathsf{sfol}}(\Sigma_m^{pd}))$

$$\text{signature} : \Sigma_{wcr,\perp} = \{$$
$$\text{sort} : \mathsf{Number}$$
$$\text{constants} : 0, 1, \perp : \mathsf{Number}$$
$$\text{total functions} : \_ + \_ , \_ \cdot \_ : \mathsf{Number} \times \mathsf{Number} \to \mathsf{Number};$$
$$- \_ : \mathsf{Number} \to \mathsf{Number}$$
$$\text{equality relation} : \_ = \_ \subseteq \mathsf{Number} \times \mathsf{Number}\}$$
$$\text{variables} : x, y, z : \mathsf{Number}$$

$$((x + y) + z =_{\mathsf{p}} x + (y + z)) = \mathsf{T} \qquad \text{(pm1a)}$$
$$(x + 0 =_{\mathsf{p}} x) = \mathsf{T} \qquad \text{(pm2a)}$$
$$(x + (-x) =_{\mathsf{p}} 0) = \mathsf{T} \qquad \text{(pm3a)}$$
$$(x \cdot (y \cdot z) =_{\mathsf{p}} (x \cdot y) \cdot z) = \mathsf{T} \qquad \text{(pm4a)}$$
$$(x \cdot y =_{\mathsf{p}} y \cdot x) = \mathsf{T} \qquad \text{(pm5a)}$$
$$(1 \cdot x =_{\mathsf{p}} x) = \mathsf{T} \qquad \text{(pm6a)}$$
$$(x \cdot (y + z) =_{\mathsf{p}} (x \cdot y) + (x \cdot z)) = \mathsf{T} \qquad \text{(pm7a)}$$
$$(y \neq_{\mathsf{p}} 0 \multimap \frac{x}{y} =_{\mathsf{p}} x \cdot \frac{1}{y}) = \mathsf{T} \qquad \text{(pm8a)}$$
$$(x \neq_{\mathsf{p}} 0 \multimap \frac{x}{x} =_{\mathsf{p}} 1) = \mathsf{T} \qquad \text{(pm9a)}$$
$$(0 \neq_{\mathsf{p}} 1) = \mathsf{T} \qquad \text{(pm10a)}$$
$$((x \neq_{\mathsf{p}} 0 \wedge y \neq_{\mathsf{p}} 0) \multimap x \cdot y \neq_{\mathsf{p}} 0) = \mathsf{T} \qquad \text{(pm11a)}$$

Definition 1. *A **partial meadow** is a structure F^{pd} with signature Σ_m^{pd} that is obtained by expanding a field F with a partial division operator (with the usual definition, i.e. $\frac{a}{b} = c$ if $b \neq 0$ and $b \cdot c = a$).*

In Σ_m^{pd} constants are supposed to have a value and functions, except division, are supposed to be total.

Starting from our definition in Sect. 2.1 of a sequential first order logic, we understand 'fracterm calculus for partial meadows', FTCpm in short, as the collection of $\mathsf{UL_{sfol}}(\Sigma_m^{pd})$-formulae ϕ (thus ϕ quantifier-free), such that ϕ is valid in all partial meadows, i.e. for each partial meadow F^{pd},

$$F^{pd} \models \phi$$

(that is, for all valuations σ, $F^{pd}, \sigma \models \phi$).

A specification of Σ_m^{pd} with a set $\mathsf{AxFTCpm}$ of axioms for FTCpm is given in Table 2. Observe that $(\frac{1}{1} =_\mathsf{p} 1) = \mathsf{T}$ follows immediately from axiom (pm9a), which in turn with axiom (pm8a) implies $(\frac{x}{1} =_\mathsf{p} x) = \mathsf{T}$. We note that axioms (pm10a) and (pm11a) capture common properties of a field: $0 \neq 1$ and absence of zero divisors.

Theorem 1 (Soundness and completeness of $\mathsf{AxFTCpm}$).

(i) *(Soundness)   The axioms of $\mathsf{AxFTCpm}$ are sound for the class of partial meadows, and*

(ii) *(Completeness)   If a universal formula $\phi \in \mathsf{UL_{sfol}}(\Sigma_m^{pd})$ is true in all partial meadows, then $\mathsf{AxFTCpm} \models \phi$.*

Table 3. The set $\mathsf{AxFTCpm}$ of axioms according to the first equivalence of (qF) (see page 6)

---

import : Σ_m^{pd} (Table 2)

variables : x, y, z : Number

$$(\forall_\mathsf{p} x.\forall_\mathsf{p} y.\forall_\mathsf{p} z. \; (x + y) + z =_\mathsf{p} x + (y + z)) = \mathsf{T} \tag{pm1b}$$

$$(\forall_\mathsf{p} x. \; x + 0 =_\mathsf{p} x) = \mathsf{T} \tag{pm2b}$$

$$(\forall_\mathsf{p} x. \; x + (-x) =_\mathsf{p} 0) = \mathsf{T} \tag{pm3b}$$

$$(\forall_\mathsf{p} x.\forall_\mathsf{p} y.\forall_\mathsf{p} z. \; x \cdot (y \cdot z) =_\mathsf{p} (x \cdot y) \cdot z) = \mathsf{T} \tag{pm4b}$$

$$(\forall_\mathsf{p} x.\forall_\mathsf{p} y. \; x \cdot y =_\mathsf{p} y \cdot x) = \mathsf{T} \tag{pm5b}$$

$$(\forall_\mathsf{p} x. \; 1 \cdot x =_\mathsf{p} x) = \mathsf{T} \tag{pm6b}$$

$$(\forall_\mathsf{p} x.\forall_\mathsf{p} y.\forall_\mathsf{p} z. \; x \cdot (y + z) =_\mathsf{p} (x \cdot y) + (x \cdot z)) = \mathsf{T} \tag{pm7b}$$

$$\forall_\mathsf{p} x.\forall_\mathsf{p} y.(y \neq_\mathsf{p} 0 \rightarrowtail \frac{x}{y} =_\mathsf{p} x \cdot \frac{1}{y}) = \mathsf{T} \tag{pm8b}$$

$$(\forall_\mathsf{p} x. \; x \neq_\mathsf{p} 0 \rightarrowtail \frac{x}{x} =_\mathsf{p} 1) = \mathsf{T} \tag{pm9b}$$

$$(0 \neq_\mathsf{p} 1) = \mathsf{T} \tag{pm10b}$$

$$(\forall_\mathsf{p} x.\forall_\mathsf{p} y.(x \neq_\mathsf{p} 0 \wedge y \neq_\mathsf{p} 0) \rightarrowtail x \cdot y \neq_\mathsf{p} 0) = \mathsf{T} \tag{pm11b}$$

Proof Soundness is obvious by inspection of the axioms of AxFTCpm. For completeness assume that ϕ is valid in all partial meadows. Now consider a model B of AxFTCpm. B is an expansion with a division function of a ring and in fact of a field. B may differ from a partial meadow because the division function may be defined for some pairs of arguments (a, b) with $b = 0$. Now let B' be obtained from B by replacing the division function of B by the standard partial division function. B' is a partial meadow and therefore $B' \models \phi$. It can be shown by induction on the structure of open formulae ψ that for all valuations σ it is the case that $B', \sigma \models \psi$ implies $B \models \psi$. We find that each model of AxFTCpm satisfies ϕ, as required. $\square$

3.2 FTCpm: Concise Notations

To enhance readability, we introduce the following convention.

Convention 1. (1) *We adopt the convention of writing ϕ instead of $\phi = \mathsf{T}$.*
(2) *$\forall_\mathsf{p}$-elimination: for expressions of the form $\forall_\mathsf{p} x.\phi$ (with $\phi \in \mathsf{L_{sfol}}(\Sigma_m^{pd})$) we adopt the convention of writing ϕ.*
If not explicitly mentioned, ϕ here either stands for a syntactic formula (an element of $\mathsf{L_{sfol}}(\Sigma_m^{pd})$), or for $\vdash \phi$, or for $\models \phi$, and this should then always be clear from the context.

Table 4. Representation of the axioms of AxFTCpm according to Convention 1.(1)

$$\text{import} : \Sigma_m^{pd} \text{ (Table 2)}$$

$$\text{variables} : x, y, z : \text{Number}$$

$$\forall_\mathsf{p} x.\forall_\mathsf{p} y.\forall_\mathsf{p} z.\ (x + y) + z =_\mathsf{p} x + (y + z) \qquad \text{(pm1c)}$$

$$\forall_\mathsf{p} x.\ x + 0 =_\mathsf{p} x \qquad \text{(pm2c)}$$

$$\forall_\mathsf{p} x.\ x + (-x) =_\mathsf{p} 0 \qquad \text{(pm3c)}$$

$$\forall_\mathsf{p} x.\forall_\mathsf{p} y.\ x \cdot (y \cdot z) =_\mathsf{p} (x \cdot y) \cdot z \qquad \text{(pm4c)}$$

$$\forall_\mathsf{p} x.\forall_\mathsf{p} y.\ x \cdot y =_\mathsf{p} y \cdot x \qquad \text{(pm5c)}$$

$$\forall_\mathsf{p} x.\ 1 \cdot x =_\mathsf{p} x \qquad \text{(pm6c)}$$

$$\forall_\mathsf{p} x.\forall_\mathsf{p} y.\ x \cdot (y + z) =_\mathsf{p} (x \cdot y) + (x \cdot z) \qquad \text{(pm7c)}$$

$$\forall_\mathsf{p} x.\forall_\mathsf{p} y.\ y \neq_\mathsf{p} 0 \multimap \frac{x}{y} =_\mathsf{p} x \cdot \frac{1}{y} \qquad \text{(pm8c)}$$

$$\forall_\mathsf{p} x.\ x \neq_\mathsf{p} 0 \multimap \frac{x}{x} =_\mathsf{p} 1 \qquad \text{(pm9c)}$$

$$0 \neq_\mathsf{p} 1 \qquad \text{(pm10c)}$$

$$\forall_\mathsf{p} x.\forall_\mathsf{p} y.\ (x \neq_\mathsf{p} 0 \wedge y \neq_\mathsf{p} 0) \multimap x \cdot y \neq_\mathsf{p} 0 \qquad \text{(pm11c)}$$

Table 5. Representation of the set AxFTCpm of axioms according to Convention 1

$$\text{import} : \Sigma_m^{pd} \ (\text{Table 2})$$
$$\text{variables} : x, y, z : \text{Number}$$

$$(x + y) + z =_\mathsf{p} x + (y + z) \tag{pm1}$$
$$x + 0 =_\mathsf{p} x \tag{pm2}$$
$$x + (-x) =_\mathsf{p} 0 \tag{pm3}$$
$$x \cdot (y \cdot z) =_\mathsf{p} (x \cdot y) \cdot z \tag{pm4}$$
$$x \cdot y =_\mathsf{p} y \cdot x \tag{pm5}$$
$$1 \cdot x =_\mathsf{p} x \tag{pm6}$$
$$x \cdot (y + z) =_\mathsf{p} (x \cdot y) + (x \cdot z) \tag{pm7}$$
$$y \neq_\mathsf{p} 0 \ \circ\!\!\rightarrow \ \frac{x}{y} =_\mathsf{p} x \cdot \frac{1}{y} \tag{pm8}$$
$$x \neq_\mathsf{p} 0 \ \circ\!\!\rightarrow \ \frac{x}{x} =_\mathsf{p} 1 \tag{pm9}$$
$$0 \neq_\mathsf{p} 1 \tag{pm10}$$
$$(x \neq_\mathsf{p} 0 \ \wedge \ y \neq_\mathsf{p} 0) \ \circ\!\!\rightarrow \ x \cdot y \neq_\mathsf{p} 0 \tag{pm11}$$

In Tables 3, 4 and 5, we display the axioms of AxFTCpm in different, equivalent formats. Table 2 represents the $\forall_\mathsf{p}$-elimination of the axioms of Table 3, and Table 5 shows the $\forall_\mathsf{p}$-elimination of the axioms of Table 4. Of course, Convention 1 is justified by the Tarski-semantics discussed in Sect. 2.2.

As an example, we give for axiom (pm9a) of Table 2 a diagram that illustrates this convention, using the first equivalence of (qF), i.e. $F^{pd} \models \phi = \mathsf{T} \iff F^{pd} \models (\forall_\mathsf{p} x.\phi) = \mathsf{T}$ (see page 6), in which the prefix "$F^{pd} \models$" is omitted:

$$\text{(Tbl.2)} \ (x \neq_\mathsf{p} 0 \circ\!\!\rightarrow \tfrac{x}{x} =_\mathsf{p} 1) = \mathsf{T} \iff (\forall_\mathsf{p} x.x \neq_\mathsf{p} 0 \circ\!\!\rightarrow \tfrac{x}{x} =_\mathsf{p} 1) = \mathsf{T} \ \text{(Tbl.3)}$$
$$\downarrow \qquad\qquad\qquad\qquad\qquad \downarrow$$
$$\text{(Tbl.5)} \quad x \neq_\mathsf{p} 0 \circ\!\!\rightarrow \tfrac{x}{x} =_\mathsf{p} 1 \quad\longleftarrow\quad \forall_\mathsf{p} x.x \neq_\mathsf{p} 0 \circ\!\!\rightarrow \tfrac{x}{x} =_\mathsf{p} 1 \quad \text{(Tbl.4)}$$

Convention 1 and these examples relate to both the axioms in Sect. 2.1 and those for partial meadows. In what follows, we will work mostly according to this convention and the axioms in Table 5, but where practical, we will use more explicit representation. A typical example is the following consequence:

If t is defined, thus $t =_\mathsf{p} t$, and $\forall_\mathsf{p} x.\phi(x)$ is a valid assertion, then so is $\phi(t)$.

This 'instantiation consequence' is justified by axiom (a1), i.e. $((t =_\mathsf{p} t \ \wedge \ \forall_\mathsf{p} x.\phi) \circ\!\!\rightarrow \phi[t/x]) = \mathsf{T}$. An example of this consequence applied to axiom (pm11) and the (derivable) identity $-1 =_\mathsf{p} -1$ is $(-1 \neq_\mathsf{p} 0 \ \wedge \ y \neq_\mathsf{p} 0) \circ\!\!\rightarrow -1 \cdot y \neq_\mathsf{p} 0$.

We end this section with a final remark on the axioms for partial meadows. Observe that the condition $(x \neq_{\mathsf{p}} 0 \;\underline{\wedge}\; y \neq_{\mathsf{p}} 0)$ of axiom (pm11a) in Table 2 and in its related versions in Tables 3–5 can be replaced by $(y \neq_{\mathsf{p}} 0 \;\underline{\wedge}\; x \neq_{\mathsf{p}} 0)$.

3.3 Some Consequences of FTCpm and $\mathsf{Eq}(\mathsf{L}_{\mathsf{sfol}}(\Sigma_m^{pd}))$

Table 6 lists some familiar consequences (in the sense of $\models$) of the axioms of AxFTCpm in the format of Table 5. Note that the order of the three conjuncts in Assertion (A6) is not relevant.

Table 6. Assertions of fracterm calculus of partial meadows (with $x, y, u, v \in V_{var}$)

$$x + y \;=_{\mathsf{p}}\; y + x \tag{A1}$$

$$0 \cdot x \;=_{\mathsf{p}}\; 0 \tag{A2}$$

$$x \neq_{\mathsf{p}} 0 \;\multimap\; -x \neq_{\mathsf{p}} 0 \tag{A3}$$

$$y \neq_{\mathsf{p}} 0 \;\multimap\; -\frac{x}{y} \;=_{\mathsf{p}}\; \frac{-x}{y} \tag{A4}$$

$$(y \neq_{\mathsf{p}} 0 \;\underline{\wedge}\; v \neq_{\mathsf{p}} 0) \;\multimap\; \frac{x}{y} \cdot \frac{u}{v} \;=_{\mathsf{p}}\; \frac{x \cdot u}{y \cdot v} \tag{A5}$$

$$(y \neq_{\mathsf{p}} 0 \;\underline{\wedge}\; u \neq_{\mathsf{p}} 0 \;\underline{\wedge}\; v \neq_{\mathsf{p}} 0) \;\multimap\; \frac{\left(\frac{x}{y}\right)}{\left(\frac{u}{v}\right)} \;=_{\mathsf{p}}\; \frac{x \cdot v}{y \cdot u} \tag{A6}$$

$$(y \neq_{\mathsf{p}} 0 \;\underline{\wedge}\; v \neq_{\mathsf{p}} 0) \;\multimap\; \frac{x}{y} + \frac{u}{v} \;=_{\mathsf{p}}\; \frac{(x \cdot v) + (y \cdot u)}{y \cdot v} \tag{A7}$$

Proposition 2. *The assertions (A1)–(A7) in Table 6 follow from* AxFTCpm.

Proof. See [7, Prop.3.3.1].   □

Definition 2. *A **flat fracterm** is an expression of the form $\frac{p}{q}$ that contains precisely one occurrence (i.e. the top level occurrence) of the division operator, thus p and q are **division free** terms.*

Theorem 2 (Conditional fracterm flattening for partial meadows). *For each term t there is a division free term s and a flat fracterm r such that*

(i) $s \neq_{\mathsf{p}} 0 \;\multimap\; t =_{\mathsf{p}} r$ holds in all partial meadows, and
(ii) $s =_{\mathsf{p}} 0 \;\underline{\wedge}\; t =_{\mathsf{p}} t$ does not hold in any partial meadow under any valuation.

In [7, Thm.3.3.3], this theorem is proven by induction on the structure of t (which may be an open term). When using the same notation as in the theorem, except that we write $\frac{p}{q}$ for r (thus, p and q division free), the following equation is not valid unless t is always defined: $(t =_{\mathsf{p}} \frac{p}{q}) = \mathsf{T}$. Also, $(t =_{\mathsf{p}} \frac{p \cdot s}{q \cdot s}) = \mathsf{T}$ fails.

To see this complication, notice that for instance $(\frac{1}{x} =_{\mathsf{p}} \frac{1}{x}) = \mathsf{T}$ fails, while $(x \neq_{\mathsf{p}} 0 \;\circ\!\!\!-\!\!\!\rightarrow\; \frac{1}{x} =_{\mathsf{p}} \frac{1}{x}) = \mathsf{T}$ holds. Hence, we also find the following $\mathsf{Eq}(\mathsf{L}_{\mathsf{sfol}}(\Sigma_m^{pd}))$ identities:

$$(s \neq_{\mathsf{p}} 0 \;\circ\!\!\!-\!\!\!\rightarrow\; x =_{\mathsf{p}} t) = (s \neq_{\mathsf{p}} 0 \;\circ\!\!\!-\!\!\!\rightarrow\; x =_{\mathsf{p}} \frac{p}{q}),$$

$$(s =_{\mathsf{p}} 0 \;\circ\!\!\!-\!\!\!\rightarrow\; x =_{\mathsf{p}} t) = (s =_{\mathsf{p}} 0 \;\circ\!\!\!-\!\!\!\rightarrow\; 0 =_{\mathsf{p}} \frac{1}{0}).$$

In $\mathsf{Eq}(\mathsf{L}_{\mathsf{sfol}}(\Sigma_m^{pd}))$, conditional fracterm flattening can be obtained in a more direct manner.

Proposition 3. *For each term t there is a division free term s and a flat fracterm $\frac{p}{q}$ such that the $\mathsf{Eq}(\mathsf{L}_{\mathsf{sfol}}(\Sigma_m^{pd}))$-identity*

$$(x =_{\mathsf{p}} t) = (x =_{\mathsf{p}} \tfrac{p \cdot s}{q \cdot s})$$

is valid in all partial meadows.

Proof. Given t, let s and $r = \frac{p}{q}$ be as found in Theorem 2. Given a partial meadow F^{pd} and a valuation σ, two cases are distinguished:

$$F^{pd}, \sigma \models s \neq_{\mathsf{p}} 0 \quad \text{and} \quad F^{pd}, \sigma \models s =_{\mathsf{p}} 0.$$

In the first case, $F^{pd}, \sigma \models t =_{\mathsf{p}} \frac{p}{q}$ and $F^{pd}, \sigma \models \frac{s}{s} =_{\mathsf{p}} 1$ so that $F^{pd}, \sigma \models t =_{\mathsf{p}} \frac{p \cdot s}{q \cdot s}$, in the second case, both t and $\frac{p \cdot s}{q \cdot s}$ are undefined in F^{pd} under valuation σ. $\square$

In $\mathsf{Eq}(\mathsf{L}_{\mathsf{sfol}}(\Sigma_m^{pd}))$, the equation $(\frac{1}{0} =_{\mathsf{p}} \frac{1}{0}) = (\frac{1}{0} \neq_{\mathsf{p}} \frac{1}{0})$ expresses that division is not total. However, this cannot be expressed in $\mathsf{L}_{\mathsf{sfol}}(\Sigma_m^{pd})$:

Proposition 4. *It is impossible to express in* FTCpm, *thus by formulae in* $\mathsf{L}_{\mathsf{sfol}}(\Sigma_m^{pd})$, *that division is not total.*

Proof. Suppose that $F^{pd} \models \phi$ for some partial meadow F^{pd}, then we may totalise division in accordance with the Suppes-Ono convention $\frac{x}{0} = 0$, thereby obtaining $\mathsf{Tot}_0(F^{pd})$. Now we claim that $\mathsf{Tot}_0(F^{pd}) \models \phi$. With simultaneous induction on the structure of ϕ one easily proves that: (i) if $F^{pd} \models \phi$ then $\mathsf{Tot}_0(F^{pd}) \models \phi$ and (ii) if $F^{pd} \models \neg\phi$ then $\mathsf{Tot}_0(F^{pd}) \models \neg\phi$. It follows that no formula ϕ can distinguish between F^{pd} and $\mathsf{Tot}_0(F^{pd})$ by being true for F^{pd} and not for $\mathsf{Tot}_0(F^{pd})$. $\square$

Two assertions in $\mathsf{L}_{\mathsf{sfol}}(\Sigma_m^{pd})$ that involve $\exists_{\mathsf{p}}$ and hold in all partial meadows are these:

$$x \neq_{\mathsf{p}} 0 \;\circ\!\!\!-\!\!\!\rightarrow\; \exists_{\mathsf{p}} y.(x \cdot y =_{\mathsf{p}} 1), \tag{1}$$

$$x \neq_{\mathsf{p}} 0 \;\circ\!\!\!-\!\!\!\rightarrow\; \exists_{\mathsf{p}} y.(y \neq_{\mathsf{p}} 0 \,\barwedge\, x =_{\mathsf{p}} \frac{1}{y}). \tag{2}$$

Note that (1) is related to axiom (pm11) and that in (2), the conjunct $y \neq_p 0$ cannot be omitted.

In the case of $F^{pd} = \mathbb{Q}^{pd}$, the partial meadow of rationals, we find a computable partial algebra. A specification of the abstract partial data type of rationals is given in Table 7, where the notation x^2 in (3) abbreviates $x \cdot x$.

Proposition 5. *The axioms in Table 7 are satisfied in $\mathbb{Q}^{pd}$ and prove each closed equation and inequation that is true in $\mathbb{Q}^{pd}$.*

Table 7. AxFTCpm/4sq: A specification of the partial meadow of rationals

$$\text{import} : \text{AxFTCpm (Table 5)}$$
$$\text{variables} : x, y, z, u : \text{Number}$$

$$1 + ((x^2 + y^2) + (z^2 + u^2)) \neq_p 0 \qquad (3)$$

4 $\perp$-Enlargements and Consequence Relations

In Sects. 4.1 and 4.2 we define a notion of 'enlargement' in order to connect partial algebras and their logic to ordinary first order logic with an absorptive element $\perp$ that models partiality. In Sect. 4.3 we provide alternative notions of computability for partial algebras, though limited to the case of minimal partial algebras. We will focus on minimal algebras only and then with much simpler definitions.

4.1 $\perp$-Enlargement and Its Converse

Let the *absorptive element* $\perp$ be a new constant symbol, intended to represent "no proper value" (i.e. $t \neq \perp$ corresponds to t being defined) and let the set of first order conditional formulas $T_\perp$ contain the assertions that express that functions produce $\perp$ on any series of arguments involving $\perp$. For instance, for a three place function f, $T_\perp$ contains

$$f(\perp, y, z) = \perp, \quad f(x, \perp, z) = \perp, \quad f(x, y, \perp) = \perp.$$

Given a partial algebra A, its $\perp$-enlargement $\mathsf{Enl}_\perp(A)$ is obtained by extending the domain with a new element, also denoted $\perp$, that serves as the interpretation of $\perp$. The notation $\mathsf{Enl}_\perp(A)$ is taken from [11].

In the opposite direction, given a total algebra B that contains an absorptive element $\perp$, and such that $B \models \exists x.x \neq \perp$, the operation $\mathsf{Pdt}_\perp$ (partial data type) as introduced in [11] creates a partial algebra $\mathsf{Pdt}_\perp(A)$ with $\perp$ removed from the domain and each operation which produces $\perp$ on some arguments made partial on these arguments. The name $\mathsf{Pdt}_\perp$ suggests that the resulting algebra is minimal, a requirement on all data types. Such was the intention in [11]. We will use the same notation also in the more general case where the resulting structure need not be minimal.

Proposition 6. *If $\perp \notin \Sigma(A)$ and $\perp \notin |A|$ then $\mathsf{Pdt}_\perp(\mathsf{Enl}_\perp(A)) = A$.*

Proposition 7. *If $\perp \in \Sigma(A)$ and $\perp \in |A|$ with $\mathsf{card}(|A|) > 1$ then*

$$\mathsf{Enl}_\perp(\mathsf{Pdt}_\perp(A)) = A.$$

4.2 Reformulating the Semantics of $\mathsf{Eq}(\mathsf{L}_{\mathsf{sfol}}(\Sigma))$ in First Order Terms

Assuming $\perp \notin \Sigma$, let $\Sigma_\perp = \Sigma \cup \{\perp\}$. A pair of transformations ψ_{true} and ψ_{false} translates formulae in $\mathsf{L}_{\mathsf{sfol}}(\Sigma)$ to first order formulae over $\Sigma_\perp$, i.e. to $\mathsf{L}_{\mathsf{fol}}(\Sigma_\perp)$. The transformation ψ_{true} translates formulae that are assumed to evaluate to true, and ψ_{false} is used as an auxiliary operator to deal with negation (i.e. $\psi_{\mathsf{true}}(\neg\phi) \equiv \psi_{\mathsf{false}}(\phi)$):

(1) $\psi_{\mathsf{true}}(\mathsf{T}) \equiv \mathsf{T}$ and $\psi_{\mathsf{true}}(\mathsf{F}) \equiv \mathsf{F}$,
(2) $\psi_{\mathsf{false}}(\mathsf{T}) \equiv \mathsf{F}$ and $\psi_{\mathsf{false}}(\mathsf{F}) \equiv \mathsf{T}$,
(3) $\psi_{\mathsf{true}}(t =_{\mathsf{p}} r) \equiv t \neq \perp \wedge r \neq \perp \wedge t = r$ (where $x \neq y$ abbreviates $\neg(x = y)$,
(4) $\psi_{\mathsf{false}}(t =_{\mathsf{p}} r) \equiv t = \perp \vee r = \perp \vee t \neq r$,
(5) $\psi_{\mathsf{true}}(\neg\phi) \equiv \psi_{\mathsf{false}}(\phi)$ (hence, $\psi_{\mathsf{true}}(t \neq_{\mathsf{p}} r) \equiv \psi_{\mathsf{false}}(t =_{\mathsf{p}} r)$),
(6) $\psi_{\mathsf{false}}(\neg\phi) \equiv \psi_{\mathsf{true}}(\phi)$ (hence, $\psi_{\mathsf{false}}(t \neq_{\mathsf{p}} r) \equiv \psi_{\mathsf{true}}(t =_{\mathsf{p}} r)$),
(7) $\psi_{\mathsf{true}}(\phi_1 \mathbin{\underset{\circ}{\vee}} \phi_2) \equiv \psi_{\mathsf{true}}(\phi_1) \vee (\psi_{\mathsf{false}}(\phi_1) \wedge \psi_{\mathsf{true}}(\phi_2))$,
(8) $\psi_{\mathsf{false}}(\phi_1 \mathbin{\underset{\circ}{\vee}} \phi_2) \equiv \psi_{\mathsf{false}}(\phi_1) \wedge \psi_{\mathsf{false}}(\phi_2)$,
(9) $\psi_{\mathsf{true}}(\forall_{\mathsf{p}} x.\phi) \equiv \forall x.(x \neq \perp \rightarrow \psi_{\mathsf{true}}(\phi))$,
(10) $\psi_{\mathsf{false}}(\forall_{\mathsf{p}} x.\phi) \equiv \exists x.(x \neq \perp \wedge \psi_{\mathsf{false}}(\phi)) \wedge \forall x.\psi_{\mathsf{true}}(\phi \mathbin{\underset{\circ}{\vee}} \neg\phi)$.

It follows easily that

$$\psi_{\mathsf{true}}(\phi_1 \mathbin{\underset{\circ}{\wedge}} \phi_2) \equiv \psi_{\mathsf{true}}(\phi_1) \wedge \psi_{\mathsf{true}}(\phi_2),$$
$$\psi_{\mathsf{false}}(\phi_1 \mathbin{\underset{\circ}{\wedge}} \phi_2) \equiv \psi_{\mathsf{false}}(\phi_1) \vee (\psi_{\mathsf{true}}(\phi_1) \wedge \psi_{\mathsf{false}}(\phi_2)),$$
$$\psi_{\mathsf{true}}(\exists_{\mathsf{p}} x.\phi) \equiv \exists x.(x \neq \perp \wedge \psi_{\mathsf{true}}(\phi)) \wedge \forall x.\psi_{\mathsf{true}}(\phi \mathbin{\underset{\circ}{\vee}} \neg\phi),$$
$$\psi_{\mathsf{false}}(\exists_{\mathsf{p}} x.\phi) \equiv \forall x.(x \neq \perp \rightarrow \psi_{\mathsf{false}}(\phi)).$$

In order to formulate key properties of the operator ψ_{true}, a consequence relation must be chosen.

4.3 Consequence Relations

Various consequence relations can be contemplated in the context of 3-valued logics. For an extensive discussion of these options we refer to [20]. We will consider the so-called *strong validity* consequence relation, notation $\models_{\mathsf{ss}}$, where both in the assumptions and in the conclusion the formulae (sentences) are considered "true" if these are valid under all valuations. Alternatively one may consider $\models_{\mathsf{sw}}$, $\models_{\mathsf{ws}}$, and $\models_{\mathsf{ww}}$ where w indicates weak validity, that is for no valuation a formula is false. We propose that in the case of elementary arithmetic, the use of $\models_{\mathsf{ss}}$ is preferable to the three alternatives just mentioned. Below we will write $\models_{\Sigma}$ instead of $\models_{\mathsf{ss}}$ in order to highlight the role and relevance of the signature involved.

Definition 3. *Define* $\phi_1, ..., \phi_n \models_{\Sigma} \phi$ *if, and only if, for each* Σ*-structure* A*: if for all valuations* σ *into* $|A|$ *it is the case that* $A, \sigma \models_{\Sigma} \phi_1,$ *...,* $A, \sigma \models_{\Sigma} \phi_n$*, then for all valuations* σ *into* $|A|$*,* $A, \sigma \models_{\Sigma} \phi$*.*

A connection between the various satisfaction relations and the transformations ψ_{true} and ψ_{false} is found under some restrictions.

Proposition 8. *For any partial* Σ*-algebra* A*, for each* $\mathsf{L}_{\mathsf{sfol}}(\Sigma)$ *formula* ϕ *and for each valuation* σ *taking values in* $|A|$*:* $A, \sigma \models_{\Sigma} \phi$ *if, and only if,* $\mathsf{Enl}_{\bot}(A), \sigma \models \psi_{\mathsf{true}}(\phi)$*.*
Proof. Straightforward by induction on the structure of ϕ. □

In the following, let A be a partial Σ-algebra and B a total Σ-algebra with $\bot \in \Sigma(B)$.

Proposition 9. $A \models_{\Sigma} \phi$ *if, and only if,* $\mathsf{Enl}_{\bot}(A) \models \psi_{\mathsf{true}}(\phi)$*.*
Proof. Immediate using Proposition 8. □

Proposition 10. *Let* $c \in \Sigma(B)$*, and assume that* $B \models c \neq \bot$*. Then* $\mathsf{Pdt}_{\bot}(B) \models_{\Sigma} \phi$ *if, and only if,* $B \models \psi_{\mathsf{true}}(\phi)$*.*

Proposition 11. $\phi_1, ..., \phi_n \models_{\Sigma} \phi$ *if, and only if,*

$$T_{\bot} \cup \{\psi_{\mathsf{true}}(\phi_1), ..., \psi_{\mathsf{true}}(\phi_n)\} \cup \{\exists x. x \neq \bot\} \models \psi_{\mathsf{true}}(\phi).$$

Proof. For "if", assume that $A \models_{\Sigma} \phi_1, ..., A \models_{\Sigma} \phi_n$, then by Proposition 9,

$$\mathsf{Enl}_{\bot}(A) \models \psi_{\mathsf{true}}(\phi_1), ..., \mathsf{Enl}_{\bot}(A) \models \psi_{\mathsf{true}}(\phi_n).$$

Because A has a non-empty domain, $A \models_{\Sigma} \exists_{\mathsf{p}} x. x \neq \bot$. Because $\mathsf{Enl}_{\bot}(A) \models T_{\bot}$ it follows with $T_{\bot} \cup \{\psi_{\mathsf{true}}(\phi_1), ..., \psi_{\mathsf{true}}(\phi_n)\} \models \psi_{\mathsf{true}}(\phi)$ that $\mathsf{Enl}_{\bot}(A) \models \psi_{\mathsf{true}}(\phi)$. Now using Proposition 9, $A \models_{\Sigma} \phi$.

For the other direction assume that $B \models T_{\bot} \cup \{\psi_{\mathsf{true}}(\phi_1), ..., \psi_{\mathsf{true}}(\phi_n)\} \cup \{\exists x. x \neq \bot\}$. Then $\mathsf{Pdt}_{\bot}(B)$ has a non-empty domain so that $A = \mathsf{Pdt}(B)$ is well-defined, and with Proposition 7, $B = \mathsf{Enl}_{\bot}(A)$. It follows with Proposition 8 that $A \models_{\Sigma} \phi_1, ..., A \models_{\Sigma} \phi_n$ so that $A \models_{\Sigma} \phi$ from which one obtains $B \models \psi_{\mathsf{true}}(\phi)$ with Proposition 9. □

Proposition 12. *The consequence relation* $\phi_1, ..., \phi_n \models_{\Sigma} \phi$ *is semi-computable.*
Proof. From Proposition 11 it follows that the consequence at hand is effectively 1-1 reducible to an instance of consequence from a semi-computable first order theory, which is known to be semi-computable. □

5 Fracterm Calculus for Common Meadows

In Sect. 5.1, we recall *common meadows* and a fracterm calculus for these, FTCcm. In Sect. 5.2, we establish that the axiomatisation of FTCcm is equivalent to the transformation $\psi_{\text{true}}(\textsf{AxFTCpm})$ with $\textsf{AxFTCpm}$ as shown in Table 4.

5.1 FTCcm, a Specification

Fracterm calculus for common meadows, FTCcm, starts by involving the absorptive element $\bot$ and by assuming $\frac{x}{0} = \bot$.

Following [12], we adopt a modular approach and first consider $\textsf{Enl}_\bot(R)$, the enlargement of a commutative unital ring R with $\bot$, with axioms in Table 8.

Table 8. Specification of commutative unital $\bot$-rings, with a set $E_{wcr,\bot}$ of axioms

$$
\begin{aligned}
\text{signature} &: \Sigma_{wcr,\bot} = \{ \\
\text{sort} &: \textsf{Number} \\
\text{constants} &: 0, 1, \bot : \textsf{Number} \\
\text{total functions} &: \_ + \_ , \_ \cdot \_ : \textsf{Number} \times \textsf{Number} \to \textsf{Number}; \\
& \quad\ - \_ : \textsf{Number} \to \textsf{Number} \\
\text{equality relation} &: \_ = \_ \subseteq \textsf{Number} \times \textsf{Number} \} \\
\text{variables} &: x, y, z : \textsf{Number}
\end{aligned}
$$

$$
\begin{aligned}
(x + y) + z &= x + (y + z) & \text{(c1)} \\
x + y &= y + x & \text{(c2)} \\
x + 0 &= x & \text{(c3)} \\
x + (-x) &= 0 \cdot x & \text{(c4)} \\
(x \cdot y) \cdot z &= x \cdot (y \cdot z) & \text{(c5)} \\
x \cdot y &= y \cdot x & \text{(c6)} \\
1 \cdot x &= x & \text{(c7)} \\
x \cdot (y + z) &= (x \cdot y) + (x \cdot z) & \text{(c8)} \\
-(-x) &= x & \text{(c9)} \\
x + \bot &= \bot & \text{(c10)} \\
0 \cdot (x \cdot x) &= 0 \cdot x & \text{(c11)}
\end{aligned}
$$

Since $\bot$ is absorptive, it follows that $-\bot = \bot + x = \bot \cdot x = \bot$, so the familiar ring identities $0 \cdot x = 0$ and $x + (-x) = 0$ are not valid, but the weaker identities

$0 \cdot (x \cdot x) = 0 \cdot x$ and $x + (-x) = 0 \cdot x$ are. In [12, Thm.2.1], the set of axioms $E_{wcr,\perp}$ is defined and it is shown that for each equation $t = r$ over $\Sigma(R) \cup \{\perp\}$,

$$E_{wcr,\perp} \vdash t = r \iff \mathsf{Enl}_\perp(R) \models t = r.$$

For example, $E_{wcr,\perp} \vdash 0 \cdot (x+y) = 0 \cdot (x \cdot y)$ (with $0 \cdot (x+y) = 0 \cdot ((x+y) \cdot (x+y))$ this follows easily). With *Mace4* [23], it quickly follows that the axioms of E_{wcr} are logically independent.

Table 9. Specification of the fracterm calculus of common meadows, with a set AxFTCcm of axioms

---

$$\text{import} : E_{wcr,\perp} \setminus \{(c11)\} \ (\text{Table 8})$$
$$\text{signature} : \Sigma^d_{md,\perp} = \Sigma_{wcr,\perp} \cup \{$$
$$\text{total functions} : \frac{-}{-} : \mathsf{Number} \times \mathsf{Number} \to \mathsf{Number}\}$$
$$\text{variables} : x, y : \mathsf{Number}$$

$$\frac{x}{y} = x \cdot \frac{1}{y} \tag{cm1}$$

$$\frac{x}{x} = 1 + \frac{0}{x} \tag{cm2}$$

$$\frac{1}{x \cdot y} = \frac{1}{x} \cdot \frac{1}{y} \tag{cm3}$$

$$\frac{1}{1 + (0 \cdot x)} = 1 + (0 \cdot x) \tag{cm4}$$

$$\perp = \frac{1}{0} \tag{cm5}$$

Definition 4. *A **common meadow** is an enlargement $F_\perp$ of a field F, which results by first extending the domain with an absorptive element $\perp$ and then expanding the structure thus obtained with a constant $\perp$ (for said absorptive element) and a division function which is made total by adopting*

$$\frac{x}{0} = \frac{x}{\perp} = \frac{\perp}{x} = \perp.$$

A common meadow provides arguably the most straightforward way to turn division into a total operator. The fracterm calculus of common meadows (as discussed in [4] and in [5]) has many different axiomatisations, see e.g. [12]. Here we combine axioms (c1)–(c10) of $E_{wcr,\perp}$ (Table 8) and axioms (cm1)–(cm5) of Table 9 that define division as a total function for each structure containing $\perp$

as an absorptive element. Table 9 lists a set AxFTCcm of axioms for FTCcm following the presentation of [4], though using fracterms instead of inverse notation x^{-1} for $\frac{1}{x}$.

With *Prover9* [23] it quickly follows that axiom (c11) is derivable from AxFTCcm, which, according to *Mace4* [23], is a set of independent axioms. Also with *Prover9*, the following familiar consequences of AxFTCcm are quickly derived:

$$\frac{x}{1} = x, \quad -\frac{x}{y} = \frac{-x}{y} = \frac{x}{-y}, \quad \frac{x}{y} \cdot \frac{u}{v} = \frac{x \cdot u}{y \cdot v}, \quad \text{and} \quad \frac{x}{y} + \frac{u}{v} = \frac{x \cdot v + y \cdot u}{y \cdot v} \ .$$

The axioms of AxFTCcm allow fracterm flattening: each expression can be proven equal to a flat fracterm. This was first shown in [4, Prop.2.2.3] with inverse notation x^{-1} for $\frac{1}{x}$ (conversely, division can be defined by $\frac{x}{y} = x \cdot y^{-1}$).

5.2 $\perp$-Enlargement: Application of $\psi_{\text{true}}()$ to FTCpm

First, we establish some properties of common meadows. By Definition 4,

$$0 \neq \perp \ \text{ and } \ 1 \neq \perp, \tag{4}$$

$$-(\perp) = \perp, \ x + \perp = \perp + x = \perp, \ x \cdot \perp = \perp \cdot x = \perp, \ \text{and} \ \frac{x}{\perp} = \frac{\perp}{x} = \perp, \tag{5}$$

$$\frac{x}{0} = \perp. \tag{6}$$

Moreover, since $\perp$ is absorbing, it easily follows that

$$-x = \perp \rightarrow x = \perp,$$
$$x + y = \perp \rightarrow (x = \perp \lor y = \perp), \ \text{ and}$$

$$x \cdot y = \perp \rightarrow (x = \perp \lor y = \perp). \tag{7}$$

The following theorem is proven in [7, Thm.5.2.1] and implies that our axiomatisation of AxFTCpm of partial meadows is sufficiently strong. We write AxFTCpm^{cl} for the axioms of partial meadows as represented in Table 4, thus with all universal quantifications made explicit, e.g.

$$\forall_\text{p} x.\forall_\text{p} y.\forall_\text{p} z.(x + y) + z =_\text{p} x + (y + z).$$

Theorem 3. *With* (4)–(7) *it follows that* $\psi_{\text{true}}(\text{AxFTCpm}^{\text{cl}}) \vdash \text{AxFTCcm}$ *and that* $\psi_{\text{true}}(\text{AxFTCpm}^{\text{cl}})$ *axiomatises a common meadow.*

6   Concluding Remarks

Short-circuit logics (SCLs) were introduced in [8] and are distinguished by sequential connectives that prescribe left-to-right (sequential) evaluation of their operands, in particular, $\mathsf{F} \wedge_{\!\!\circ} x = \mathsf{F}$, while $x \wedge_{\!\!\circ} \mathsf{F} = \mathsf{F}$ is not necessarily true (in the case of a partial meadow, take $(\frac{1}{0} =_{\mathsf{p}} 0)$ for x).

Depending on the strength of possible atomic side-effects, different *short-circuit* logics were defined and axiomatised, both for the two-valued and three-valued case, see [9,24]. In [6], three-valued CℓSCL is introduced, which differs from Guzmán and Squier's Conditional logic [18] only by the use of sequential connectives. CℓSCL with only the constants T and F and none for the value undefined (CℓSCL$_2$) is also introduced in [6] and most closely resembles propositional logic: side-effects are not modelled and full left-sequential conjuction $\wedge$, definable by $x \wedge y = (x \wedge_{\!\!\circ} y) \vee_{\!\!\circ} (y \wedge_{\!\!\circ} x)$, is commutative. Moreover, adding $x \wedge_{\!\!\circ} \mathsf{F} = \mathsf{F}$ to CℓSCL$_2$ yields a sequential version of propositional logic and excludes the use of a third truth value undefined (because with a constant U for undefined, it would follow that $\mathsf{U} = \mathsf{U} \wedge_{\!\!\circ} \mathsf{F} = \mathsf{F}$).

Starting from CℓSCL$_2$ and partial equality $(=_{\mathsf{p}})$, we here introduced partial meadows together with axioms and rules split into a part for general, partial Σ-algebras (using rules for weak substitution from [3]) and a part specific to partial meadows (with signature Σ_m^{pd}). We have taken a pragmatic approach and included only axioms and rules that were used in our proofs. The new quantifiers $\forall_{\mathsf{p}}$ and $\exists_{\mathsf{p}}$ were introduced for readability and comprehensibility, but could have been replaced by their familiar counterparts $\forall$ and $\exists$.

It is an open question whether the axioms of FTCpm (AxFTCpm in Table 5) are independent. It is certainly the case that axioms (pm1)–(pm7) are independent (*Mace4*) and imply $x + y =_{\mathsf{p}} y + x$ (Proposition 2), and it seems that the two axioms (pm8) and (pm9) for division, i.e.

$$y \neq_{\mathsf{p}} 0 \;\circ\!\!\to\; \frac{x}{y} =_{\mathsf{p}} x \cdot \frac{1}{y} \quad \text{and} \quad x \neq_{\mathsf{p}} 0 \;\circ\!\!\to\; \frac{x}{x} =_{\mathsf{p}} 1,$$

are both mutually independent and also from the first seven. Axioms (pm10) and (pm11), i.e. $0 \neq_{\mathsf{p}} 1$ and $(x \neq_{\mathsf{p}} 0 \wedge_{\!\!\circ} y \neq_{\mathsf{p}} 0) \circ\!\!\to x \cdot y \neq_{\mathsf{p}} 0$, express that a partial meadow is an expansion of a field, and their independence is not clear.

We expect that an extension of AxFTCpm can be designed, including its proof system, for which a suitable completeness theorem can be obtained so that it becomes rewarding to investigate the model theory of these axioms, perhaps in a manner comparable to [15,16] where the model theory of the axioms for common meadows has been worked out in considerable detail.

Partial data types for arithmetic arise in different ways, for instance the transreals of Anderson et al. [1,25] can be turned into partial transreals where division is more often defined than in a partial meadow ($\frac{1}{0} = +\infty$, and $\frac{-1}{0} = -\infty$, while $\frac{0}{0}$ is undefined) and where addition and multiplication are partial: $\infty + (-\infty)$ and $0 \cdot \infty$ are undefined (while in transreals $\infty + (-\infty) = 0 \cdot \infty = \Phi$). Just as in a common meadow where $\frac{1}{0} = \bot$ which we replace by undefined to obtain a partial meadow, viewing Φ as a representation of undefinedness leads to partial transreals and to its substructure of partial transrationals.

The entropic transreals of [13] are a modification of transreals which can be turned into partial entropic transreals where division and multiplication are total while addition is partial. Again the idea is to have t undefined (in the partial entropic transreals) in case $t = \perp$ in entropic transreals. In the partial entropic transreals one has $\frac{1}{0} = +\infty$, $\frac{0}{0} = 0 \cdot \infty = 0$, while $\infty + (-\infty)$ is undefined.

Wheels (see Carlström's [14]) can be made partial also by having t undefined if $t = \perp$ in a wheel. In a partial wheel division, addition, and multiplication are each partial. We notice that a wheel contains a single unsigned infinite element ∞ rather than a pair of signed infinite elements $+\infty$ and $-\infty$ (as in transreals and entropic transreals) and that in a partial wheel, $\infty + \infty$ is undefined.

Acknowledgments. We are grateful to the reviewers for their helpful comments, which have led to several improvements. We thank the editors of this volume for their assistance and for organising this celebration.

Disclosure of Interests. The authors have no competing interests to declare that are relevant to the content of this article.

References

1. Anderson, J.A.D.W., Völker, N., Adams, A.A.: Perspex Machine VIII, axioms of transreal arithmetic. In: Latecki, J., Mount, D.M., Wu, A.Y. (eds.) Proc. SPIE 6499, Vision Geometry XV, 649902 (2007). https://doi.org/10.1117/12.698153

2. Bergstra, J.A., Bethke, I., Rodenburg, P.H.: A propositional logic with 4 values: true, false, divergent and meaningless. J. Appl. Non-Class. Logics **5**(2): 199–217 (1995). https://doi.org/10.1080/11663081.1995.10510855 (also available as report P9406 at https://ivi.fnwi.uva.nl/tcs/publications.php)

3. Bergstra, J.A., Broy, M., Tucker, J.V., Wirsing, M.: On the power of algebraic specifications. In: Gruska, J., Chytil, M. (eds.) Mathematical Foundations of Computer Science 1981 (MFCS 1981), LNCS, vol. 118, pp. 193–204, Springer, Berlin, Heidelberg (1981). https://doi.org/10.1007/3-540-10856-4_85

4. Bergstra, J.A., Ponse, A.: Division by zero in common meadows. In De Nicola, R., Hennicker, R. (eds.) Software, Services, and Systems: Essays dedicated to Martin Wirsing. LNCS, vol. 8950, pp. 46–61, Springer, Cham (2015). https://doi.org/10.1007/978-3-319-15545-6_6 Also available in improved form as arXiv:1406.6878v4 (22 March 2021). https://doi.org/10.48550/arXiv.1406.6878

5. Bergstra, J.A., Ponse, A.: Fracpairs and fractions over a reduced commutative ring. Indigationes Mathematicae **27**(3), 727–748 (2016). https://doi.org/10.1016/j.indag.2016.01.007

6. Bergstra, J.A., Ponse, A.: Conditional logic as a short-circuit logic. Sci. Ann. Comput. Sci. **35**(2): 161–196 (2025). https://doi.org/10.47743/SACS.2025.2.161

7. Bergstra, J.A., Ponse, A.: Fracterm calculus for partial meadows. arXiv:2502.13812 (7 October 2025). https://doi.org/10.48550/arXiv.2502.13812

8. Bergstra, J.A., Ponse, A., Staudt, D.J.C.: Short-circuit logic. arXiv:1010.3674v4 (12 March 2013). https://doi.org/10.48550/arXiv.1010.3674

9. Bergstra, J.A., Ponse, A., Staudt, D.J.C.: Non-commutative propositional logic with short-circuit evaluation. J. Appl. Non-Classical Logics **31**(3–4), 234–278 (2021). https://doi.org/10.1080/11663081.2021.2010954

10. Bergstra, J.A., Tucker, J.V.: The rational numbers as an abstract data type. J. ACM **54**(2), Article 7, 25 pages (2007). https://doi.org/10.1145/1219092.1219095

11. Bergstra, J.A., Tucker, J.V.: Partial arithmetical data types of rational numbers and their equational specification. J. Logical Algeb. Methods Programm. **128**, Article 100797, 16 (2022). https://doi.org/10.1016/j.jlamp.2022.100797

12. Bergstra, J.A., Tucker, J.V.: On the axioms of common meadows: fracterm calculus, flattening and incompleteness. Comput. J. **66**(7), 1565–1572 (2022). https://doi.org/10.1093/comjnl/bxac026

13. Bergstra, J.A., Tucker, J.V.: On defining expressions for entropy and cross-entropy: the entropic transreals and their fracterm calculus. Entropy **27**(1), Article 31, 13 (2025). https://doi.org/10.3390/e27010031

14. Carlström, J.: Wheels - on division by zero. Math. Struct. Comput. Sci. **14**(1), 143–184 (2004). https://doi.org/10.1017/S0960129503004110

15. Dias, J., Dinis, B.: Towards an enumeration of finite common meadows. Internat. J. Algebra Comput. **24**(06), 837–855 (2024). https://doi.org/10.1142/S0218196724500310

16. Dias, J., Dinis, B.: Strolling through common meadows. Comm. Algebra **52**(12), 5015–5042 (2024). https://doi.org/10.1080/00927872.2024.2362932

17. Diertens, B.: PSF - Process Specification Formalism. https://bob.diertens.org/cs/psf/. Accessed 24 Oct 2024

18. Guzmán, F., Squier, C.C.: The algebra of conditional logic. Algebra Universalis **27**, 88–110 (1990). https://doi.org/10.1007/BF01190256

19. Jones, C.B., Middelburg, C.A.: A typed logic of partial functions, reconstructed classically. Acta Informatica **31**, 399–430 (1994). https://doi.org/10.1007/BF01178666

20. Konikowska, B., Tarlecki, A., Blikle, A.: A three-valued logic for software specification and validation: Tertium tamen datur. In: Bloomfield, R.E., Marshall, L.S., Jones, R.B. (eds.) VDM '88 VDM – The Way Ahead (VDM 1988). LNCS, vol. 328, pp. 218–242, Springer, Berlin, Heidelberg (1988). https://doi.org/10.1007/3-540-50214-9_19

21. Mauw, S.: A constructive version of the approximation induction principle. In: Proceedings of the SION Conference on Computing Science in the Netherlands (CSN'87), pp. 235–252, CWI, Amsterdam (1987)

22. Mauw, S., Veltink, G.J.: Algebraic specification of communication protocols. Cambridge Tracts in Theoretical Computer Science, vol. 36. Cambridge University Press, Cambridge (1993). https://doi.org/10.1017/CBO9780511721625

23. McCune, W.: The GUI: Prover9 and Mace4 with a graphical user interface. Prover9-Mace4 Version 0.5B. (Prover9-Mace4-v05B.zip, March 14, 2008). https://www.cs.unm.edu/~mccune/prover9/gui/v05.html, last accessed 2025/11/17

24. Ponse, A., Staudt, D.J.C.: An independent axiomatisation for free short-circuit logic. J. Appl. Non-Classical Logics **28**(1), 35–71 (2018). https://doi.org/10.1080/11663081.2018.1448637

25. dos Reis, T.S., Gomide, W., Anderson, J.A.D.W.: Construction of the transreal numbers and algebraic transfields. IAENG Int. J. Appl. Math. **46**(1): 11–23 (2016). https://www.iaeng.org/IJAM/issues_v46/issue_1/IJAM_46_1_03.pdf

Ethics in Computer Science Research

Francien Dechesne[1][(✉)] and Olga Gadyatskaya[2]

[1] eLaw Center for Law and Digital Technologies, Leiden Institute for Advanced
Computer Science, Leiden, The Netherlands
`f.dechesne@law.leidenuniv.nl`
[2] Leiden Institute for Advanced Computer Science, Leiden University,
Leiden, The Netherlands
`o.gadyatskaya@liacs.leidenuniv.nl`

Abstract. This position paper argues that professional responsibility
and ethical reflection are relevant to *everyone* educated and working in
the computational sciences: not only in areas with direct applications
in the center of societal developments (such as cybersecurity and artificial intelligence), but also in more theoretical parts of the field. While
work has been done to translate (parts of) ethical issues into formalized
requirements, implementation guidelines, and performance measures for
moral values (such as trust, privacy, fairness), the engagement with ethics
and moral responsibility of the field is yet to be adopted more systematically. We aim to clarify the need for the incorporation of ethical reflection
across the computational sciences and to address the role of education
in getting there.

Keywords: ethics · professional responsibility · cybersecurity ·
artificial intelligence · theoretical computer science · software
engineering

1   Introduction

If any scientific activity seems, at first glance, to be devoid of personal biases,
it would be mathematics and computation. They are analytical rather than
empirical disciplines, with results based on explicit and unambiguous definitions,
axioms, and reasoning rules rather than on situated and mediated observations.
Proofs can be verified as necessary implications by those explicit and precise
premises.

What then is the relevance of moral reflection and responsibility for the
researchers working in these fields? In this position paper, we argue that ethics
and responsibility matter – albeit in different ways – for researchers in *all* parts
of computer science (CS), from the fields developing computational and analysis
techniques that will be more applied (such as cybersecurity or machine learning
research), all the way to more theoretical parts of the discipline.

With the vast digitization of crucial parts of our lives and society, the attention to ethics around computational technologies has made it onto the agendas of

B. Fila et al. (Eds.): Sjouke Mauw Festschrift, LNCS 16365, pp. 54–72, 2026.
https://doi.org/10.1007/978-3-032-20684-8_4

governments and boardrooms. Questions around responsibility, privacy, fairness, the relations of network architectures to power structures, the use of technology for military purposes or by malicious actors, all the way to the desirable structure of our society (democracy and markets, rule of law), have become intricately related to developments in digital technologies such as the internet, social media, smartphones and the internet of things, digital currencies, data collection and processing, and artificial intelligence.

For a long time, as confirmed in our own experience and surroundings, addressing how ethics is relevant to computer science research and the work of the computer scientist has not been an obvious or very active part of computer science, especially branches of research primarily concerned with abstractions (such as theory of computation, algorithmics, formal structures, and models) [21].

To be clear: we do not mean to say that attention for ethics and professional responsibility was never there. Both individuals and institutions have articulated positions and guidelines around the role of the work in the larger societal context and the professional responsibility that it brings [65,71]. What we observe is that computer science researchers often tend to focus on modeling aspects of moral questions as computational problems. For example, in the bodies of work that focus on developing techniques to formalize and codify moral values, such as trust, security, privacy, etc., into (non-functional) requirements, aiming to contribute to promoting those values [2,32].

Such work, while arguably of instrumental value to moral deliberations around digital technologies, does not inherently train awareness of, and active engagement with, the moral character of those questions. Turning them into computational specifications may also obscure the fact that moral problems have inherently contested understandings and no (universal) solutions. There should be a reflection on the link between analytic work and moral guidance or evaluation: what can a discipline focused on abstraction and formalization contribute to context-sensitive moral problems, but also: what are the moral implications of the field itself, in light of its embedded logics, methods, culture, and measures for success [37,54,65,69].

In this paper, we highlight past as well as current instances and moments of awareness of the moral character of work in the computational sciences to underline the importance of ethical reflection across the entire field: from the current discussions around artificial intelligence, which in fact go back to the very early days of the field, via the moral issues in cybersecurity and software engineering, to the professional responsibilities for the computational sciences in general – including the more theoretical parts.

Ethical reflection should take place on the research itself, on the position of the research in larger (power) structures (e.g., regarding the collective norms and standards of the field or regarding finance and infrastructure), and in educating new researchers and practitioners. This requires changes in culture, through new institutional structures (such as ethical review processes) and in curricula.

We signal important developments in this direction that are specific to computer science research, e.g., in the emergence of ethics committees, professional codes of conduct, and curricula adopting modules on (moral) responsibility specific to research in the computational sciences. In particular, we address the crucial role of continuous education in making ethical reflection and deliberation part of a culture, accepting the responsibility that comes with the development and application of the specific knowledge and skills of the field.

2   Ethics in the Computational Sciences

Over the (relatively short) history of the research field of computer science, several individual and institutional actors have taken steps to incorporate an awareness and culture of professional responsibility [71].

In the 2010s, growing awareness of the implications of the -by then-widespread use of the internet, as well as the widespread collection of the accompanying data traces, led to a number of calls for renewed ethical awareness for people working in the field. For example, in 2012, the Department of Homeland Security adopted the Menlo Report [6], proposing "guidelines for ethical assessment of computer and information security research" based on key principles derived from the reputable Belmont report on ethical guidelines for human subjects research [57]. The Menlo report noted that these core principles are applicable to broader ICT research fields and other disciplines beyond computer science [6]. In the wake of the 2013 Snowden revelations, cryptographer Phil Rogaway called for attention to the "moral character of cryptographic work" [65].

In this section, we discuss several prominent cases calling for ethical awareness in computer science research, starting with some of the earliest examples.

2.1   Earlier Calls for Ethical Awareness

On the individual level, several prominent researchers in the computational sciences have been explicit in their concern about the impacts of possible applications of their work from the very beginning. Norbert Wiener, who coined the term *cybernetics* for the study of interactions between biological and mechanical or electronic systems, warned of the potential societal implications of such technology in the early days of the development of electronic computers [83].[1]

At another stage of development, Joseph Weizenbaum warned about the potential psychological impact of computers programmed to mimic a human conversation partner. In the 1960s, he had developed a simple chatbot called ELIZA:

---

[1] Quote:"It has long been clear to me that the modern ultra-rapid computing machine was in principle an ideal central nervous system to an apparatus for automatic control; and that its input and output need not be in the form of numbers or diagrams but might very well be, respectively, the readings of artificial sense organs, such as photoelectric cells or thermometers, and the performance of motors or solenoids... We are already in a position to construct artificial machines of almost any degree of elaborateness of performance. Long before Nagasaki and the public awareness of the atomic bomb, it had occurred to me that we were here in the presence of another social potentiality of unheard-of importance for good and for evil." [83, p.39].

"a computer program for the study of Natural Language Communication between Man and Machine" [81]. With a relatively small number of instructions, the system turned out to produce human-like responses that were convincing to people interacting with it. Dialogues with a specific persona called DOCTOR, coded to mimic a psychotherapy session, were perceived to be actually therapeutic. This has since been called the ELIZA-effect. From these findings, Weizenbaum went on to write about the implications of introducing computational technologies into society and human relations, arguing for putting limits on the delegation of tasks to computers. He had concerns [82] about the lack of accountability and contestability when decisions were to be made using computers [9].[2]

These examples show ethical concerns from individual researchers in the early computational sciences, asking their professional community to reflect on the role of their – sometimes seemingly abstract – work and their responsibilities towards society as professionals in the field.

2.2   Ethics as Part of Defining the Profession

Collective reflection on responsibilities in the new scientific field around electronic computers also took place. With the accelerated development towards operational electronic computers during World War II, a new profession had started shaping – as marked by the founding of the Association for Computing Machinery (ACM) in 1947, "to advance the science, development, construction, and application of the new machinery for computing, reasoning, and other handling of information." Over the years, this constitutional description of the organization has evolved to explicitly include the aim to serve "both professional and public interests by fostering the open interchange of information and by promoting the highest professional and ethical standards." [1]

The development of ethical standards and guidelines is often associated with the definition of a profession and a professional community, as Parker [59] writes in the context of the development of the first code of ethics for the ACM in 1968. This is echoed in the guiding article for a revision of the ACM Code of Ethics in 1992: "Historically, professional associations have viewed codes of ethics as mechanisms to establish their status as a profession or as a means to regulate their membership and thereby convince the public that they deserve to be self-regulating." [4] Such a new profession comes with specific ethical issues (Parker [59] mentions, a.o., privacy or copyrighting code), that interact with (more general) "personal ethics" of the professional. The ACM published their "Guidelines for Professional Conduct in Information Processing" in 1966, which were succeeded by the ACM Code for Professional Conduct (1972), the ACM Code of Ethics and Professional Conduct (1992), and the current 2018 revision of the 1992 Code.[3]

---

[2] Weizenbaum was, e.g., concerned that "the introduction of computers into our already technological society has [...] merely reinforced and amplified those antecedent pressures that have driven man to an ever more highly rationalistic view of his society and an ever more mechanistic image of himself" [80, p.11].

[3] See https://ethics.acm.org/code-of-ethics/previous-versions/. [19].

Tracing back the origin of norms for the emerging research area of *computing machinery*, we should note that the foundation of the ACM was predated by the formation of communities around the emerging field of electrical *engineering* in the late 19th century, such as the AIEE and the IRE in the US. These grew rapidly and merged in 1963 to form the IEEE, which is now claimed to be the world's largest professional society.[4] Taking an approach to ethics focusing less on the professional responsibility of the engineer[5] and more on "foster[ing] technological innovation and excellence for the benefit of humanity",[6] they launched the *Global Initiative on Ethics of Autonomous and Intelligent Systems* in 2016 to answer to the need for more active ethical awareness and guidance in computational *engineering* coming with the increase of the attention and resources put into Artificial Intelligence (AI), for both research and development of applications. Note that the IEEE efforts, especially through their initiatives on developing Standards[7] are more explicitly focused on engineering and building applications in industry (rather than on research and research communities).

2.3   Developments in AI Ethics

As the above-mentioned IEEE initiative shows, the developments in *Artificial Intelligence* of the past decade have drawn particular attention to ethics among engineering communities. *AI* can be framed as a long-term interdisciplinary project, with a strong grounding in the computational sciences, to build machines to simulate behavior and/or perform tasks that we would say require (human) intelligence [50]. In his seminal 1950 paper*"Computing Machinery and Intelligence"* [77], Alan Turing avoided the challenge of establishing a general definition of intelligence by introducing the thought experiment of the *imitation game*. This has since been called the *Turing test*, and it has become adopted as a benchmark for AI: a machine is said to pass the test if a human evaluator cannot distinguish, with a high enough degree of certainty, whether they converse with another human or with a machine. This early benchmark can be seen to have steered foundational strands of the project of Artificial Intelligence on the track of processing natural language, as well as producing language that successfully simulates "natural" language. From the start, ethical (and psychological) effects of such an endeavour were acknowledged (see the discussion of the ELIZA-effect [81] above).

The increased availability of data and computing power, and the developments in the field of machine learning over the past couple of decades have led to renewed and increased investment – and co-development between science

---

[4] https://www.ieee.org/about/ieee-history.html.

[5] For example, while the roots of the IEEE predate the founding of the ACM, the ACM was earlier in formulating their code of ethics. [59].

[6] Cf. the IEEE Mission statement: https://www.ieee.org/about/vision-mission.html.

[7] This happens via the IEEE Standards Association, see for example the (P)7000-standard series for Autonomous and Intelligent systems: https://standards.ieee.org/initiatives/autonomous-intelligence-systems/standards/.

and industry – in the project of Artificial Intelligence towards applications with societal impact.

One of the most prominently debated examples of the risks of machine learning *"solutions"* in societal contexts was the *COMPAS* case in 2016: the analysis and discussion of a recidivism scoring tool used in several courts in the USA. The data journalists of the platform *ProPublica* had analyzed how the system assigned the scores, and whether those scores could be seen as justified. It found a clear bias against people of color. The producer of the system refused to give transparency about how the system produces the scores, but rebutted with statistics, claiming there was no disparity in the distribution of the scores between colored and white subjects. However, the work of ProPublica had also shown the inaccuracy of a large percentage of the scores. On closer inspection, the discrimination did not lie in a disparate distribution of scores, but in the distribution of false-positives versus the false-negatives over the two groups. A mathematical impossibility result shows that the one disparity cannot be resolved without increasing the other [18]. The COMPAS case has led to fundamental research on patterns found in data through machine learning, reflecting and promoting harmful biases and discrimination.

This confrontation with consequences in the real world of the outcomes of abstract research in the computational sciences has called for more active and broader consideration of the ethical implications of the work in the field [26, 42]. When machine learning increasingly moved towards applications in societal processes, some researchers with concerns started workshops co-located with the large Machine Learning conferences. These workshops led to the establishment of a new interdisciplinary community focusing on "Fairness, Accountability and Transparency" (in Machine Learning) (FAccT). The first independent conference was held in 2018; at the third edition in 2020, the conference series was brought under the auspices of the ACM.[8] The FAccT-community becoming part of an organization covering such a broad range of computational fields has helped *cross-pollinate* its results: consideration of FAccT-aspects has become a frequent requirement across other AI publication venues and conferences.

Further, recent developments at the intersection of AI and Natural Language Processing (NLP) [78] have drawn public attention, in particular, since the public launch of the so-called *Large Language Model (LLM)* ChatGPT by OpenAI in November 2022. The societal implications had been anticipated in the work of Hovy and Spruit [41], who connected growing discussions around responsible engineering, ethics, and digital technologies, in particular ethics for data-intensive computational fields (in the wake of the *big data*-hype) with Natural Language Processing. Their paper provided "some of the relevant terminology from the literature on ethics of technology, namely the concepts of exclusion, overgeneralization, bias confirmation, topic under- and overexposure, and dual use" [41]. In 2019, computational linguist Emily Bender argued, together with

---

several leading members of the Google AI Ethics team [8],[9] that current applications of NLP (such as the LLM-based applications currently being rolled out under disputable claims of utility), in general, come with a whole range of visible and invisible costs and risk of harms to users, non-users, society at large, and to our natural resources. These developments raised new questions about professional responsibilities and the development of a culture around ethics within computational linguistics and natural language processing. The Association of Computational Linguistics (ACL) adopted the 2018 ACM Code of Ethics in 2020 [19]. The first ACL conference to explicitly point to the Code of Ethics in its call for papers (and reviewing processes) was Empirical Methods in NLP in 2020 [7].

To summarize, the past decade has seen a rapid impulse for technical developments in artificial intelligence via the increased variety and availability of data and computational resources. The growing awareness of societal implications of these developments has led a wide range of nations, international organisations, companies, government agencies, etc. to develop AI Ethics policies and steps towards technical standards and (legal but also self-)regulation. [28,30]

At the same time, we note that moral issues arise that are less directly related to the computational sciences, but are tied to the increased economic importance of the field and its products: challenges around the (lack of) distribution of resources, responsibility, and power in a market increasingly dominated by just a handful of actors (companies and states). For researchers in the field, this will raise general moral questions around the independence of their work in case they have to rely on commercial resources (such as funding, data, or compute). It also raises general moral questions around personal responsibility: people working for the Big Tech companies, if the policies of the company go against personal or public values.[10]

2.4 Ethics in Cybersecurity

Cybersecurity, also referred to as computer security, has emerged as a field where ethical considerations are now paramount [23,85]. Whereas discussions and publications about ethics appeared regularly within the community, in recent years, the attention to ethics peaked when one of the top conferences, USENIX Security Symposium 2025, demanded in its Call for Papers that all submissions explicitly discuss the applicable ethical considerations[11] and provided its own ethical guidelines for authors.[12]

Several prominent research directions and methods in the cybersecurity domain demand attention to ethics. First, security research frequently aims to

---

[9] Note that Google subsequently fired some team members, and others then resigned. Arguably industry, or at least one of its biggest representatives in the field, did not foster a culture of ethics.

[10] See also Moshe Vardi's reflections in the Communications of the ACM in December 2024: https://cacm.acm.org/opinion/i-was-wrong-about-the-ethics-crisis/.

[11] https://www.usenix.org/conference/usenixsecurity25/call-for-papers.

[12] https://www.usenix.org/conference/usenixsecurity25/ethics-guidelines.

discover, report, and mitigate vulnerabilities in popular software or hardware systems. However, the interests of the security researcher who discovered an impactful vulnerability may not be fully aligned with the interests of the system owner or society. To balance the interests of all involved parties, the *coordinated vulnerability disclosure* (CVD) process, sometimes also called responsible vulnerability disclosure, has been established [56]. It requires the researcher to first confidentially notify the system owner about the vulnerability and agree to wait a reasonable amount of time until the vulnerability is patched [40]. However, there are many additional ethical concerns that the researchers have to address in conjunction with the CVD. For example, some large-scale studies lead to the discovery of so many vulnerabilities that it might not be feasible to notify the system owners [17,53], or some vulnerabilities might be "unpatchable" [25,47].

Second, in recent years, *human studies* have become more and more popular in the field. Given that many cyber attacks involve social engineering or human errors [79] and that the success or failure of many security tools depends on how well the users can wield them [67] – the community has recognized the need to study users and professionals and their interaction with cybersecurity [44]. Human studies demand special attention to the protection of the participants and, more broadly, the involved or affected populations, for example, by guaranteeing their privacy and minimizing potential harm to them [6]. Moreover, some technology-focused studies might be human studies *in disguise*, when there are no explicitly recruited participants, but human subjects (or their data or personal systems) are still being observed and studied [11]. A notable example is the Encore study [13], which measured internet censorship in different regions by deploying scripts on websites accessed by internet users who were not able to consent to participation [48,60].

Finally, another example topic worth mentioning here is the potential misuse (or dual-use) of the developed technology and methods and, more broadly, research that has potential future applications or implications that go beyond the intention of the authors [15,64]. Cybersecurity research frequently falls under this category, which is not surprising, as the motto of the field is "think like an attacker". Different methods and tools for vulnerability finding and cryptanalysis inherently introduce a risk of misuse, as they might enable adversaries to find weaknesses in third-party systems. It is thus important to balance the benefits of proactively identifying weaknesses when done by the "good guys" with the risks of these methods being misused by adversaries.

We note that the list of potential ethical concerns related to cybersecurity does not stop here. For more extensive discussions and guidance about ethical considerations in the cybersecurity field and cyberspace, we refer the reader to [45,70,74]. Recognizing the pervasiveness of ethical concerns in security, the community has started to organize itself by providing reference papers [14,29,31,47,49,52,68,85], operationalizing recommendations for Ethics Review Boards [64], proposing improvements to the current ethical review practices [23], and organizing topical workshops, such as the Workshop on Ethics in Computer Security (EthiCS) or Cyber-security Research Ethics Dialog &

Strategy Workshop (CREDS). The influential Menlo report [6] is the key reference document for the field, being originally written for information security researchers and decision makers as the primary audience.

However, there are indications that more ethical awareness is still needed in the field [23, 48, 68, 85]. In 2020–2021, the "Hypocrite Commits" paper[13] was recognized by many as a wake-up call that the existing ethics review processes were inadequate and that the security community had to become better in proactively designing and executing ethical research [23]. Much has been improved since then (including strengthening the ethical review processes of the leading conferences). However, just at the beginning of 2025, a security researcher from Snyk was caught red-handed when they were "pentesting" the security of Cursor AI by uploading data-stealing packages to the leading open source package library npm.[14] This case shows that some researchers and practitioners are still not able to properly examine consequences and apply careful ethical consideration.

2.5 Other Developments

We have named the ethical developments in Cybersecurity and AI as cases in point that ethical awareness and reflection are increasingly being recognized within the computational sciences. We chose to highlight these as these are the fields in which we, the authors, are currently active. However, we do not mean to suggest that no important developments take place in other areas, or in general. In this section, we briefly mention two of those developments.

Ethics in Software/Systems Engineering. Software engineering is another CS field where attention to ethics has been substantial [3, 5, 63, 73]. For example, the Software Engineering Code of Ethics supported by both ACM and IEEE was developed already in the 90 s [35].

Software Engineering conferences such as the ACM/IEEE International Conference on Software Engineering (ICSE), the International Conference on Evaluation and Assessment in Software Engineering (EASE), and the ACM/IEEE International Symposium on Empirical Software Engineering and Measurement (ESEM) have increasingly started to pay attention to the legal and ethical implications and considerations in the field, e.g. around themes such as privacy and fairness, and responsible practices such as data protection, documentation, and software engineering for trustworthiness [72].

Dutch Advice for Ethical Review in the Computational Sciences. In 2016, in our national context of the Netherlands, a special advisory committee of the Dutch Academy of Sciences (KNAW) published their findings on the assignment "to identify ways to assess the ethical and legal aspects of computer science research." Their conclusions very explicitly ask for the field to take action (from the English language summary of the report [46]):

---

[13] https://www.ieee-security.org/TC/SP2021/downloads/2021_PC_Statement.pdf.
[14] https://sourcecodered.com/snyk-malicious-npm-package/.

C2.1 To develop an ethical infrastructure for computer science.

C4.1 To install an Ethical Review Board for Informatics (ERBI) [...] and reflect on the lessons learned in this manner – with the recommendations [R4.1] for all governing bodies of institutes or departments active in computer science research to install an ERBI, either on their own or in collaboration; and [R4.2] in light of the relative immaturity for ethical review of computer science, and the dynamics of the field, to develop methods and sets of standards in close collaboration with other ERBIs.

The KNAW report was followed by an additional recommendation from the national ICT-Research Platform IPN in June 2019 to establish ethics committees for the STEM disciplines. In the wake of these reports, research institutions in the Netherlands have followed up in roughly two ways: either with informatics participating in broader STEM review boards (e.g., in Leiden[15]), or in establishing specific review boards for computational disciplines (as, for example, in Twente [64]).

2.6 What Is the Relevance of Ethics in Theoretical Computer Science?

After discussing the developments towards ethical awareness and active reflection in several more obviously application-oriented research fields, we will now take on the challenge to argue that such developments should also take place in the more explicitly theory-oriented fields of computational sciences.

It is not straightforward to argue that ethics (and education in ethics) also has relevance to theoretical computer science research. Intuitively, theoretical computer science is as morally neutral as any scientific activity can be, with its basis on agreed and fully transparent axioms and reasoning rules. Furthermore, as long as no direct application is envisioned, pure theory seemingly evades questions of morality. This is, for example, argued in *A Mathematician's Apology*, where George Hardy (a known pacifist) writes [36]:

It is sometimes suggested that pure mathematicians glory in the uselessness of their work, and make it a boast that it has no practical applica- tions. [...] If the theory of numbers could be employed for any practical and obviously honourable purpose, if it could be turned directly to the furtherance of human happiness or the relief of human suffering, as physiology and even chemistry can, then surely neither Gauss nor any other mathematician would have been so foolish as to decry or regret such applications. But science works for evil as well as for good (and particularly, of course, in time of war)[p. 13] ... There is one comforting conclusion which is easy for a real mathematician. Real mathematics has no effects on war. No one has yet discovered any warlike purpose to be served by the theory of numbers

---

[15] https://www.organisatiegids.universiteitleiden.nl/en/faculties-and-institutes/science/committees/ethics-review-committee.

or relativity, and it seems very unlikely that anyone will do so for many years. [p. 44]

What Hardy writes about mathematics seems to be valid intuitively for theoretical computer science research as well. For example, cryptographer Phil Rogaway's writes in the introduction to the course *Ethics in an age of technology*: "When I teach [...] *Theory of Computation*, I don't think that my religious inclinations, say, color what I do." [66]

However, over the past decade, Hardy's position has been explicitly challenged by the emergence of initiatives around *ethics in mathematics*, most noticeably at his own Alma Mater, with the founding in 2016 of the Cambridge University Ethics in Mathematics Society.[16]

We want to present two reasons why the intuitive (and quite widespread) *ethics-as-irrelevant-for-theory* position can be questioned. The first one is about the morality of assuming the authority to decide what is "pure theory" and to establish that "pure theory" is morally neutral. The second one is challenging the implication that the human practices aimed at "pure theory" are morally neutral.

As even Hardy acknowledges,[17] an (initially theoretical) frame may afford applications, in yet unknown near or far future circumstances, with moral implications. There is moral relevance in the assessment of a research question or result as "purely theoretical": it implies, or sets, norms on "pure" and "theory", and on when the researcher is supposedly absolved from responsibility. But whether the "theoretical" result stems from the intention to apply it in practice or not, a concept or a mathematical result that is useful for theory could later turn out to be useful for applications – directly or indirectly.

The development of the electronic computer, and with it the field of computer science, could serve as a case in point. In the 19th century, with the development of non-Euclidean geometries came the explicit study of *meta-mathematics* at the intersection of philosophy and mathematics, studying the nature of mathematics, and its relation to the (physical) world. Set theory and logic emerged as ways of grounding mathematics and afforded people like Church and Turing in the 1930s to express a precise conception of computation in formalism. In particular, Turing's conceptual construct of the 'a-machine' (for automatic machine, now known as Turing machine) demonstrated how computational instructions as well as inputs and outputs can be implemented as binary numbers [20]. This idea was then instrumental for the building of the early electronic computers in the 1940s (in which Turing was famously involved himself).

---

[16] Initiative by Maurice Chiodo, see https://www.ethics-in-mathematics.com/ and https://cueims.soc.srcf.net/: *"Mathematics is a profession. As such, we carry a responsibility to be aware of the harm we might do with our skills. CUEiMS was formed to promote awareness and discuss ethical issues faced by working mathematicians."*

[17] *"No one foresaw the applications of matrices and groups and other purely mathematical theories to modern physics, and it may be that some of the 'highbrow' applied mathematics will become 'useful' in as unexpected a way"* [36, p. 39].

Similarly, earlier investigations into developing neural networks and current investigations into quantum computing can be argued to have started as "purely theoretical".

To be clear, by making the point that ethical *reflection* is also relevant for research aimed at "pure theory", we do not mean to say such research should also undergo ethical *review*, as becomes more and more standard practice in branches of computer science research that more directly and clearly impact humans or society (see above). The point here is that moral reflection is also warranted when the (initial) motivation of the research is 'for the sake of theory'. This means that researchers in theoretical computer science, as members of society, involved in the important but specific societal practice of knowledge production, should be equipped with a basic understanding of the role their work may come to play when, expectedly or unexpectedly, the theory leads to applications.

Indeed, as researchers, we all hope that our scientific endeavors contribute to society – by adding to the advancement of knowledge, of what is theoretically and/or practically (im)possible, and under what preconditions. It may be necessary for those with deep knowledge of the theory to be involved in assessing how these contributions can be 'beneficial,' for which we should (be able and willing to) apply our moral evaluation framework.

Our second reason for questioning the *ethics-as-irrelevant-for-theory* position is more concrete in that it relates to the (current) structures wherein the research practices take place. Internally, researchers, also in more fundamental fields, are involved in framing what counts as worthwhile research. The resulting standards and norms on what counts as computer science may be biased and lead to exclusive research cultures [37]. But they may also be positively informed by moral principles, such as individual autonomy and democracy: a case in point is the work of people like David Chaum, who pioneered theoretical work on network architectures and communication protocols to afford privacy-preserving computational applications like digital cash and voting systems [16].

More externally, research funding frequently comes with expectations of serving societal (in case of public funding) or competitive (in case of private funding) interests. There is arguably a responsibility in weighing the acceptance of the funding with the expectation to serve those interests. Do those expectations and/or interests give a different perspective on what is "purely theoretical"? Researchers, even in theoretical computer science, should be prepared to assess such questions.

The Dutch KNAW commission acknowledged in an interview about its report on ethical review in computational sciences [46] that the field needs to engage with potential implications and applications of the research in the field: "as computational techniques become more important for sensitive parts of our society, ethical and also legal impacts will play an increasingly large role. But at this moment [2016], there is no mechanism in place to shape the ethical assessment. [...] As researchers, we mostly see the power and potential of the internet and the technology, but we have to acknowledge that there could be undesirable consequences" [43].

The committee also acknowledges it to be impossible to make a road map for laying out all possible scenarios and – even more – what the solutions should be: with both the rapid developments of the technology and the emergent ways in which they are adopted, such an endeavor would be highly speculative. This apparent limitation stems from the fact that the implications of the computational sciences are highly socio-technical. This supports the conclusion that awareness and reflection on implications are relevant and should be practiced across the computational sciences, in conversation with other relevant perspectives (scientific as well as societal).

3   Education as Path Forward

We argue that education is a viable path forward to create more ethical awareness in students, who are future CS researchers. [33,38]. Not everyone around in the academic profession is currently taking this responsibility seriously, or cites considerations of competitiveness of the computer science degree, or other priorities in the packed curricula. Such arguments point at implicit norms and standards around the profession that deserve questioning – also as part of the ethics conversation.

Education is not a one-way street. It can offer a two-way conversation between students and their professors, providing a unique opportunity to jointly reflect on what is morally at stake in the area of knowledge production of the computational sciences (in the current societal context), and what that means for professional and civic responsibility. It also provides a unique context for practicing normative argumentation, for both students and professors, and for becoming aware that this is different from the analytical reasoning that is characteristic for the field. Here is also where interaction with other disciplines and methodologies (philosophy and ethics, law, social sciences, and humanities) may be required.

The need for systematic reflection on the norms and standards in the computational sciences is slowly but increasingly being recognized, especially around AI. Curricula incorporate single courses on (general) philosophy of science, and provide electives on *responsible AI* or *AI and Society*. However, ethics education would ideally be more integrated into the whole curriculum and inter-disciplinary: interventions limited to singular courses might have limited impact [61] and multiple (yet not too many) modules engaging with ethics are recommended [39]. The community engaged in CS education has surveyed the available literature [10,58,62], shared educational designs [12,15,27,55] and best practices [34,51,76], and made recommendations [84] on integrating ethics and social responsibility in higher education for computational sciences.

Yet still, some students, as well as teachers, perceive ethics not to be fundamental to be a practicing computer scientist and not enhancing their employability [21]. This challenge came up as well in an inventory conducted by the *Teaching Responsible AI* initiative (TRAI) for higher education in the Netherlands [22].[18] The TRAI inventory also demonstrated, on the other hand, a clear demand from many teachers and students to be trained in using frameworks, vocabularies, and connections to other disciplines, in order to be able to engage with the moral implications and responsibilities of our work.

While higher education should strive to provide adequate and integrated ethical foundations, it is still the task for all of us to actively shape the future computing profession that will value ethics and societal responsibility.

4   Concluding Remarks

In this position paper we have argued that professional responsibility and ethical reflection are relevant to *everyone* educated and working in the computational sciences: not only in areas with direct applications in the center of societal developments (cybersecurity and artificial intelligence, for example), but even – albeit at a more abstract, meta-level – in more theoretical parts of the field.

This engagement with ethics and moral responsibility of the field should go beyond offering computational models and measures for (parts of) ethical issues: it should be systematically incorporated in the professional culture of the field. One step is the installation of an ethics review for the computational sciences, as recommended by the KNAW. Good steps in that direction are currently being made. We argue that, for true culture change and for those review boards to be meaningful, we also need to commit to incorporating the professional responsibilities of the field into our education.

To be clear: this paper does not mean to frame implications of the computational sciences as the sole responsibility of the computational scientist: computational systems are deeply socio-technical, and many stakeholders are involved in their embedding in societal practices and institutions (as expressed in the *problem of many hands* [75]). But we want to signal that with the particular knowledge of the discipline comes particular responsibility – while the discipline does not inherently provide us with the tools, vocabularies, and methods to handle it. Juggling the moral implications of the work – in applied as well as theoretical areas of the field – with the abstract nature of our work requires training and regular practice [24].

Acknowledgments. The work presented in this paper has profited significantly from vivid interactions at a panel discussion on Ethics in Computer Science that took place at the Alice and Eve workshop on October 25, 2024, in Leiden, convened by the second author and with the first author as panelist. The authors acknowledge the invaluable contributions of Hugo Jonker to the panel and the discussions that ultimately led to this paper. We also thank the two anonymous reviewers for their constructive comments that helped us sharpen the points we wanted to bring across.

The authors and Hugo would like to thank Sjouke Mauw for the many stimulating conversations over the years each of us worked with him, whether on our work or

---

[18] The initiative is linked to the Dutch Coalition for AI (AIC4NL, https://aic4nl.nl/). The first author is one of the founding members of the initiative and was actively involved in the inventory.

on seemingly random other activities (such as juggling, lindy hop, or unicycles). Like three juggling balls following disjoint trajectories, but thrown up and caught by the same hand, you may appreciate that we have been *bien étonnés de se trouver ensemble* recently around ethics education and ethics review committees for the computational sciences, and in writing this piece.

Disclosure of Interests. The authors have no competing interests to declare that are relevant to the content of this article.

References

1. ACM History Committee: ACM history. https://www.acm.org/about-acm/acm-history
2. Alcalde, B., Dubois, E., Mauw, S., Mayer, N., Radomirovic, S.: Towards a decision model based on trust and security risk management. In: Proceedings of the 7th Australasian Information Security Conference - AISC'09, volume 98 of Conferences in Research and Practice in Information Technology (CRPIT), pp. 61–69 (2009)
3. Alidoosti, R., Lago, P., Razavian, M., Tang, A.: Ethics in software engineering: A systematic literature review (2022). https://research.vu.nl/ws/portalfiles/portal/179576160/Ethics_in_SE_TR_2022.pdf
4. Anderson, R.E., Johnson, D.G., Gotterbarn, D., Perrolle, J.: Using the new ACM code of ethics in decision making. Commun. ACM **36**(2), 98–107 (Feb 1993). https://doi.org/10.1145/151220.151231
5. Aydemir, F.B., Dalpiaz, F.: A roadmap for ethics-aware software engineering. In: Proceedings of the International Workshop on Software Fairness, pp. 15–21 (2018)
6. Bailey, M., Dittrich, D., Kenneally, E., Maughan, D.: The Menlo report. IEEE Secur. Priv. **10**(2), 71–75 (2012)
7. Bender, E., Fort, K.: NAACL ethics review process report-back. blog (2021). https://2021.naacl.org/blog/ethics-review-process-report-back/
8. Bender, E.M., Gebru, T., McMillan-Major, A., Shmitchell, S.: On the dangers of stochastic parrots: Can language models be too big? In: Proceedings of the 2021 ACM Conference on Fairness, Accountability, and Transparency, pp. 610–623. FAccT '21, Association for Computing Machinery, New York, NY, USA (2021). https://doi.org/10.1145/3442188.3445922
9. Berry, D.M.: The limits of computation: Joseph Weizenbaum and the ELIZA chatbot. Weizenbaum J. Digital Soc. **3**(3) (Nov 2023). https://ojs.weizenbaum-institut.de/index.php/wjds/article/view/106
10. Brown, N., Xie, B., Sarder, E., Fiesler, C., Wiese, E.S.: Teaching ethics in computing: a systematic literature review of ACM computer science education publications. ACM Trans. Comput. Educ. **24**(1), 1–36 (2024)
11. Buchanan, E., Aycock, J., Dexter, S., Dittrich, D., Hvizdak, E.: Computer science security research and human subjects: emerging considerations for research ethics boards. J. Empir. Res. Hum. Res. Ethics **6**(2), 71–83 (2011)
12. Bullock, B.B., Nascimento, F.L., Doore, S.A.: Computing ethics narratives: teaching computing ethics and the impact of predictive algorithms. In: Proceedings of the 52nd ACM Technical Symposium on Computer Science Education, pp. 1020–1026 (2021)
13. Burnett, S., Feamster, N.: Encore: Lightweight measurement of web censorship with cross-origin requests. In: Proceedings of the 2015 ACM Conference on Special Interest Group on Data Communication. pp. 653–667 (2015)

14. Burstein, A.J.: Conducting cybersecurity research legally and ethically. LEET **8**, 1–8 (2008)
15. Cassing, K., Weydner-Volkmann, S.: Dual-use in cybersecurity research. Towards a new culture of research ethics. In: Gestreamt, gelikt, flüchtig–schöne neue Kulturwelt? pp. 349–360. Nomos Verlagsgesellschaft mbH & Co. KG (2024)
16. Chaum, D.L.: Untraceable electronic mail, return addresses, and digital pseudonyms. Commun. ACM **24**(2), 84–90 (Feb 1981). https://doi.org/10.1145/358549.358563
17. Chen, T.H., Tagliaro, C., Lindorfer, M., Borgolte, K., Van Der Ham-De Vos, J.: Are you sure you want to do coordinated vulnerability disclosure? In: 2024 IEEE European Symposium on Security and Privacy Workshops (EuroS&PW), pp. 307–314. IEEE (2024)
18. Chouldechova, A.: Fair prediction with disparate impact: a study of bias in recidivism prediction instruments. Big Data **5**, 153–163 (2017)
19. for Computational Linguistics, A.: ACL Code of Ethics (3 2020). https://www.aclweb.org/portal/content/acl-code-ethics
20. Copeland, B.J.: The Church-Turing Thesis. In: Zalta, E.N., Nodelman, U. (eds.) The Stanford Encyclopedia of Philosophy. Metaphysics Research Lab, Stanford University, Winter 2024 edn. (2024)
21. Darling-Wolf, H., Patitsas, E.: "Not my priority:" Ethics and the boundaries of computer science identities in undergraduate CS education. Proc. ACM Human-Comput. Interact. **8**(CSCW1), 1–28 (2024)
22. Dechesne, F., Harbers, M., Peeters, M., van Riemsdijk, B., Wiggers, P.: Verantwoorde AI in AI-opleidingen in Nederland: Uitdagingen en kansen (2025). https://aic4nl.nl/wp-content/uploads/2025/12/TRAI-document-.pdf, report of the Teaching Responsible AI (TRAI) initiative, Stichting AICoalitie4NL
23. Dirksen, A., Giessler, S., Erz, H., Johns, M., Fiebig, T.: Don't patch the researcher, patch the game: a systematic approach for responsible research via federated ethics boards. In: Proceedings of the New Security Paradigms Workshop, pp. 126–141 (2024)
24. Engels, A., Mauw, S.: Why men (and octopuses) cannot juggle a four ball cascade. In: Brune, M., Deursen, van, A., Heering, J. (eds.) Dat is dus heel interessant. Liber Amicorum Paul Klint 25 jaar SMC/CWI, pp. 109–115. CWI (1997)
25. Ethembabaoglu, A., van Wegberg, R., Zhauniarovich, Y., van Eeten, M.: The unpatchables: Why municipalities persist in running vulnerable hosts. In: 33rd USENIX Security Symposium (USENIX Security 24), pp. 7049–7066 (2024)
26. Favaretto, M., De Clercq, E., Gaab, J., Elger, B.S.: First do no harm: an exploration of researchers' ethics of conduct in Big Data behavioral studies. PLoS ONE **15**(11), e0241865 (2020)
27. Fiesler, C., Garrett, N., Beard, N.: What do we teach when we teach tech ethics? A syllabi analysis. In: Proceedings of the 51st ACM Technical Symposium on Computer Science Education, pp. 289–295 (2020)
28. Fjeld, J., Achten, N., Hilligoss, H., Nagy, A., Srikumar, M.: Principled artificial intelligence: Mapping consensus in ethical and rights-based approaches to principles for AI. Research Publication 2020-1, Berkman Klein Center, http://dx.doi.org/10.2139/ssrn.3518482 (January 2020)
29. Flechais, I., Chalhoub, G.: Practical cybersecurity ethics: Mapping CyBOK to ethical concerns. In: Proceedings of the 2023 New Security Paradigms Workshop, pp. 62–75 (2023)

30. Floridi, L.: The end of an era: from self-regulation to hard law for the digital industry. Philos. Technol. **34**(4), 619–622 (2021). https://doi.org/10.1007/s13347-021-00493-0

31. Formosa, P., Wilson, M., Richards, D.: A principlist framework for cybersecurity ethics. Comput. Secur. **109**, 102382 (2021)

32. Friedman, B.: Value-sensitive design. ACM Interact. **3**, 16–23 (1996). https://doi.org/10.1145/242485.242493

33. Garcia, R., et al.: Beyond "awareness": If we teach inclusive design, will students act on it? In: Proceedings of the 2024 ACM Conference on International Computing Education Research-Volume 1, pp. 434–451 (2024)

34. Garrett, N., Beard, N., Fiesler, C.: More than "if time allows". The role of ethics in AI education. In: Proceedings of the AAAI/ACM Conference on AI, Ethics, and Society, pp. 272–278 (2020)

35. Gotterbarn, D., Miller, K., Rogerson, S.: Software engineering code of ethics. Commun. ACM **40**(11), 110–118 (1997)

36. Hardy, G.H.: A Mathematician's Apology. Cambridge University Press, Canto (1992)

37. Hermans, F., Schlesinger, A.: A case for feminism in programming language design. In: Proceedings of the 2024 ACM SIGPLAN International Symposium on New Ideas, New Paradigms, and Reflections on Programming and Software, pp. 205–222. Onward! '24, Association for Computing Machinery, New York, NY, USA (2024)

38. Horton, D., Liu, D., McIlraith, S.A., Coyne, S., Wang, N.: Do embedded ethics modules have impact beyond the classroom? In: Proceedings of the 55th ACM Technical Symposium on Computer Science Education V. 1, pp. 533–539 (2024)

39. Horton, D., Liu, D., McIlraith, S.A., Wang, N.: Is more better when embedding ethics in CS courses? In: Proceedings of the 54th ACM Technical Symposium on Computer Science Education V. 1, pp. 652–658 (2023)

40. Householder, A.D., Wassermann, G., Manion, A., King, C.: The CERT guide to coordinated vulnerability disclosure. Software Engineering Institute (Carnegie Mellon University) (2017). available via https://bit.ly/3CSCaz5

41. Hovy, D., Spruit, S.L.: The social impact of natural language processing. In: Proceedings of the 54th Annual Meeting of the Association for Computational Linguistics (Volume 2: Short Papers), pp. 591–598. Association for Computational Linguistics, Berlin, Germany (Aug 2016). https://aclanthology.org/P16-2096

42. Huang, C., Zhang, Z., Mao, B., Yao, X.: An overview of artificial intelligence ethics. IEEE Trans. Artif. Intell. **4**(4), 799–819 (2022)

43. Ingenieur, R.D.: Ethische commissies voor informatica (2016). https://deingenieur.nl/artikelen/ethische-commissies-voor-informatica

44. Kaur, M., van Eeten, M., Janssen, M., Borgolte, K., Fiebig, T.: Human factors in security research: Lessons learned from 2008-2018. arXiv preprint arXiv:2103.13287 (2021)

45. Kizza, J.M.: Ethical and secure computing: A concise module. Springer (2023)

46. KNAW: Ethische en juridische aspecten van informaticaonderzoek (2016). https://storage.knaw.nl/2022-07/20160919-summary-ENG-advisory-ethische-en-juridische-aspecten-van-informaticaonderzoek-web.pdf

47. Kohno, T., Acar, Y., Loh, W.: Ethical frameworks and computer security trolley problems: Foundations for conversations. In: 32nd USENIX Security Symposium (USENIX Security 23), pp. 5145–5162 (2023)

48. Macnish, K., Van der Ham, J.: Ethics in cybersecurity research and practice. Technol. Soc. **63**, 101382 (2020)

49. Matwyshyn, A.M., Cui, A., Keromytis, A.D., Stolfo, S.J.: Ethics in security vulnerability research. IEEE Secur. Priv. **8**(2), 67–72 (2010)
50. McCarthy, J., Minsky, M., Rochester, N., Shannon, C.: A proposal for the Dartmouth summer research project on artificial intelligence. Available on John McCarthy's website: http://jmc.stanford.edu/articles/dartmouth.html (1955)
51. McDonald, N., et al.: Responsible computing: a longitudinal study of a peer-led ethics learning framework. ACM Trans. Comput. Educ. (TOCE) **22**(4), 1–21 (2022)
52. Mersinas, K., Bada, M., Furnell, S.: Cybersecurity behavior change: a conceptualization of ethical principles for behavioral interventions. Comput. Secur. **148**, 104025 (2025)
53. Moura, G.C., Heidemann, J.: Vulnerability disclosure considered stressful. ACM SIGCOMM Comput. Commun. Rev. **53**(2), 2–10 (2023)
54. Mulligan, D.K., Kroll, J.A., Kohli, N., Wong, R.Y.: This thing called fairness: disciplinary confusion realizing a value in technology. Proc. ACM Hum.-Comput. Interact. **3**(CSCW) (Nov 2019)
55. Narayanan, A., Zevenbergen, B.: No encore for encore? Ethical questions for web-based censorship measurement, Technology Science (2015)
56. Nationaal Cyber Security Centrum: Coordinated vulnerability disclosure: de leidraad (2018). https://www.ncsc.nl/documenten/publicaties/2019/mei/01/cvd-leidraad
57. National Commission for the Protection of Human Subjects of Biomedical and Behavioral Research: The Belmont report. Ethical principles and guidelines for the protection of human subjects of research (1978). https://www.hhs.gov/ohrp/regulations-and-policy/belmont-report/index.html
58. Padiyath, A.: A realist review of undergraduate student attitudes towards ethical interventions in technical computing courses. ACM Trans. Comput. Educ. **24**(2), 1–19 (2024)
59. Parker, D.B.: Rules of ethics in information processing. Commun. ACM **11**(3), 198–201 (mar 1968). https://doi.org/10.1145/362929.362987
60. Partridge, C., Allman, M.: Ethical considerations in network measurement papers. Commun. ACM **59**(10), 58–64 (2016)
61. Petelka, J., Finn, M., Roesner, F., Shilton, K.: Principles matter: integrating an ethics intervention into a computer security course. In: Proceedings of the 53rd ACM Technical Symposium on Computer Science Education-Volume 1, pp. 474–480 (2022)
62. Ranade, N., Saravia, M.: Teaching AI ethics in technical and professional communication: a systematic review. IEEE Trans. Profess. Commun. (2024)
63. Rashid, A., Weckert, J., Lucas, R.: Software engineering ethics in a digital world. Computer **42**(6), 34–41 (2009)
64. Reidsma, D., van der Ham, J., Continella, A.: Operationalizing cybersecurity research ethics review: From principles and guidelines to practice. In: 2nd International Workshop on Ethics in Computer Security, EthiCS 2023. Internet Society (2023)
65. Rogaway, P.: The moral character of cryptographic work. Cryptology ePrint Archive, Paper 2015/1162 (2015). https://eprint.iacr.org/2015/1162, for more context: https://web.cs.ucdavis.edu/~rogaway/papers/moral.html
66. Rogaway, P.: ECS 188: Ethics in an age of technology - Phil's teaching notes. On the author's homepage (2018). https://web.cs.ucdavis.edu/~rogaway/classes/188/teaching/

67. Sasse, M.A., Flechais, I.: Usable security: Why do we need it? How do we get it? O'Reilly (2005)
68. Schrittwieser, S., Mulazzani, M., Weippl, E.: Ethics in security research. Which lines should not be crossed? In: 2013 IEEE Security and Privacy Workshops, pp. 1–4. IEEE (2013)
69. Selbst, A.D., Boyd, D., Friedler, S.A., Venkatasubramanian, S., Vertesi, J.: Fairness and abstraction in sociotechnical systems. In: Proceedings of the Conference on Fairness, Accountability, and Transparency, pp. 59–68. FAT* '19, Association for Computing Machinery (2019)
70. Spinello, R.: Cyberethics: Morality and law in cyberspace. Jones & Bartlett Publishers (2010)
71. Stahl, B.C., Timmermans, J., Mittelstadt, B.D.: The ethics of computing: a survey of the computing-oriented literature. ACM Comput. Surv. (CSUR) **48**(4), 1–38 (2016)
72. Staron, M., Abraháo, S., Serebrenik, A., Penzenstadler, B., Horkoff, J., Honnenahalli, C.: Laws, ethics, and fairness in software engineering. IEEE Softw. **42**(1), 110–113 (2025). https://doi.org/10.1109/MS.2024.3469488
73. Takaoka, A.J.W., Cutrupi, C.M., Jaccheri, L.: Intersectional software engineering as a field. Software **4**(3), 18 (2025)
74. Tavani, H.T.: Ethics and technology: Controversies, questions, and strategies for ethical computing. John Wiley & Sons (2016)
75. Thompson, D.F.: The Problem of Many Hands, pp. 11–32. Cambridge University Press (2004)
76. Tran, M., Fiesler, C.: "It's not exactly meant to be realistic": Student perspectives on the role of ethics in computing group projects. In: Proceedings of the 2024 ACM Conference on International Computing Education Research-Volume 1, pp. 517–526 (2024)
77. Turing, A.M.: Computing machinery and intelligence. Mind **49**, 433–460 (1950)
78. Vaswani, A., et al.: Attention is all you need. CoRR **abs/1706.03762** (2017). http://arxiv.org/abs/1706.03762
79. VerizonDBIR2024: Data breach investigations report 2024 (DBIR) (2024). https://www.verizon.com/business/resources/reports/dbir/
80. Weizenbaum, J.: Computer Power and Human Reason: From Judgement To Calculation. W. H, Freeman and Company (1976)
81. Weizenbaum, J.: ELIZA – A computer program for the study of natural language communication between man and machine. Commun. ACM **9**(1), 36–45 (1 1966https://doi.org/10.1145/365153.365168
82. Weizenbaum, J.: On the impact of the computer on society. Science **176**(4035), 609–614 (1972). https://www.science.org/doi/abs/10.1126/science.176.4035.609
83. Wiener, N.: Cybernetics or Control and Communication in the Animal and the Machine. The MIT Press (10 1948/2019). https://doi.org/10.7551/mitpress/11810.001.0001
84. Wortman, K.A., et al.: Reflecting on practices to integrate socially responsible computing in introductory Computer Science courses. In: Proceedings of the 56th ACM Technical Symposium on Computer Science Education V. 1, pp. 1253–1259 (2025)
85. Zhang, Y., Liu, M., Zhang, M., Lu, C., Duan, H.: Ethics in security research: Visions, reality, and paths forward. In: 2022 IEEE European Symposium on Security and Privacy Workshops (EuroS&PW), pp. 538–545. IEEE (2022)

A Formal Treatment of the Limits of Authenticated Key Exchange Security

Michèle Feltz[1] and Cas Cremers[2]($\boxtimes$) (iD)

[1] Institute of Information Security, ETH Zurich, Zurich, Switzerland
mmc.feltz@gmail.com
[2] CISPA Helmholtz Center for Information Security, Saarbrücken, Germany
cremers@cispa.de

Abstract. Authenticated Key Exchange (AKE) protocols are a core building block of all modern communications, connecting the distribution benefits of public-key cryptography to the performance benefits of symmetric-key cryptography. Modern AKE protocols are proven secure in game-based security models that offer considerably more security guarantees than the seminal Bellare-Rogaway model from 1993, in order to capture real-world security properties such as various notions of forward secrecy and resistance against predictable or bad pseudorandom number generators. For most of these security models, it is claimed that they offer "the best possible security", based on informal arguments that at best hold under unstated assumptions. This has led to a fragmented landscape of AKE security models with seemingly contradictory results.

We provide the first systematization of the limits of game-based security models for two-party AKE protocols. Our treatment covers classical stateless protocols as well as a restricted class of modern stateful protocols. Our analysis uncovers how the details of the considered protocol class have crucial implications for (im)possibility results, and reveals how different security goals can be achieved in different relevant classes of AKE protocols. From our formal impossibility results, we derive strong security models for these classes and give protocols that satisfy them.

1 Introduction

Authenticated Key Exchange (AKE) protocols have been a core building block of secure systems since the invention of public-key, a.k.a. asymmetric, cryptography. To address challenges of key distribution, public-key cryptography allows parties to communicate as long as they know each other's public keys. However, because asymmetric encryption is orders of magnitude slower than symmetric cryptography, it is desirable if the two parties first communicate to establish a fresh temporary symmetric key, which is then used to efficiently encrypt subsequent data streams using symmetric cryptography. AKE protocols perform exactly this critical function: starting from two parties that know each other's

Michèle Feltz – This work was conducted when the author was at ETH Zurich, Switzerland.

B. Fila et al. (Eds.): Sjouke Mauw Festschrift, LNCS 16365, pp. 73–97, 2026.
https://doi.org/10.1007/978-3-032-20684-8_5

public key, establish a fresh shared symmetric key between them. While this may seem a straightforward task, new key exchange protocols are still proposed every year, and dozens of designs are deployed in practice. They differ in efficiency, assumptions, and critically, in the threat models that they aim to be secure against. Given their critical role in global communications, their formal security analysis has become a prominent and important application of formal cryptographic security proofs. Such proofs set out to establish that a protocol meets a certain security goal with respect to a threat model, together known as the *security model*.

The first formal security model for evaluating the security of AKE protocols was introduced in 1993 by Bellare and Rogaway [4]. Since then, there has been a steady stream of new AKE protocols and associated security models. The most influential additions and modifications to the original Bellare-Rogaway model incorporate further security guarantees or increase the capabilities of the adversary [5,11,29,31], for example, to learn some long-term private keys or random values used in the computations.

This leads to the question: what is the strongest security that can be achieved by an AKE protocol? However, few results exist on the exact limits of AKE security and, consequently, on the strongest security guarantees achievable by AKE protocols. Most impossibility results in the literature are stated as restrictions on the adversary's capabilities, with the implicit (unproven) assumption that it is impossible to construct a protocol secure with respect to a stronger adversary. These observations on strongest possible adversaries are often incorrect or only hold under unstated protocol restrictions. For example, the claim that the eCK model [31] is the strongest possible model for analyzing two-message AKE protocols [12,31,32] was refuted in [19], proving that stronger guarantees than eCK security can be achieved for two-message protocols. We give more examples of incorrect statements at the end of this section. In fact, most AKE security models are formally incomparable (e.g., see [13,16]). Technically, there are nearly as many security models as there are protocol proposals. The sometimes subtle differences between the models are in fact critical for security, because they determine whether the security model covers practically relevant attack scenarios. We argue that rigorous impossibility results for key exchange protocol design and subsequent systematic security models are still missing in the context of ever stronger AKE security guarantees.

In this work we revisit the notions of strongest possible security models for AKE protocols, and show that many of the restrictions posed on the behavior of the adversary in the models stem from unstated assumptions on the considered protocol class. For example, our formal impossibility results reveal a previously unstated assumption on the protocols analyzed in AKE security models: the protocols do not modify memory shared among sessions, i.e., they only modify session-specific memory. We also consider several classes of protocols that modify memory shared between the (local) sessions of a user, which can be used to implement counters or to incorporate data from previous sessions.

Contributions. Our main contributions are the following.

First, building on our previous work [23], we develop a systematization of the limits of game-based AKE security. We identify several relevant classes of two-party AKE protocols for which we show formal impossibility results, which (a) clarify which security guarantees cannot be achieved by any protocol in the respective class, and (b) allow us to systematically develop strong security models for each class. For each class we show a concrete protocol that is secure in the corresponding strong model.

Second, our exploration of the limits of game-based security leads to a protocol hierarchy based on the constructed protocols. Our hierarchy highlights the security guarantees that can be achieved by each class. We define generic protocol transformations meaning that, given a protocol secure in one model, the transformed protocol will be secure in the stronger model.

Paper Structure. In the remainder of this section we discuss related work. In Sect. 2 we recall the formal AKE framework from [23]. In Sect. 3 we define several classes of two-party AKE protocols on the basis of message structure and the way that protocol state is shared and updated between a user's sessions. For each class based on message structure that is stateless (which includes the majority of AKE protocols), we provide in Sect. 4 impossibility results and derive strong security models from them. We repeat the same steps for a class of stateful protocols whose state updates can only occur at the creation of sessions in Sect. 5. In Sect. 6 we provide a security protocol hierarchy that visualizes the relative differences and benefits of the constructed security models and of the protocols that satisfy these models. We conclude in Sect. 7.

In the long version [24] of this paper we provide all proofs, the study of the relations between the constructed security models, and further details.

Dedication. This paper is dedicated to the 65th birthday of Sjouke Mauw, who was PhD supervisor of Cas Cremers. Their work on protocol analysis is in active use in teaching and research to this day [21]. Sjouke inspires students by warmly sharing his scientific curiosity, interest in puzzles, and search for clarity in formal modeling, together with a belief in his students that allows them to blossom. This paper's juggling of the interactions between long-term and temporary secrets, and their corresponding clauses in a protocol's security guarantees, reminds of the formal analysis of juggling [22] that combined two of Sjouke's passions, but sadly didn't involve dancing.

Related Work. *Impossibility results.* In general, proposals for AKE protocols are motivated by either claiming stronger security guarantees or improved efficiency. This has resulted in a large number of works that suggest to provide security against the strongest possible adversary [9,12,26,27,29,31,32]. Until now, such comments mostly relied on informal impossibility results. For example, Krawczyk [29] sketched a generic perfect forward secrecy attack, for which it claimed that it breaks the security of any "implicitly authenticated" two-message AKE protocol. This attack has led to the statements that (a) no two-message protocol can provide Perfect Forward Secrecy (PFS) [29, p. 56], and (b) the eCK model capturing only Weak Perfect Forward Secrecy is the strongest possible model for analyzing two-message AKE protocols [31,32]. Krawczyk's claim is often cited as fact [14,31,36,37] when it is in fact not true. In [19], it is shown that two-message protocols can achieve PFS even for eCK-like adversaries. The eCK security model [31] that only captures weak PFS was described in the literature as the strongest possible security model for two-message AKE protocols [31,32].

[39, p. 120] states that no protocol can be secure against *reset-and-replay attacks* on the target session. In [23] it was shown that their impossibility result only holds for stateless protocols, which do not modify memory that is shared among a user's sessions, and provided a stateful protocol, namely CNX, that is secure even against reset-and-replay attacks on the target session.

[37] claims that "any protocol which allows the adversary to reveal ephemeral keys, cannot provide full PFS" [37] and "[...] when using any two-message protocol that provides full PFS we also must have that the corresponding security model does not allow the ephemeral secrets as formally shown in Appendix E" [37]. The paper cites [25] as its definition of PFS. The core problem is that the statement is based on mixing arguments about specific executions (the adversary can win in certain protocol classes if it can trigger two queries together) with arguments about security models (PFS is a security model, not a statement about a specific execution with arbitrary queries). Concretely, the definition of PFS from [25] (as used by [37]) is a security model that has no query for revealing ephemeral keys. The argument in Appendix E of [37] involves constructing an attack using ephemeral key reveal. Because this query is not possible in the PFS definition from [25], the argument does not prove that protocols cannot achieve PFS. Instead, what it shows is that a security model that would allow this combination of queries *in a single execution*, would not be satisfied by two-message protocols. However, a security model can still allow ephemeral key reveal in other executions, and can still encode PFS as in [25]. As a consequence, and contrary to statements about related work in [37], protocols like those in [18] can satisfy PFS.

Similarly, in earlier work, [9] claims that one-round AKE protocols that do not provide message replay detection cannot achieve PFS if the adversary can also reveal session-specific randomness of the target session's peer. The argument of [9] is based on a variant of Krawczyk's PFS attack [29] that involves a replay attack together with leakage of session-specific randomness of the session the replayed message originates from. Again, their argument mixes a conclusion about a specific experiment with a security model. Concretely, [9] defines PFS in an informal way and formally defines a variant of the CK model that incorporates PFS in a specific way [9, Section 2.1]. The problem is that their generic attack shows that one-round AKE protocols violate their CK security definition (incorporating PFS) as it allows ephemeral key reveal queries on the partner party to the test session, from which they informally draw conclusions about encoding PFS. However, their generic attack does not violate their own informal PFS definition (as this definition does not take into account ephemeral key reveal queries), similar to [37].

[23] defines a generic AKE framework and shows that no stateless protocol can achieve security in a model that permits the adversary to choose the randomness of sessions and to reveal certain session keys. It shows that there are in fact one-round protocols that do not require replay detection and are only vulnerable to the [9] attack if the target session is activated with a message replayed from the first session of its peer. [23] shows that there exists a protocol that achieves security even under compromise of the target session's randomness and the actor of that session's long-term secret key as long as the randomness of at least one of the previous sessions of the same user has not been compromised. We build on [23] and extend its results to larger classes of protocols.

Stateless and Stateful AKE Protocols. Many AKE protocols (e. g., HMQV [29], NAXOS [31], CMQV [38]) are stateless in the sense that only session-specific memory is modified, which is lost after the session ends: no user memory is modified. In contrast, stateful protocols can modify the user's local memory shared between sessions. E.g., Blake-Wilson et al. [6] propose to modify their Protocol 2 by concatenating the secret value with a user-specific counter. We denote this as Protocol 2C. Instead of running the protocol each time a session key is required, a new session key is obtained by simply incrementing the counter and computing a new hash value [6]. No security proof of Protocol 2C was given. Provably secure stateful AKE protocols (CNX and NXPR) were proposed in [23].

Post-Compromise Security and Continuous Key Exchange. Continuous Key Exchange occurs after an initial key exchange [1,35] and can potentially achieve Post-Compromise Security [15]. Such protocols and properties are out of scope of our work, and we leave their analysis for future work.

AKE Protocol Classes and Bad Randomness. In our previous work [23], we developed a framework and defined several protocol classes that we re-use and build on in this work. However, the focus of the previous work was entirely on bad and chosen randomness. In contrast, in this work our goal is to systematize impossibility results, and establish a full hierarchy of (im)possibility results in this domain, culminating in Fig. 4.

2   Background: Authenticated Key Exchange Framework

We build on the framework from [23] to reason about the security of different AKE protocol classes against various adversarial capabilities.

2.1   Security Model

Sessions and session-specific memory. Let $\mathcal{P}$ be a finite set of N user identifiers. Each user can execute multiple protocol instances, called sessions, concurrently. We identify a user's sessions by referring to the order in which they are created. Thus, we denote the i-th session of user $\hat{P}$ by the tuple $(\hat{P}, i) \in \mathcal{P} \times \mathbb{N}$. The state of each user $\hat{P}$ can be derived from its random numbers, long term keys, and public information. We differentiate between session-specific memory and

Table 1. Elements of session state

actor	the session's actor (the user running the session)
peer	the session's peer (the intended communication partner)
role	taken role; either $\mathcal{I}$ (initiator) or $\mathcal{R}$ (responder)
sent, recv	concatenation of all messages sent, respectively received, in the session
status	session status; either `active`, `accepted`, or `rejected`
key	key established in the session
rand	randomness used in the session
data	any additional session-specific or protocol-specific data
step	protocol step to be executed (in the session)

user memory, which is shared among different sessions. We take an abstract view on the session-specific memory and assume that it can be separated into distinct named fields, referred to as variables, listed in Table 1. Initially we assume that each session-specific variable is undefined, denoted by $\bot$. The next step to be executed by the protocol is stored in the variable *step*. Alternatively, this value could be stored in the variable *data*. We choose to store it in a separate variable for clarity. We say that a session s has accepted (or is completed) if the value of its *status* variable taking values in the set $\{\texttt{active}, \texttt{accepted}, \texttt{rejected}\}$ is `accepted`. We denote by st_s the session-specific memory related to session s.

User Memory. The user memory of some user stores the user's long-term public/secret key pair, the public key of all other users $\hat{Q} \in \mathcal{P}$ as well as additional variables that might be required by the protocol. The information stored in the user memory is accessed and possibly updated by sessions of the user according to the protocol specification. In contrast to session-specific information, data stored in the user memory of some user $\hat{P}$ is shared among different sessions of the user $\hat{P}$. We denote by $st_{\hat{P}}$ the user memory of user $\hat{P} \in \mathcal{P}$.

Game State and Game Behavior (see also [10]). The adversary, modeled as a probabilistic polynomial-time algorithm, interacts with users within a game through queries in a set Q. The state of the game contains session-specific state information st_s for all sessions s, user-specific information $st_{\hat{P}}$ for each user $\hat{P} \in \mathcal{P}$ as well as other information related to the game such as some bit that the adversary attempts to guess. The game behavior, which we denote by Φ, describes how the game processes the queries in Q. More precisely, the game behavior Φ is an algorithm taking as input the current state of the game GST, a query $q \in Q$, a protocol π, and a security parameter 1^k, and returning a new state GST' and a response $\mathsf{response} \in \{0,1\}^* \cup \{\bot, \star\}$ to the adversary's query q.

Definition 1 (h-message protocol [23]). *Let 1^k be the security parameter. An h-message protocol π, where h is the sum of the number of messages sent* *and received during a protocol session, consists of the following (publicly known) algorithms and parameters:*

- *a set of domain parameters,*
- *a probabilistic polynomial-time key generation algorithm KeyGen, which takes as input the security parameter and outputs a public/secret key pair, and*
- *a deterministic polynomial-time algorithm Ψ executed by a user in a session. This algorithm takes as input the security parameter 1^k, the session-specific memory st_s of a session s, the user memory $st_{\hat{P}}$ of the actor $\hat{P}$ of session s, and a message $m \in \{0,1\}^*$, and outputs a triple of elements $(m', st'_s, st'_{\hat{P}})$, where $m' \in \{0,1\}^* \cup \{\star\}$ is a message, st'_s is an updated internal session state, and $st'_{\hat{P}}$ is an updated state of the user memory of user $\hat{P}$.*

If h is even, then the number of messages $m' \neq \star$ output by Ψ during a protocol session is $\frac{h}{2}$ for both roles initiator and responder. If h is odd, then the number of messages $m' \neq \star$ output by Ψ during a protocol session is $\frac{h+1}{2}$ for the initiator role and $\frac{h-1}{2}$ for the responder role.

The output of the key exchange algorithm Ψ (see Definition 1) may include the value $\star$ to indicate that the session does not generate an outgoing message.

Game Setup. A setup algorithm *SetupG* generates a set of a fixed number N of user identifiers and to initialize the user memory of each user. The algorithm *SetupG* takes as input the protocol π and the security parameter 1^k, and outputs an initial game state GST_{init}:

1. generate a set $\mathcal{P} = \{\hat{P}_1, ..., \hat{P}_N\}$ of N distinct user identifiers,
2. for all users $\hat{P} \in \mathcal{P}$: generate a long-term public/secret key pair $(\text{pk}_{\hat{P}}, \text{sk}_{\hat{P}})$ using algorithm KeyGen,
3. for all users $\hat{P} \in \mathcal{P}$: store the key pair $(\text{pk}_{\hat{P}}, \text{sk}_{\hat{P}})$ together with the set $\{(\hat{P}, \text{pk}_{\hat{P}}) \mid \hat{P} \in \mathcal{P} \setminus \{\hat{P}\}\}$ in the user memory $st_{\hat{P}}$, and
4. initialize all other user-specific variables used by the protocol.

Queries. The specification of some of the queries that we define below is similar to queries defined in the framework of Boyd et al. [8]. The public-info query, which was informally introduced in [10, p. 4], allows the adversary to obtain information that was generated during the setup phase of the game such as the users' identifiers and their public keys.

- public-info(). The query returns a set $\mathcal{L}$ of information which contains the set $\{(\hat{P}, \text{pk}_{\hat{P}}) \mid \hat{P} \in \mathcal{P}\}$ as well as the initial values of all other variables stored in the user memory of each user, except for the users' long-term secret key.

The queries in the set $Q_R = \{\text{create}, \text{send}\}$ that we define next model regular execution of the protocol.

- create$(\hat{P}, r[, \hat{Q}])$. The query models the creation of a new session s for the user with identifier $\hat{P}$. It requires that $\hat{P} \in \mathcal{P}, \hat{Q} \in \mathcal{P}$, and that $r \in \{\mathcal{I}, \mathcal{R}\}$; otherwise, it returns $\perp$. Session variables are initialized as

$$(s_{actor}, s_{role}, s_{sent}, s_{recv}, s_{status}, s_{key}, s_{step}) \leftarrow (\hat{P}, r, \epsilon, \epsilon, \texttt{active}, \perp, 1) \ .$$

A bitstring in $\{0, 1\}^k$ is sampled uniformly at random and assigned to s_{rand}; we assume that all randomness required during the execution of session s is deterministically derived from s_{rand}. If the optional peer identifier $\hat{Q}$ is provided, the variable s_{peer} is set to $\hat{Q}$.

The key exchange algorithm Ψ is executed on input $(1^k, st_s, st_{\hat{P}}, \epsilon)$. The algorithm returns a triple of elements $(m', st'_s, st'_{\hat{P}})$. We set $st_s \leftarrow st'_s$ and $st_{\hat{P}} \leftarrow st'_{\hat{P}}$. The query returns m'.

- send$(\hat{P}, i, m)$. The query models sending message m to the i'th session of $\hat{P}$, which we denote by s. It requires that $s_{status} = \texttt{active}$; otherwise it returns $\perp$. The algorithm Ψ is run on input $(1^k, st_s, st_{\hat{P}}, m)$, and outputs a triple $(m', st'_s, st'_{\hat{P}})$. We set $st_s \leftarrow st'_s$ and $st_{\hat{P}} \leftarrow st'_{\hat{P}}$. The query returns m'.

The queries in the set $Q_\mathsf{C} = \{\mathsf{session\text{-}key}, \mathsf{corrupt}, \mathsf{randomness}, \mathsf{cr\text{-}create}\}$ that we define next model the corruption of a user's secrets. The $\mathsf{randomness}$ query models the adversary's capability of learning the randomness s_{rand} of a particular session s. In contrast, the $\mathsf{cr\text{-}create}$ query models the adversary's capability of choosing the randomness used within a session. The $\mathsf{session\text{-}key}$ query allows us to model known-key attacks [34], unknown-key share (UKS) attacks [7,17], and replay attacks combined with chosen-randomness attacks [39]. In the definition of the queries $\mathsf{session\text{-}key}$ and $\mathsf{randomness}$ we denote the i'th session of user $\hat{P}$ by s.

- session-key$(\hat{P}, i)$. The query requires that $s_{status} = \texttt{accepted}$; otherwise, it returns $\perp$. The query returns the session key s_{key} of session s.
- corrupt$(\hat{P})$. If $\hat{P} \notin \mathcal{P}$, then S returns $\perp$. Otherwise the query returns the long-term secret key $\mathsf{sk}_{\hat{P}}$ of user $\hat{P}$.
- randomness$(\hat{P}, i)$. If $s_{status} \neq \perp$, then the randomness s_{rand} used in session s is returned. Otherwise, the query returns $\perp$.
- cr-create$(\hat{P}, r, rnd[, \hat{Q}])$. The query models the creation of a new session s, using randomness rnd chosen by the adversary, for the user $\hat{P}$. The query requires that $\hat{P} \in \mathcal{P}, \hat{Q} \in \mathcal{P}, rnd \in \{0, 1\}^k$, and that $r \in \{\mathcal{I}, \mathcal{R}\}$; otherwise, it returns $\perp$. The session is initialized using

$$(s_{actor}, s_{role}, s_{sent}, s_{recv}, s_{status}, s_{key}, s_{rand}, s_{step}) \leftarrow (\hat{P}, r, \epsilon, \epsilon, \texttt{active}, \perp, rnd, 1) \ .$$

If the optional peer identifier $\hat{Q}$ is provided, the variable s_{peer} is set to $\hat{Q}$. The key exchange algorithm Ψ is executed on input $(1^k, st_s, st_{\hat{P}}, \epsilon)$. The algorithm returns a triple $(m', st'_s, st'_{\hat{P}})$. We set $st_s \leftarrow st'_s$ and $st_{\hat{P}} \leftarrow st'_{\hat{P}}$. The query returns m'.

The set $Q_{\mathsf{noCR}} = Q_{\mathsf{R}} \cup (Q_{\mathsf{C}} \setminus \{\mathsf{cr\text{-}create}\})$ contains all execution and corruption queries, except the query $\mathsf{cr\text{-}create}$. The notion of matching sessions specifies when two sessions are supposed to be intended communication partners. It is formalized below via matching conversations as in [19,31].

Definition 2 (Matching sessions). *Let π be an h-message protocol. We say that two sessions s and s' of π are* matching *if $s_{status} = s'_{status} = \mathsf{accepted}$ and $s_{actor} = s'_{peer} \wedge s_{peer} = s'_{actor} \wedge s_{sent} = s'_{recv} \wedge s_{recv} = s'_{sent} \wedge s_{role} \neq s'_{role}$.*

We define a family of AKE security models, parameterized by (i) a subset Q of the above adversary queries, and (ii) a freshness predicate F that restricts certain combinations of queries.

Definition 3 (AKE security model [23]). *Let π be an h-message protocol. Let Q be a set of adversary queries such that $Q_{\mathsf{R}} \subseteq Q \subseteq Q_{\mathsf{R}} \cup Q_{\mathsf{C}}$. Let F be a freshness predicate, i.e., a predicate on a session of π and a sequence of queries (including arguments and results) in Q. We call (Q, F) an AKE security model.*

2.2   Security Experiment

We associate to each AKE security model $X = (Q, F)$ a security experiment $W(X)$, defined below, played by an adversary E against a challenger. To win the experiment, the adversary aims to distinguish a real session key from a random key, modelled through the following query.

- $\mathsf{test\text{-}session}(s)$. This query requires that $s_{status} = \mathsf{accepted}$; otherwise, it returns $\perp$. A bit b is chosen at random. If $b = 0$, then s_{key} is returned. If $b = 1$, then a random key is returned according to the probability distribution of keys generated by the protocol.

Definition 4 (Security Experiment $W(X)$). *Let π be an h-message protocol. Let $X = (Q, F)$ be an AKE security model. We define experiment $W(X)$, between an adversary E and a challenger who implements all the users, as follows:*

1. *The game is initialized with domain parameters for security parameter 1^k and the setup algorithm SetupG is executed.*
2. *The adversary E first issues the query $\mathsf{public\text{-}info}$, and then performs any sequence of queries from the set Q.*
3. *At some point in the experiment, E issues a $\mathsf{test\text{-}session}$ query to a session s that has accepted and satisfies F at the time the query is issued.*
4. *The adversary may continue with queries from Q, under the condition that the test session must continue to satisfy F.*
5. *Finally, E outputs a bit b' as its guess for b.*

The adversary E wins the security experiment $W(X)$ if it correctly guesses the bit b chosen by the challenger during the $\mathsf{test\text{-}session}$ query (i. e., if $b = b'$, where b' is E's guess). Success of E in the experiment is expressed in terms of E's advantage in distinguishing whether it received the real or a random session key in response to the test-session query. The advantage of adversary E in the above security experiment against a key exchange protocol π for security parameter k is defined as $Adv_{W(X)}^{\pi,E}(k) = |2P(b = b') - 1|$.

Definition 5 (AKE Security). *A key exchange protocol π is said to be* secure *in AKE security model (Q, F) if, for all PPT adversaries E, it holds that*

- *if two users successfully complete matching sessions, then they compute the same session key,*
- *the probability of event* Multiple-Match$_{\pi,E}^{W(X)}(k)$ *is negligible, where* Multiple-Match$_{\pi,E}^{W(X)}(k)$ *denotes the event that there exists a session that has accepted with at least two matching sessions, and*
- *E has no more than a negligible advantage in winning the $W(X)$ security experiment, that is, there exists a negligible function negl in the security parameter k such that $Adv_{W(X)}^{\pi,E}(k) \leq negl(k)$.*

3   Protocol Classes

In this section we define a series of protocol classes. The distinction between these classes enables the systematic development of strong security models.

3.1   Classes **AKE**, **INDP**, and **INDP-DH**

We start by defining a large class of AKE protocols. Such protocols are required to be executable, i. e., if the messages of two users $\hat{A}$ and $\hat{B}$ are faithfully relayed to each other, then both users end up with a shared session key (see also [3–5]). A second requirement ensures that protocol messages depend on session-specific randomness. We use both properties for proving impossibility results in Sect. 4.

Definition 6 (Protocol class AKE [23]). *We define AKE as the class of all h-message protocols for which, in the presence of an eavesdropping adversary:*

- *two users $\hat{A}$ and $\hat{B}$ can complete matching sessions, in which case they hold the same session key, and*
- *the probability that two sessions of the same user output in all protocol steps identical messages is negligible in the security parameter.*

We next consider a subclass of two-message AKE protocols, namely the class INDP of one-round AKE protocols, where the outgoing message can be computed before any message is received.

Definition 7 (Protocol class INDP). *The protocol class INDP consists of all two-message protocols in AKE for which the outgoing message of any session s with status $s_{status} \neq$ rejected does not depend on the incoming message.*

We define the class INDP-DH of one-round Diffie-Hellman type protocols as a subclass of INDP as follows.

Definition 8 (Protocol class INDP-DH).

The protocol class INDP-DH *consists of all protocols in the class* INDP *of the following form, specified by polynomial-time computable functions* $f_\mathcal{I}, f_\mathcal{R}, F_\mathcal{I}, F_\mathcal{R}$:

- *Domain parameters* (G, g, q), *where* $G = \langle g \rangle$ *is a group of prime order* q *generated by* g.
- KeyGen(): *Choose* $a \in_R [0, q-1]$. *Set* $A \leftarrow g^a$. *Return secret key* sk $= a$ *and public key* pk $= A$.
- *When the initiator is activated to create a new session* s *with a* create$(\hat{A}, \mathcal{I}, \hat{B})$ *query, the initiator computes an outgoing ephemeral public key* $X \leftarrow g^{f_\mathcal{I}(s_{rand}, st_{\hat{A}})}$ *and returns as an outgoing message* $g^{f_\mathcal{I}(s_{rand}, st_{\hat{A}})}$.
- *The responder is activated to create a new session* s' *with* create$(\hat{B}, \mathcal{R}, \hat{A})$.
- *When the responder is activated in a session* s' *with a* send$(s', M = X)$ *query, the responder computes an outgoing ephemeral public key* $Y \leftarrow g^{f_\mathcal{R}(s'_{rand}, st_{\hat{B}})}$ *and returns as an outgoing message* Y. *The responder computes a session key* $s'_{key} \leftarrow F_\mathcal{R}(f_\mathcal{R}(s'_{rand}, st_{\hat{B}}), st_{\hat{B}}, s'_{recv})$, *and accepts:* $s'_{status} \leftarrow$ accepted.
- *When the initiator is activated in a session* s *with a* send$(s, M = Y)$, *the initiator computes a session key* $s_{key} \leftarrow F_\mathcal{I}(f_\mathcal{I}(s_{rand}, st_{\hat{A}}), st_{\hat{A}}, s_{recv})$, *and accepts:* $s_{status} \leftarrow$ accepted.

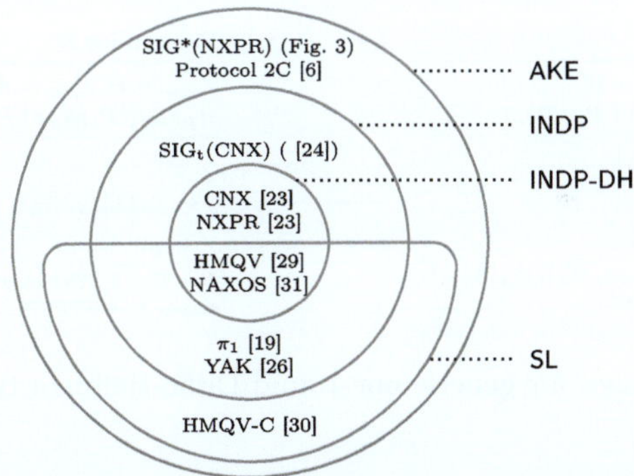

Fig. 1. Venn Diagram of the protocol classes and example protocols

3.2   Stateless and Stateful Protocols

As in [23], we distinguish between stateless and stateful protocols. Additionally, we analyze protocols outside of the class INDP-DH. Stateless protocols do not change the memory shared among sessions (Fig. 2). We give examples of stateless and stateful protocols Fig. 1, and recall the definitions from [23].

Definition 9 (Stateless protocol [23]). *Let $\mathcal{A}, \mathcal{B}$, and $\mathcal{C}$ be sets. Let $\mathrm{proj}_3 :$ $\mathcal{A} \times \mathcal{B} \times \mathcal{C} \to \mathcal{C}$ be the map given by $\mathrm{proj}_3(a, b, c) = c$ for all $(a, b, c) \in \mathcal{A} \times \mathcal{B} \times \mathcal{C}$. Let π be a protocol in the class* AKE. *We say that π is a* stateless protocol *if $\mathrm{proj}_3\big(\Psi(1^k, st_s, st_{\hat{P}}, m)\big) = st_{\hat{P}}$, for all $(k, st_s, st_{\hat{P}}, m) \in \mathbb{N} \times \{st_s \mid s \in \mathcal{P} \times \mathbb{N}\} \times \{st_{\hat{P}} \mid \hat{P} \in \mathcal{P}\} \times \{0, 1\}^*$. We denote by* SL *all stateless* AKE *protocols.*

Definition 10 (Stateful Protocol [23]). *Let π be a protocol in the class* AKE. *We say that π is a* stateful protocol *if π is not in* SL.

The class ISM defined below contains all stateless AKE protocols as well as all stateful AKE protocols that only access and update user memory upon creation of sessions (Initial State Modification). Protocols that rely on the synchronization of state between two parties (see, e.g., [15]) do not belong to the class ISM.

Definition 11 (Class ISM). *Let π be a protocol in the class* AKE. *We say that π is in the class* ISM *if it belongs to the class* SL *or if it only accesses and updates user memory upon creation of sessions.*

Remark 1. Note that [23] only considers the subclass INDP-DH $\cap$ SL (denoted by Λ in [23]) of AKE. Compared to [23], we consider a range of protocol classes (see Fig. 1), provide impossibility results for protocols in the respective classes, and derive a hierarchy of security models from these results.

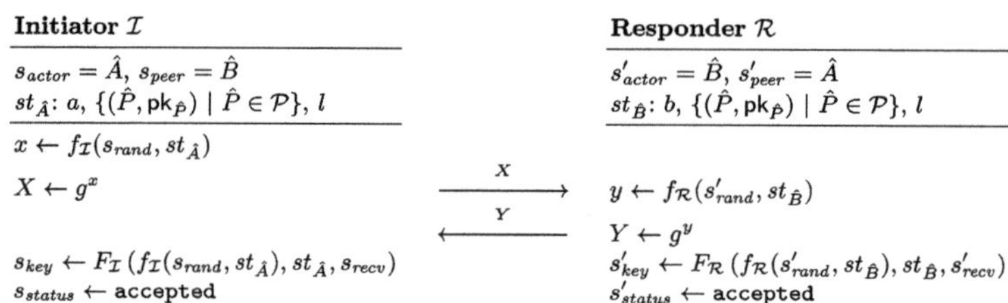

Initiator $\mathcal{I}$

$s_{actor} = \hat{A}$, $s_{peer} = \hat{B}$
$st_{\hat{A}}$: a, $\{(\hat{P}, \mathsf{pk}_{\hat{P}}) \mid \hat{P} \in \mathcal{P}\}$, l

$x \leftarrow f_{\mathcal{I}}(s_{rand}, st_{\hat{A}})$
$X \leftarrow g^x$

$s_{key} \leftarrow F_{\mathcal{I}}\left(f_{\mathcal{I}}(s_{rand}, st_{\hat{A}}), st_{\hat{A}}, s_{recv}\right)$
$s_{status} \leftarrow$ **accepted**

Responder $\mathcal{R}$

$s'_{actor} = \hat{B}$, $s'_{peer} = \hat{A}$
$st_{\hat{B}}$: b, $\{(\hat{P}, \mathsf{pk}_{\hat{P}}) \mid \hat{P} \in \mathcal{P}\}$, l

$y \leftarrow f_{\mathcal{R}}(s'_{rand}, st_{\hat{B}})$
$Y \leftarrow g^y$

$s'_{key} \leftarrow F_{\mathcal{R}}\left(f_{\mathcal{R}}(s'_{rand}, st_{\hat{B}}), st_{\hat{B}}, s'_{recv}\right)$
$s'_{status} \leftarrow$ **accepted**

Message X is sent from Initiator to Responder; message Y is sent from Responder to Initiator.

Fig. 2. Messages for generic one-round Diffie-Hellman type protocol

4 Impossibilities and Strong Models for Stateless Protocols

In this section we provide impossibility results for protocols in the classes AKE $\cap$ SL, INDP $\cap$ SL and INDP-DH $\cap$ SL with respect to an adversary with access to the queries in the set $Q_{\mathsf{noCR}} = Q_{\mathsf{R}} \cup (Q_{\mathsf{C}} \setminus \{\mathsf{cr\text{-}create}\})$. We then derive strong security models for reasoning about the security of protocols in the respective classes from these impossibility results. We thereby build on, and extend, results from [19] and [23]. We start by defining the notion of partially matching sessions.

Definition 12 (Partially Matching Sessions). *Let π be an h-message protocol, where $h \geq 2$. Let s denote a session of π with $s_{status} = \texttt{accepted}$. We say that session s is partially matching session s' in status $s'_{status} \neq \perp$ if:*

- *$s_{role} \neq s'_{role} \wedge s_{actor} = s'_{peer} \wedge s_{peer} = s'_{actor}$ and either*
- *$s_{role} = \mathcal{I} \wedge s_{send}\,[1..m] = s'_{recv}\,[1..m] \wedge s_{recv}\,[1..m] = s'_{send}\,[1..m]$ with $m = \frac{h}{2}$ if h is even and $m = \frac{h-1}{2}$ if h is odd, or*
- *$s_{role} = \mathcal{R} \wedge s_{send}\,[1..(m-1)] = s'_{recv}\,[1..(m-1)] \wedge s_{recv}\,[1..m] = s'_{send}\,[1..m]$ with $m = \frac{h}{2}$ if h is even and $m = \frac{h+1}{2}$ if h is odd,*

where $s_{send}\,[1..l]$ denotes the concatenation of the first l messages sent by session s and $s_{recv}\,[1..l]$ similarly denotes the first l received messages.

Partially matching sessions does not require the last message sent by one session to be received by the partner session. This allows us to capture combinations of randomness and corrupt attacks on such sessions as well.

To relate a received message that was not constructed by the adversary to the session it originates from, we use the concept of origin-session, which was first introduced in [18]. The existence of an origin-session for a given session implies integrity of the received messages.

Definition 13 (origin-session [18]). *We say that a session s' with $s'_{status} \neq \perp$ is an origin-session for a session s with $s_{status} = \texttt{accepted}$ if $s'_{send} = s_{recv}$.*

Theorem 1 (Impossibility Result for AKE∩SL). *Let π be an arbitrary protocol in the class AKE∩SL. Let $X = (Q_{\mathsf{noCR}}, F)$ be the AKE security model with F being true for all sessions s and all sequences of queries. Let s^* denote the test session and let s' denote a session such that s^* is partially matching session s'. There exist adversaries who win the security experiment $W(X)$ against protocol π with non-negligible probability by issuing either*

1. *a query $\mathsf{session\text{-}key}(s^*)$, or*
2. *a query $\mathsf{session\text{-}key}(\tilde{s})$, where $\tilde{s}$ and s^* are matching sessions, or*
3. *a query $\mathsf{corrupt}(s^*_{actor})$ and a query $\mathsf{randomness}(s^*)$, or*
4. *a query $\mathsf{corrupt}(s^*_{peer})$ as well as a query $\mathsf{randomness}(s')$, or*
5. *a query $\mathsf{corrupt}(s^*_{peer})$ before creation of session s^* via a create query or as long as $s^*_{status} = \texttt{active}$ and $s^*_{recv} = \epsilon$, and impersonating the peer to s^*.*

Theorem 1 gives rise to the security model $\Omega_{\mathsf{AKE∩SL}}$ defined as follows. The associated freshness notion restricts the adversary from performing the generic attacks specified in Theorem 1.

Definition 14 ($\Omega_{\mathsf{AKE∩SL}}$). *The $\Omega_{\mathsf{AKE∩SL}}$ model is defined by (Q, F), where $Q = Q_{\mathsf{R}}$ and a session s is said to satisfy F if the following conditions hold:*

1. *no $\mathsf{session\text{-}key}(s)$ query has been issued,*
2. *for all sessions s^* such that s^* matches s, no $\mathsf{session\text{-}key}(s^*)$ has been issued,*

3. *not both queries* corrupt(s_{actor}) *and* randomness(s) *have been issued,*
4. *for all sessions* s' *such that* s *is partially matching session* s', *not both queries* corrupt(s_{peer}) *and* randomness(s') *have been issued, and*
5. *if there exists no origin-session for session* s, *then no* corrupt(s_{peer}) *query has been issued before creation of session* s *via a* create *query or as long as* $s_{status} =$ active *and* $s_{recv} = \epsilon$.

To see that there exist protocols in the class AKE ∩ SL that are secure in the model $\Omega_{\mathsf{AKE \cap SL}}$, consider the protocol SIG*(NAXOS) ∈ AKE ∩ SL obtained by applying the signature transformation SIG with optional fields from [18] to the NAXOS protocol ([24]).[1] The outgoing message of a SIG*(NAXOS) initiator session of user $\hat{A}$ is of the form $(X, Sign_{\hat{A}}(X, \hat{B}))$ while the outgoing message of a SIG*(NAXOS) responder session of user $\hat{B}$ is of the form $(Y, Sign_{\hat{B}}(Y, X, \hat{A}))$. SIG*(NAXOS) does not belong to the class INDP ∩ SL since the outgoing message of a responder session depends on the Diffie-Hellman exponential contained in the incoming message. It follows from [20, Corollary 1] and from the fact that the existence of a unique origin-session s for the test-session s^* implies the existence of a unique partially matching session s' for s^* with $s = s'$, that protocol SIG*(NAXOS) is secure in the model $\Omega_{\mathsf{AKE \cap SL}}$ under the same assumptions as SIG(NAXOS) being secure in the eCK-PFS model [20].

Even though security in model $\Omega_{\mathsf{AKE \cap SL}}$ can be achieved by protocols in the class AKE ∩ SL, we next show that no protocol in the class INDP can provide these strong security guarantees.

Proposition 1 (Impossibility result for INDP). *No protocol in the class* INDP *can satisfy security in the model* $\Omega_{\mathsf{AKE \cap SL}}$.

We next define c-origin-session, which is stronger than origin-session because it additionally requires distinct roles and agreement on the communicating users.

Definition 15 (c-origin-session). *We say that a session* s' *with* $s'_{status} \neq \perp$ *is a c-origin-session for a session* s *with* $s_{status} =$ accepted *if* $s_{actor} = s'_{peer} \wedge s_{peer} = s'_{actor} \wedge s_{recv} = s'_{sent} \wedge s_{role} \neq s'_{role}$.

Note that for protocols in the class INDP the last condition of Definition 14 can be simplified: a created initiator session s of any protocol in INDP completes upon receipt of a valid message m and the variable $s_{recv} = \epsilon$ is then updated with message m, i.e. $s_{recv} \leftarrow (s_{recv}, m)$. Consequently, the point in time of receipt of the first message m in an initiator session s coincides with the completion of session s. The same reasoning applies to responder sessions. If we combine this with the model $\Omega_{\mathsf{AKE \cap SL}}$ and Proposition 1, we establish a strong model for analyzing protocols in the class INDP ∩ SL, i.e., model $\Omega_{\mathsf{INDP \cap SL}}$:

---

[1] The SIG transformation with optional fields takes a two-message protocol and transforms it to sign each message, the peer's identity, and, for the responder role, the received Diffie-Hellman exponential with the long-term secret key. We assume a unique signature scheme [33]; alternatively, the session key of the transformed protocol can be computed as the hash of the message transcript concatenated with the session key of the original protocol, as shown in [20].

Definition 16 ($\Omega_{\mathsf{INDP\cap SL}}$). *The $\Omega_{\mathsf{INDP\cap SL}}$ model is defined by (Q, F), where $Q = Q_{\mathsf{R}}$, and a session s is said to satisfy F if the following conditions hold:*

1. *no* session-key(s) *query has been issued,*
2. *for all sessions s^* such that s^* matches s, no* session-key(s^*) *has been issued,*
3. *not both queries* corrupt(s_{actor}) *and* randomness(s) *have been issued,*
4. *for all sessions s' such that s' is a c-origin-session for session s, not both queries* corrupt(s_{peer}) *and* randomness(s') *have been issued, and*
5. *if there exists no origin-session for session s, then no* corrupt(s_{peer}) *query has been issued before the completion of session s.*

Remark 2. Compared to the notion of freshness in model $\Omega_{\mathsf{AKE\cap SL}}$, freshness of a session s in $\Omega_{\mathsf{INDP\cap SL}}$ requires that the adversary does not issue a corrupt query to the peer of session s as well as a randomness query to a c-origin-session for session s. This restriction prevents the attack used in the proof of Proposition 1.

Consider the protocol $\mathrm{SIG}_t(\mathrm{NAXOS}) \in \mathsf{INDP} \cap \mathsf{SL}$ obtained by applying a tagged version of the signature transformation SIG from [19] to the NAXOS protocol ([24]; the outgoing message of a $\mathrm{SIG}_t(\mathrm{NAXOS})$ initiator session of user $\hat{A}$ is of the form $(X, Sign_{\hat{A}}(0, X, \hat{B}))$ while the outgoing message of a $\mathrm{SIG}_t(\mathrm{NAXOS})$ responder session of user $\hat{B}$ is of the form $(Y, Sign_{\hat{B}}(1, Y, \hat{A}))$. It follows from [20, Corollary 1] and from the fact that the existence of a unique origin-session s for the test-session s^* implies the existence of a unique c-origin-session s' for s^* with $s = s'$, that protocol $\mathrm{SIG}_t(\mathrm{NAXOS})$ is secure in model $\Omega_{\mathsf{INDP\cap SL}}$ under the same assumptions as SIG(NAXOS) being secure in the eCK-PFS model [20].

We next show that any protocol in the class INDP-DH is insecure in $\Omega_{\mathsf{INDP\cap SL}}$.

Proposition 2 (Impossibility result for INDP-DH). *No one-round Diffie-Hellman type protocol in* INDP-DH *can satisfy security in the model* $\Omega_{\mathsf{INDP\cap SL}}$.

Any protocol $\pi \in \mathsf{INDP\text{-}DH} \cap \mathsf{SL}$ that does not contain sufficient public information in the outgoing message is insecure in the model derived from model $\Omega_{\mathsf{INDP\cap SL}}$ and Proposition 2. This follows from the fact that a redirect event of a message from a session of a different user than the test session's peer can cause the existence of an origin-session that is not a c-origin-session for the test session. Combining this with Proposition 2, we derive the following security model.

Definition 17 ($\Omega_{\mathsf{INDP\text{-}DH\cap SL}}$). *The $\Omega_{\mathsf{INDP\text{-}DH\cap SL}}$ model is defined by (Q_{R}, F), where a session s is said to satisfy F if the following conditions hold:*

1. *no* session-key(s) *query has been issued, and*
2. *for all sessions s^* such that s^* matches s, no* session-key(s^*) *query has been issued, and*
3. *not both queries* corrupt(s_{actor}) *and* randomness(s) *have been issued, and*
4. *for all sessions s' such that s' is an origin-session for session s, not both queries* corrupt(s_{peer}) *and* randomness(s') *have been issued, and*
5. *if there exists no origin-session for s, then no* corrupt(s_{peer}) *has been issued.*

The model $\Omega_{\mathsf{INDP\text{-}DH}\cap\mathsf{SL}}$ is similar to the eCK^w model [19]; the concepts of matching and freshness are defined in the same way, only the query set is different since in the eCK^w model, the send query models both the creation of a new session and the sending of a message to a session. Note that whereas the eCK^w model has been obtained by modifying the eCK model [31] to incorporate a slightly stronger form of weak perfect forward secrecy, the $\Omega_{\mathsf{INDP\text{-}DH}\cap\mathsf{SL}}$ has been derived via a series of impossibility results on various protocol classes. The NAXOS protocol [31] ([24]) is an example of a protocol in the class $\mathsf{INDP\text{-}DH} \cap \mathsf{SL}$ that is secure in the eCK^w model [19, Proposition 6], and hence also in the $\Omega_{\mathsf{INDP\text{-}DH}\cap\mathsf{SL}}$ model.

4.1   Deriving Models with Chosen-Randomness

As an immediate consequence of Theorem 1, we obtain Theorem 2, which generalizes our impossibility results on protocol class $\mathsf{AKE} \cap \mathsf{SL}$ to adversaries who are in addition given access to the query $\mathsf{cr\text{-}create}$.

Theorem 2 (Impossibility result for AKE $\cap$ SL under chosen-randomness). *Let π be an arbitrary protocol in the class $\mathsf{AKE} \cap \mathsf{SL}$. Let $X = (Q_{\mathsf{noCR}} \cup \{\mathsf{cr\text{-}create}\}, F)$ be the AKE security model with F being true for all sessions s and all sequences of queries. Let s^* denote the test session and let s' denote a session such that s^* is partially matching session s'. There exist adversaries who win the security experiment $W(X)$ against protocol π with non-negligible probability by issuing*

1. *a query $\mathsf{session\text{-}key}(s^*)$, or*
2. *a query $\mathsf{session\text{-}key}(\tilde{s})$, where $\tilde{s}$ and s^* are matching sessions, or*
3. *a query $\mathsf{corrupt}(s^*_{actor})$ and a (randomness or $\mathsf{cr\text{-}create}$) query to s^*, or*
4. *a query $\mathsf{corrupt}(s^*_{peer})$ as well as a (randomness or $\mathsf{cr\text{-}create}$) query to s', or*
5. *a query $\mathsf{corrupt}(s^*_{peer})$ before creation of session s^* via a (create or $\mathsf{cr\text{-}create}$) query or as long as $s^*_{status} = \mathsf{active}$ and $s^*_{recv} = \epsilon$, and impersonating the peer to the test session s^*.*

The previous theorem gives rise to the intermediate security model $\Omega^{-}_{\mathsf{AKE}\cap\mathsf{ISM}}$ below. We will later show that this model cannot be satisfied by protocols in SL and that we can construct an even stronger model for $\mathsf{AKE} \cap \mathsf{ISM}$. We use the "$-$" superscript in the $\Omega^{-}_{\mathsf{AKE}\cap\mathsf{ISM}}$ notation to indicate it is non-optimal.

Definition 18 ($\Omega^{-}_{\mathsf{AKE}\cap\mathsf{ISM}}$). *The $\Omega^{-}_{\mathsf{AKE}\cap\mathsf{ISM}}$ model is defined by (Q, F), where $Q = Q_{\mathsf{noCR}} \cup \{\mathsf{cr\text{-}create}\}$, and a session s is said to satisfy F if the following conditions hold:*

1. *no $\mathsf{session\text{-}key}(s)$ query has been issued,*
2. *for all sessions s^* such that s^* matches s, no $\mathsf{session\text{-}key}(s^*)$ has been issued,*
3. *not both queries $\mathsf{corrupt}(s_{actor})$ and (randomness(s) or $\mathsf{cr\text{-}create}(.)$ creating session s) have been issued,*

4. *for all sessions s' such that s is partially matching session s', not both queries* corrupt(s_{peer}) *and (*randomness(s') *or* cr-create(.) *creating session s') have been issued, and*

5. *if there exists no origin-session for session s, then no* corrupt(s_{peer}) *query has been issued before creation of session s via a (*create *or* cr-create*) query or as long as $s_{status} =$* active *and $s_{recv} = \epsilon$.*

The models $\Omega^{-}_{\mathsf{INDP} \cap \mathsf{ISM}}$ and $\Omega^{-}_{\mathsf{INDP\text{-}DH} \cap \mathsf{ISM}}$, defined below, are obtained from the models $\Omega_{\mathsf{INDP} \cap \mathsf{SL}}$ and $\Omega_{\mathsf{INDP\text{-}DH} \cap \mathsf{SL}}$, respectively, in a similar way as model $\Omega^{-}_{\mathsf{AKE} \cap \mathsf{ISM}}$ is obtained from model $\Omega_{\mathsf{AKE} \cap \mathsf{SL}}$. As shown in [23], security in models that capture chosen randomness attacks implies security against attacks exploiting repeated randomness failures.

Definition 19 ($\Omega^{-}_{\mathsf{INDP} \cap \mathsf{ISM}}$). *The $\Omega^{-}_{\mathsf{INDP} \cap \mathsf{ISM}}$ model is defined by (Q, F), where $Q = Q_{\mathsf{noCR}} \cup \{$*cr-create*$\}$, and a session s is said to satisfy F if the following conditions hold:*

1. *no* session-key(s) *query has been issued,*
2. *for all sessions s^* such that s^* matches s, no* session-key(s^*) *has been issued,*
3. *not both queries* corrupt(s_{actor}) *and (*randomness(s) *or* cr-create(.) *creating session s) have been issued,*
4. *for all sessions s' such that s' is a c-origin-session for session s, not both queries* corrupt(s_{peer}) *and (*randomness(s') *or* cr-create(.) *creating session s') have been issued, and*
5. *if there exists no origin-session for session s, then no* corrupt(s_{peer}) *query has been issued before the completion of session s.*

Definition 20 ($\Omega^{-}_{\mathsf{INDP\text{-}DH} \cap \mathsf{ISM}}$). *The $\Omega^{-}_{\mathsf{INDP\text{-}DH} \cap \mathsf{ISM}}$ model is defined by (Q, F), where $Q = Q_{\mathsf{noCR}} \cup \{$*cr-create*$\}$ and a session s is said to satisfy F if the following conditions hold:*

1. *no* session-key(s) *query has been issued, and*
2. *for all s^* such that s^* matches s, no* session-key(s^*) *has been issued, and*
3. *not both queries* corrupt(s_{actor}) *and (*randomness(s) *or* cr-create(.) *creating session s) have been issued, and*
4. *for all sessions s' such that s' is an origin-session for session s, not both queries* corrupt(s_{peer}) *and (*randomness(s') *or* cr-create(.) *creating session s') have been issued, and*
5. *if there exists no origin-session for session s, then no* corrupt(s_{peer}) *query has been issued.*

Note that $\Omega^{-}_{\mathsf{INDP\text{-}DH} \cap \mathsf{ISM}}$ is identical to CR-eCK^w in [23]. Whereas the model CR-eCK^w [23] was constructed on top of the model eCK^w [19], the model $\Omega^{-}_{\mathsf{INDP\text{-}DH} \cap \mathsf{ISM}}$ above has been obtained from the model $\Omega_{\mathsf{INDP\text{-}DH} \cap \mathsf{SL}}$, which in turn has been deduced via impossibility results.

4.2   Insecurity of Stateless Protocols Against Chosen-Randomness

The following proposition states that no stateless protocol is secure in model $\Omega^-_{\mathsf{INDP\text{-}DH}\cap\mathsf{ISM}}$. We will show in Sect. 6 that stateful protocols can in fact achieve these stronger security guarantees.

Proposition 3 (Impossibility result for AKE $\cap$ SL under chosen-randomness). *No protocol in the class AKE $\cap$ SL can satisfy security in the model $\Omega^-_{\mathsf{INDP\text{-}DH}\cap\mathsf{ISM}}$.*

Corollary 1. *No protocol in the class AKE $\cap$ SL can satisfy security in either model $\Omega^-_{\mathsf{INDP}\cap\mathsf{ISM}}$ or model $\Omega^-_{\mathsf{AKE}\cap\mathsf{ISM}}$.*

5   Impossibility Results and Strong Models for the Class ISM

In the previous section we only considered stateless protocols. In this section, we extend our work to the class ISM (Initial State Modification) and provide strong models for analyzing protocols in this class.

Recall that the class ISM contains all AKE protocols that are either stateless or *only* access and update user memory upon creation of sessions. This class contains, e. g., the protocols NAXOS and HMQV, but also some stateful protocols such as the CNX and NXPR protocols [23] (see Fig. 1). This class excludes protocols that offer PCS [15] since this requires updating user memory on the basis of received messages. We leave the analysis of protocols that update user memory at later steps in the protocol execution as future work.

We next present a generalized impossibility result and its derived model for the broad class AKE $\cap$ ISM, taking into account the adversary's ability to choose session-specific randomness. Recall that the completion of a session occurs at the time at which the status of the session is set to `accepted`.

Theorem 3. (Impossibility result for AKE $\cap$ ISM). *Let π be an arbitrary protocol in the class AKE $\cap$ ISM. Let $X = (Q_{\mathsf{noCR}} \cup \{\mathsf{cr\text{-}create}\}, F)$ be the AKE security model with F being true for all sessions s and all sequences of queries. Let s^* denote the test session and let s' denote a session such that s^* is partially matching session s'. There exist adversaries who win the security experiment $W(X)$ against protocol π with non-negligible probability by issuing either*

1. *a query* session-key(s^*), *or*
2. *a query* session-key$(\tilde{s})$, *where $\tilde{s}$ and s^* are matching sessions, or*
3. *a query* corrupt(s^*_{actor}) *as well as (*randomness *or* cr-create*) queries on all sessions s with $s_{actor} = s^*_{actor}$, where the query* create *or* cr-create *creating session s occurred before or at creation of session s^*, or*
4. *a query* corrupt(s^*_{peer}) *as well as (*randomness *or* cr-create*) queries on all sessions s with $s_{actor} = s'_{actor}$, where the query* create *or* cr-create *creating session s occurred before or at creation of session s', or*

5. *a query* corrupt(s^*_{peer}) *before creation of session* s^* *via a query (*create *or* cr-create *) or as long as* s^*_{status} = active *and* s^*_{recv} = ϵ, *and impersonating the peer to the test session* s^*.

From Theorem 3, we derive the following model.

Definition 21 ($\Omega_{\mathsf{AKE \cap ISM}}$). *The model* $\Omega_{\mathsf{AKE \cap ISM}}$ *is defined by* (Q, F), *where* $Q = Q_{\mathsf{noCR}} \cup \{$cr-create$\}$ *and a session* s *is said to satisfy* F *if the following conditions hold:*

1. *no* session-key(s) *has been issued,*
2. *for all sessions* s^* *such that* s^* *matches* s, *no* session-key(s^*) *has been issued,*
3. *not all queries* corrupt(s_{actor}) *as well as (*randomness *or* cr-create*) on all sessions* $\tilde{s}$ *with* $\tilde{s}_{actor} = s_{actor}$, *where the query* create *or* cr-create *creating session* $\tilde{s}$ *occurred before or at creation of session* s, *have been issued,*
4. *for all sessions* s' *such that* s *is partially matching session* s', *not all queries* corrupt(s_{peer}) *as well as (*randomness *or* cr-create*) on all sessions* $\tilde{s}$ *with* $\tilde{s}_{actor} = s'_{actor}$, *where the query* create *or* cr-create *creating session* $\tilde{s}$ *occurred before or at creation of session* s', *have been issued, and*
5. *if there exists no origin-session for session* s, *then no* corrupt(s_{peer}) *query has been issued before creation of session* s *via a query (*create *or* cr-create*) or as long as* s_{status} = active *and* s_{recv} = ϵ.

Unlike the models we saw previously, the adversary in the $\Omega_{\mathsf{AKE \cap ISM}}$ model is allowed to compromise both the randomness of the target session and the actor's long-term secret key as long as the randomness of at least one of the previous sessions of the actor has not been compromised.

The $\mathrm{SIG^*(NXPR)}$ protocol in Fig. 3 is in the class AKE $\cap$ ISM. Each user maintains a variable $l \in \{0, 1\}^*$ initialized with ϵ. We write $st_{\hat{P}}.l$ to access the variable l stored in the user memory of user $\hat{P}$. In contrast to NAXOS, $\mathrm{SIG^*(NXPR)}$ additionally includes the randomness of all sessions that have been previously created as input to the hash function H_1 and each user signs a message using its long-term secret key and checks that the received signature is valid with respect to the long-term public key of its peer.

Proposition 4 below follows from [23, Proposition 7], [20, Theorem 1] and from the fact that the existence of a unique origin-session s for the test-session s^* implies the existence of a unique partially matching session s' for s^* with $s = s'$.

Proposition 4. *Under the GAP-CDH assumption in the cyclic group* G *of prime order* q, *using a unique strongly existentially unforgeable under an adaptive chosen-message signature scheme, the* $\mathrm{SIG^*(NXPR)}$ *protocol is secure in the* $\Omega_{\mathsf{AKE \cap ISM}}$ *model, when* H_1, H_2 *are modelled as independent random oracles.*

Definition 21 and Proposition 1 give rise to the model $\Omega_{\mathsf{INDP \cap ISM}}$ below. The third condition in Definition 22 prevents the adversary from both corrupting the actor of the target session and revealing the randomness of all sessions of this user that were created prior to creation of the target session as well as the

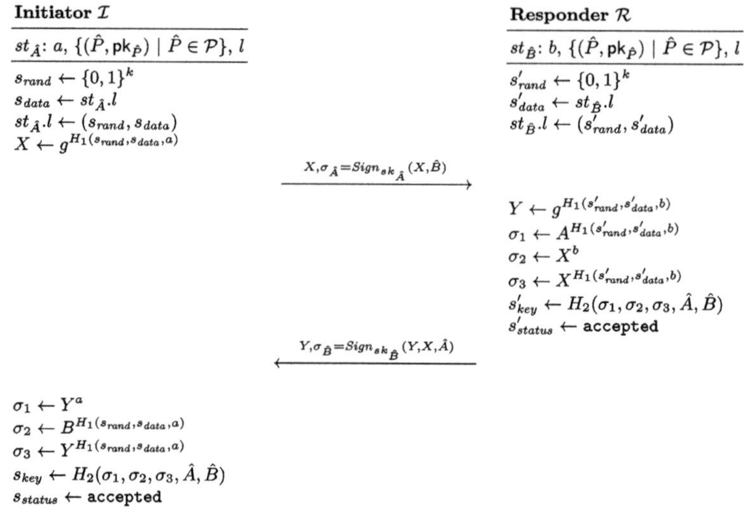

Fig. 3. SIG*(NXPR) protocol, where $H_1 : \{0,1\}^* \to \mathbb{Z}_q$ (with $||q|| = k$, where k is the security parameter) and $H_2 : \{0,1\}^* \to \{0,1\}^k$ denote two hash functions. Users additionally perform signature verification, which we leave implicit in the figure.

randomness of the target session itself. Because only initial state modification is possible, the responses for the previous queries would allow the adversary to emulate the protocol execution steps for the target session. The fourth condition specifies a similar requirement c-origin-sessions for the target session.

Definition 22 ($\Omega_{\mathsf{INDP}\cap\mathsf{ISM}}$). *The model $\Omega_{\mathsf{INDP}\cap\mathsf{ISM}}$ is defined by (Q, F), where $Q = Q_{\mathsf{noCR}} \cup \{\mathsf{cr\text{-}create}\}$ and a session s is said to satisfy F if:*

1. *no* session-key(s) *has been issued,*
2. *for all sessions s^* such that s^* matches s, no* session-key(s^*) *has been issued,*
3. *not all queries* corrupt(s_{actor}) *as well as (*randomness *or* cr-create*) on all sessions $\tilde{s}$ with $\tilde{s}_{actor} = s_{actor}$, where the query* create *or* cr-create *creating session $\tilde{s}$ occurred before or at creation of session s, have been issued,*
4. *for all sessions s' such that s' is a c-origin-session for session s, not all queries* corrupt(s_{peer}) *as well as (*randomness *or* cr-create*) on all sessions $\tilde{s}$ with $\tilde{s}_{actor} = s'_{actor}$, where the query* create *or* cr-create *creating session $\tilde{s}$ occurred before or at creation of session s', have been issued, and*
5. *if there exists no origin-session for session s, then no* corrupt(s_{peer}) *query has been issued before the completion of session s.*

Definition 21 and Propositions 1 and 2 give rise to the model $\Omega_{\mathsf{INDP\text{-}DH}\cap\mathsf{ISM}}$:

Definition 23 ($\Omega_{\mathsf{INDP\text{-}DH}\cap\mathsf{ISM}}$). *The model $\Omega_{\mathsf{INDP\text{-}DH}\cap\mathsf{ISM}}$ is defined by (Q, F), where $Q = Q_{\mathsf{noCR}} \cup \{\mathsf{cr\text{-}create}\}$ and a session s is said to satisfy F if the following conditions hold:*

1. *no* session-key(s) *has been issued,*

2. *for all sessions s^* such that s^* matches s, no* session-key(s^*) *has been issued,*

3. *not all queries* corrupt(s_{actor}) *as well as (*randomness *or* cr-create*) on all sessions $\tilde{s}$ with $\tilde{s}_{actor} = s_{actor}$, where the query* create *or* cr-create *creating session $\tilde{s}$ occurred before or at creation of session s, have been issued,*

4. *for all sessions s' such that s' is an origin-session for session s, not all queries* corrupt(s_{peer}) *as well as (*randomness *or* cr-create*) on all sessions $\tilde{s}$ with $\tilde{s}_{actor} = s'_{actor}$, where the query* create *or* cr-create *creating session $\tilde{s}$ occurred before or at creation of session s', have been issued, and*

5. *if there exists no origin-session for s, then no* corrupt(s_{peer}) *has been issued.*

Note that $\Omega_{\mathsf{INDP\text{-}DH}\cap\mathsf{ISM}}$ was obtained via a series of impossibility results on various protocol classes, but in fact corresponds to the Ω_Λ model in [23], which has been deduced via impossibility results on the narrow protocol class $\mathsf{INDP\text{-}DH} \cap \mathsf{ISM}$.

6   Construction of a Protocol-Security Hierarchy

A so-called *protocol-security hierarchy* [2] has been introduced by Basin and Cremers and allows to classify the relative strength of protocols against different attacker models. In Fig. 4 we show the protocol-security hierarchy with respect to our security models.

We recall notions of relative strengths of security between game-based security models from [8,19]. Let secure(M, π) be a predicate that is true if and only if the protocol π is secure in security model M.

Definition 24 ([19]). *Let Π be a class of AKE protocols. We say that a security model M' is at least as strong as a security model M with respect to Π, denoted by $M \leq^{\Pi} M'$, if $\forall \pi \in \Pi, secure(M', \pi) \implies secure(M, \pi)$. We say that model M' is stronger than model M with respect to protocol class Π, if $M \leq^{\Pi} M'$ and not $M' \leq^{\Pi} M$.*

The rounded rectangles in Fig. 4 identify protocol classes. For each class, we identify the security guarantees that cannot be achieved by any of its members. For example, because NAXOS is in $\mathsf{INDP\text{-}DH} \cap \mathsf{SL}$, it cannot provide PFS nor message origin authentication. Additionally, NAXOS is insecure if the RNG is compromised or fails (see [23]). The protocols in the figure that belong to the class $\mathsf{AKE} \setminus \mathsf{SL}$ are secure even against attacks based on bad randomness such as reset-and-replay attacks. In contrast to CNX, $\mathrm{SIG}_t(\mathrm{CNX})$, and $\mathrm{SIG}^*(\mathrm{CNX})$, the protocols NXPR, $\mathrm{SIG}_t(\mathrm{NXPR})$, and $\mathrm{SIG}^*(\mathrm{NXPR})$, achieve security even under compromise of the randomness of the target session and the long-term secret key of the actor of that session as long as the randomness of at least one of the previous sessions of the same user has not been compromised.

The protocols in the class INDP can provide PFS, but cannot provide *recent aliveness*. Recent aliveness means that, after completion of a session, the user executing the session has a guarantee that its peer has been alive during the execution of the protocol [28]. For example, the protocol $\mathrm{SIG}_t(\mathrm{NAXOS})$ provides

PFS as it is secure in the model $\Omega_{\mathsf{INDP} \cap \mathsf{SL}}$, but it does not provide recent aliveness, because the messages of initiator and responder can be generated independently of each other. In contrast, the protocols SIG*(NAXOS), SIG*(CNX), and SIG*(NXPR) provide recent aliveness to the initiator in the models $\Omega_{\mathsf{AKE} \cap \mathsf{SL}}$, $\Omega_{\overline{\mathsf{AKE}} \cap \mathsf{ISM}}$, and $\Omega_{\mathsf{AKE} \cap \mathsf{ISM}}$, respectively. The responder not only signs its own Diffie-Hellman exponential but also the exponential that it received from the initiator. Thus, the latter protocols also achieve security against replay attacks to the initiator. Recent aliveness for both initiator and responder can be achieved in three-message protocols, e. g., by adding a third message that contains a signature on the Diffie-Hellman exponential that the initiator received from its peer.

7   Conclusions

We provided the first formal, systematic, analysis of the limits of authenticated key exchange security by collecting and providing generic attacks on protocols classes and deriving strong security models. If a protocol designer aims to develop a protocol in a certain class, our results demonstrate which strong guarantees

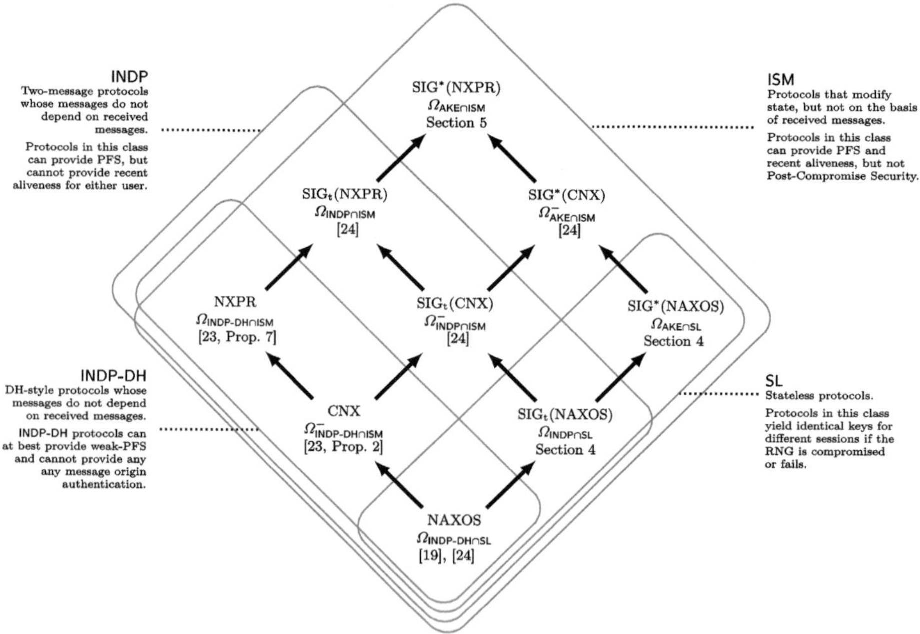

Fig. 4. Protocol-security hierarchy. Nodes list the protocols and the corresponding strong security model that they satisfy. The rounded rectangles denote protocol classes. The side annotations describe the classes and their guarantees. Nodes also refer to the proof of the protocol in the model. Edges refer to the proof of the model relations. We provide proofs for all implication edges in the long version of this paper [24].

can at best be achieved. Conversely, if a certain security guarantee is required, our results indicate in which protocol classes it can be achieved.

In this work we did not consider adversarial registration of public keys: the generic approach from [8] can be used to achieve strong security guarantees for such cases. As future work we would like to extend our impossibility results to the broad class of protocols AKE, thus lifting the restriction of the subclass ISM, and to provide a strong model for analyzing protocols in AKE.

Disclosure of Interests. The authors have no competing interests to declare that are relevant to the content of this article.

References

1. Alwen, J., Coretti, S., Dodis, Y.: The Double Ratchet: Security Notions, Proofs, and Modularization for the Signal Protocol. Cryptology ePrint Archive, Paper 2018/1037 (2018). https://eprint.iacr.org/2018/1037
2. Basin, D., Cremers, C.: Degrees of security: Protocol guarantees in the face of compromising adversaries. In: Computer Science Logic, 24th International Workshop, CSL 2010, 19th Annual Conference of the EACSL. LNCS, vol. 6247. Springer (2010)
3. Bellare, M., Pointcheval, D., Rogaway, P.: Authenticated key exchange secure against dictionary attacks. In: 19th International Conference on Theory and Application of Cryptographic Techniques, pp. 139–155. EUROCRYPT'00, Springer (2000)
4. Bellare, M., Rogaway, P.: Entity authentication and key distribution. In: 13th Annual International Cryptology Conference on Advances in Cryptology, pp. 232–249. CRYPTO '93, Springer New York, NY, USA (1994)
5. Bellare, M., Rogaway, P.: Provably secure session key distribution: the three party case. In: 27th Annual ACM Symposium on Theory of computing, pp. 57–66. STOC '95, ACM New York, NY, USA (1995)
6. Blake-Wilson, S., Johnson, D., Menezes, A.: Key agreement protocols and their security analysis. In: Darnell, M. (ed.) Cryptography and Coding 1997. LNCS, vol. 1355, pp. 30–45. Springer, Heidelberg (1997). https://doi.org/10.1007/BFb0024447
7. Blake-Wilson, S., Menezes, A.: Unknown key-share attacks on the Station-to-Station (STS) protocol. In: Proceedings of the Second International Workshop on Practice and Theory in Public Key Cryptography. LNCS, vol. 1560. Springer (1999)
8. Boyd, C., Cremers, C., Feltz, M., Paterson, K.G., Poettering, B., Stebila, D.: ASICS: Authenticated Key Exchange Security Incorporating Certification Systems. In: Crampton, J., Jajodia, S., Mayes, K. (eds.) ESORICS 2013. LNCS, vol. 8134, pp. 381–399. Springer, Heidelberg (2013). https://doi.org/10.1007/978-3-642-40203-6_22
9. Boyd, C., Nieto, J.G.: On forward secrecy in one-round key exchange. In: Chen, L. (ed.) IMACC 2011. LNCS, vol. 7089, pp. 451–468. Springer, Heidelberg (2011). https://doi.org/10.1007/978-3-642-25516-8_27
10. Brzuska, C., Fischlin, M., Warinschi, B., Williams, S.: Composability of Bellare-Rogaway key exchange protocols. In: Proceedings of the 18th ACM conference on Computer and communications security, pp. 51–62. CCS '11, ACM (2011)

11. Canetti, R., Krawczyk, H.: Analysis of key-exchange protocols and their use for building secure channels. In: EUROCRYPT'01. LNCS, vol. 2045, pp. 453–474. Springer London, UK (2001)
12. Cheng, Q., Ma, C., Hu, X.: A new strongly secure authenticated key exchange protocol. In: Park, J.H., Chen, H.-H., Atiquzzaman, M., Lee, C., Kim, T., Yeo, S.-S. (eds.) ISA 2009. LNCS, vol. 5576, pp. 135–144. Springer, Heidelberg (2009). https://doi.org/10.1007/978-3-642-02617-1_14
13. Choo, K.K.R., Boyd, C., Hitchcock, Y.: Examining indistinguishability-based proof models for key establishment protocols. In: Proceedings of the 11th international conference on Theory and Application of Cryptology and Information Security. ASIACRYPT'05, Springer-Verlag (2005)
14. Chow, S.S.M., Choo, K.-K.R.: Strongly-secure identity-based key agreement and anonymous extension. In: Garay, J.A., Lenstra, A.K., Mambo, M., Peralta, R. (eds.) ISC 2007. LNCS, vol. 4779, pp. 203–220. Springer, Heidelberg (2007). https://doi.org/10.1007/978-3-540-75496-1_14
15. Cohn-Gordon, K., Cremers, C.J.F., Garratt, L.: On post-compromise security. In: CSF, pp. 164–178. IEEE Computer Society (2016)
16. Cremers, C.: Examining indistinguishability-based security models for key exchange protocols: the case of CK, CK-HMQV, and eCK. In: Proceedings of ACM Symposium on Information, Computer and Communications Security. ASIACCS '11, ACM (2011)
17. Cremers, C., Feltz, M.: One-round strongly secure key exchange with perfect forward secrecy and deniability. Cryptology ePrint Archive, Report 2011/300 (2011). http://eprint.iacr.org/2011/300
18. Cremers, C., Feltz, M.: Beyond eCK: perfect forward secrecy under actor compromise and ephemeral-key reveal. In: Proceedings of the 17th European Conference on Research in Computer Security. ESORICS, Springer-Verlag (2012)
19. Cremers, C., Feltz, M.: Beyond eCK: Perfect Forward Secrecy Under Actor Compromise and Ephemeral-key Reveal. Designs, Codes and Cryptography (2013)
20. Cremers, C., Feltz, M.: Beyond eCK: Perfect Forward Secrecy under Actor Compromise and Ephemeral-Key Reveal. Cryptology ePrint Archive, Report 2012/416 (2012). http://eprint.iacr.org/2012/416
21. Cremers, C., Mauw, S.: Operational Semantics and Verification of Security Protocols. Springer, Information Security and Cryptography (2012)
22. Engels, A., Mauw, S.: Why men (and octopuses) cannot juggle a four ball cascade (1997). https://satoss.uni.lu/members/sjouke/papers/EnMa02.pdf
23. Feltz, M., Cremers, C.: Strengthening the security of authenticated key exchange against bad randomness. Designs, Codes Cryptograph. **86**(3), 481–516 (Mar 2018). https://doi.org/10.1007/s10623-017-0337-5
24. Feltz, M., Cremers, C.: A Formal Treatment of the Limits of Key Exchange Security (Long Version) (2025). https://people.cispa.io/cas.cremers/downloads/papers/akelimits-SMLXV-long.pdf
25. Gennaro, R., Krawczyk, H., Rabin, T.: Okamoto-Tanaka revisited: fully authenticated Diffie-Hellman with minimal overhead. In: ACNS'10. Springer (2010)
26. Hao, F.: On robust key agreement based on public key authentication. In: Financial Cryptography. LNCS, vol. 6052, pp. 383–390. Springer (2010)
27. Kim, M., Fujioka, A., Ustaoglu, B.: Strongly secure authenticated key exchange without NAXOS' approach. In: IWSEC'09, pp. 174–191 (2009)
28. Krawczyk, H.: SIGMA: The 'SIGn-and-MAc' approach to authenticated Diffie-Hellman and its use in the IKE-Protocols. In: CRYPTO, pp. 400–425 (2003)

29. Krawczyk, H.: HMQV: a high-performance secure Diffie-Hellman protocol. In: Shoup, V. (ed.) CRYPTO 2005. LNCS, vol. 3621, pp. 546–566. Springer, Heidelberg (2005). https://doi.org/10.1007/11535218_33
30. Krawczyk, H.: HMQV: A High-Performance Secure Diffie-Hellman Protocol. Cryptology ePrint Archive, Report 2005/176 (2005). http://eprint.iacr.org/2005/176
31. LaMacchia, B., Lauter, K., Mityagin, A.: Stronger security of authenticated key exchange. In: Susilo, W., Liu, J.K., Mu, Y. (eds.) ProvSec 2007. LNCS, vol. 4784, pp. 1–16. Springer, Heidelberg (2007). https://doi.org/10.1007/978-3-540-75670-5_1
32. Lee, J., Park, J.: Authenticated key exchange secure under the computational Diffie-Hellman assumption. Cryptology ePrint Archive, Report 2008/344 (2008). https://eprint.iacr.org/2008/344
33. Lysyanskaya, A.: Unique signatures and verifiable random functions from the DH-DDH separation, pp. 597–612. Springer Berlin Heidelberg (2002)
34. Menezes, A., van Oorschot, P., Vanstone, S.: Handbook of Applied Cryptography. CRC Press, Boca Raton, FL, USA (1996)
35. Poettering, B., Rösler, P.: Asynchronous ratcheted key exchange. Cryptology ePrint Archive, Report 2018/296 (2018). https://eprint.iacr.org/2018/296
36. Sarr, A., Elbaz-Vincent, P., Bajard, J.C.: A new security model for authenticated key agreement. Secur. Cryptograph. Netw. 219–234 (2010)
37. Schäge, S.: TOPAS: 2-pass key exchange with full perfect forward secrecy and optimal communication complexity. In: Proceedings of the 22nd ACM SIGSAC Conference on Computer and Communications Security, pp. 1224–1235. ACM (2015)
38. Ustaoglu, B.: Obtaining a secure and efficient key agreement protocol from (H)MQV and NAXOS. Cryptology ePrint Archive, Report 2007/123 (2007), https://eprint.iacr.org/2007/123
39. Yang, G., Duan, S., Wong, D.S., Tan, C.H., Wang, H.: Authenticated key exchange under bad randomness. In: Proceedings of the 15th International Conference on Financial Cryptography and Data Security, pp. 113–126. FC'11, Springer-Verlag (2012)

A Quadratic Lower Bound for Simulation

Jan Friso Groote[1]([✉])[iD] and Jan Martens[2][iD]

[1] Eindhoven University of Technology, Eindhoven, The Netherlands
j.f.groote@tue.nl
[2] Leiden University, Leiden, The Netherlands
j.j.m.martens@liacs.leidenuniv.nl

Abstract. We show that deciding simulation equivalence and simulation preorder have quadratic lower bounds assuming that the Strong Exponential Time Hypothesis holds. This result matches the best known quadratic upper bounds of simulation equivalence. This means that, assuming the Strong Exponential Time Hypothesis, deciding simulation is inherently quadratic. A consequence of our result is that computing simulation equivalence is fundamentally harder than computing bisimilarity.

1 Introduction

Commonly, processes are abstractly represented as directed graphs with states and transitions where states or transitions are labelled. One process is simulated by another if each step of the first process can be simulated by the second. Two processes are simulation equivalent if they can both simulate each other. Simulation preorders for the comparison of the behaviour of programs have been defined in [13]. Algorithms for deciding simulation equivalences and simulation preorders on finite graphs were only defined decades later [1,2,8] and their worst case complexity is bounded by the number of states times the number of transitions. In [3,6,15,16] these algorithms are improved by reducing both the required memory footprint and the time complexity to the number of simulation equivalence classes times the number of transitions, but as the number of equivalence classes can be the number of states this essentially means that all algorithms have worst case quadratic time complexity in terms of the input.

This raises the question whether calculating simulation preorder and simulation equivalence over finite graphs is inherently quadratic. Hitherto, the literature presents no real answer to this question. The only analysis is that determining simulation is at least as hard as computing bisimilarity [12]. This follows from the observation that via a polynomial translation of the process graph bisimulation equivalence reduces to simulation equivalence, showing that modulo this transformation simulation can be used to calculate bisimilarity. For bisimilarity there is a quasi-linear lower bound assuming partition refinement is used [7].

In this paper we provide an answer to the above-mentioned question by showing that if the Strong Exponential Time Hypothesis (SETH) holds, then

B. Fila et al. (Eds.): Sjouke Mauw Festschrift, LNCS 16365, pp. 98–105, 2026.
https://doi.org/10.1007/978-3-032-20684-8_6

determining simulation preorder on deterministic transition systems and simulation equivalence on non-deterministic transition systems must be quadratic in complexity.

The Strong Exponential Time Hypothesis (SETH) states that satisfiability of a propositional formula with n propositional variables cannot be solved in time $O(2^{\delta n})$ for any $\delta < 1$ [10]. There is also the Exponential Time Hypothesis (ETH), also occurring in [10], which says that determining satisfiability of propositional formulas in conjunctive normal form where each clause has length 3 needs at least time $O(2^{\epsilon n})$ for some $\epsilon > 0$. The strong exponential time hypothesis is a stronger hypothesis than ETH which in turn is stronger than $P \neq NP$. This means that SETH implies ETH implies $P \neq NP$ but the converse does not need to be the case. Both hypotheses ETH and SETH state that in essence no algorithm for satisfiability significantly outperforms brute-force methods. They are especially useful to prove lower bounds for problems within P [14,18].

For us the results in [14] are particularly interesting. They deal with the problem of determining the non-emptiness of the intersection for k deterministic finite state machines (k-DFA-NEI). This problem is defined as follows. Given k deterministic finite state machines $A_1, \ldots, A_k$, each over an alphabet Σ and having n states, determine whether

$$\bigcap_{i=1}^{k} \mathcal{L}(A_i) \stackrel{?}{=} \emptyset$$

where $\mathcal{L}(A_i)$ is the set of accepted strings by state machine A_i. For unbounded k this problem is PSPACE-complete [11]. If the number of input DFAs k is fixed, this problem can be solved naively in $O(n^k)$ time by constructing the product automaton of the input. Under the assumption ETH, it cannot be solved significantly faster in $O(n^{o(k)})$ [4, Prop. 3]. Furthermore, under the stronger assumption SETH, an algorithm running in $O(n^{k-\epsilon})$ is impossible for any constant $\epsilon > 0$, which is more interesting to us.

We show in a quite straightforward way that if simulation of two DFAs can be determined in time $O(n^{2-\epsilon})$, both with n states, then 2-DFA-NEI can be solved in time $O(n^{2-\epsilon})$, which would imply that the assumption SETH does not hold. As a corollary it follows that computing simulation equivalence for the initial states of two nondeterministic automata is also inherently quadratic.

2 SETH Implies that DFA-NEI has Quadratic Complexity

In this section we rephrase in more detail that the strong exponential time hypothesis (SETH) implies that calculating the non-emptiness of the intersection of two deterministic finite state machines requires quadratic time. In particular, we illustrate by example how a slightly improved algorithm for the non-emptiness of language intersection would mean an exponential improvement for CNF-SAT. More detailed proofs of this construction can be found in [19, Theorem 7.21].

We start out with some preliminaries and the common notion of a deterministic finite automaton. An alphabet is a finite set of letters Σ. A word is a finite sequence of letters over an alphabet where we write ϵ for the empty sequence. For a number $i \in \mathbb{N}$ the set Σ^i is the set of all sequences of length i. The set $\Sigma^* = \bigcup_{i \in \mathbb{N}} \Sigma^i$ is the Kleene closure and contains all finite words over Σ. Given a word $w \in \Sigma^*$ and a position $1 \le i \le |w|$, we write $w[i]$ for the i-th symbol in w.

Definition 1. A Deterministic Finite Automaton (DFA) $A = (S, \Sigma, \delta, F, q_0)$ is a five-tuple consisting of:

- a finite set of states S,
- a finite set of labels Σ called the alphabet,
- a transition function $\delta : S \times \Sigma \to S$,
- a set of final states $F \subseteq S$, and
- an initial state $q_0 \in S$.

The *language* accepted by a DFA $A = (S, \Sigma, \delta, F, q_0)$, denoted as $\mathcal{L}(A)$, is the set of words $w \in \Sigma^*$ such that the path with labels from w starting in q_0 ends up in an accepting state.

$$\mathcal{L}(A) = \{w \mid w \in \Sigma^* \text{ and } \delta(q_0, w) \in F\}$$

where we use the generalised transition function δ by taking $\delta(q, \epsilon) = q$ and $\delta(q, a\,w) = \delta(\delta(a, q), w)$ for any state q.

Given a finite number k of DFAs the non-empty intersection problem of DFAs asks whether there is a word which is accepted by all DFAs. More concretely, it contains all k-tuples of DFAs of which the intersection of the accepted languages is not empty.

Definition 2. The decision problem k-DFA-NEI is the following set of tuples of DFAs

$$k\text{-DFA-NEI} = \{\langle A_1, \ldots, A_k \rangle \mid \bigcap_{i \in [1,k]} \mathcal{L}(A_i) \ne \emptyset\}.$$

We define DFA-NEI as the union of k-DFA-NEI for all k. This problem is well known to be PSPACE-complete [11]. For a fixed k the problem is naively solvable in $O(n^k)$ by computing the product automaton. Surprisingly, it turns out that if this can be computed more efficiently, it also means more efficient algorithms for deciding CNF-SAT [19]. We elaborate on that below.

Given an $\ell \in \mathbb{N}$, the decision problem ℓ-CNF-SAT is the variant of the boolean satisfiability problem over formulas in conjunctive normal form (CNF) with at most ℓ literals per clause. The computational complexity of deciding ℓ-CNF-SAT, for increasing values of ℓ is studied in [10]. Let

$$s_\ell = \inf\{\delta \mid \ell\text{-CNF-SAT is solvable in time } 2^{\delta n}\},$$

for each $\ell \in \mathbb{N}$, where inf is the infimum. The exponential time hypothesis (ETH) asserts that $s_3 > 0$, i.e., 3-CNF-SAT cannot be solved in less than exponential time. The strong exponential time hypothesis (SETH) asserts that

$$\lim_{\ell \to \infty} s_\ell = 1.$$

Equivalently SETH asserts that for any $\delta < 1$ there is no algorithm solving CNF-SAT that has a runtime of $O(2^{\delta n})$.

We consider a CNF-formula Φ with m clauses $C_1, \ldots, C_m$ over an even number n of propositional variables $x_1, \ldots, x_n$. We construct the languages $L_1^\Phi, L_2^\Phi \subseteq \{0,1\}^*$ that consist of words $w \in \Sigma^{n+m}$ in which the first n letters comprise a bitstring in which for each $1 \le i \le n$ the bit $w[i]$ encodes the truth assignment for x_i. The second part of m letters encode a gadget which assigns each clause to either L_1^Φ or L_2^Φ. We require that $w \in L_1^\Phi$ if and only if $w = w_\rho b_1 \cdots b_m$ for a word $w_\rho \in \Sigma^n$ modelling a truth assignment and $b_1, \ldots, b_m \in \{0,1\}$ such that if $b_i = 0$ then C_i is satisfied by the assignment to the variables $x_1, \ldots, x_{\frac{1}{2}n}$. Similarly, $w_\rho b_1 \cdots b_m \in L_2^\Phi$ if and only if for all $1 \le i \le m$ if $b_i = 1$ then C_i is satisfied by the assignment of some variable $x_{\frac{1}{2}n+1}, \ldots, x_n$.

For example, consider $\Psi = (x_1 \vee \overline{x_2}) \wedge (\overline{x_1} \vee x_2)$. In Fig. 1 the minimal automata that accept the languages L_1^Ψ and L_2^Ψ are given.

Observe that, given a formula Φ, for each truth assignment $w_\rho \in \{0,1\}^n$ there is an extension $w_C \in \{0,1\}^m$ such that $w_\rho w_C \in L_1^\Phi \cap L_2^\Phi$ if and only if w_ρ models a satisfying assignment for Φ. This means the intersection $L_1^\Phi \cap L_2^\Phi$ is not empty if and only if there is a satisfying assignment for Φ.

This allows us to prove satisfiability of Φ by constructing L_1^Φ and L_2^Φ and show that their intersection is not empty. Now note that the minimal DFAs that accept L_1^Φ and L_2^Φ both contain at most $m \, n2^{\frac{1}{2}n}$ states.

Assume that we can calculate language intersection on two graphs with N states each in time $O(N^{2-\epsilon})$, then we can construct L_1^Φ and L_2^Φ, and calculate their intersection in time $O((mn2^{\frac{1}{2}n})^{2-\epsilon}) = O(n^{2-\epsilon}m^{2-\epsilon}2^{n(1-\frac{1}{2}\epsilon)})$ determining CNF-SAT. But this refutes the Strong Exponential Time Hypothesis, saying that CNF-SAT cannot be solved $O(2^{\delta n})$ for any $\delta < 1$.

Theorem 3. [19, Theorem 7.21] If 2-DFA-NEI can be solved in $O(n^{2-\epsilon})$ for some constant $\epsilon > 0$, then SETH is false.

3   SETH Implies Simulation has Quadratic Complexity

In this section we show that determining simulation preorder on deterministic, and simulation equivalence on non-deterministic transition systems is necessarily quadratic, assuming SETH is valid. Simulation is typically defined on labelled transition systems which divert slightly from DFAs.

Definition 4. A Labelled Transition System (LTS) $M = (S, \Sigma, \rightarrow, s_0)$ is a four-tuple consisting of:

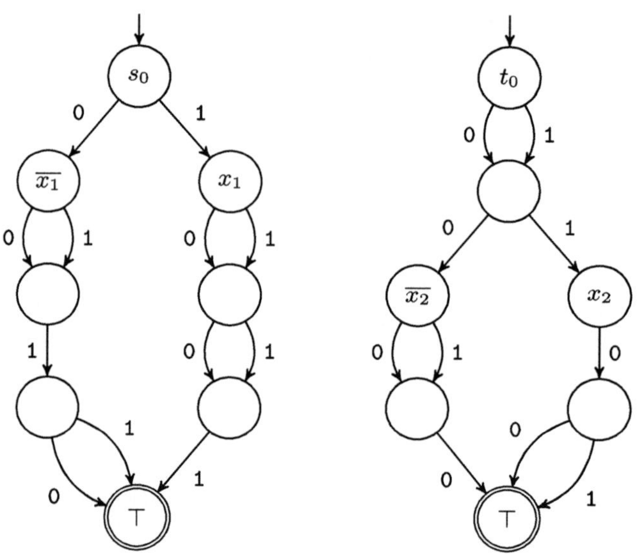

Fig. 1. Automata accepting L_1^Ψ (left), and L_2^Ψ (right) for $\Psi = (x_1 \vee \overline{x_2}) \wedge (\overline{x_1} \vee x_2)$.

- a finite set of states S,
- a finite set of action labels Σ,
- a transition relation $\rightarrow \subseteq S \times \Sigma \times S$, and
- the initial state $s_0 \in S$.

Given an LTS $L = (S, \Sigma, \rightarrow, s_0)$, we write $s \xrightarrow{a} s'$ when $(s, a, s') \in \rightarrow$. The LTS L is called *deterministic* iff there is at most one outgoing transition for every combination of state $s \in S$ and action label $a \in \Sigma$, i.e. $|\{s' \mid s \xrightarrow{a} s'\}| \leq 1$ for every $(s, a) \in S \times \Sigma$.

Definition 5. Given an LTS $M = (S, \Sigma, \rightarrow, s_0)$, a relation $R \subseteq S \times S$ is called a *simulation relation* iff for all $(s, t) \in R$ it holds that

- for each $s \xrightarrow{a} s'$ there is a transition $t \xrightarrow{a} t'$ such that $(s', t') \in R$.

The largest simulation relation, written as $\sqsubseteq$, is called similarity. Given an LTS $M_1 = (S_1, Act_1, \rightarrow_1, s_1)$ and two states $s, t \in S_1$ we say s is simulated by t iff $s \sqsubseteq t$. Given a second LTS $M_2 = (S_2, Act_2, \rightarrow_2, s_2)$, we write $M_1 \sqsubseteq M_2$ iff $s_1 \sqsubseteq s_2$ in the combined LTS $M = (S_1 \cup S_2, Act_1 \cup Act_2, \rightarrow_1 \cup \rightarrow_2, s_1)$, where we assume w.l.o.g. that the states of M_1 and M_2 are disjoint, e.g. $S_1 \cap S_2 = \emptyset$.

We say two states s, t are *simulation equivalent*, written $s \simeq t$, iff they simulate each other. A simulation relation which is symmetric is called a bisimulation relation.

We introduce a mapping α from automata to deterministic LTSs such that given two DFAs A_1, A_2, for the projected deterministic LTSs $M_1 = \alpha(A_1), M_2 = \alpha(A_2)$ it holds that $M_1 \sqsubseteq M_2$ if and only if $\mathcal{L}(A_1) \subseteq \mathcal{L}(A_2)$.

Informally, the mapping α maintains the same transition structure in the deterministic LTSs but adds one state and action label that encodes the accepting states of the automata. More formally, given a DFA $A = (S, \Sigma, \delta, F, q_0)$, we define the deterministic LTS $\alpha(A) = (S \cup \{\top\}, \Sigma \cup \{\checkmark\}, \to, q_0)$, with fresh symbols $\top \notin S, \checkmark \notin \Sigma$, and where the transition relation $\to$ is defined as:

$$\to \; = \{(q, a, \delta(q, a)) \mid \text{for each } (q, a) \in Q \times \Sigma\} \cup \{(q, \checkmark, \top) \mid \text{for each } q \in F\}.$$

As the construction above is quite straightforward, it is easy to see that we have the following theorem.

Theorem 6. Let A, B be DFAs over the alphabet Σ, then

$$\mathcal{L}(A) \subseteq \mathcal{L}(B) \iff \alpha(A) \sqsubseteq \alpha(B)$$

The construction $\alpha(A)$ is computable in linear time. This allows us to compute 2-DFA-NEI by translating the involved DFAs to deterministic LTSs using α.

Theorem 7. If for some time function f similarity on two deterministic LTSs with n states can be decided in $f(n)$ steps then 2-DFA-NEI for input DFAs of n states is computable in $f(n) + O(n)$ steps.

Proof. Note that deciding $\mathcal{L}(A) \cap \mathcal{L}(B) = \emptyset$ is equivalent to deciding $\mathcal{L}(A) \subseteq \Sigma^* \setminus \mathcal{L}(B)$. The DFA $\overline{B}$ is the complement of B, e.g. with all accepting and non-accepting states swapped, such that $\mathcal{L}(\overline{B}) = \Sigma^* \setminus \mathcal{L}(B)$.

Now by Theorem 6 it holds that $\alpha(A) \sqsubseteq \alpha\left(\overline{B}\right)$ if and only if $\mathcal{L}(A) \cap \mathcal{L}(B) = \emptyset$. Computing $\alpha(A), \alpha(\overline{B})$ can be done in $O(n)$, and hence any $f(n)$ algorithm for similarity could be translated to 2-DFA-NEI.

$\square$

This immediately translates to the following corollary.

Corollary 8. SETH implies that similarity for deterministic LTSs can not be decided in $O(n^{2-\epsilon})$.

On deterministic structures simulation equivalence coincides with bisimilarity. Meaning that deciding simulation equivalence on deterministic structures can be done in almost linear time [5,9,17], where 'almost' refers to a multiplicative factor with the inverse Ackermann's function. However, using one non-deterministic transition a faster than quadratic algorithm for simulation equivalence on LTSs in general violates SETH.

Corollary 9. SETH implies that simulation equivalence cannot be decided in $O(n^{2-\epsilon})$.

Proof. In order to see that deciding simulation equivalence is also computationally equivalent to deciding 2-DFA-NEI we reduce from deciding similarity on deterministic LTSs by adding one non-deterministic state. Given LTSs $M_1 = (S_1, \Sigma, \rightarrow_1, s_0)$ and $M_2 = (S_2, \Sigma, \rightarrow_2, t_0)$, we construct the LTS $M = (S_1 \cup S_2 \cup \{s, t\}, \rightarrow_1 \cup \rightarrow_2 \cup \{(s, a, s_0), (s, a, t_0), (t, a, t_0)\}, (s_0, t_0))$ with two fresh states $s, t \notin S_1 \cup S_2$ for some $a \in \Sigma$. See Fig. 2. Now in M it holds that $s \simeq t \iff s_0 \sqsubseteq t_0$. If simulation equivalence for LTSs is solvable in $O(n^{2-\epsilon})$, then, using this construction, similarity is solvable in $O(n^{2-\epsilon})$. In that case it follows from Corollary 8 that SETH is false.

$\square$

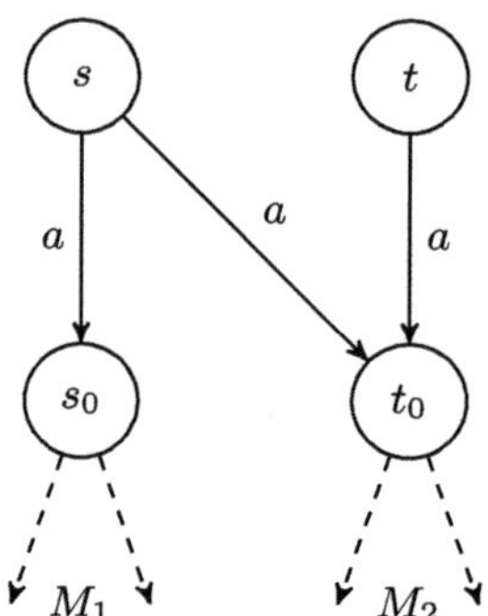

Fig. 2. The LTS M.

The proof technique employed in this paper appears to be quite universal. It promises to be useable to show fine-grained, i.e., sub-exponential, lower bounds for a much wider classes of problems in the domain of process theory and model checking. Unfortunately, as yet, we were not able to do so.

Disclosure of Interests. The authors have no competing interests to declare that are relevant to the content of this article.

References

1. Bloom, B., Paige, R.: Transformational design and implementation of a new efficient solution to the ready simulation problem. Sci. Comput. Program. **24**(3), 189–220 (1995). https://doi.org/10.1016/0167-6423(95)00003-B
2. Bustan, D., Grumberg, O.: Simulation-based minimization. ACM Trans. Comput. Log. **4**(2), 181–206 (2003). https://doi.org/10.1145/635499.635502
3. Crafa, S., Ranzato, F., Tapparo, F.: Saving space in a time efficient simulation algorithm. Fundam. Informaticae **108**(1–2), 23–42 (2011). https://doi.org/10.3233/FI-2011-412
4. Fernau, H., Krebs, A.: Problems on finite automata and the exponential time hypothesis. Algorithms **10**(1), 24 (2017)

5. Fischer, M.J.: Efficiency of equivalence algorithms. In: Miller, R.E., Thatcher, J.W. (eds.) Proceedings of a symposium on the Complexity of Computer Computations, held March 20-22, 1972, at the IBM Thomas J. Watson Research Center, Yorktown Heights, New York, USA. pp. 153–167. The IBM Research Symposia Series, Plenum Press, New York (1972). https://doi.org/10.1007/978-1-4684-2001-2_14

6. van Glabbeek, R., Ploeger, B.: Correcting a space-efficient simulation algorithm. In: Gupta, A., Malik, S. (eds.) CAV 2008. LNCS, vol. 5123, pp. 517–529. Springer, Heidelberg (2008). https://doi.org/10.1007/978-3-540-70545-1_49

7. Groote, J.F., Martens, J., de Vink, E.P.: Lowerbounds for bisimulation by partition refinement. Log. Methods Comput. Sci. **19**(2) (2023). https://doi.org/10.46298/LMCS-19(2:10)2023

8. Henzinger, M.R., Henzinger, T.A., Kopke, P.W.: Computing simulations on finite and infinite graphs. In: 36th Annual Symposium on Foundations of Computer Science, Milwaukee, Wisconsin, USA, 23-25 October 1995. pp. 453–462. IEEE Computer Society (1995). https://doi.org/10.1109/SFCS.1995.492576

9. Hopcroft, J.E., Karp, R.M.: A linear algorithm for testing equivalence of finite automata. Tr 114, Cornell University (1971)

10. Impagliazzo, R., Paturi, R.: On the complexity of k-SAT. J. Comput. Syst. Sci. (2001). https://doi.org/10.1006/jcss.2000.1727

11. Kozen, D.: Lower bounds for natural proof systems. In: Proceedings of SFCS 1977, pp. 254–266. IEEE, IEEE (1977). https://doi.org/10.1109/SFCS.1977.16

12. Kučera, A., Mayr, R.: Why is simulation harder than bisimulation? In: Brim, L., Křetínský, M., Kučera, A., Jančar, P. (eds.) CONCUR 2002. LNCS, vol. 2421, pp. 594–609. Springer, Heidelberg (2002). https://doi.org/10.1007/3-540-45694-5_39

13. Milner, R.: An algebraic definition of simulation between programs. In: Cooper, D.C. (ed.) Proceedings of the 2nd International Joint Conference on Artificial Intelligence. London, UK, September 1-3, 1971. pp. 481–489. William Kaufmann (1971). http://ijcai.org/Proceedings/71/Papers/044.pdf

14. de Oliveira Oliveira, M., Wehar, M.: On the fine grained complexity of finite automata non-emptiness of intersection. In: Jonoska, N., Savchuk, D. (eds.) DLT 2020. LNCS, vol. 12086, pp. 69–82. Springer, Cham (2020). https://doi.org/10.1007/978-3-030-48516-0_6

15. Ranzato, F.: An efficient simulation algorithm on Kripke structures. Acta Informatica **51**(2), 107–125 (2014). https://doi.org/10.1007/S00236-014-0195-9

16. Ranzato, F., Tapparo, F.: A new efficient simulation equivalence algorithm. In: 22nd IEEE Symposium on Logic in Computer Science (LICS 2007), 10–12 July 2007, Wroclaw, Poland, Proceedings, pp. 171–180. IEEE Computer Society (2007). https://doi.org/10.1109/LICS.2007.8

17. Tarjan, R.E.: Efficiency of a good but not linear set union algorithm. J. ACM (JACM) **22**(2), 215–225 (1975). https://doi.org/10.1145/321879.321884

18. Vassilevska Williams, V.: Hardness of easy problems: basing hardness on popular conjectures such as the strong exponential time hypothesis. In: Husfeldt, T., Kanj, I. (eds.) Proceedings of IPEC 2015. Leibniz International Proceedings in Informatics (LIPIcs), vol. 43, pp. 17–29. Schloss Dagstuhl – Leibniz-Zentrum für Informatik (2015). https://doi.org/10.4230/LIPIcs.IPEC.2015.17

19. Wehar, M.: On the complexity of intersection non-emptiness problems. Ph.D. thesis, University at Buffalo (2016)

How to Carve Out-of-Order Fragmented Files

Nick Huijsmans[1], Bart Kuijsten[1], Hugo Jonker[1,2](✉) (iD), and Harm van Beek[1,3]

[1] Open Universiteit, Heerlen, Netherlands
`hugo.jonker@ou.nl`, `harm.vanbeek@ou.nl`
[2] Radboud Universiteit, Nijmegen, Netherlands
[3] Netherlands Forensic Institute, The Hague, Netherlands

Abstract. The contents of files are typically stored on disk in a consecutive manner. However, ∼4% of files are *fragmented* – the contents is not stored on-disk in one continuous part. The fragments that together constitute the file may even be stored in non-consecutive order on-disk. This turns out to be a common occurrence: the `WildFrag` dataset (gathered by Van der Meer et al.) showed that almost half of fragmented files (∼46%) are fragmented out of order. This is a type of fragmentation that, while not entirely overlooked, has received scant attention in the file carving literature.

In this paper, we further analyse the `WildFrag` dataset to find insights which may impact the design of file carvers. Second, we propose an initial design and proof-of-concept implementation of a carver capable of handling out-of-order fragmentation. Lastly, we note a dearth of suitable disk image sets to test our implementation. We construct a test set generator which can generate disk images with tunable fragmentation patterns, setting fragmentation percentage, number of fragments per file, and the degree of 'out-of-order'ness. We conclude that while this work shows out-of-order carving is feasible, it is still an open question how to do so efficiently in practical settings.

1 Introduction

In contemporary file systems, including NTFS,[1] file storage is managed through a file table structure—in NTFS terms a Master File Table (MFT)—that preserves metadata about each file. This table includes information regarding the physical location(s) where the data constituting each file is stored, by specifically documenting the clusters allocated to each file. When a process requests a file from the file system, the file system uses this metadata to reconstruct the file's content from the clusters in which the file's data was stored. Files can also be reconstructed from their constituent clusters *without* relying on file system metadata, though this is an arduous process. This process is referred to as **file carving**. File carving tools are designed to retrieve data from storage media

---

[1] New Technology File System —The default file system on Windows computers.

B. Fila et al. (Eds.): Sjouke Mauw Festschrift, LNCS 16365, pp. 106–121, 2026.
https://doi.org/10.1007/978-3-032-20684-8_7

in scenarios where a file table is (partially) missing. This is a common scenario when files have been deleted. For NTFS, when a file is deleted, the file system does not actually zero out the clusters assigned to the file. Instead, it marks the clusters as de-allocated in the MFT, indicating their availability. The original data in these marked clusters remains on disk until overwritten by new data. This enables recovery of the data.

Table 1. Storage patterns of a two-cluster file, $\boxed{A}$ and $\boxed{B}$. Only the storage pattern $\boxed{A\,|\,B}$ is not fragmented, all other storage patterns are fragmented files. Image due to Van der Meer et al. [14].

	Contiguous	*Non-contiguous*
In-order	A B	A $\cdots$ B
Out-of-order	B A	B $\cdots$ A

In file systems, files are stored in fixed-size clusters.[2] Files larger than the cluster size are stored in multiple clusters. **File fragmentation** occurs when the cluster numbers assigned to a file are non-contiguous, non-consecutive or both (Table 1). Note that this implies that files with less than two assigned clusters cannot be fragmented. A study by Van der Meer et al. [14] found that about 4.4% of files are fragmented, and that almost half of the fragmented files are fragmented out of order. While these numbers may seem low, due to the ever-increasing capacity of storage mediums, the amount of fragmented data has increased even as the percentage of fragmented files has reduced.

File carving has been an active academic and engineering field. A significant body of academic and practical works exist, focusing on file recovery. However, fragmented files have received far less attention – and out-of-order fragmented files only a sliver of that. Thus, while many file carvers and file carving algorithms have been developed, few have specifically addressed the challenges posed by out-of-order fragmentation.

Contributions. The goal of this paper is to provide a foundation for carving fragmented files. First, we note that a deep analysis of fragmentation as encountered in the real world may lead to insights which impact the design of file carvers for fragmented files. We analyse the WildFrag dataset (gathered by Van der Meer et al. [14]) with a focus on fragmentation patterns in Sect. 3).

Next, we propose a basic two-stage carving strategy for recovering fragmented files from a disk containing both fragmented and non-fragmented data (Sect. 4). This leverages the insights gained from the analysis.

---

[2] In case the file contents is smaller than the cluster size, this data can sometimes be stored in its entirety in the MFT. Files whose contents is stored entirely in the MFT are called *resident files* and are not further considered here.

Lastly, there is a lack of comprehensive test sets with specific characteristic fragmentation patterns. This is necessary to test developed carving algorithms. We design a test generator that can be tuned to generate disk images with the desired fragmentation patterns and test a proof-of-concept implementation of our design (Sect. 5).

2   Related Work

In 2013, Alherbawi et al. [1] provided a systematic literature review on data carving.

In absence of file system metadata, file carvers have to rely on knowledge about the structure of a file to recover its contents. The first generation file carvers used knowledge about byte-sequences—also called magic numbers, signatures or markers—found in *headers* and optionally *footers* of a file. The process involves searching the data for headers. Upon locating a header, the corresponding footer needs to be found. The data found in between (and including) the header and footer is considered the content of the file. In the case the file formats lacks a footer, such as bitmap files (BMP), the length of the file, can be extracted from the header data. Based on this length, data following header are considered to be the content of the file. This method was used in tools such as Foremost and Scalpel [10,12]. The carving algorithms of these carvers did not take fragmentation into account, not to mention out-of-order fragmentation. Consequently, the recovery process resulted in an incomplete, wrong or overcomplete reconstruction of the original file set.

In 2007, Garfinkel [4] conducted and presented an analysis on over 300 hard drives. He discovered that although overall only 6% of the files were fragmented, the forensically interesting files are more likely to be fragmented than other file types, emphasizing the need for carvers that handle fragmentation. Garfinkel presented a carving strategy for dealing with fragmentation, called BiFragment Gap Carving (BGC). If the contiguous clusters between a found header and footer do not validate as a file, the algorithm systematically tests if the data does validate as a file for all possible (single) gaps in the data between the header and footer. This method handles fragmentation, but is only designed to handle in-order bi-fragmentation. BGC's exhaustive gap testing method significantly increases computational cost as the number of potential gap sizes grows, making it less suitable for large disks. Furthermore, since the method relies on sequentially searching for a footer after identifying a header, it does not allow for out-of-order fragmentation.

In 2002, Shanmugasundaram et al. [13] presented Graph Theoretic Carvers for dealing with the limitation of the first generation file carvers. Their idea treats fragment reassembly for text documents as a Hamiltonian path problem. The idea is that the correct permutation of clusters maximizes the sum of candidate weights. These weights are assigned based on *prediction by partial matching* (PPM), where the likelihood of neighboring clusters is determined by analyzing which text characters would most likely follow the characters in the current fragment. The task thus becomes one of finding the shortest (cheapest) path by identifying the most likely neighbor for each cluster, which can be considered the Traveling Salesman Problem (TSP).

Where this Hamiltonian Path Problem focuses on single files, Memon and Pal [8] reformulated the problem as a k vertex disjoint path problem in their work on automated assembly of multiple fragmented JPEG images. With the total search space consisting of n fragments, they identify k vertex disjoint paths, where each vertex (representing a fragment) belongs to exactly one file's path. Each file then has its own disjoint path within the graph. A vertex initially assigned to one path might better suit another path. So during the carving process itself, these paths cannot be treated as strictly disjoint. This insight forms the basis for their `Enhanced Greedy Heuristic` algorithm [8], where path candidates are determined by weights assigned through pixel examination using Sum of Differences and Median Edge Detection. Memon and Pal developed several algorithms out of which the *Parallel Unique Path (PUP)* algorithm showed the most promising. The PUP algorithm starts with a set of headers and selects the best available cluster for each header based on pre-assigned weights. This creates a set of clusters, from which the best match is chosen and added to the corresponding file's path. This process repeats until all clusters are assigned, and thus all files are recovered. The PUP algorithm requires the calculation of all weights in advance. To reduce this computational costs, it was later modified to analyze adjacent clusters sequentially until detecting a fragmentation point [11]. A slightly different approach was developed by Cohen [2]. Although he also treated carving as an optimization problem, the validator, which he calls *discriminator*, plays a crucial role. The idea is that a disk image is read and preprocessed. In this stage headers are identified using header recognition. A file carver is constructed for each potential file, comprising two key components. A *mapping function generator* is responsible for creating mapping functions that associates a file's logical offsets with its corresponding location in the disk image. A *discriminator* (or *validator*) is used to determine the validity of the mapping function, by validating the correctness of the reconstructed file. Here, correctness refers to whether the file conforms to the expected structure of its type (e.g., a valid JPEG header, proper segment markers, and consistent encoding). Ideally it would not only detect the correctness of the entire file, but also report back where exactly the file became corrupted [2], making testing an iterative process. After all discontinuities are handled, the resulting map is saved, completing the carving of that file. Although certain assumptions were made regarding fragmentation to simplify the mapping function, this can be extended to cover Out-of-Order (OoO) fragmentation.

While other validation-focused approaches, such as hash-based carving [5], are valuable for identifying specific files within fragmented data, we excluded them from this comparative analysis. The focus of this study is on search strategies rather than specific validation methods.

When evaluating the effectiveness of file carving algorithms for Out-of-Order fragmentation, we observe a clear evolution. Earlier approaches such as the structure based carvers in the first generation, and simplified approaches like

BiFragment Gap Carving are limited by their assumptions on fragmentation and orderedness.

Current approaches have their advantages and disadvantages. More advanced techniques such as Cohen's discriminator and Memon and Pal's PUP algorithm are capable of handling OoO fragmentation. Although PUP's weight-based approach can handle OoO fragmentation, the cost of calculating weights between all possible cluster pairs is a limiting factor. Cohen's discriminator approach offers high probability of reconstruction correctness but requires multiple validation passes. Advanced classification during the collating phase can significantly reduce the search space, but requires more sophisticated preprocessing.

We hypothesize that a carving strategy can be most effective when combining these strategies: using preprocessing to reduce the search space, weight-based metrics for initial matching, and validation for verification.

3 Analysis of Fragmentation Patterns in the `WildFrag` dataset

Between October 2018 and January 2019, data from 220 laptops was collected as part of a study by Van der Meer et al. [14]. The data was preserved using privacy-conscious methods and stored in a database referred to as the `WildFrag` dataset. We only analysed that portion of the `WildFrag` dataset pertaining to (1) NTFS-formatted storage volumes with (2) a cluster size of 4096 bytes. The latter constraint is necessary as there are too few storage volumes with other cluster sizes to draw conclusions from. A total of 707 disks (out of `WildFrag`'s 733 disks) satisfy both requirements.

Table 2. Number of fragments of fragmented files.

# fragments	`WildFrag` # files	% of total	Garfinkel # files	% of total
2	953,149	56%	22,984	32%
3	309,813	18%	6,474	9%
4	145,973	9%	3,653	5%
5	86,390	5%		
6	51,770	3%		
7	24,153	1%		
8	16,743	1%	13,139	18%
9	11,909	1%		
10	9,083	1%		
≥11	88,305	5%	26,324	36%
Total	**1,692,288**		**72,574**	

3.1   Number of Fragments

Analysis of the `WildFrag` dataset shows that 4.4% of all potentially fragmented files are indeed fragmented, which is **lower than reported** in previous studies [4,9]. This coincides with the increase in average size of storage volumes, offering more free space. Since lack of free space correlates with fragmentation [4], this increase in storage space offers a partial explanation for the reduction of fragmentation.

Garfinkel demonstrated in 2007 that files with more than three fragments are rare [4]. While our analysis confirms that bi-fragmented and tri-fragmented files constitute a substantial portion of the dataset, we observed files with **three or four fragments at a significantly higher frequency** than reported by Garfinkel. Table 2 compares the number of fragments per fragmented file in the `WildFrag` dataset with that in Garfinkel's dataset.

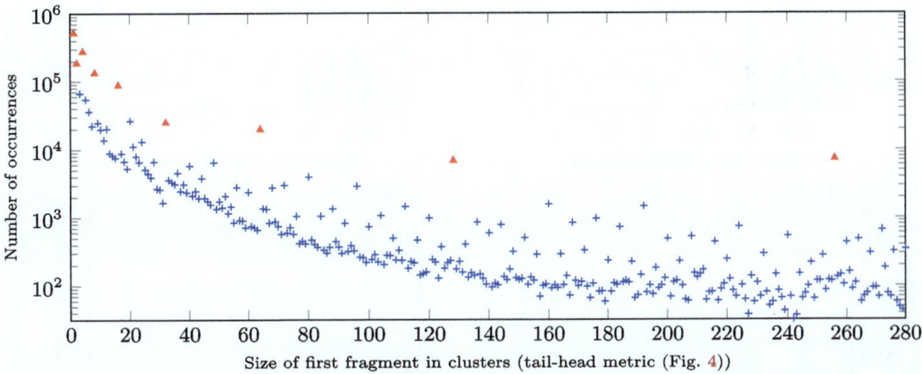

Fig. 1. Distribution of size of the first fragment of a file plotted on a y-axis with logarithmic scale. Peaks occur at sizes with powers of two, highlighted by red triangles. (Color figure online)

3.2   Initial and Relative Fragment Size

The most commonly observed size for the *initial* fragment among all fragmented files is a single cluster ($\sim$524,000 occurrences), followed by four clusters ($\sim$278,000), then two ($\sim$189,000), eight ($\sim$134,000) and 16 clusters ($\sim$88,000). Note that all these lengths are powers of two. While the distribution of initial fragment size quickly drops, we continue to find a significant higher incidence of lengths that are powers of two for the initial fragment length. These are depicted by red triangles in Fig. 1, which has a log scale for the fragment length.

This pattern of fragment lengths extends to subsequent fragments, suggesting that the tendency toward power-of-two sizes is a consistent feature across all fragments within a file. Analogous patterns have been observed in prior studies

[4,14]. These findings underscore a systematic organization in fragment alloca-
tion, potentially indicative of underlying mechanisms within the file system that
favour power-of-two allocations.

We also examined the ratio between the sizes of consecutive fragments. We
analysed ratios between successive fragments up to the fifth fragment. Figure 2
presents a graph plotting the ratio between consecutive fragments. For all considered ratios, we found that **in ∼75% of cases, the next fragment is as
large as or larger than the current fragment.** Related, we also found
distinct peaks appear at ratios of 0.5 and 1. The first means that the next fragment is exactly double the size of the current fragment, whereas the second ratio
occurs when both fragments have equal size.

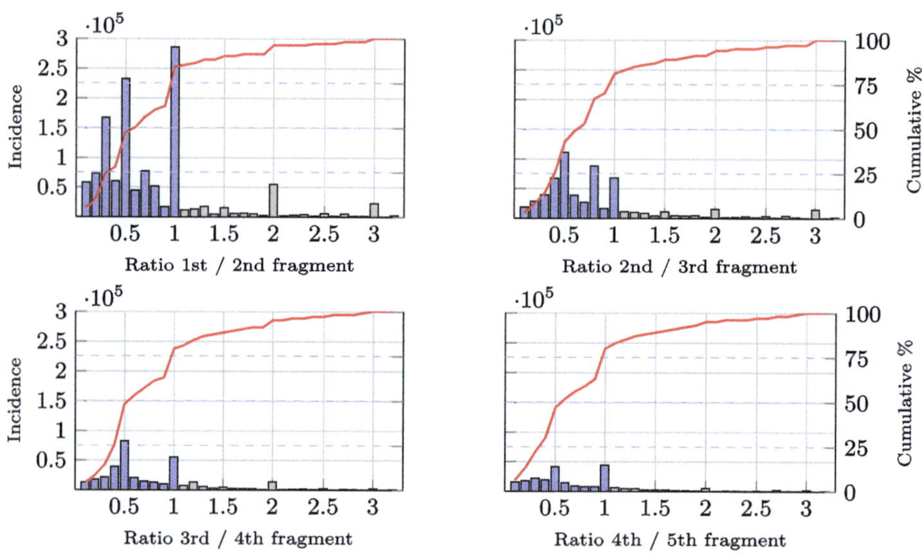

Fig. 2. Ratio of sizes between consecutive file fragments. Blue bars when the next
fragment is as large or larger, gray otherwise. The red lines show the cumulative distribution. (Color figure online)

3.3   Gap Sizes

The dataset exhibits a wide range of gap lengths between file fragments. Across
all file types, the shortest observed gap is one cluster, while the longest reaches
nearly 243 million clusters. Consistent with previous studies on bi-fragmented
files [14], spikes occur at **power-of-two intervals** in the gap sizes between
fragments for all fragmented files. These spikes are particularly pronounced up
to a gap size of 4096 clusters. For larger gap sizes, variance diminishes, likely due
to decreased data density at these higher gap sizes. In Fig. 3 the distribution of
small gap sizes is plotted, to illustrate this insight.

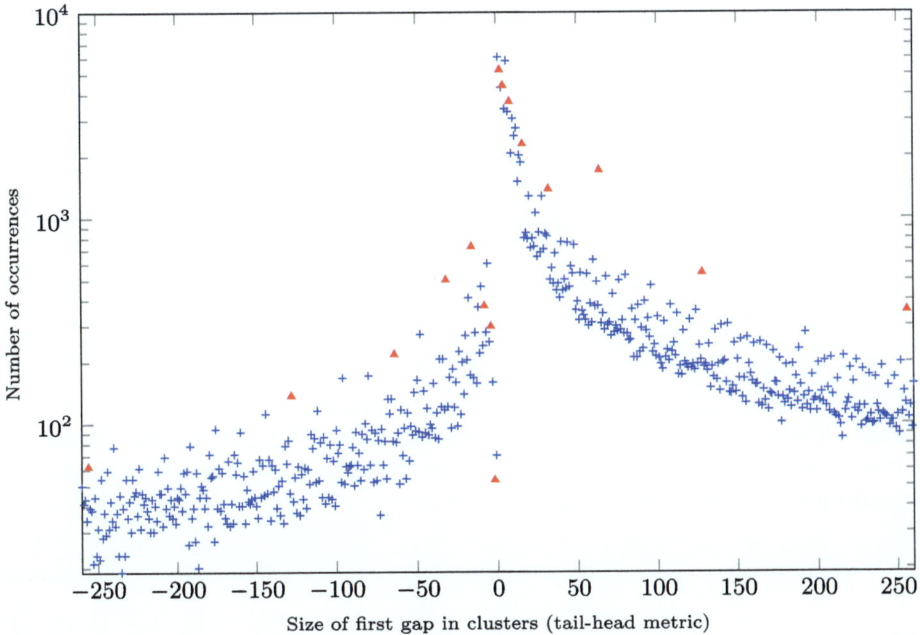

Fig. 3. Distribution of gap sizes up to 250 clusters. Peaks occur at sizes with powers of two, highlighted by red triangles. (Color figure online)

Gap size for Out-of-Order Fragments. There is only one measure that makes sense to define the gap size between two in-order fragments: the number of clusters between the tail of the first fragment and the head of the subsequent fragment (Fig. 4, right column). However, as discussed by Van der Meer et al. [14], there are different ways to define the gap size in case the fragments are out of order, depending on whether the length of the fragments is taken into consideration (Fig. 4, left column). For this paper, we use the `tail-head` metric, as it aligns best with the implementation of our carver.

The analysis of gap sizes across fragmented files reveals that **smaller gaps occur more frequently** than larger ones. Figure 5 shows the distribution of these gap sizes. Gaps containing between 1 and 40,000 clusters appear in 12% of the files, while reverse gaps—where out-of-order fragmentation is present—of the same size range appear in 9.75% of the files. For gap sizes between 40,000 and 80,000 clusters the occurrence decreases to 8.76% of the files. The occurrence of sizes beyond 360,000 clusters further declines to less than 3%.

The distribution of gap sizes follows a **normal distribution**, with a sharper decline in frequency for negative gap sizes compared to positive gap sizes. Within the range of gap sizes from -560,000 to 560,000, the standard deviation σ is 233,000 clusters for the first gap.

These observations provide a valuable insight for optimizing carving strategies. The likelihood of identifying successive clusters is higher in closer proximity

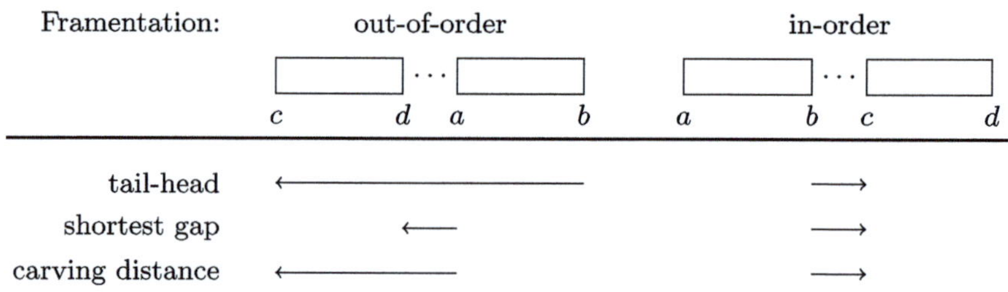

Fig. 4. Possible metrics for gap sizes of out-of-order fragmented files. Adapted from Van der Meer et al. [14].

compared to those further away. Consequently, in terms of assigning weights, candidate clusters situated nearer should be attributed higher weights. Moreover, if the location of a candidate cluster corresponds to a power-of-two value, the probability of identification increases further.

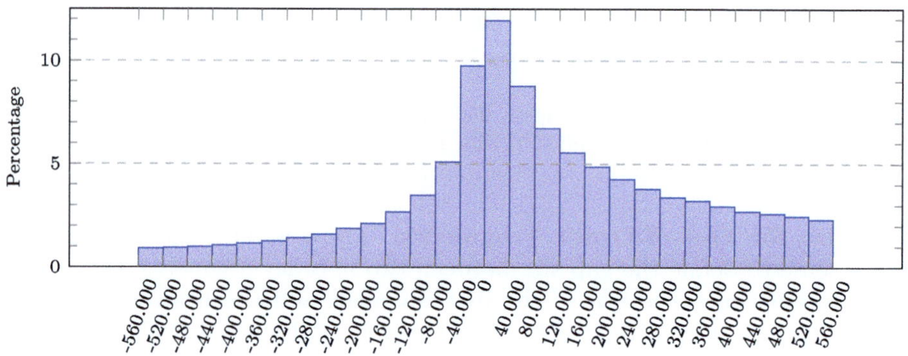

Fig. 5. Distribution of gap sizes for the first gap. The x-axis represents the number of clusters that spans the gap.

3.4   Fragmentation Patterns of .jpg files

Image files have received detailed attention in forensic literature. However, details on their fragmentation were only first reported by Van der Meer et al. [14]. In this work, we focus on JPEG files, more specifically, files with the extension .jpg. Van der Meer et al. found that .jpg files are more often fragmented than the average: $\sim 8.5\%$ instead of $\sim 4\%$. Moreover, .jpg files were more often fragmented out of order: $\sim 57\%$ instead of $\sim 46\%$. In short, the .jpg file **fragmentation pattern is more complex than average**. Thus, this poses a challenge for carving tools, depending on more specific characteristics of how such files are fragmented.

The dataset contains 26,776 fragmented `.jpg` files. The average file size of those files around 826 kilobytes. In Table 3 we show the distribution of number of fragments for fragmented `.jpg` files. Note that 43% of these files consists of only two fragments, while 93% consists of ten or less fragments.

Table 3. Number of fragments of `.jpg` files.

	# fragments	#files
2	11,422	43%
3	4,665	17%
4	2,837	11%
5	2,003	7%
6	1,199	4%
7	1,000	4%
8	817	3%
9	617	2%
10	428	2%
$\geq$11	1,788	7%
Total 26,776		

In-Order vs Out-of-Order. When a file consists of three or more fragments, the likelihood of it containing at least one out-of-order fragment exceeds 50% [14]. Notably, this effect is even stronger for `.jpg` files. Specifically, for `.jpg` files with three fragments, the likelihood rises to 64%.

Fragment and Gap Sizes. For fragmented sizes, in Sect. 3.2, we discussed that the distribution of fragment sizes shows distinct peaks at sizes that align with powers of two.

Figure 6 illustrates the distribution of initial fragment sizes for JPEG files, revealing a consistent pattern with other files. Fragment sizes exceeding 100 clusters are excluded from the plot due to their rarity in the dataset, with fewer than 10 instances observed. The mean fragment size for the first fragment is 35 clusters, with a standard deviation σ of 266 clusters, highlighting the variability in fragment lengths.

The pattern illustrated by Fig. 2 is also observed for JPEG files. The likelihood of the next fragment being the same size or larger than the current fragment is **notably higher for JPEG files**, ranging between 4 and nearly 6 times as likely, compared to approximately 3 times for all file types. Furthermore, the likelihood of the next fragment being larger than the current fragment is approximately 3 for JPEG files. This indicates a stronger tendency for sequential fragments in JPEG files to maintain or exceed the size of their predecessors.

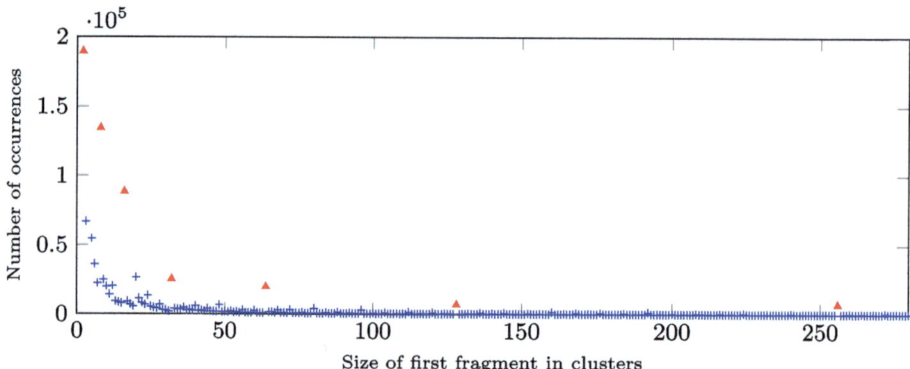

Fig. 6. Distribution of size of the first fragment of a `.jpg` file. To improve clarity, the peaks for size 1 (524.000) and size 4 (278.000) were excluded from this graph. Peaks occur at sizes with powers of two, highlighted by red triangles.

Table 4. Distribution of gap sizes in number of clusters for JPEG files.

Gap size	% of files
$-120,000$ to $-80,000$	2.4
$-80,000$ to $-40,000$	4.3
$-40,000$ to 0	15.7
1 to 40,000	31.8
40,000 to 80,000	8.0
80,000 to 120,000	5.4
120,000 to 160,000	3.6

The normal distribution for gap sizes, seen in Fig. 5, is also present for JPEG files. For JPEG files, gap sizes vary significantly, similar to the pattern observed in other file types. Within the corpus, gap sizes range up to 230 million clusters. However, almost 32% of all JPEG files have a gap size between 0 and 40,000 cluster, while almost 16% have a negative size up to -40,000 clusters. See Table 4 for the most common gap sizes, covering more than 70% of the files.

Within the range of gap sizes from -560,000 to 560,000, we found a smaller standard deviation σ than for all files. For JPEG files σ is approximately 175,000 clusters for the first gap.

In conclusion, **for JPEG files, the same insights observed in the overall dataset hold.** During the carving process, the validity of a candidate fragment is more probable when located in close proximity to the last validated fragment, particularly when the location aligns with a power-of-two value. Additionally, candidate fragments with sizes equal to or larger than the last validated fragment have an even higher probability of being valid.

4   A Carver Capable of Handling Out-of-Order Fragmentation

We design and implement an initial approach for a carver capable of recovering out-of-order fragmented files. For brevity, we will refer to this concept carver as 'OoO carver' or, simply, carver. We design the carver to recover as many files as possible, irrespective of a specific target file or file type, assuming that there is no metadata available. Note emark that this is (very) far from a realistic setting. For example, typically a file system structure with metadata on most files would be available. However, this change of perspective allows us to explore various considerations that otherwise would be swept under the table.

First, the carver makes an initial pass over the disk image to recover contiguous files and mark initial fragments as such. Next, it goes through the list of initial fragments and tries to complete each. There are two sets of design decisions to consider:

- in what order to process the initial fragments.
  This boils down to the recovery priority of each file type.
- the order in which to attempt recovery of the known first fragments.

Having decided, albeit theoretically, which file type to carve first, we can now determine which clusters to evaluate first when searching for the next fragment of a given partial file.

This decision is informed by the analysis conducted in Sect. 3, where we made several observations. We will exclude the observation regarding the fragment size favoring a power-of-two size because this information is not available as fragments are merged into larger candidate fragments. This leaves us with four key insights:

- The likelihood of out-of-order fragmentation reaches over 90% for files with six or more fragments (see Huijsmans and Kuijsten [6]).
- Gap sizes frequently occur at power-of-two intervals (see Fig. 3).
- Successive fragments are often of equal or greater in size compared to a current fragment (see Fig. 2).
- Gap distances follow a normal distribution, with smaller gaps being more prevalent (see Fig. 5).

4.1   Proof-of-Concept Implementation

We have developed a proof-of-concept implementation of the OoO carver, publicly available.[3] This obviously necessitated making the implicit weighing formulas of the file types and the remaining fragments explicit. For the latter, the weighing formula used gave 93.2% of candidate fragments lower weight than the correct one.

---

[3] https://git.cs.ou.nl/file-carving-optimization/file-carving-optimization.

5 Generating Suitable Disk Images for Testing File Carvers

The discovery of the prevalence of out-of-order fragmentation by Van der Meer et al. [14] has various consequences. One of these is that test sets for file carving should be updated to incorporate appropriate levels of fragmentation. However, as Van der Meer et al. found, specific fragmentation characteristics vary by file type. One way to approximate conditions as encountered in the wild is to instead create a generator which can generate disk images with specific characteristics. More specifically, the generator is to account for three variables pertaining to fragmentation – the *fragmentation pattern*. This pattern is denoted as (Fragmentation Percentage – Internal Fragmentation – Out-of-Orderness), where:

- **Fragmentation percentage:** the percentage of fragmented files
- **Internal fragmentation:** the percentage of clusters of a fragmented file after which a fragmentation point occurs (i.e., [14, def. 2])
- **Out-of-Orderness:** the percentage of fragmentation points where the logically next cluster is located earlier on disk

For example, a pattern of (09–14–34) denotes that 9% of files will be fragmented, that for each fragmented file, a fragmentation point will occur after 14% of its allocated clusters (i.e., the file is split into roughly 7 fragments), and that for 34% of the file's fragmentation points (i.e., 2 out of 7 fragments), the next fragment is found earlier on disk than the fragmentation point.

We design and implement[4] our disk image generator therefore as follows:

1. Read files from a specified directory.
2. Split a percentage of files into fragments, based on fragmentation percentage; for each file selected for fragmentation do:
   (a) Divide the file into n fragments, where n is determined by the amount of internal fragmentation specified. Fragment sizes are 'randomly' chosen as multiples of the cluster size.
   (b) Reorder the fragments in accordance with the desired out-of-orderness degree provided to the algorithm.
3. Write all fragments to a raw image using a weighted random selection approach.

For testing file carvers, it makes sense to test their performance without any fragmentation, as well as when facing various forms of fragmentation. Our test set generator is sufficiently versatile to accommodate a wide range of in-order as well as out-of-order fragmentation patterns, given a set of files to store in a disk image. For these files, we use the collection of JPEGs gathered by Van der Meer and Van den Bos [7]. Note that this introduces the unrealistic aspects that most files have roughly the same order of magnitude of size. This limitation allows us to ignore file size in generating disk images.

---

[4] Source code is available from
https://git.cs.ou.nl/file-carving-optimization/file-carving-optimization.

We let our tool generate 10 disk images for each of the following fragmentation patterns:

- No fragmentation: (0-0-0)
- Real World JPEG fragmentation [14, Table 3]: (09-14-34)
- Heavy in-order (only) fragmentation: (50-50-0)
- Heavy in-order and Out-of-Order fragmentation: (50-50-50)
- Extreme fragmentation: (99-99-99)

Generating 10 disk images per fragmentation pattern thus results in a test set of 50 disk images. We note that this set aims to offer a good way to test a carver's capability to handle fragmentation. Do note that the goal of these disk images is to stress-test file carvers; the generated disk images in no way resemble real world disk images.

5.1 Testing the Proof-of-Concept OoO Carver

We tested the proof-of-concept implementation of our OoO carver design. For each of the five fragmentation pattern discussed above, we generated 10 disk images. For each disk image, the OoO carver was successfully able to recover all files with no false positives (phantom files) and no false negatives (missed actual files). This shows that, in principle, OoO carving is possible.

However, whether this is feasible in practice remains an open question. Note that the disk images we generated for this test were never intended to be realistic. For practical reasons, we had to limit to very small disk images containing only .jpg files. In other words, a brute-force approach to file carving would have been feasible on these disk images. The success of the proof-of-concept should thus only be taken as indicating that the concept is viable, no more, but certainly also no less. A detailed analysis of the tests is available in the bachelor thesis of Huijsmans and Kuijsten [6].

6 Conclusions

In this work, we further analysed the WildFrag dataset to uncover data useful for guiding design decisions in out-of-order (OoO) carvers. Based on these findings, we presented the main design decisions involved in building an OoO carver, discussed the range of options available for each decision, and implemented a proof-of-concept carver that demonstrates the viability of this approach. Lastly, we addressed the lack of a comprehensive test set for fragmented disk images. More specifically, we designed and implemented a generator for creating disk images containing files fragmented according to desired fragmentation percentage, the number of fragments, and the 'out-of-orderness'. This generator enables controlled experimentation by producing test cases that reflect realistic or extreme fragmentation patterns. However, the resulting disk images are (by design) unrealistically small.

Although the generator enables generation of data that resembles fragmented files, there is a need for real-world reference sets of disk images against which file carvers can be tested, benchmarked and compared. Without such standardized datasets, it remains difficult to fully validate or fairly evaluate carving approaches across different tools and research efforts.

Several limitations remain when implementing and using OoO carvers. First, detailed file structures must be known for determining fragmentation points, and for most file formats, such structures are rarely available. Second, the current approach requires multiple passes over the entire data, which is very time consuming and therefore not always suitable for large-scale application (e.g., in criminal investigations on terabytes of data). Finally, the current work does not yet take into account partially missing or broken fragments that may occur due to disk space reuse, an important challenge for real-world carving scenarios. All in all, we have shown that out-of-order carving is feasible, but how to make efficient use of it in practical settings, such as recovering files in criminal investigations, remains an open question.

The discussion of relevance is also important when considering the future of file carving. On the one hand, carving remains highly relevant for data recovery applications, where fragmented files on disks must be reconstructed to salvage lost information. On the other hand, its significance in digital forensics is waning. Increasingly, user data resides in the cloud rather than on local storage devices, making traditional disk carving less central to investigations. Additionally, much raw data—such as that stored on smartphones—is encrypted and only accessible through the operating system. Legal distinctions between allocated and unallocated data, also limits the use of data recovered from unallocated disk space for evidential purposes. Finally, the growing prevalence of databases as primary storage systems further diminishes the role of traditional file carving in forensic analysis.

Acknowledgement. Sjouke Mauw was instrumental in the start of two of the authors academic careers (Hugo and Harm). In both cases, he acted as daily supervisor of their PhD project. Harm's interests led his career to exploring digital forensics. Sjouke's work on mCarve [3] served as Hugo's first encounter with this field. This eventually led to a PhD project on file recovery, co-supervised by Hugo. The contributions of that project serve as the foundation for the current paper.

Disclosure of interest. The authors have no competing interests to declare that are relevant to the content of this article.

References

1. Alherbawi, N., Shukur, Z., Sulaiman, R.: Systematic literature review on data carving in digital forensic. Procedia Technology **11**, 86–92 (2013). https://doi. org/10.1016/j.protcy.2013.12.165, https://www.sciencedirect.com/science/article/ pii/S2212017313003198, 4th International Conference on Electrical Engineering and Informatics, ICEEI 2013

2. Cohen, M.: Advanced carving techniques. Digit. Investig. **4**(3), 119–128 (2007). https://doi.org/10.1016/j.diin.2007.10.001
3. van Deursen, T., Mauw, S., Radomirović, S.: mCarve: Carving attributed dump sets. In: 20th USENIX Security Symposium (USENIX Security 11). USENIX Association, San Francisco, CA (Aug 2011). https://www.usenix.org/conference/usenix-security-11/mcarve-carving-attributed-dump-sets
4. Garfinkel, S.: Carving contiguous and fragmented files with fast object validation. Digital Invest. **4**, 2–12 (09 2007). https://doi.org/10.1016/j.diin.2007.06.017
5. Garfinkel, S.L., McCarrin, M.: Hash-based carving: Searching media for complete files and file fragments with sector hashing and hashdb. Digit. Investig. **14**, S95–S105 (2015). https://doi.org/10.1016/j.diin.2015.05.001, the Proceedings of the Fifteenth Annual DFRWS Conference
6. Huijsmans, N., Kuijsten, B.: Reconstructing files with out-of-order fragmentation (2025), bSc. thesis
7. van der Meer, V., van den Bos, J.: JPEG file fragmentation point detection using Huffman Code and Quantization Array Validation. In: Proceedings of the 16th International Conference on Availability, Reliability and Security. ARES '21, Association for Computing Machinery, New York, NY, USA (2021). https://doi.org/10.1145/3465481.3470061
8. Memon, N., Pal, A.: Automated reassembly of file fragmented images using greedy algorithms. IEEE Trans. Image Process. **15**(2), 385–393 (2006). https://doi.org/10.1109/TIP.2005.863054
9. Meyer, D.T., Bolosky, W.J.: A study of practical deduplication. ACM Trans. Storage **7**(4) (2012). https://doi.org/10.1145/2078861.2078864
10. Pal, A., Memon, N.: The evolution of file carving. Signal Process. Mag., IEEE **26**, 59 – 71 (04 2009). https://doi.org/10.1109/MSP.2008.931081
11. Pal, A., Sencar, T., Memon, N.: Detecting file fragmentation point using sequential hypothesis testing. Digital Invest. **5** (09 2008). https://doi.org/10.1016/j.diin.2008.05.015
12. Richard, G.G., Roussev, V.: Scalpel: A frugal, high performance file carver. In: Proceedings of the Digital Forensic Research Workshop (DFRWS) (2005)
13. Shanmugasundaram, K., Memon, N.D.: Automatic reassembly of document fragments via data compression. In: 2nd Digital Forensics Research Workshop, Syracuse (2002)
14. van der Meer, V., Jonker, H., van den Bos, J.: A contemporary investigation of NTFS file fragmentation. Forensic Sci. Int.: Digital Invest. **38**, 301125 (2021). https://doi.org/10.1016/j.fsidi.2021.301125

Encrypted and Signed File Transfer with PostGuard

Daniel Ostkamp$^{(\boxtimes)}$ and Bart Jacobs

Radboud Universiteit, Nijmegen, Netherlands
`{daniel.ostkamp,bart.jacobs}@ru.nl`

Abstract. File sharing is an important aspect of modern (business) communication. Sharing via email is often constrained by file size limits. To overcome such limitations, users often turn to external file transfer services like Dropbox's DocSend, WeTransfer, or SURFfilesender (in the academic world). File encryption typically requires choosing a password that must be exchanged out-of-band with recipients. As an alternative, Identity-Based Encryption (IBE) provides a more seamless solution, leveraging recipients' identities to eliminate the need for password sharing. This paper introduces PostGuard, a practical implementation of IBE for securely sharing large files. PostGuard integrates an identity wallet for authentication. The paper details PostGuard's cryptographic design and protocol, analyzes its confidentiality guarantees via attack trees, and proposes countermeasures for the potential attacks. Furthermore, PostGuard is compared with other file transfer services, with respect to general and security-related criteria. The scores of the different tools show considerable variation. This study bridges the gap between theoretical IBE research and practical secure file transfer implementations, contributing to the broader adoption of IBE-based solutions.

1 Introduction

People often need to share files online for work-related matters, such as presentations or large PDFs. As email is still the most used communication channel in business contexts, files are often shared via emails.[1] However, most email providers limit the size of attached files. Because of such limitations, people often use file transfer services, such as Dropbox DocSend [8], WeTransfer [32], or SURFfilesender [28]. These tools have in common that people can upload files to an external service via a web interface and provide the email address of the intended recipient(s), who, subsequently, receive an email with a download link. Most such tools claim to offer the option to encrypt files locally, at the sender's side, so that the server does not have access to the file content. However, as

---

Dedicated to Sjouke Mauw on the occasion of his 65th birthday.

[1] See the following article summarizing a study about email usage in business contexts: https://theamericangenius.com/email-remains-top-communication-tool-businesses/.

B. Fila et al. (Eds.): Sjouke Mauw Festschrift, LNCS 16365, pp. 122–140, 2026.
https://doi.org/10.1007/978-3-032-20684-8_8

files are encrypted with an *ad hoc* password, the sender still needs to use an out-of-band channel to share the password with possible multiple recipients.[2]

An alternative approach that avoids the need of explicitly exchanging passwords is Identity-Based Encryption (IBE). In 1984 Adi Shamir [24] introduced the concept of identity-based signatures (IBS). Building on Shamir's idea, Boneh and Franklin [1], and roughly at the same time, Cocks [6], presented the first IBE schemes. We observe that most IBE-related research focuses on the mathematical and cryptographic aspects (see for an overview presentation of Boneh [2]) or usability (such as Ruoti *et al.* [21] or Botros *et al.* [3]). There is less research on designing and analyzing actual software implementations using IBE and IBS, with regard to practical security. This paper addresses this imbalance and investigates the challenges in applications of identity wallets, in particular by analyzing the security of IBE and IBS for encrypted and signed file transfer, for a prototype system called PostGuard.[3] In particular, this paper looks at the file sending functionality of PostGuard, and its use of the identity wallet Yivi.[4] To analyze the security we use attack trees [16,23] to identify possible attacks. Based on the analysis, we can determine countermeasures to mitigate the risks of potential attacks. Moreover, we put PostGuard into perspective by comparing it with existing file transfer tools.

Within IBE, a trusted third party, the *Private Key Generator* (PKG), is responsible for key creation and distribution. The PKG creates a master key pair during initial setup of the system. Based on the master public key the sender can encrypt a message for (multiple) recipients based on their individual identities. Then, after a recipient successfully authenticates to the PKG, the PKG generates a personal private key and transfers it to the recipient. Finally, the recipient can decrypt the message with the received own private key.

Our main contributions are as follows: (1) Explaining PostGuard's cryptographic design decisions and protocol; (2) Analyzing PostGuard's current security, focusing on confidentiality aspects, via an elementary attack tree. Based on our analysis, we identify several countermeasures to mitigate potential vulnerabilities; (3) Comparing PostGuard with other file transfer services, such as the previously mentioned ones, based on general and security-related criteria; Implicitly, this paper demonstrates that identity wallets form a useful building block that can boost new IBE-applications.

The paper is organized as follows. In Sect. 2 we provide background information on IBS and IBE, on Yivi (the identity wallet app used in PostGuard), and on our method to analyze PostGuard's security via attack trees. In Sect. 3 we describe PostGuard by providing sequence charts [18] to visualize the file trans-

---

[2] Email is not advised as emails are not end-to-end encrypted by default.

[3] PostGuards source code is publicly available under https://github.com/encryption4all.

[4] Postguard's file transfer is operational and accessible on the website https://postguard.eu/#filesharing. It is maintained by the PostGuard team at Radboud University in Nijmegen (within the iHub research center) together with the company Procolix (see https://procolix.com). PostGuard also offers encryption and signing of emails but that service is less developed and is not discussed here.

fer protocol, and cryptographic design decisions. In section Sect. 4 we conduct a threat analysis. In Sect. 5 we compare some popular file sending services. Finally, Sect. 6 contains several concluding remarks.

One of the authors (BJ) of the current paper is roughly from the same generation as Sjouke Mauw and has had a similar scientific trajectory: a PhD in theoretical computer science and a follow-up in computer security. Sjouke is among the first people who developed security as an academic discipline within computer science, building on existing mathematical research in cryptography. His contributions to shaping this community, first in The Netherlands and then in Luxemburg, are highly appreciated. Sjouke's early work in process algebra [19] formed a good preparation for subsequent work in security protocols and their verification [7]. This paper builds in particular on his highly successful work on graphical methods for security, in particular message sequence charts [17,18] and attack trees [15,16].

2   Background

This section introduces Identity Based Encryption (IBE) and Identity Based Signature (IBS) in more detail by providing algorithms used and typical session examples. Additionally, it explains what the biggest risks are with identity-based systems in general, how the Yivi identity wallet works, and finally, how the rest of this paper proceeds.

2.1   Identity Based Encryption (IBE) and Identity Based Signature (IBS)

With IBE and IBS it is possible to reduce, from a user's perspective, encryption and signing to authentication [3]. This is relevant, since many (ordinary) users do not understand what encryption (or signing) entails. The simple mental model that can be used with IBE is: only the intended recipient can read your message. For this reason, recipients must prove who they are - technically to obtain the required private key from the PKG. A dual story applies to signing where senders have to prove who they are. This makes it easier for users to create a fitting mental model: for encryption 'I need to prove that I am the right person to get access to the message' and for signing 'I need to prove that I am the person that actually sent the message'.

At a more technical level, in the literature, a common definition of IBE consists of four (polynomial-time) algorithms [1,6].

$Setup() \rightarrow$ (MSK, MPK). Upon starting the private key generator (PKG) for the first time, this step generates a key pair: a master public key (MPK) and master private/secret key (MSK), where the latter needs to be kept secret.

$Encrypt(M, ID, MPK) \rightarrow CT$. This step encrypts a message M (which may be a session key for symmetric encryption) using the master public key MPK and a uniquely identifying set of attributes ID of the receiver.

$KeyGen(\mathsf{ID}, \mathrm{MSK}) \to \mathrm{USK}_{\mathsf{ID}}$. In this step the private key generator (PKG) generates the asymmetric user private/secret key $\mathrm{USK}_{\mathsf{ID}}$ after the receiver has authenticated successfully to the PKG, involving the receiver's identity ID.

$Decrypt(\mathrm{CT}, \mathrm{USK}_{\mathsf{ID}}) \to \mathrm{M}$. Via the step the receiver decrypts the ciphertext CT with her own key $\mathrm{USK}_{\mathsf{ID}}$, producing the plaintext M.

An IBE scheme is correct if decrypting an encrypted messages returns the original, that is, if $Decrypt(Encrypt(\mathrm{M}, \mathsf{ID}, \mathrm{MPK}), KeyGen(\mathsf{ID}, \mathrm{MSK})) = \mathrm{M}$.

We turn to IBS: in the literature a common definition of IBS consists of four (polynomial-time) algorithms [24].

$Setup() \to (\mathrm{MSK}, \mathrm{MPK})$. As in the first step described above.

$KeyGen(\mathsf{ID}, \mathrm{MSK}) \to \mathrm{USK}_{\mathsf{ID}}$. After authentication of the signer to the PKG with (self-selected) identity ID, the PKG generates the associated asymmetric private/secret key USK_{ID} for the signer.

$Sign(\mathrm{M}, USK_{\mathsf{ID}}) \to \sigma$. In this step the signer/sender signs a message M using her own key USK_{ID}, resulting in a signature σ.

$Verify(\sigma, \mathrm{MPK}, \mathrm{M}, \mathsf{ID}) \to \{\mathrm{yes}, \mathrm{no}\}$. The receiver verifies that the signature σ checks out (corresponding to outcome yes), or not (no), by using the master public key MPK and the signer's identity ID, used for creating the signature.

An IBS scheme is correct if only for the right triple $\mathrm{MPK}, \mathrm{M}, \mathsf{ID}$ the verification of the signature succeeds, as in: $Verify(Sign(\mathrm{M}, KeyGen(\mathsf{ID}, \mathrm{MSK})), \mathrm{MPK}, \mathrm{M}, \mathsf{ID}) = true$.

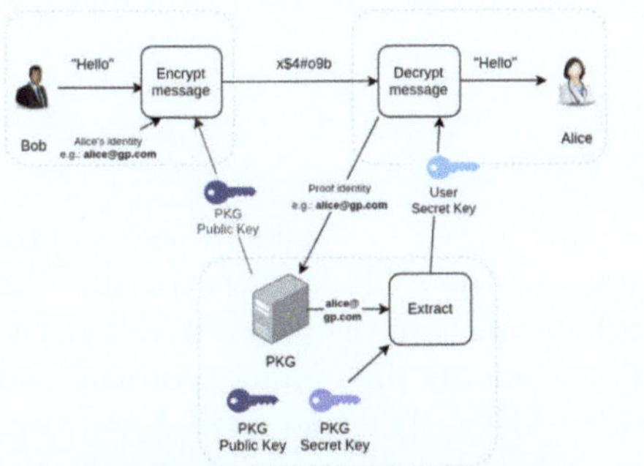

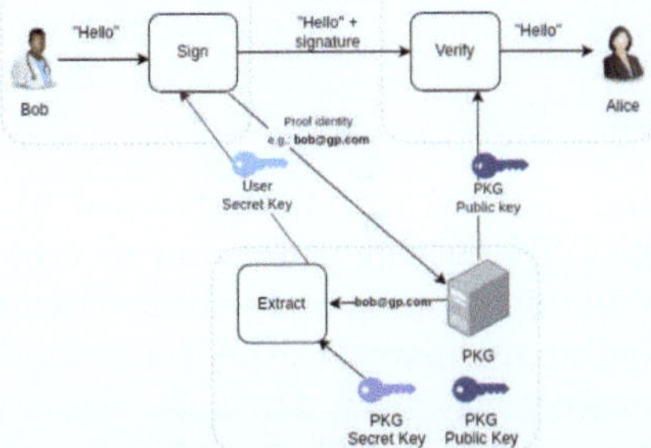

(a) Identity-Based Encryption (b) Identity-Based Signature

Fig. 1. Exchanges for identity-based encryption and signing in a general setting.

Figure 1a shows a typical IBE session. Bob wishes to encrypt a message for GP Alice, for instance, to send her a detailed description of his sickness symptoms. First, Bob (actually: his mail or web client) derives a public key based on the master public key for the attributes of Alice that he selects (*e.g.* her medical registration number). Subsequently, with this derived public key, Bob can encrypt the sensitive message for Alice and send it to her. Before Alice can decrypt, she must authenticate to the PKG by proving that she possesses the identity attributes that Bob used for the encryption key. After the PKG verifies her proof of identity, it produces Alice's private key (USK), based on the master private key and her disclosed identity attributes (such as her registration number) and transfers the USK to Alice via a secure communication channel, for instance via a SSL connection between PKG and client. Finally, with her USK, Alice can decrypt the message—provided that Alice has indeed disclosed the right attributes, as selected by Bob.

Figure 1b shows a typical IBS session. Here, Bob chooses a set of attributes of himself that he wishes to use to sign the message, for instance, a registration request. Then, he proves that he possesses this set of attributes towards the PKG to receive the USK, for actually signing the message. Finally, Alice can verify the signature based on the MPK and identity of the sender.

An important issue with any identity-based system for encryption and signing is that all users need to rely on the PKG as trusted third party. This results in two main challenges. First, imagine the PKG behaves untrustworthy or is compromised by adversaries. Compromise in this context means that adversaries possess, or somehow control the usage of, the master key pair, in particular if they control the generation of user secret keys. This is a nightmare scenario, since those adversaries can then compute private keys USKs for all identities. Consequently, they can decrypt all ciphertexts that they can find and also create signatures for any identity. Thus, the PKG is a single point of attack to break confidentiality and integrity. Second, the PKG is also a single point of failure for availability. If the PKG becomes unavailable, no recipient can receive a USK needed to sign or decrypt.[5] For both challenges mitigations exist, via multiple PKGs, see our analysis in Sect. 4.

2.2　Yivi

Yivi[6] is used within PostGuard to authenticate users: the senders to generate the USK for signatures and receivers to generate the USK for decryption. Yivi is an open-source and privacy-friendly identity wallet, developed initially at the Radboud University, the Netherlands. Yivi implements the Idemix protocol, and consequently uses *Attribute-based credentials* (ABCs) [22] and *Zero-Knowledge Proofs* (ZKPs) [10]. An ABC is a container, consisting of one or more personal attributes, including the user's secret key, digitally signed by the issuer of the ABC. An attribute describes a part of an identity of a person—Fig. 2 shows some of Alice's partial identities. A partial identity is a subset of all the attributes that belong to Alice. An attribute can be identifying in a certain context, such as one's full name or social security number, or not identifying, such as a birth date or postal code.

---

[5] However, an implementation could cache keys for some time to not have to contact the PKG every time a user wants to decrypt data.

[6] See the official documentation here: https://yivi.app/docs/what-is-irma/.

Zero-knowledge proofs (ZKPs) are a cryptographic technique to prove that a value satisfies a certain property without revealing the actual value.[7] Yivi uses ZKPs for the following two scenarios: (1) when a user discloses attributes of an attribute-based credential (ABC), she hides the other attributes and can still convince the verifier to possess a valid issuer signature for the whole ABC; (2) when the issuer creates a signature over attributes in an ABC, including the user's secret key, the actual value of the key remains secret.

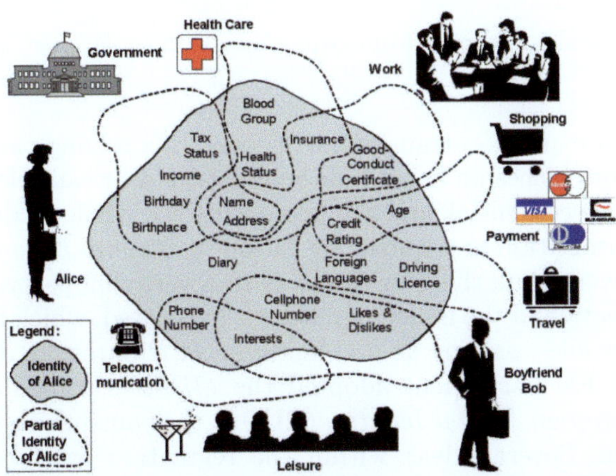

Fig. 2. Alice's partial identities (from Clauß and Köhntopp [5])

Figure 3 shows the two main Yivi processes for issuance and disclosure of credentials. First, in an issuance session, after a user authenticates successfully, an organization or institution generates one or more credentials, signs them with its private key, and transfers the credential(s) to the user's Yivi wallet app. Second, in a disclosure session, a verifying party asks a user to prove that she has ownership of one or more attributes. After a user selects the matching attributes in one ore more credentials in the Yivi app and agrees to their disclosure, the selected attributes are directly sent to the verifier, which in turn can check the validity of the disclosed attributes by using the public key of the issuer. Because the two processes are independent, an issuer never learns when a user uses the credentials in a disclosure session, as the disclosed attributes are sent directly from the user to the verifying party. This is different from currently employed systems such as Facebook Connect, as Facebook learns which attributes from which users are disclosed to which verifying party.

Yivi can be considered privacy-friendly, as ABCs and ZKPs are secure and privacy-enhancing technologies due to several reasons. First, when credentials are issued, they are associated with the user's secret key, which is stored partly on the user's device and partly on a central "keyshare server". Consequently,

---

[7] See Yivis ZKPs documentation: https://docs.yivi.app/zkp/.

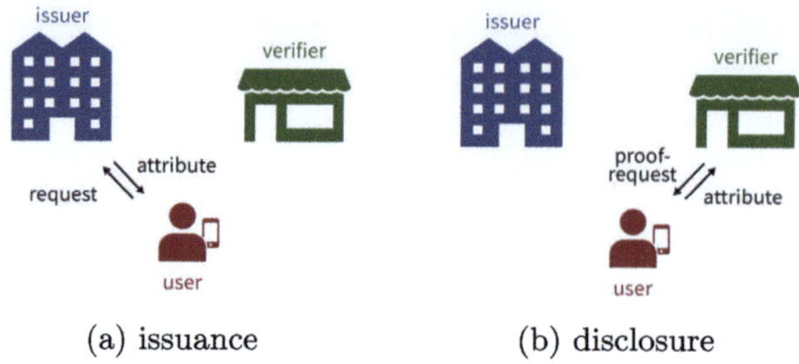

Fig. 3. Yivi sessions (copied from https://www.yivi.app/en/more_about_yivi/).

ABCs are authentic and non-transferable. Second, if a relying party provides the user with different choices on how to authenticate, a user can selectively disclose attributes from one credential, and not necessarily the whole credential. This can lead to data minimization as required by Europe's *General Data Protection Regulation.* Third, every time the user discloses to a verifying party, due to ZKP, a unique transformation of the issuer signature is generated, which makes disclosed credentials unlinkable—as long as no identifying attributes are disclosed.

Recently, the EU parliament adopted the *eIDAS 2.0* regulation [29], also referred to as *European Digital Identity* (EUDI), that amends the existing (first) eIDAS regulation. Several ideas within the regulation overlap with those of Yivi, such as ABCs, selective disclosure, and data minimization. This EUDI provides EU-citizens with (free) identity wallets. EU member states need to ensure that *personal identification data* (PID) can be issued to such wallet, including attributes commonly stored in passports.[8]

2.3   Threat Modeling via Attack Trees

For analyzing the security of PostGuard we use attack trees [16,23]. An attack tree is a visual tool to outline possible attacks to breach one or more security properties of a system. Countermeasures can be added to such trees. Attack trees are easy to set up, extensible and understandable. Moreover, they come with tool support—we use the *ADTool 2*, created by Gadyatskaya *et al.* [11].

Figure 4 shows a simple example of an attack tree to open a safe. Three attacks are identified: use a lock-picker, cut open the safe, or learn the combination (combo). Learning the combo can then be achieved by either getting the combination from a target, who knows it, or by finding the combination written somewhere (or guessing it by luck).

---

[8] See   https://eu-digital-identity-wallet.github.io/eudi-doc-architecture-and-referen ce-framework/1.4.0/annexes/annex-3/annex-3.01-pid-rulebook/\#232-overview.

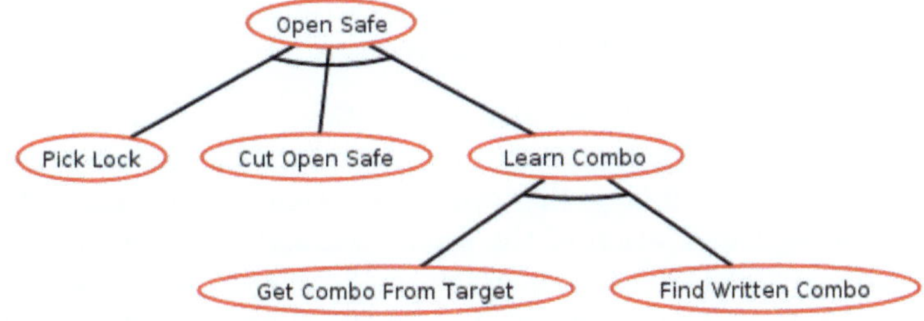

Fig. 4. Example attack tree to open a safe box.

3 PostGuard's System Design

This section elaborates on the system design of PostGuard. It starts by explaining the most important cryptographic design decisions. Then, it describes the PostGuard file transfer protocol with the different actors and their interactions. We use a sequence chart [18] to visualize the protocol.

3.1 Cryptographic Design Decisions

IBE and IBS schemes used. The current protocol uses a CCA-secure variant [31, p. 41] of the scheme CGW15 [4, p. 6] for encryption. The scheme is built on top of the BLS12-381 pairing-friendly curves. Those curves reach close to 128-bit security levels, see [33] for details.

For signing, the current protocol uses concatenated Schnorr signatures [12]. They are simple to implement and efficient. We instantiated our hash functions with SHAKE128 and SHA3, respectively. We chose SHAKE128 for performance reasons and for its second preimage resistance of 128 bits—enough to protect against forgeries.

Hybrid Encryption. Instead of encrypting the file(s) via IBE, we use an hybrid encryption approach for efficiency. Hence, we employ an identity-based key encapsulation mechanism (KEM) to generate a symmetric session key. The KEM is probabilistic, and thus, this session key is different every time. Subsequently, the session key is used to encrypt the file(s) via AES-256 [20].

We implemented a multi-recipient identity-based key encapsulation mechanism (mIBKEM). The idea is that mIBKEM can be used to encapsulate the same shared secret for multiple recipients, which saves re-encrypting the file(s). Two additional algorithms are needed for mIBKEM.

$Encaps(\mathsf{MPK}, \mathsf{IDs}) \rightarrow (\mathrm{CT}, \mathrm{K})$. This step encapsulates a single session key for all receivers IDs, and returns the encrypted session key CT together with the session key K itself. Consequently, on the sender side the files are encrypted once, for all recipients, with the same session key K.

Decaps(CT, *USK*) → K. This step decapsulates the encrypted session key CT with the private/secret key *USK* of the receiver.

Streaming. With regular authenticated encryption, a decrypting user has to decrypt all data before verifying the authenticity of the data. This is impractical for PostGuard file-sharing if large files are shared. Hence, the current PostGuard protocol uses an implementation of the *online authenticated encryption* scheme designed by Hoang *et al.* [13]. Consequently, smaller chunks of data are encrypted and signed by PostGuard while simultaneously uploading already encrypted and signed chunks. This mechanism allows authenticity verification before the download of the whole file.

Sign-then-Encrypt. PostGuard uses a *Sign-then-Encrypt* composition to hide possible sensitive data that the sender used to sign. First, a signature is set on the data that is to be transferred. The data and signature are then encrypted using the hybrid encryption approach, as explained above. This signature is used to sign the data with potentially sensitive attributes of the sender. The attributes should only be visible to the recipients specified by the sender in the encryption policy after decryption. Also, the attributes used for signing are sent along with the signature and data as those are needed to verify the signature by the recipient's client. Furthermore, the header is signed separately by the sender, which in case of file sharing uses the sender's email address as only attribute. This email address is information that will be seen by recipients anyway. The goal of the separate header signature is to provide authenticity on data that the recipient requires to further decrypt: the header specifies which credentials the recipient must present to receive the *USK*.

Use Yivi's mutual authentication. Yivi offers the feature of registering a relying party (RP) as a "trusted verifier", leading to mutual authentication. This means that both the user and the RP are authenticated. To use mutual authentication within Yivi the domain of the RP is added, after proper checks by the organization behind Yivi, to the official Yivi scheme together with a logo of the RP. Those checks include verifying the name of the RP, the RP domain name, and the logo, so that users can trust how these parties present themselves as verifiers in the Yivi app. Then, when users see a disclosure request within Yivi, they see the official name and logo of the RP. Hence, they can trust that they disclose data to the intended RP.

The currently running PostGuard prototype is registered as such a trusted verifier within Yivi. Consequently, before users disclose data to the PKG, they see the PostGuard logo and domain name.

3.2   PostGuard File Share Protocol

The sequence chart in Fig. 5 shows the different actors and interactions between them in a PostGuard file-sharing session. To keep the diagram simple, we depict the signing operation for the data and omit the separate signature on the header. Additionally, we do not include details of the streaming algorithm, but just assume that first the files are encrypted and uploaded, respectively downloaded and decrypted. Fore details about signing and streaming, see the previous Subsect. 3.1.

Before explaining the interactions between actors, we first describe the different actors themselves. The sender represents both the actual user wishing to send one or more files to one or more recipients and the user's PostGuard file sharing web client. Similarly, the recipient represents both the actual user receiving and decrypting the encrypted files and their web client. The central private key generator (PKG) offers an API making the Yivi session management accessible only to the file storage. In the current setup, the Yivi authentication service runs on the same server as the PKG. The file storage exposes a separate API for file upload and download. Both PKG and this file storage are hosted at different hosting parties, where the PKG sees the keys (and identities), but not the files, and the file storage sees the (encrypted) files, but not the keys. When these parties collude, the system breaks.

On the sending side, initially, the PostGuard web client requests the master public key for encryption (MPK_e) from the PKG. Then, in the web interface, the sender adds one identity per recipient by choosing a set of attributes and the values that the recipients need to prove to be in possession of with their Yivi app (IDs_r). Subsequently, the sender adds the file(s) she wants to share with the recipients. To receive the user secret key for signing (USK_s) the file(s), the sender discloses her chosen signing identity ID_s with Yivi to the PKG. The sender then signs the files with the resulting USK_s before encryption. The client generates the shared secret K via the *Encaps* function, which is then used to encrypt the file(s). Subsequently, the client uploads the metadata required for decryption and the encrypted file(s) to the file storage. The file storage, in turn, informs the sender about the upload status. Once uploading is finished, the file storage sends emails to the recipients to inform them that files are available for download.

After receiving such an email, the recipient can click on a link that opens the session within the PostGuard file sharing web client. To verify the signature later, the client needs to receive the master public key for signing, MPK_s, from the PKG. Also, the client automatically downloads the metadata, including the ID_s, ID_r and ciphertext, with the encrypted shared secret CT. After disclosing the requested identity via Yivi to the PKG, the recipient receives the private key USK_r for decryption. Subsequently, the recipient decrypts CT via the *Decaps* function to reveal the session key K. After receiving the payload, the client locally decrypts the files with K, symmetrically. Moreover, the verification of the signature happens locally in the receiver's client automatically by using the MPK_s and ID_s, telling whether the signature provided is valid.

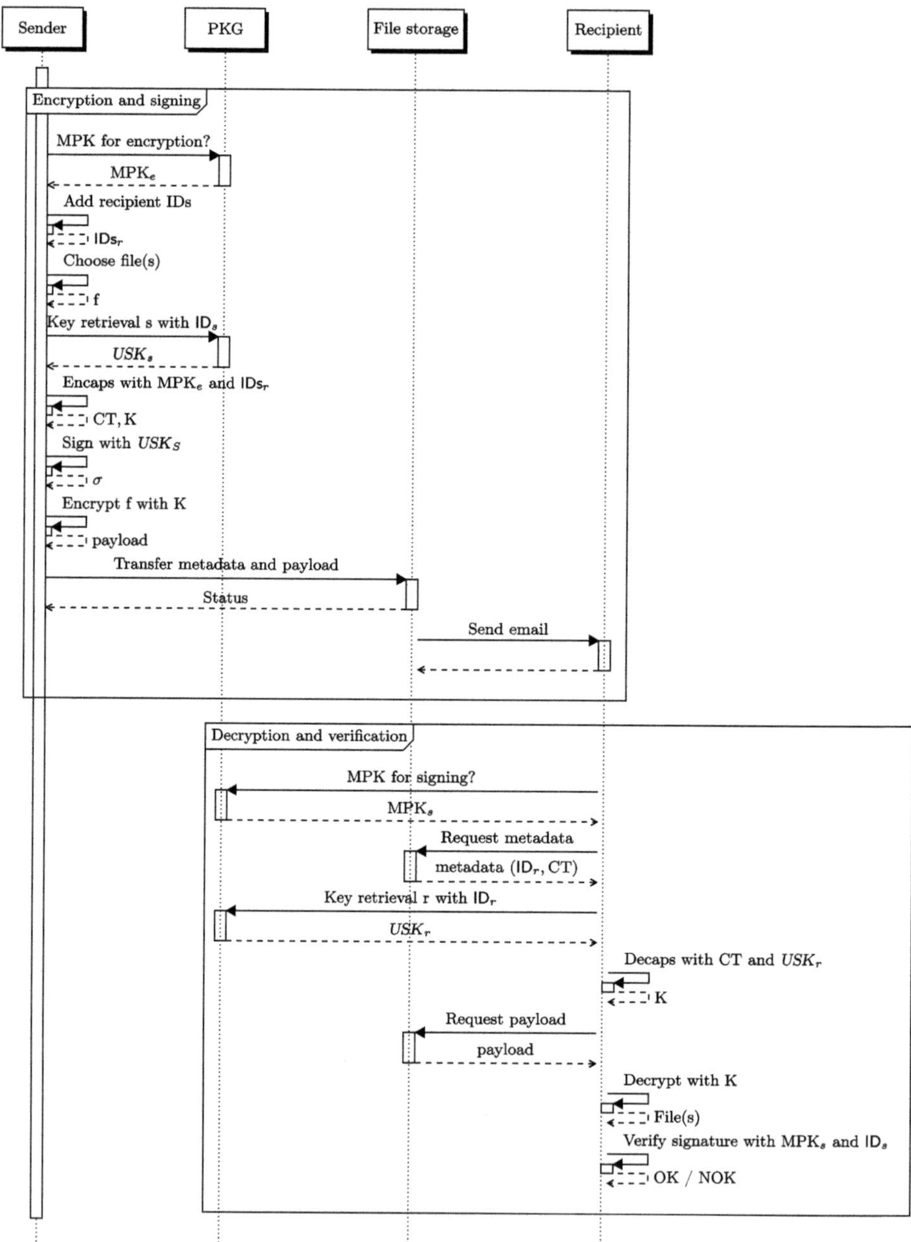

Fig. 5. The PostGuard file transfer protocol visualized via a sequence chart. The solid arrows show a request, the dashed arrows a response. Actors can execute a function within their own boundary whereby both arrows point back to that same actor.

4   Threat Analysis

The goal of this section is to conduct an informal, high-level threat analysis to identify threats that may emerge in the current PostGuard file-sharing system. Specifically, we focus on the threat of *information disclosure* [25] to limit the scope of our analysis. Information disclosure means that an unauthorized entity is able to access protected resources, as in PostGuard file-sharing case would be the content of the transferred files. We use a simple attack tree to identify possible points of attack in the system, see Subsect. 2.3 for an explanation. After identifying the points of attack, we describe some potential countermeasures.

In implementing PostGuard, we adopted a security-by-design methodology. This approach resulted in two crucial countermeasures: the separation of the Private Key Generator (PKG) and file storage across distinct hosting providers, and the integration of Yivi's mutual authentication protocol (between sender/receiver and PKG). These design decisions, detailed in Sect. 3, demonstrate how proactive security considerations mitigate possible vulnerabilities as we identify related threats in what follows.

We make several assumptions to limit the scope of our analysis: (1) HTTP communication channels between actors are always encrypted, via a recent version of TLS; (2) the credentials stored within the Yivi app belong to the person owning the phone; (3) the Yivi protocols are secure, and are not attacked. Consequently, we do not include any replay or identity theft attacks.

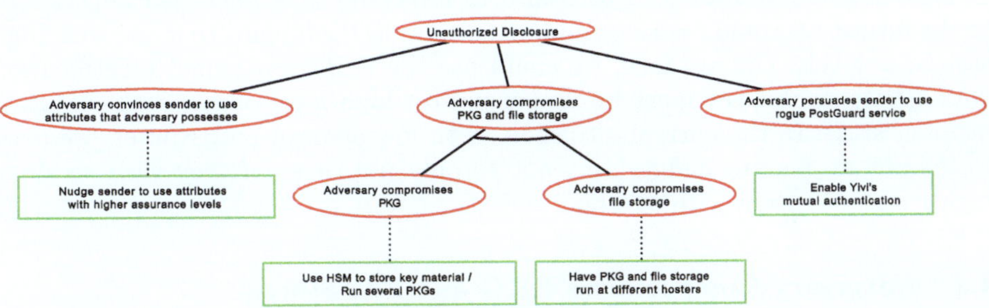

Fig. 6. Attack tree for the goal of unauthorized disclosure of information.

Figure 6 shows our attack tree. Its goal is to gain access to the protected data by an unauthorized adversary, leading to unauthorized disclosure of file contents. It does not matter whether this access happens on the sender or recipient side. We add countermeasures to the attack tree, indicated by the green rectangles. In what follows we briefly describe the identified attacks and possible countermeasures.

4.1 The Adversary Convinces the Sender to Use Attributes of the Adversary for Encryption

In this potential attack, initially, the adversary communicates with the sender before the sender uses PostGuard. Then, the adversary somehow convinces the sender to use the adversary's attributes to encrypt the files with, for instance, a mail address owned by the adversary that seems to be genuine and related to the intended recipient. After receiving the PostGuard mail, the adversary can decrypt the encrypted files that were not intended for her.

Currently within PostGuard, the sender can choose from the following set of attributes the recipients needs to prove to possess: mobile number, full name and date of birth. Yivi offers more attributes, but this list is hardcoded into PostGuard, for simplicity. However, the current PostGuard system does not provide details about the levels of assurance for each attribute. Levels of assurance (LoA) means the certainty with which a claim (= attribute) to a particular identity can be trusted to actually be from the right individual. Within the EU, three levels are distinguished: low, medium, and high.[9] For instance, on the one hand, everyone can create an email address and get it into Yivi via a simple challenge-message sent to that address. Hence, an email address has a low level of assurance. On the other hand, the identity card issued by the Dutch government has a high level of assurance, as citizens requesting this identity card need to prove who they are with a high level of certainty. For instance, they are required to show up in person at the municipality with a valid ID card.

Countermeasure 1: Restrict PostGuard to attributes with high assurance levels. In the future, we could restrict (Yivi) attributes in PostGuard to those with high assurance levels. For instance, we could use the EUDI's personal identification data (PID) as this set must be issued with a high level of assurance by each member state. In the current situation, with low assurance attributes, we need to investigate how to nudge users not to only use those, if they wish to share highly sensitive data with others.

4.2 Adversary Compromises PKG and File Storage

In this potential attack, the adversary compromises both the private key generator (PKG) and the file storage, to get access to the master private/secret key (MSK) and to the encrypted files. With the MSK the adversary can compute the user secret key (USK) needed to decrypt the encrypted files, retrieved from the file storage. PostGuard does not guarantee forward secrecy, hence, also previously encrypted files could be decrypted.

Countermeasure 2: Have PKG and file storage run at different hosters. To prevent that an adversary only needs to compromise one hosting party, in the current PostGuard setup we have both the PKG and file storage hosted at different hosting parties. If the compromise of the file storage leads to a denial of service,

---

[9] See the eIDAS Levels of Assurance website: https://ec.europa.eu/digital-building-blocks/sites/display/DIGITAL/eIDAS+Levels+of+Assurance.

i.e. by deleting all encrypted content, users can just resend their files again. We strongly recommend that everyone who wishes to run their own PostGuard service to apply the same measure.

Countermeasure 3: Run multiple PKGs. There are several approaches to have multiple PKGs participate in a system rather than relying on a single PKG. Smetters and Durfee [26] propose to distribute the trust per domain, such that an institution or organization can run its own PKG. Information about how to reach this PKG can then be communicated via DNS. However, still, only one PKG would be used per session, and if that PKG is compromised, an adversary could compute all possible USKs.

Another approach is to use a multi-authority ciphertext-policy attribute-based encryption scheme, as proposed by Venema *et al.* [30]. Here, several PKGs work together to compute a valid user secret key (USK). Then, an adversary would need to compromise all participating PKGs to be able to compute a valid USK. However, as far as we know, there are no practical implementations of this architecture.

Countermeasure 4: Use an HSM to store key material. Currently, within Post-Guard the master key pair is generated by the PKG and stored in the server's own file system. Thus, an adversary who can access this file system as root can also access the master secret key (MSK). A *hardware security module* (HSM) [27] could be used to make it harder for adversaries to access such key material. One of features of a HSM is that it allows only authenticated and authorized applications to access key material. However, HSMs are costly and hard to maintain.

4.3 Adversary Persuades the Sender to Use a Rogue PostGuard Service Run by the Adversary

In this scenario, the adversary sets up her own PostGuard service. This is easy as PostGuard is completely open-source. The adversary then changes the software (locally) such that the file(s) to be transferred are not encrypted at all, while telling the user that they are. The adversary persuades the sender to use that rogue PostGuard instance and share the files with the intended recipients. However, as the files are not encrypted, the adversary can also access the content.

Countermeasure 5: Enable Yivi's mutual authentication. To mitigate this risk, PostGuard currently uses Yivi's mutual authentication protocol, the so-called "trusted verifier", which we explained in our design decisions (see Sect. 3). If now a user is requested to disclose to a rogue PKG run by the adversary, she would see an unauthenticated verifier, and hence, could refrain from disclosing the identity data.

4.4 Elaboration

As visible in our attack tree in Fig. 6 we can identify five countermeasures to mitigate the risk of possible attacks succeeding. As already stated before, two countermeasures are already covered in the current PostGuard implementation: the separation of Private Key Generator (PKG) and file storage, and Yivi's mutual authentication protocol. Most focus for PostGuard in the future should be to protect the key material by distributing it over several PKGs and store the keys in an HSM. Moreover, senders can be better informed about the assurances of attributes chosen.

5   Comparison

This section compares PostGuard file sharing with four other deployed file sharing services: Dropbox Doc Send, WeTransfer, Proton drive file sharing, and SURFfilesender.

The following six properties are used in the comparison.

Open source. Releasing software as open source can lead to an increase in security as bad code is visible to anyone and anyone can contribute in fixing identified flaws [14]. Moreover, such transparancy can contribute to user trust.

E2EE. End-to-end encryption (E2EE) ensures that no one but the sender and intended recipients see the plain files, as the files are encrypted and decrypted on the end-user devices. Then, intermediate service providers cannot see the content of the files.

E2EE free of charge. Indicates whether E2EE is free of charge or users need to pay to use for it as additional service.

Download confirmation. After a recipient downloads the files, the sender is informed about the download.

Sender authentication. This property indicates whether senders are authenticated such that recipients can trust that the transferred files are indeed originating from the claimed sender.

Signatures. This means that a sender can generate a signature over the content of the files such that (source) authenticity and (message) integrity is guaranteed, *i.e.* that the claimed sender is the actual sender and that the content has not been tampered with.

Table 1 shows how the five services that we consider score on these six properties. In the following paragraphs we briefly explain the scores per property. Finally, we provide observations on our comparison.

Table 1. Comparing five different file sender systems based on six properties.

	PostGuard	Dropbox DocSend	WeTransfer	Proton file sharing	SURFfilesender
Open source	yes	no	partly	partly	yes
E2EE	yes (weaker)	yes	no	yes	yes
E2EE free of charge	yes	no	-	yes	yes
Download confirmation	no	yes	yes	yes	yes
Sender authentication	yes	yes	yes	yes	yes
Signatures	yes	yes	no	no	no

We observe that all five services score differently. Only PostGuard and SURF-filesender run with a complete open source software stack, WeTransfer and Proton file sharing have their clients open sourced. PostGuard is the only service which uses identity-based cryptography. However, using this cryptography leads to a weaker form of E2EE, because a rogue PKG can also generate all valid user secret keys. The four other services rely on protecting files via passwords, that need to be shared with recipients via a separate, possible insecure, private channel. WeTransfer is the only platform that does not support end-to-end encryption as users can change passwords on the server on already protected file(s). Dropbox DocSend is the only service that offers E2EE with a paid subscription. PostGuard is the only tool not providing download confirmation. All services offer some kind of sender authentication, whereby three different types are used: (1) identity-based signature in case of PostGuard; (2) accounts linked to an email address, with optional MFA, in case of Dropbox DocSend, WeTransfer, and Proton file sharing; (3) authentication via a single-sign-on (via SURFConext for SURFfilesender). PostGuard and DropBox DocSend[10] are tools that support the creation of signatures to guarantee integrity.

6   Conclusion

This paper explores the design and implementation of the PostGuard file sharing system, based on Identity-Based Encryption (IBE) and Identity-Based Signatures (IBS) for secure file transfer (Sect. 3). This work bridges the gap between theoretical IBE research and real-world applications by providing an informal, brief security analysis for the PostGuard system. The analysis uses a simple attack tree to identify possible attacks to break confidentiality of the system (Sect. 4). To mitigate those attacks, several countermeasures are described, two of which are already implemented within the current PostGuard system.

In Sect. 5 PostGuard file sharing is compared to four other popular file transfer tools. This shows that no other tools use identity-based cryptography, but most provide free E2EE by having the sender specify a password. Also, all tools have some kind of sender authentication, by either using a single sign on or creating a user account bound to an email address. PostGuard thus sets a new standard for hardened file share based on advanced cryptography.

Future work could explore extending PostGuard file sharing with distributed key management, to avoid one centralized private key generator. Additionally, one could provide threat analysis for other aspects than confidentiality, such as integrity and availability. Also, one can explore whether PostGuard could become an official "Qualified Electronic Registered Delivery Service", as defined under the eIDAS 1 regulation [9]. Finally, another topic to further explore is a systematic security analysis of the PostGuard file sharing protocol through formal verification methods.

---

[10] See https://help.docsend.com/hc/en-us/articles/360015518794-Create-signable-documents-with-eSignature for details about their eSignature solution.

Acknowledgements. We wish to thank Leon Botros for documenting cryptographic details and for helping to create the sequence chart in Fig. 5. Furthermore, we thank NWO for funding the Encryption4All project within which the PostGuard system was designed and built.

Disclosure of Interests. The authors have no competing interests to declare that are relevant to the content of this article.

References

1. Boneh, D., Franklin, M.: Identity-Based Encryption from the Weil Pairing. In: Kilian, J. (ed.) CRYPTO 2001. LNCS, vol. 2139, pp. 213–229. Springer, Heidelberg (2001). https://doi.org/10.1007/3-540-44647-8_13
2. Boneh, D.: An overview of identity based encryption. https://csrc.nist.gov/csrc/media/Presentations/2023/stppa5-ibe/images-media/20230209-stppa5-Dan-Boneh--IBE.pdf (2023)
3. Botros, L., Brandon, M., Jacobs, B., Ostkamp, D., Schraffenberger, H., Venema, M.: Postguard: towards easy and secure email communication. In: Extended Abstracts of the 2023 CHI Conference on Human Factors in Computing Systems, pp. 1–6 (2023). https://doi.org/10.1145/3544549.3585622
4. Chen, J., Gay, R., Wee, H.: Improved dual system abe in prime-order groups via predicate encodings. In: Oswald, E., Fischlin, M. (eds.) EUROCRYPT 2015. LNCS, vol. 9057, pp. 595–624. Springer, Heidelberg (2015). https://doi.org/10.1007/978-3-662-46803-6_20
5. Clauß, S., Köhntopp, M.: Identity management and its support of multilateral security. Comput. Netw. **37**(2), 205–219 (2001). https://doi.org/10.1016/S1389-1286(01)00217-1
6. Cocks, C.: An identity based encryption scheme based on quadratic residues. In: Honary, B. (ed.) Cryptography and Coding 2001. LNCS, vol. 2260, pp. 360–363. Springer, Heidelberg (2001). https://doi.org/10.1007/3-540-45325-3_32
7. Cremers, C., Mauw, S.: Operational semantics and verification of security protocols. Information Security and Cryptography, Springer Berlin, Heidelberg (2012). https://doi.org/10.1007/978-3-540-78636-8
8. Dropbox: Dropbox Docsend. https://www.docsend.com/how-it-works/ (2024). Accessed 11 Nov 2024
9. European Parliament, Council of the European Union: Regulation (EU) No 910/2014 of the European Parliament and of the Council of 23 July 2014 on electronic identification and trust services for electronic transactions (Jul 2014). https://eur-lex.europa.eu/legal-content/EN/TXT/?uri=CELEX:32014R0910, articles 43-44 specifically address Qualified Electronic Registered Delivery Services (QERDS)
10. Fiege, U., Fiat, A., Shamir, A.: Zero knowledge proofs of identity. In: Proceedings of the Nineteenth Annual ACM Symposium on Theory of Computing, pp. 210–217 (1987). https://doi.org/10.1145/28395.2841
11. Gadyatskaya, O., Jhawar, R., Kordy, P., Lounis, K., Mauw, S., Trujillo-Rasua, R.: Attack trees for practical security assessment: ranking of attack scenarios with ADTool 2.0. In: Agha, G., Van Houdt, B. (eds.) QEST 2016. LNCS, vol. 9826, pp. 159–162. Springer, Cham (2016). https://doi.org/10.1007/978-3-319-43425-4_10

12. Galindo, D., Garcia, F.D.: A Schnorr-like lightweight identity-based signature scheme. In: Preneel, B. (ed.) AFRICACRYPT 2009. LNCS, vol. 5580, pp. 135–148. Springer, Heidelberg (2009). https://doi.org/10.1007/978-3-642-02384-2_9

13. Hoang, V.T., Reyhanitabar, R., Rogaway, P., Vizár, D.: Online authenticated-encryption and its nonce-reuse misuse-resistance. In: Gennaro, R., Robshaw, M. (eds.) CRYPTO 2015. LNCS, vol. 9215, pp. 493–517. Springer, Heidelberg (2015). https://doi.org/10.1007/978-3-662-47989-6_24

14. Hoepman, J., Jacobs, B.: Increased security through open source. it may seem counterintuitive, but going "open" all the way offers the most security. Communications of the Association for Computing Machinery **50** (2007). https://doi.org/10.1145/1188913.1188921

15. Kordy, B., Mauw, S., Radomirović, S., Schweitzer, P.: Foundations of Attack–Defense Trees. In: Degano, P., Etalle, S., Guttman, J. (eds.) FAST 2010. LNCS, vol. 6561, pp. 80–95. Springer, Heidelberg (2011). https://doi.org/10.1007/978-3-642-19751-2_6

16. Mauw, S., Oostdijk, M.: Foundations of attack trees. In: Won, D.H., Kim, S. (eds.) ICISC 2005. LNCS, vol. 3935, pp. 186–198. Springer, Heidelberg (2006). https://doi.org/10.1007/11734727_17

17. Mauw, S., Reniers, M.: An algebraic semantics of basic message sequence charts. Comput. J. **37**(4), 269–277 (1994). https://doi.org/10.1093/comjnl/37.4.269

18. Mauw, S., Reniers, M.: High-level message sequence charts. In: SDL'97: Time for Testing, pp. 291–306. Elsevier Science, Amsterdam (1997). https://doi.org/10.1016/B978-044482816-3/50020-4

19. Mauw, S., Veltink, G.: A process specification formalism. Fund. Inform. **13**(2), 85–139 (1990). https://doi.org/10.3233/FI-1990-13202

20. Andriani, R., Wijayanti, S.E., Wibowo, F.W.: Comparision of aes 128, 192 and 256 bit algorithm for encryption and description file. In: 2018 3rd International Conference on Information Technology, Information System and Electrical Engineering (ICITISEE), pp. 120–124. IEEE (2018). https://doi.org/10.1109/ICITISEE.2018.8720983

21. Ruoti, S., Andersen, J., Hendershot, T., Zappala, D., Seamons, K.: Private Webmail 2.0: Simple and Easy-to-Use Secure Email. In: Proceedings of the 29th Annual Symposium on User Interface Software and Technology, pp. 461–472. UIST '16, ACM (2016). https://doi.org/10.1145/2984511.2984580

22. Sabouri, A., Rannenberg, K.: ABC4Trust: protecting privacy in identity management by bringing privacy-ABCs into real-life. In: Camenisch, J., Fischer-Hübner, S., Hansen, M. (eds.) Privacy and Identity 2014. IAICT, vol. 457, pp. 3–16. Springer, Cham (2015). https://doi.org/10.1007/978-3-319-18621-4_1

23. Schneier, B.: Academic: Attack trees—schneier on security (1999). https://www.schneier.com/academic/archives/1999/12/attack_trees.html

24. Shamir, A.: Identity-based cryptosystems and signature schemes. In: Blakley, G.R., Chaum, D. (eds.) CRYPTO 1984. LNCS, vol. 196, pp. 47–53. Springer, Heidelberg (1985). https://doi.org/10.1007/3-540-39568-7_5

25. Shirey, R.: Internet security glossary, version 2. Tech. rep. (2007). https://doi.org/10.17487/RFC4949

26. Smetters, D.K., Durfee, G.: Domain-Based Administration of Identity-Based Cryptosystems for Secure Email and IPSEC. In: 12th USENIX Security Symposium (USENIX Security 03) p. 15 (2003)

27. Sommerhalder, M.: Hardware security module. Trends in Data Protection and Encryption Technologies, pp. 83–87 (2023). https://doi.org/10.1007/978-3-031-33386-6

28. SURF: SURFfilesender. https://www.surf.nl/en/services/surffilesender (2024). Accessed 11 Nov 2024
29. The European Parliament and Council: Regulation (EU) 2024/1183 of the European Parliament and of the Council of 11 April 2024 amending Regulation (EU) No 910/2014 as regards establishing the European Digital Identity Framework (2024). https://eur-lex.europa.eu/eli/reg/2024/1183/oj/eng
30. Venema, M., Alpár, G., Hoepman, J.: Systematizing Core Properties of Pairing-Based Attribute-Based Encryption to Uncover Remaining Challenges in Enforcing Access Control in Practice. Designs, Codes and Cryptography p. 57 (2023). https://doi.org/10.1007/s10623-022-01093-5
31. Venema, M., Botros, L.: Efficient and generic transformations for chosen-ciphertext secure predicate encryption. Cryptology ePrint Archive, Paper 2022/1436 (2022). https://eprint.iacr.org/2022/1436
32. WeTransfer: WeTransfer | Send Large Files Fast. https://wetransfer.com/. Accessed 11 Nov 2024
33. ZKcrypto: Bls12 381 curve security. https://github.com/zkcrypto/bls12_381?tab=readme-ov-file#curve-security (2024). Accessed 02 01 2025

Deciding Impossible Futures

Maurice Laveaux[iD] and Tim A.C. Willemse[(✉)][iD]

Eindhoven University of Technology, Eindhoven, The Netherlands
`{m.laveaux,t.a.c.willemse}@tue.nl`

Abstract. Stepwise refinement is crucial in software development, but typical refinement relations like *stable failures refinement* and *failures-divergences refinement* have drawbacks in how they deal with divergences. Mauw and Voorhoeve's *impossible futures* preorder has more pleasing properties, yet lacks a practical verification algorithm. This paper presents a novel algorithm for checking *impossible futures* refinement, enhanced by antichains and further optimisations.

1 Introduction

Stepwise refinement is a fundamental principle in software development, enabling the transformation of high-level specifications into detailed implementations. This approach is prevalent in Formal Methods; in particular, the concept underlies the design methodology proposed by the process algebra CSP by Hoare [5,12]. It is also the basis of commercial Model-Driven Engineering approaches such as Dezyne [15], which typically generate provably correct executable code from high-level specifications.

Various refinement relations have been proposed and studied. In the context of the process algebra CSP, *stable failures refinement* [2,12] and *failures-divergences refinement* [8,12] are commonly employed. However, these preorders have some drawbacks when dealing with divergences (infinite sequences of unobservable actions). In particular, *stable failures* refinement may fail to detect harmful divergences in implementations. *Failures-divergences* refinement, on the other hand, can disqualify implementations due to divergences that are mere modelling artefacts.

In 2001, Mauw and Voorhoeve [18] proposed the *impossible futures* refinement relation, a missing link in the lattice of Van Glabbeek [16]. Compared to the aforementioned preorders, the *impossible futures* refinement relation handles divergences in a potentially more meaningful manner. While the theoretical aspects of this preorder have been thoroughly studied, a practical algorithm that allows to verify whether an implementation is indeed an *impossible futures* refinement of a specification has been lacking.

In this paper, we address exactly this gap, describing a series of algorithmic developments, beginning with a naive algorithm, for deciding the *impossible futures* refinement. We then demonstrate how to incorporate *antichains* in the naive algorithm. In [8], antichains were shown to speed-up checking *weak*

B. Fila et al. (Eds.): Sjouke Mauw Festschrift, LNCS 16365, pp. 141–159, 2026.
https://doi.org/10.1007/978-3-032-20684-8_9

trace inclusion and *stable-failures refinement*, but as we show in Sect. 5, naively adding antichains to the *impossible futures* refinement checking algorithm does not lead to a performant algorithm. We therefore introduce three optimisations, which, together yield the required performance improvements, allowing *impossible futures* refinement checking of systems of reasonable size. The contributions of this paper aim to bridge the gap between the theoretical appeal of *impossible futures* and its practical application.

Outline. In Sect. 2, we introduce the notion of labelled transition systems, and define the notions of weak trace inclusion and weak impossible futures inclusion on transition systems. We describe a naive algorithm for checking weak impossible futures inclusion in Sect. 3, and in Sect. 4 we show how antichains can be used to effectively improve the performance of the naive algorithm. We finish with a section illustrating the performance gains of our optimised algorithm over the naive algorithm in Sect. 5. We wrap up with closing remarks in Sect. 6.

Dedication. This paper was written especially for the 65th birthday of Sjouke Mauw. In his career, Sjouke has consistently strived to realise seemingly impossible futures (among others by literally defining the notion), setting an example for many others. The second author is one of those inspired by him; he is indebted to Sjouke for the many pleasant adventures, both academically and recreationally, not just during his journey as a PhD candidate, but even to this day.

2   Preliminaries

In this section the preliminaries of labelled transition systems and the notion of weak trace inclusion and weak impossible futures inclusion of [18] are introduced.

2.1   Labelled Transition Systems

For the remainder of this paper, we fix a finite set Act of actions. We furthermore presuppose a special constant τ, not part of Act, which we use to model *internal* activity. We let Act_τ denote the set $Act \cup \{\tau\}$.

Definition 1. *A labelled transition system over Act_τ is a tuple $\mathcal{L} = (S, \iota, \rightarrow)$ where S is a set of states; $\iota \in S$ is the initial state and $\rightarrow \subseteq S \times Act_\tau \times S$ is the transition relation.*

Henceforward, we assume an arbitrary LTS $\mathcal{L} = (S, \iota, \rightarrow)$ over Act_τ, and adopt the following notational conventions and notions. States are typically indicated by letters s, t, u; sets of states are indicated by U, V, and a, b denote arbitrary actions. A transition $(s, a, t) \in \rightarrow$ is typically denoted by $s \xrightarrow{a} t$. The LTS $\mathcal{L}$ is said to be deterministic iff for all $s, t, u \in S$ and all $a \in Act_\tau$ for which $s \xrightarrow{a} t$ and $s \xrightarrow{a} u$, we have $t = u$.

A finite sequence of actions is denoted by $a_0 a_1 \cdots a_{n-1}$ where $a_i \in Act_\tau$ for all $i < n$, and ϵ denotes the empty sequence of actions. The sets Act^* and

Act^*_τ denote the set of all finite sequences of actions ranging over Act and Act_τ, respectively. The transition relation of an LTS is lifted to sequences of actions $\sigma \in Act^*_\tau$ as follows: $s \xrightarrow{\epsilon} t$ holds iff $s = t$, and $s \xrightarrow{\sigma a} t$ holds iff there is a state u such that $s \xrightarrow{\sigma} u$ and $u \xrightarrow{a} t$. Furthermore, the *weak transition* relation $\Longrightarrow \subseteq S \times Act \times S$ is defined as follows: $s \xRightarrow{a} t$ holds iff there are some u, u' such that $s\,(\xrightarrow{\tau})^*\,u$, $u \xrightarrow{a} u'$ and $u'\,(\xrightarrow{\tau})^*\,t$. The weak transition relation is generalised to sequences of actions $\rho \in Act^*$ in the obvious way.

Definition 2. *The set* $\mathsf{TR}(s)$ *of traces starting in state* s, *the set* $\mathsf{WT}(s)$ *of weak traces starting in state* s *and the set* $\mathsf{IF}(s)$ *of weak impossible futures starting in state* s *are defined as follows:*

- $\mathsf{TR}(s) = \{\sigma \in Act^*_\tau \mid \exists t \in S : s \xrightarrow{\sigma} t\}$,
- $\mathsf{WT}(s) = \{\rho \in Act^* \mid \exists t \in S : s \xRightarrow{\rho} t\}$,
- $\mathsf{IF}(s) = \{(\rho, X) \in Act^* \times 2^{Act^*} \mid \exists t \in S : s \xRightarrow{\rho} t \wedge X \cap \mathsf{WT}(t) = \emptyset\}$.

The set of traces of $\mathcal{L}$ is given by $\mathsf{TR}(\iota)$, the weak traces of $\mathcal{L}$ is given by $\mathsf{WT}(\iota)$, and the set of weak impossible futures of $\mathcal{L}$ is given by $\mathsf{IF}(\iota)$. We define two preorders on LTSs, *viz.*, *weak trace inclusion* and the *weak impossible futures* preorder. The latter was first studied in [18] by Voorhoeve and Mauw.

Definition 3. *Let* $\mathcal{L}_1 = (S_1, \iota_1, \rightarrow_1)$ *and* $\mathcal{L}_2 = (S_2, \iota_2, \rightarrow_2)$ *be arbitrary LTSs. We write:*

- $s_1 \sqsubseteq_{\mathsf{wt}} s_2$ *if and only if* $\mathsf{WT}(s_1) \subseteq \mathsf{WT}(s_2)$;
- $s_1 \sqsubseteq_{\mathsf{if}} s_2$ *if and only if* $\mathsf{IF}(s_1) \subseteq \mathsf{IF}(s_2)$.

Let $\mathcal{L}_1 \sqsubseteq_{\mathsf{wt}} \mathcal{L}_2$ *denote* $\iota_1 \sqsubseteq_{\mathsf{wt}} \iota_2$; $\mathcal{L}_1 \sqsubseteq_{\mathsf{if}} \mathcal{L}_2$ *denotes* $\iota_1 \sqsubseteq_{\mathsf{if}} \iota_2$.

Observe that $s_1 \sqsubseteq_{\mathsf{if}} s_2$ implies $s_1 \sqsubseteq_{\mathsf{wt}} s_2$; this follows immediately from the fact that for any state s, we have $\rho \in \mathsf{WT}(s)$ iff $(\rho, \emptyset) \in \mathsf{IF}(s)$. The reverse does not hold true, as illustrated by the example below.

Example 1. The job ad for a university professor position at a certain university is accompanied by the transition system depicted on the left, characterising all tasks and secondary benefits of working at the university, which prominently includes a vibrant, swinging dance scene. Years later and closer to retirement, the appointed professor proposes the transition system depicted on the right would be a better characterisation, with teaching often preempting dancing in the past, but no longer in the future.

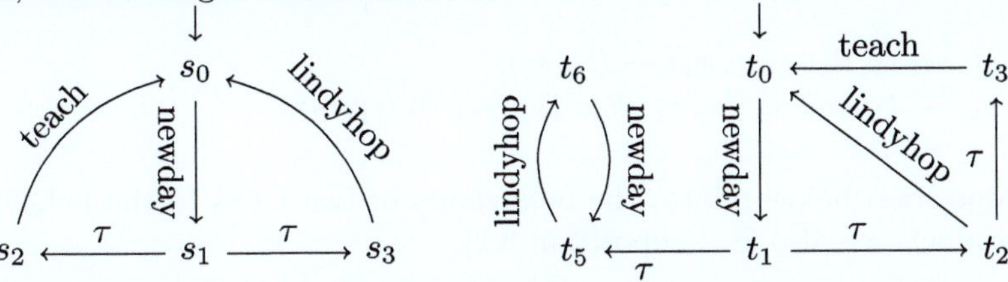

Observe that s_0 and t_0 are weak trace equivalent: both $s_0 \sqsubseteq_{\mathsf{wt}} t_0$ and $t_0 \sqsubseteq_{\mathsf{wt}} s_0$ hold true. However, $t_0 \sqsubseteq_{\mathsf{if}} s_0$ fails to hold true: the weak impossible future (newday, {lindyhop newday teach}) belongs to $\mathsf{IF}(t_0)$ but not to $\mathsf{IF}(s_0)$.   □

3 Towards Deciding Weak Impossible Futures

Deciding whether $\mathcal{L}_1 \sqsubseteq_{\text{if}} \mathcal{L}_2$ requires reasoning about the set of weak impossible futures of $\mathcal{L}_1$ and $\mathcal{L}_2$. Note that the set of weak impossible futures of any given LTS is generally of infinite size, so a simple enumerative strategy cannot work. We draw inspiration from [8,12] and employ a normalisation procedure for deciding weak trace inclusion between two LTSs. The normal form of an LTS is obtained using a more-or-less standard subset construction, typically used when determinising a transition system, and leads to a deterministic LTS without τ-labelled transitions.

Definition 4. *The normalisation of* $\mathcal{L} = (S, \iota, \to)$*, denoted* $\mathsf{norm}(\mathcal{L})$*, is the LTS* $(S', \iota', \to')$*, where* $S' = 2^S$*,* $\iota' = \{s \in S \mid \iota \overset{\epsilon}{\Longrightarrow} s\}$ *and* $\to'$ *is defined as follows:* $U \overset{a}{\to}' V$ *if and only if* $V = \{t \in S \mid \exists s \in U : s \overset{a}{\Longrightarrow} t\}$ *for all sets of states* $U, V \subseteq S$ *and actions* $a \in Act$.

Observe that $\emptyset$ is a state in a normalised LTS. The three lemmas stated below relate the set of weak traces of $\mathcal{L}$ to the set of traces of $\mathsf{norm}(\mathcal{L})$; see also [8, Lemmas 3.4, 3.5 and 3.6].

Lemma 1. *Let* $\mathcal{L} = (S, \iota, \to)$ *and* $\mathsf{norm}(\mathcal{L}) = (S', \iota', \to')$*. For all* $\rho \in Act^*$ *and states* $U \in S'$ *such that* $\iota' \overset{\rho}{\to}' U$*, it holds that* $\iota \overset{\rho}{\Longrightarrow} s$ *for all* $s \in U$.

Lemma 2. *Let* $\mathcal{L} = (S, \iota, \to)$ *and* $\mathsf{norm}(\mathcal{L}) = (S', \iota', \to')$*. For all* $\rho \in Act^*$ *and for all states* $s \in S$ *such that* $\iota \overset{\rho}{\Longrightarrow} s$*, there is a state* $U \in S'$ *such that* $s \in U$ *and* $\iota' \overset{\rho}{\to}' U$.

Lemma 3. *Let* $\mathcal{L} = (S, \iota, \to)$ *and* $\mathsf{norm}(\mathcal{L}) = (S', \iota', \to')$*. For all* $\rho \in Act^*$ *it holds that* $\rho \notin \mathsf{WT}(\mathcal{L})$ *if and only if* $\iota' \overset{\rho}{\to}' \emptyset$.

The normalisation of an LTS can be combined with another LTS to obtain a one-sided product. Such a one-sided product allows for deciding weak trace inclusion.

Definition 5. *Let* $\mathcal{L}_1 = (S_1, \iota_1, \to_1)$ *and* $\mathcal{L}_2 = (S_2, \iota_2, \to_2)$*. The* one-sided product *of* $\mathcal{L}_1$ *and* $\mathcal{L}_2$*, denoted by* $\mathcal{L}_1 \ltimes \mathcal{L}_2$*, is an LTS* $(S, \iota, \to)$ *where* $S = S_1 \times S_2$ *and* $\iota = (\iota_1, \iota_2)$*. The transition relation* $\to$ *is the smallest relation such that for all* $s_1, t_1 \in S_1$*, and* $s_2, t_2 \in S_2$ *and* $a \in Act$:

- *If* $s_1 \overset{\tau}{\to}_1 t_1$ *then* $(s_1, s_2) \overset{\tau}{\to} (t_1, s_2)$.
- *If* $s_1 \overset{a}{\to}_1 t_1$ *and* $s_2 \overset{a}{\to}_2 t_2$ *then* $(s_1, s_2) \overset{a}{\to} (t_1, t_2)$.

The proposition below relates the behaviours of two LTSs to the behaviours of their product; see also [8, Proposition 3.2].

Proposition 1. *Let* $\mathcal{L}_1 = (S_1, \iota_1, \to_1)$ *and* $\mathcal{L}_2 = (S_2, \iota_2, \to_2)$*. Assume* $\mathcal{L}_1 \ltimes \mathcal{L}_2 = (S, \iota, \to)$*. For all state pairs* $(s_1, t_1), (s_2, t_2) \in S$ *and all* $\rho \in Act^*$ *it holds that* $(s_1, s_2) \overset{\rho}{\Longrightarrow} (t_1, t_2)$ *if and only if* $s_1 \overset{\rho}{\Longrightarrow}_1 t_1$ *and* $s_2 \overset{\rho}{\Longrightarrow}_2 t_2$.

The one-sided product and the normalisation can be combined to search for violations of weak trace inclusion between two LTSs, see [8]. With minor adaptations, however, they can be used to search for violations of weak impossible futures, too. To this end, we have the following lemma.

Lemma 4. *Let $\mathcal{L}_1$ and $\mathcal{L}_2$ be LTSs. $\mathcal{L}_1 \sqsubseteq_{if} \mathcal{L}_2$ fails to hold iff for some $\rho \in \mathsf{WT}(\mathcal{L}_1)$ and state s_1 satisfying $\iota_1 \overset{\rho}{\Longrightarrow}_1 s_1$, and all states s_2 satisfying $\iota_2 \overset{\rho}{\Longrightarrow}_2 s_2$, $s_2 \sqsubseteq_{wt} s_1$ fails to hold.*

Proof. We consider both implications separately; we first prove the contrapositive.

- Suppose $\mathcal{L}_1 \sqsubseteq_{if} \mathcal{L}_2$ holds true. Then $\mathsf{IF}(\iota_1) \subseteq \mathsf{IF}(\iota_2)$. Let $\rho \in \mathsf{WT}(\iota_1)$, and suppose s_1 is such that $\iota_1 \overset{\rho}{\Longrightarrow}_1 s_1$. Then $(\rho, Act^* \setminus \mathsf{WT}(s_1)) \in \mathsf{IF}(\iota_1)$. Since $\mathsf{IF}(\iota_1) \subseteq \mathsf{IF}(\iota_2)$, we therefore also have $(\rho, Act^* \setminus \mathsf{WT}(s_1)) \in \mathsf{IF}(\iota_2)$. Hence, there must be a state s_2 such that $\iota_2 \overset{\rho}{\Longrightarrow}_2 s_2$. Moreover, we have $(Act^* \setminus \mathsf{WT}(s_1)) \cap \mathsf{WT}(s_2) = \emptyset$. But this means that $\mathsf{WT}(s_2) \subseteq \mathsf{WT}(s_1)$, *i.e.*, we have $s_2 \sqsubseteq_{wt} s_1$.
- Suppose $\mathcal{L}_1 \sqsubseteq_{if} \mathcal{L}_2$ does not hold true. That means $\mathsf{IF}(\iota_1) \subseteq \mathsf{IF}(\iota_2)$ does not hold, and therefore $\mathsf{IF}(\iota_1) \setminus \mathsf{IF}(\iota_2) \neq \emptyset$. Let $(\rho, X) \in \mathsf{IF}(\iota_1) \setminus \mathsf{IF}(\iota_2)$. Hence, for some s_1 such that $\iota_1 \overset{\rho}{\Longrightarrow}_1 s_1$ we have $X \cap \mathsf{WT}(s_1) = \emptyset$. Let s_1 be such. Pick an arbitrary s_2 in $\mathcal{L}_2$, and assume that $\iota_2 \overset{\rho}{\Longrightarrow}_2 s_2$. Since $(\rho, X) \notin \mathsf{IF}(\iota_2)$ we also have $X \cap \mathsf{WT}(s_2) \neq \emptyset$. Towards a contradiction, suppose that $\mathsf{WT}(s_2) \subseteq \mathsf{WT}(s_1)$. Then also $X \cap \mathsf{WT}(s_1) \neq \emptyset$. Contradiction. Hence, not $\mathsf{WT}(s_2) \subseteq \mathsf{WT}(s_1)$, and therefore $s_2 \sqsubseteq_{wt} s_1$ does not hold true. $\square$

We use this lemma to obtain the following characterisation of the state pair that indicates a violation to the weak impossible futures inclusion is reached in the product of an LTS and a normalised LTS.

Definition 6. *Let $\mathcal{L}_1$ and $\mathcal{L}_2$ be arbitrary LTSs. The state pair (s, U) of product $\mathcal{L}_1 \ltimes \mathsf{norm}(\mathcal{L}_2)$ is called:*

- *a WT-witness to a violation of weak trace inclusion iff $U = \emptyset$; and*
- *an IF-witness to a violation of weak impossible futures inclusion iff:*
  - *$U = \emptyset$; or*
  - *$U \neq \emptyset$ and $t \sqsubseteq_{wt} s$ fails to hold for all $t \in U$.*

Example 2. Reconsider the LTSs of Example 1, and assume that $\mathcal{L}_1$ is the LTS depicted on the right and $\mathcal{L}_2$ is the LTS depicted on the left. Then $(t_5, \{s_1, s_2, s_3\})$ is an IF-witness since $s_1 \not\sqsubseteq_{wt} t_5$, $s_2 \not\sqsubseteq_{wt} t_5$ and $s_3 \not\sqsubseteq_{wt} t_5$. $\square$

The following lemmas and theorem formalise that weak trace inclusion can be decided by checking reachability of a WT-witness in the one-sided product $\mathcal{L}_1 \times \mathsf{norm}(\mathcal{L}_2)$; see also [8, Lemmas 3.9 and 3.10].

Lemma 5. *Let $\mathcal{L}_1, \mathcal{L}_2$ be two LTSs. If $\mathcal{L}_1 \sqsubseteq_{wt} \mathcal{L}_2$ holds true then no WT-witness is reachable in $\mathcal{L}_1 \times \mathsf{norm}(\mathcal{L}_2)$.*

Lemma 6. *Let $\mathcal{L}_1, \mathcal{L}_2$ be two LTSs. If no WT-witness is reachable in $\mathcal{L}_1 \ltimes \mathsf{norm}(\mathcal{L}_2)$ then $\mathcal{L}_1 \sqsubseteq_{\mathsf{wt}} \mathcal{L}_2$.*

As a consequence, the problem of deciding weak trace inclusion can be reduced to the problem of reaching a WT-witness; see also [8, Theorem 3.11].

Theorem 1. *For all LTSs $\mathcal{L}_1, \mathcal{L}_2$, $\mathcal{L}_1 \sqsubseteq_{\mathsf{wt}} \mathcal{L}_2$ holds if and only if no WT-witness is reachable in $\mathcal{L}_1 \ltimes \mathsf{norm}(\mathcal{L}_2)$.*

Algorithm 1 uses exactly that observation: for LTSs $\mathcal{L}_1, \mathcal{L}_2$, given a pair of states $(s_1, s_2) \in S_1 \times S_2$, the algorithm computes whether a WT-witness is reachable from $(s_1, \{s' \in S_2 \mid s_2 \overset{\epsilon}{\Longrightarrow}_2 s'\})$ in the one-sided product of $\mathcal{L}_1$ and $\mathsf{norm}(\mathcal{L}_2)$. Weak trace inclusion of $\mathcal{L}_1$ in $\mathcal{L}_2$ can then be computed by running the algorithm on the input (ι_1, ι_2).

Algorithm 1. The weak trace inclusion checking algorithm. Upon termination, WEAK-TRACE(s_1, s_2) returns *true* if $s_1 \sqsubseteq_{\mathsf{wt}} s_2$, and *false* if $s_1 \not\sqsubseteq_{\mathsf{wt}} s_2$, where $\mathcal{L}_i = (S_i, \iota_i, \rightarrow_i)$ and $s_i \in S_i$.

```
 1: procedure WEAK-TRACE(s₁, s₂)
 2:     let working be a stack containing the pair (s₁, {s ∈ S₂ | s₂ ⇒₂ s})
 3:     let discovered := {(s₁, {s ∈ S₂ | s₂ ⇒₂ s})}
 4:     while working ≠ ∅ do
 5:         pop (impl, spec) from working
 6:         for impl →₁ impl' do
 7:             if a = τ then
 8:                 spec' := spec
 9:             else
10:                 spec' := {s' ∈ S₂ | ∃s ∈ spec : s ⇒₂ s'}
11:             if spec' = ∅ then
12:                 return false
13:             if (impl', spec') ∉ discovered then
14:                 discovered := discovered ∪ {(impl', spec')}
15:                 push (impl', spec') into working
16:     return true
```

Next, taking cue from the observations we made so far, we formalise the relation between deciding weak impossible futures inclusion and reaching an IF-witness.

Lemma 7. *Let $\mathcal{L}_1, \mathcal{L}_2$ be two LTSs. If $\mathcal{L}_1 \sqsubseteq_{\mathsf{if}} \mathcal{L}_2$ holds true then no IF-witness is reachable in $\mathcal{L}_1 \ltimes \mathsf{norm}(\mathcal{L}_2)$.*

Proof. Suppose $\mathcal{L}_1 \sqsubseteq_{\mathsf{if}} \mathcal{L}_2$ holds true. Towards a contradiction, assume an IF-witness is reachable in $\mathcal{L}_1 \ltimes \mathsf{norm}(\mathcal{L}_2)$. We distinguish two cases:

- Suppose there is an IF-witness (s, U) such that $U = \emptyset$. Then (s, U) is also a WT-witness. By Theorem 1, we find that $\mathcal{L}_1 \sqsubseteq_{\mathsf{wt}} \mathcal{L}_2$ fails to hold. Since weak trace inclusion is weaker than weak impossible futures inclusion we arrive at a contradiction.

– Suppose that for all IF-witnesses (s, U) we have $U \neq \emptyset$. Then $\mathcal{L}_1 \sqsubseteq_{\mathsf{wt}} \mathcal{L}_2$. Consider an arbitrary IF-witness (s, U). Since (s, U) is a reachable state in our one-sided product, there must be some weak trace $\rho \in \mathsf{WT}(\iota_1)$ such that $(\iota_1, \iota) \overset{\rho}{\Longrightarrow} (s, U)$, where $\iota = \{s' \in S_2 \mid \iota_2 \overset{\epsilon}{\Longrightarrow} s'\}$. Let ρ be this weak trace. By Proposition 1, we then have $\iota_1 \overset{\rho}{\Longrightarrow} s$ and $\iota \overset{\rho}{\to} U$. By Lemma 1, we then also have $\iota_2 \overset{\rho}{\Longrightarrow} t$ for all $t \in U$. Furthermore, by Lemma 2, and the fact that $\mathsf{norm}(\mathcal{L}_2)$ is deterministic, it follows that all states t such that $\iota_2 \overset{\rho}{\Longrightarrow} t$ belong to U. Since (s, U) is an IF-witness and $U \neq \emptyset$, $t \sqsubseteq_{\mathsf{wt}} s$ fails to hold for all $t \in U$. By Lemma 4, we can then also conclude that $\mathcal{L}_1 \sqsubseteq_{\mathsf{if}} \mathcal{L}_2$ fails to hold true, so we arrive at a contradiction.

Since both cases lead to a contradiction, we conclude that no IF-witness is reachable in $\mathcal{L}_1 \ltimes \mathsf{norm}(\mathcal{L}_2)$. $\qquad\square$

Lemma 8. *Let $\mathcal{L}_1, \mathcal{L}_2$ be two LTSs. If no IF-witness is reachable in $\mathcal{L}_1 \ltimes \mathsf{norm}(\mathcal{L}_2)$ then $\mathcal{L}_1 \sqsubseteq_{\mathsf{if}} \mathcal{L}_2$ holds.*

Proof. We proceed by proving the contrapositive. Assume that $\mathcal{L}_1 \sqsubseteq_{\mathsf{if}} \mathcal{L}_2$ fails to hold. We show that in that case, some IF-witness is reachable. We distinguish cases based on $\mathcal{L}_1 \sqsubseteq_{\mathsf{wt}} \mathcal{L}_2$ and not $\mathcal{L}_1 \sqsubseteq_{\mathsf{wt}} \mathcal{L}_2$.

– Suppose $\mathcal{L}_1 \sqsubseteq_{\mathsf{wt}} \mathcal{L}_2$ does not hold true. Then by Lemma 6, we conclude a WT-witness $(s, \emptyset)$ is reachable in $\mathcal{L}_1 \ltimes \mathsf{norm}(\mathcal{L}_2)$. Note that any WT-witness is also an IF-witness, so we conclude that some IF-witness is reachable in $\mathcal{L}_1 \ltimes \mathsf{norm}(\mathcal{L}_2)$.

– Assume that $\mathcal{L}_1 \sqsubseteq_{\mathsf{wt}} \mathcal{L}_2$ holds true. Since $\mathcal{L}_1 \sqsubseteq_{\mathsf{if}} \mathcal{L}_2$ fails, by Lemma 4, there must be some $\rho \in \mathsf{WT}(\mathcal{L}_1)$ and state s_1 satisfying $\iota_1 \overset{\rho}{\Longrightarrow}_1 s_1$, such that for all states s_2 satisfying $\iota_2 \overset{\rho}{\Longrightarrow}_2 s_2$, $s_2 \sqsubseteq_{\mathsf{wt}} s_1$ fails to hold true. Let $\rho \in \mathsf{WT}(\mathcal{L}_1)$ be this weak trace and s_1 be this state. Denote $\iota = \{s' \in S_2 \mid \iota_2 \overset{\epsilon}{\Longrightarrow} s'\}$. Since $\mathcal{L}_1 \sqsubseteq_{\mathsf{wt}} \mathcal{L}_2$, $\rho \in \mathsf{WT}(\mathcal{L}_2)$. Let s_2 be such that $\iota_2 \overset{\rho}{\Longrightarrow}_2 s_2$. By Lemma 2, there is a state $U \in \mathsf{norm}(\mathcal{L}_2)$ such that $s_2 \in U$ and $\iota \overset{\rho}{\to} U$. So, pick such a state U. Notice that (s_1, U) is reachable in $\mathcal{L}_1 \ltimes \mathsf{norm}(\mathcal{L}_2)$. Moreover, since $\mathsf{norm}(\mathcal{L}_2)$ is deterministic, state U is the only state reachable in $\mathsf{norm}(\mathcal{L}_2)$ by ρ, and we have, in fact, $U = \{s' \in S_2 \mid \iota_2 \overset{\rho}{\Longrightarrow}_2 s'\}$. We proceed to show that (s_1, U) is an IF-witness. Pick some $s \in U$. Recall that we already concluded that for all s_2 such that $\iota_2 \overset{\rho}{\Longrightarrow}_2 s_2$, $s_2 \sqsubseteq_{\mathsf{wt}} s_1$ fails to hold true. So also $s \sqsubseteq_{\mathsf{wt}} s_1$ fails to hold true. So (s_1, U) is both reachable and an IF-witness. $\qquad\square$

Theorem 2. *For all LTSs $\mathcal{L}_1, \mathcal{L}_2$, $\mathcal{L}_1 \sqsubseteq_{\mathsf{if}} \mathcal{L}_2$ holds if and only if no IF-witness is reachable in $\mathcal{L}_1 \ltimes \mathsf{norm}(\mathcal{L}_2)$.*

Proof. This follows directly from Lemmas 7 and 8. $\qquad\square$

As an immediate consequence of Theorem 1 and Theorem 2, we can conclude that a state pair (s, U) of the one-sided product $\mathcal{L}_1 \ltimes \mathsf{norm}(\mathcal{L}_2)$ is an IF-witness if either $U = \emptyset$, or $U \neq \emptyset$ and for each $t \in U$, a WT-witness is reachable from $(t, \{s' \in S_1 \mid s \overset{\epsilon}{\Longrightarrow}_1 s\})$ in $\mathcal{L}_2 \ltimes \mathsf{norm}(\mathcal{L}_1)$. This is exploited in Algorithm 2.

The performance of the resulting algorithm is rather poor, see also Table 2 in Sect. 5: the algorithm even hits the timeout of 10 min for several cases.

Algorithm 2. A weak impossible futures inclusion checking algorithm. Upon termination, WEAK-IMPOSSIBLE-FUTURES(s_1, s_2) returns *true* if $s_1 \sqsubseteq_{\mathsf{if}} s_2$ and *false* if $s_1 \not\sqsubseteq_{\mathsf{if}} s_2$, where $\mathcal{L}_i = (S_i, \iota_i, \rightarrow_i)$ and $s_i \in S_i$.

1: **procedure** WEAK-IMPOSSIBLE-FUTURES(s_1, s_2)
2:     let *working* be a stack containing the pair $(s_1, \{s \in S_2 \mid s_2 \overset{\epsilon}{\Longrightarrow}_2 s\})$
3:     let *discovered* $:= \{(s_1, \{s \in S_2 \mid s_2 \overset{\epsilon}{\Longrightarrow}_2 s\})\}$
4:     **while** *working* $\neq \emptyset$ **do**
5:         pop $(impl, spec)$ from *working*
6:         **if** $\neg\exists_{t \in spec} :$ WEAK-TRACE$(t, impl)$ **then**
7:             **return** false
8:         **for** $impl \overset{a}{\rightarrow}_1 impl'$ **do**
9:             **if** $a = \tau$ **then**
10:                 $spec' := spec$
11:             **else**
12:                 $spec' := \{s' \in S_2 \mid \exists s \in spec : s \overset{a}{\Longrightarrow}_2 s'\}$
13:             **if** $spec' = \emptyset$ **then**
14:                 **return** false
15:             **if** $(impl', spec') \notin discovered$ **then**
16:                 $discovered := discovered \cup \{(impl', spec')\}$
17:                 push $(impl', spec')$ into *working*
18:     **return** true

---

4   Antichain Algorithms for Impossible Futures

In [8,19], *antichains* have been shown to speed up checking, among others, the language inclusion problem and the universality problem on finite automata, and the (weak) trace inclusion, stable failures refinement and failures-divergences refinement on LTSs. Since Algorithm 2 for checking weak impossible futures inclusion is a variation on the algorithm for checking weak trace inclusion, it is to be expected that antichains are equally likely to speed up checking weak impossible futures inclusion. We explore the options in this section.

4.1   Antichains for Impossible Futures

Formally, an antichain is a subset $\mathcal{A} \subseteq X$ of a poset $(X, \sqsubseteq)$ in which all distinct $x, y \in \mathcal{A}$ are incomparable; *i.e.*, neither $x \sqsubseteq y$ nor $y \sqsubseteq x$. Given an antichain $\mathcal{A}$ of a poset $(X, \sqsubseteq)$, a 'membership' test $\in_{\sqsubseteq}$ checks whether $\mathcal{A}$ 'contains' a particular element; *i.e.*, $x \in_{\sqsubseteq} \mathcal{A}$ holds true exactly when there is some $y \in \mathcal{A}$ such that $y \sqsubseteq x$. The operation $\uplus_{\sqsubseteq}$ is used to 'extend' the antichain with a new element; for $x \in X$, we define $\mathcal{A} \uplus_{\sqsubseteq} x$ as the set $\{y \mid y = x \vee (y \in \mathcal{A} \wedge x \not\sqsubseteq y)\}$. Note that this operation only yields an antichain whenever $x \not\in_{\sqsubseteq} \mathcal{A}$.

In our context, the state space of the one-sided product $(S, \iota, \rightarrow)$ of an LTS $\mathcal{L}_1$ and a normalised LTS $\mathcal{L}_2$ induces a poset as follows. For $(s, U), (t, V) \in S$, we define $(s, U) \leq (t, V)$ iff $s = t$ and $U \subseteq V$; informally, we say that (s, U) is *more precise* than (t, V). We remark that the set $(S, \leq)$ is indeed a poset. To simplify notation, we write $\Subset$ and $\mathbb{U}$ instead of $\Subset_{\leq}$ and $\mathbb{U}_{\leq}$, and we only use the more verbose $\Subset_{\sqsubseteq}$ and $\mathbb{U}_{\sqsubseteq}$ for orderings $\sqsubseteq$ different from $\leq$.

In weak trace inclusion, antichains typically allow for pruning the search space by observing that in case a state (s, V) in the one-sided product can reach a WF-witness, then so can all more precise states (s, U). This leads to Algorithm 3, taken from [8].

Algorithm 3. The antichain-based weak trace inclusion checking algorithm of [8]. Upon termination, $\textsc{Weak-Trace}_{ac}(s_1, s_2)$ returns *true* if $s_1 \sqsubseteq_{\mathsf{wt}} s_2$, and *false* if $s_1 \not\sqsubseteq_{\mathsf{wt}} s_2$, where $\mathcal{L}_i = (S_i, \iota_i, \to_i)$ and $s_i \in S_i$.

1: **procedure** $\textsc{Weak-Trace}_{ac}(s_1, s_2)$
2:     let *working* be a stack containing the pair $(s_1, \{s \in S_2 \mid s_2 \overset{\epsilon}{\Longrightarrow}_2 s\})$
3:     let *antichain* $:= \emptyset \,\mathbb{U}\, (s_1, \{s \in S_2 \mid s_2 \overset{\epsilon}{\Longrightarrow}_2 s\})$
4:     **while** *working* $\neq \emptyset$ **do**
5:         pop $(impl, spec)$ from *working*
6:         **for** $impl \overset{a}{\longrightarrow}_1 impl'$ **do**
7:             **if** $a = \tau$ **then**
8:                 $spec' := spec$
9:             **else**
10:                 $spec' := \{s' \in S_2 \mid \exists s \in spec : s \overset{a}{\Longrightarrow}_2 s'\}$
11:             **if** $spec' = \emptyset$ **then**
12:                 **return** false
13:             **if** $(impl', spec') \notin antichain$ **then**
14:                 $antichain := antichain \,\mathbb{U}\, (impl', spec')$
15:                 push $(impl', spec')$ into *working*
16:     **return** true

Below, we show that a similar result holds true for weak impossible futures. First, observe that we have the following result; see [7, Proposition 2].

Proposition 2. *For all states* $(s, U), (s, V)$ *of* $\mathcal{L}_1 \ltimes \mathsf{norm}(\mathcal{L}_2)$ *satisfying* $(s, U) \leq (s, V)$ *and for every sequence* $\sigma \in Act_\tau^*$ *such that* $(s, V) \overset{\sigma}{\to} (t, V')$ *there is a state* (t, U') *such that* $(s, U) \overset{\sigma}{\to} (t, U')$ *and* $(t, U') \leq (t, V')$.

Next, we find that if a state pair of a one-sided product is an IF-witness, then so are all state pairs that are more precise.

Lemma 9. *For all states* $(s, U), (s, V)$ *of* $\mathcal{L}_1 \ltimes \mathsf{norm}(\mathcal{L}_2)$ *satisfying* $(s, U) \leq (s, V)$ *it holds that if* (s, V) *is an IF-witness then* (s, U) *is an IF-witness.*

Proof. Suppose (s, V) is an IF-witness, and assume that $(s, U) \leq (s, V)$. We distinguish two cases.

- Case $V = \emptyset$. Then also $U = \emptyset$ and therefore (s, U) is an IF-witness.
- Case $V \neq \emptyset$. Then for all $t \in V$, $t \sqsubseteq_{\mathsf{wt}} s$ fails to hold. Since $(s, U) \leq (s, V)$, we have $U \subseteq V$. But then also for all $t \in U$, $t \sqsubseteq_{\mathsf{wt}} s$ fails to hold true. Hence, (s, U) is an IF-witness. $\qquad\square$

The corollary below is then an immediate consequence of the above proposition and lemma. This result is the basis for an antichain-based algorithm for checking weak impossible futures inclusion.

Corollary 1. *For all states $(s, U), (s, V)$ of $\mathcal{L}_1 \ltimes \mathsf{norm}(\mathcal{L}_2)$ where $(s, U) \leq (s, V)$ and for every sequence $\rho \in Act^*$ it holds that if (s, V) can reach an IF-witness with ρ then (s, U) can reach an IF-witness with ρ as well.*

Using this corollary, Algorithm 2 can be implemented using an antichain that only keeps track of the minimal elements that have been discovered, and that avoids exploring states in the one-sided product that are less precise when a more precise state has already been discovered. The algorithm relies on the antichain-based algorithm for deciding weak trace inclusion, see Algorithm 3.

Algorithm 4. An antichain-based weak impossible futures inclusion checking algorithm. Upon termination, $\textsc{Weak-Impossible-Futures}_{ac}(s_1, s_2)$ returns *true* if $s_1 \sqsubseteq_{\mathsf{if}} s_2$, and *false* if $s_1 \not\sqsubseteq_{\mathsf{if}} s_2$, where $\mathcal{L}_i = (S_i, \iota_i, \rightarrow_i)$ and $s_i \in S_i$.

```
 1: procedure WEAK-IMPOSSIBLE-FUTURESac(s1, s2)
 2:     let working be a stack containing the pair (s1, {s ∈ S2 | s2 =ε⇒2 s})
 3:     let antichain := ∅ ⊎ (s1, {s ∈ S2 | s2 =ε⇒2 s})
 4:     while working ≠ ∅ do
 5:         pop (impl, spec) from working
 6:         if ¬∃t∈spec : WEAK-TRACEac(t, impl) then
 7:             return false
 8:         for impl —a→1 impl' do
 9:             if a = τ then
10:                 spec' := spec
11:             else
12:                 spec' := {s' ∈ S2 | ∃s ∈ spec : s =a⇒2 s'}
13:             if spec' = ∅ then
14:                 return false
15:             if (impl', spec') ∉ antichain then
16:                 antichain := antichain ⊎ (impl', spec')
17:                 push (impl', spec') into working
18:     return true
```

4.2 Optimising the Antichain Algorithm for Impossible Futures

The antichain-based variant of the weak impossible futures inclusion algorithm offers a performance improvement over the naive variant. However, it turns out that it does not help to reduce the number of cases for which the weak impossible futures inclusion check runs into a timeout, see Table 2 in Sect. 5. We therefore explore a number of further optimisations that, together, ensure that in most cases, weak impossible futures inclusion checking remains feasible.

We start with the observation that in a sequence of silent steps in the one-sided product, the check whether a state pair in the one-sided product is an IF-witness can be delayed. This is captured by the following lemma.

Lemma 10. *Let* $(s, U), (s', U)$ *be states of* $\mathcal{L}_1 \ltimes \mathsf{norm}(\mathcal{L}_2)$. *If* $(s, U) \xrightarrow{\tau} (s', U)$ *and* (s, U) *is an IF-witness, then also* (s', U) *is an IF-witness.*

Proof. Suppose $(s, U) \xrightarrow{\tau} (s', U)$ and assume that (s, U) is an IF-witness. We distinguish two cases.

- Case $U = \emptyset$. Then we can immediately conclude that also (s', U) is an IF-witness.
- Case $U \neq \emptyset$. Since (s, U) is an IF-witness, $t \sqsubseteq_{\mathsf{wt}} s$ fails to hold true for all $t \in U$. Pick some $t \in U$. Suppose we have $t \sqsubseteq_{\mathsf{wt}} s'$. Because $s \xrightarrow{\tau}_1 s'$, we may conclude that $s' \sqsubseteq_{\mathsf{wt}} s$. By transitivity, also $t \sqsubseteq_{\mathsf{wt}} s$. But this contradicts that $t \sqsubseteq_{\mathsf{wt}} s$ fails to hold true. Hence, $t \sqsubseteq_{\mathsf{wt}} s'$ does not hold true. Consequently, (s', U) is an IF-witness. $\square$

In case $\mathcal{L}_1$ is convergent, *i.e.*, when there are no infinite τ-paths, this lemma allows to run the rather expensive check of line 6 only when the state of $\mathcal{L}_1$ that is reached is stable; *i.e.*, when it has no τ-transition.

Of course, the LTS involved may not be convergent. In this case, we can simply first compute the strongly connected components with respect to τ-transitions, and collapse all such states. This guarantees that the resulting LTS is convergent. Computing the strongly connected components and collapsing these can be done in time linear in the number of states and τ-transitions, using, *e.g.*, Tarjan's algorithm. Note that the strongly connected component collapse preserves the impossible futures inclusion relation; see the lemma below.

Lemma 11. *Let* $\mathcal{L}_1 = (S_1, \iota_1, \rightarrow_1)$ *and* $\mathcal{L}_2 = (S_2, \iota_2, \rightarrow_2)$. *Let* $s_1, \bar{s}_1 \in S_1$ *and* $s_2 \in S_2$. *Suppose* $s_1 \xRightarrow{\epsilon}_1 \bar{s}_1 \xRightarrow{\epsilon}_1 s_1$. *Then* $s_1 \sqsubseteq_{\mathsf{if}} s_2$ *iff* $\bar{s}_1 \sqsubseteq_{\mathsf{if}} s_2$.

Proof. Let $s_1, \bar{s}_1$ and s_2 be as stated, and suppose $s_1 \xRightarrow{\epsilon}_1 \bar{s}_1 \xRightarrow{\epsilon}_1 s_1$. Assume that $s_1 \sqsubseteq_{\mathsf{if}} s_2$. Then $\mathsf{IF}(s_1) \subseteq \mathsf{IF}(s_2)$. We show that also $\mathsf{IF}(\bar{s}_1) \subseteq \mathsf{IF}(s_2)$. Pick $(\rho, X) \in \mathsf{IF}(\bar{s}_1)$. Since $s_1 \xRightarrow{\epsilon}_1 \bar{s}_1$, we must have $(\rho, X) \in \mathsf{IF}(s_1)$. But then also $(\rho, X) \in \mathsf{IF}(s_2)$. Hence, we conclude that $\bar{s}_1 \sqsubseteq_{\mathsf{if}} s_2$. The argument that $\bar{s}_1 \sqsubseteq_{\mathsf{if}} s_2$ implies $s_1 \sqsubseteq_{\mathsf{if}} s_2$ follows the same reasoning. $\square$

A second observation is that each call to Weak-Trace$_{ac}$ in line 6 involves exploring a 'fresh' one-sided product, and, upon termination, all information about the states that were visited is discarded. This means that state pairs in $\mathcal{L}_2 \ltimes \mathsf{norm}(\mathcal{L}_1)$ are potentially inspected multiple times, impacting the overall execution time of the algorithm.

We distinguish two scenarios. In case the call to Weak-Trace$_{ac}$ terminates and finds that no WT-witness was found, all relevant reachable state pairs of the one-sided product have been explored, and as a result, the antichain that was constructed by $\textsc{Weak-Trace}_{ac}$ will contain all state pairs for which no WT-witness was reachable. This means that by saving the antichain of each $\textsc{Weak-Trace}_{ac}$ call when the algorithm returns *true* the weak impossible futures check can potentially be sped-up since we can use the saved antichain to avoid reexploring state pairs already explored previously.

However, whenever the call to $\textsc{Weak-Trace}_{ac}$ terminates and returns *false*, we cannot simply save the antichain that was constructed in $\textsc{Weak-Trace}_{ac}$. For instance, there may be state pairs (t, U) in the antichain that have successors that are not yet fully explored; for such state pairs, we do not yet know whether or not they will be able to reach a WT-witness, so storing information about these state pairs is not necessarily helpful. Still, some information can be preserved: all state pairs in the antichain that *can* reach the identified WT-witness could be stored in a 'negative' antichain, say $\mathcal{A}$. Moreover, since all these states are able to reach a WT-witness, also all state pairs that are *more precise* are able to reach a WT-witness, see also Proposition 2. As a consequence, the ordering used for this negative antichain needs to be the converse of the one we have used so far, viz.: $(s, U) \geq (t, V)$ iff $s = t$ and $U \supseteq V$. We can thus extend the negative antichain $\mathcal{A}$ with a new element x if no element y, larger than x, is already present in $\mathcal{A}$. Since it can be costly to search for all state pairs that are able to reach a WT-witness, we here opt, as a heuristic, to save only the initial state pair for which the search was conducted.

Algorithm 6 incorporates all three optimisations, and crucially relies on Algorithm 5. The latter modifies Algorithm 3 in a trivial way to return both a verdict (*true/false*) and an antichain, and which takes an antichain and a negative antichain as input. Our optimisations are reflected in lines 7-16 of Algorithm 6, which refine lines 6-7 of Algorithm 4. The loop, introduced in these lines, calls $\textsc{Weak-Trace}_{ac-opt}$ only for stable states of $\mathcal{L}_1$. Moreover, $\textsc{Weak-Trace}_{ac-opt}$ uses the antichains $antichain^-$ and $antichain^+$ to short-circuit the weak trace inclusion checks. As soon as one of those weak trace inclusion checks returns *true*, we store the updated positive antichain and set the Boolean b to *false*, causing the algorithm to exit the loop. For each weak trace inclusion check that returns *false*, we store the updated negative antichain. The correctness of Algorithm 6 relies on the correctness of Algorithm 3, which is asserted by the following proposition.

Proposition 3. *Let $\mathcal{L}_1 = (S_1, \iota_1, \rightarrow_1)$ and $\mathcal{L}_2 = (S_2, \iota_2, \rightarrow_2)$. Let $\mathcal{L} = \mathcal{L}_1 \ltimes \mathrm{norm}(\mathcal{L}_2)$. Suppose that $antichain^-$ is an antichain that satisfies that for all $(impl, spec) \in_{\geq} antichain^-$ a WT-witness is reachable in the one-sided product $\mathcal{L}$. Furthermore, assume that $antichain^+$ is an antichain that satisfies that for all $(impl, spec) \in_{\leq} antichain^+$, no WT-witness is reachable in the one-sided product $\mathcal{L}$. Upon termination $\textsc{Weak-Trace}_{ac-opt}(\iota_1, \iota_2, antichain^+, antichain^-)$ returns* true *if $\mathcal{L}_1 \sqsubseteq_{\mathsf{wt}} \mathcal{L}_2$ and* false *if $\mathcal{L}_1 \not\sqsubseteq_{\mathsf{wt}} \mathcal{L}_2$.*

Based on this, the theorem below claims the correctness of Algorithm 6.

Theorem 3. *Let $\mathcal{L}_1 = (S_1, \iota_1, \rightarrow_1)$ and $\mathcal{L}_2 = (S_2, \iota_2, \rightarrow_2)$ be finite LTSs, and assume that $\mathcal{L}_1$ is convergent. Then* WEAK-IMPOSSIBLE-FUTURES$_{ac-opt}$ (ι_1, ι_2) *terminates, and it returns* true *if $\mathcal{L}_1 \sqsubseteq_{if} \mathcal{L}_2$, and* false *if $\mathcal{L}_1 \not\sqsubseteq_{if} \mathcal{L}_2$ otherwise.*

Algorithm 5. An antichain-based weak trace inclusion checking algorithm that is optimised for repeated checks. Upon termination, WEAK-TRACE$_{ac-opt}(s_1, s_2, antichain^+, antichain^-)$ returns $(true, antichain_e^+)$ if $s_1 \sqsubseteq_{wt} s_2$, and $(false, antichain_e^-)$ if $s_1 \not\sqsubseteq_{wt} s_2$, where $\mathcal{L}_i = (S_i, \iota_i, \rightarrow_i)$, $s_i \in S_i$ and $antichain_e^+$, resp. $antichain_e^-$, extend $antichain^+$, resp. $antichain^-$.

```
 1: procedure WEAK-TRACE_ac-opt(s1, s2, antichain+, antichain-)
 2:     if (s1, {s ∈ S2 | s2 ⇒ε 2 s}) ∈ antichain+ then
 3:         return (true, antichain+)
 4:     else if (s1, {s ∈ S2 | s2 ⇒ε 2 s}) ∈≥ antichain- then
 5:         return (false, antichain-)
 6:     let working be a stack containing the pair (s1, {s ∈ S2 | s2 ⇒ε 2 s})
 7:     let antichain := ∅ ⊎ (s1, {s ∈ S2 | s2 ⇒ε 2 s})
 8:     while working ≠ ∅ do
 9:         pop (impl, spec) from working
10:         for impl →a 1 impl' do
11:             if a = τ then
12:                 spec' := spec
13:             else
14:                 spec' := {s' ∈ S2 | ∃s ∈ spec : s ⇒a 2 s'}
15:             if (impl, spec') ∈≥ antichain- ∨ spec' = ∅ then
16:                 return (false, antichain- ⊎≥ (s1, {s ∈ S2 | s2 ⇒ε 2 s}))
17:             if (impl', spec') ∉ antichain ∧ (impl', spec') ∉ antichain+ then
18:                 antichain := antichain ⊎ (impl', spec')
19:                 push (impl', spec') into working
20:     return (true, antichain+ ∪ antichain)
```

We wrap up this section by illustrating the workings of the algorithm on the LTSs of Example 1; while it does not show all the benefits of using antichains, it does illustrate the general idea of the algorithm. The execution of the algorithm, using s_0 as the specification and t_0 as the implementation, proceeds as follows. Initially, we check the pair $(t_0, \{s_0\})$. This pair is added to *working* and *antichain*, both of which are initially empty, so:

$$antichain = \{(t_0, \{s_0\})\}$$
$$working = \{(t_0, \{s_0\})\}$$

The antichains $antichain^-$ and $antichain^+$ are initialised to be empty. Since *working* is not empty, we pop the pair $(t_0, \{s_0\})$ from *working* in line 6, assigning t_0 to *impl* and $\{s_0\}$ to *spec*. Next, we check for weak trace inclusion for all

---

Algorithm 6. An antichain-based weak impossible futures inclusion checking algorithm that is optimised to take advantage of the optimised weak trace inclusion checking algorithm. Upon termination, WEAK-IMPOSSIBLE-FUTURES$_{ac-opt}(s_1, s_2)$ returns *true* if $s_1 \sqsubseteq_{if} s_2$, and *false* if $s_1 \not\sqsubseteq_{if} s_2$, where $\mathcal{L}_i = (S_i, \iota_i, \rightarrow_i)$, and $s_i \in S_i$ and $\mathcal{L}_1$ is convergent.

```
 1: procedure WEAK-IMPOSSIBLE-FUTURESac−opt(s1, s2)
 2:     let working be a stack containing the pair (s1, {s ∈ S2 | s2 ⇒ε2 s})
 3:     let antichain := ∅ ⊎ (s1, {s ∈ S2 | s2 ⇒ε2 s})
 4:     let (antichain−, antichain+) := (∅, ∅)
 5:     while working ≠ ∅ do
 6:         pop (impl, spec) from working
 7:         (b, spec′) := (true, spec)
 8:         while impl ↛τ1 ∧ spec′ ≠ ∅ ∧ b do
 9:             pop t from spec′
10:             (b′, antichain′) := WEAK-TRACEac−opt(t, impl, antichain+, antichain−)
11:             if b′ then
12:                 (b, antichain+) := (false, antichain′)
13:             else
14:                 antichain− := antichain′
15:         if b = true ∧ impl ↛τ1 then
16:             return false
17:         for impl →a1 impl′ do
18:             if a = τ then
19:                 spec′ := spec
20:             else
21:                 spec′ := {s′ ∈ S2 | ∃s ∈ spec : s ⇒a2 s′}
22:             if spec′ = ∅ then
23:                 return false
24:             if (impl′, spec′) ∉ antichain then
25:                 antichain := antichain ⊎ (impl′, spec′)
26:                 push (impl′, spec′) into working
27:     return true
```

---

elements in *spec* against t_0, since $t_0 \not\rightarrow_1^\tau$; the procedure WEAK-TRACE$_{ac-opt}$ receives the arguments s_0, t_0, $antichain^+$ and $antichain^-$.

As we concluded earlier in Example 1 this check should pass; procedure WEAK-TRACE$_{ac-opt}$ thus returns true and a new antichain, which we assign to $antichain^+$. We then have:

$$antichain^+ = \{(s_0, \{t_0\}), (s_1, \{t_1, t_2, t_3, t_5\}), (s_2, \{t_1, t_2, t_3, t_5\}),$$
$$(s_3, \{t_1, t_2, t_3, t_5\})\}$$

Since the weak trace inclusion check passes, we bail out of the loop (lines 8–14). This also causes the test on line 15 to fail, so we skip to line 17 and consider the (only) transition $impl \xrightarrow{newday}_1 t_1$. That transition can be matched from $\{s_0\}$, leading to the set $\{s_1, s_2, s_3\}$, which we assign to $spec'$. Since the pair $(t_1, \{s_1, s_2, s_3\})$ is not represented in $antichain$, we extend both $antichain$ and *working* with the pair. Note that at this point we have:

$$antichain = \{(t_0, \{s_0\}), (t_1, \{s_1, s_2, s_3\})\}$$
$$working \ = \{(t_1, \{s_1, s_2, s_3\})\}$$

We pop the pair $(t_1, \{s_1, s_2, s_3\})$ from *working* in line 6, assigning t_1 to *impl* and $\{s_1, s_2, s_3\}$ to *spec*. The computation in lines 9–14 is skipped since $impl \xrightarrow{\tau}_1$. Likewise, the check in line 15 fails since $impl \xrightarrow{\tau}_1$, so the computation continues in line 17. Since $impl \xrightarrow{\tau}_1 t_2$ and $impl \xrightarrow{\tau}_1 t_5$, and neither the pair $(t_2, spec')$, nor $(t_5, spec')$, for $spec' = spec = \{s_1, s_2, s_3\}$ are represented in *antichain*, we add both pairs to *antichain* and *working*. At this point, we have:

$$antichain = \{(t_0, \{s_0\}), (t_1, \{s_1, s_2, s_3\}), (t_2, \{s_1, s_2, s_3\}), (t_5, \{s_1, s_2, s_3\})\}$$
$$working \ = \{(t_2, \{s_1, s_2, s_3\}), (t_5, \{s_1, s_2, s_3\})\}$$

We pop the pair $(t_2, \{s_1, s_2, s_3\})$ from *working* in line 6, assigning t_2 to *impl* and $\{s_1, s_2, s_3\}$ to *spec*. Again, the computation in lines 9–14 and 15–16 is skipped since $impl \xrightarrow{\tau}_1$, so the computation continues in line 17. Since $impl \xrightarrow{\tau}_1 t_3$ and the pair $(t_3, spec')$, for $spec' = spec = \{s_1, s_2, s_3\}$ is not represented in *antichain*, we add the pair to both *antichain* and *working*. Furthermore, transition $impl \xrightarrow{\text{lindyhop}}_1 t_0$ can be matched from $\{s_1, s_2, s_3\}$, leading to $\{s_0\}$. Since the pair $(t_0, \{s_0\})$ is already represented in *antichain*, we do not add this pair to *antichain*, nor to *working*. At this point, we have:

$$antichain = \{(t_0, \{s_0\}), (t_1, \{s_1, s_2, s_3\}), (t_2, \{s_1, s_2, s_3\}),$$
$$(t_5, \{s_1, s_2, s_3\}, (t_3, \{s_1, s_2, s_3\})\}$$
$$working \ = \{(t_5, \{s_1, s_2, s_3\}), (t_3, \{s_1, s_2, s_3\})\}$$

We next pop $(t_5, \{s_1, s_2, s_3\})$ from *working* in line 6, assigning t_5 to *impl* and $\{s_1, s_2, s_3\}$ to *spec*. Next, since $impl \xrightarrow{\tau} \!\!\!\!\!/\,_1$, we need to check for weak trace inclusion for all elements in $\{s_1, s_2, s_3\}$ against t_5. Procedure WEAK-TRACE$_{ac-opt}$ receives the arguments s_1, t_5, $antichain^+$ and $antichain^-$. Note that $antichain^+$ and $antichain^-$ are as follows:

$$antichain^+ = \{(s_0, \{t_0\}), (s_1, \{t_1, t_2, t_3, t_5\}), (s_2, \{t_1, t_2, t_3, t_5\}),$$
$$(s_3, \{t_1, t_2, t_3, t_5\})\}$$
$$antichain^- = \emptyset$$

Since s_1 is not weak trace included in t_5, procedure WEAK-TRACE$_{ac-opt}$ returns false and a new antichain $\{(s_1, \{t_5\})\}$, which is assigned to $antichain^-$. Next, procedure WEAK-TRACE$_{ac-opt}$ receives the arguments s_2, t_5, $antichain^+$ and the updated $antichain^-$. Again, since s_2 is not weak trace included in t_5, procedure WEAK-TRACE$_{ac-opt}$ returns false and a new antichain $\{(s_1, \{t_5\}), (s_2, \{t_5\})\}$, which is assigned to $antichain^-$. Finally, procedure WEAK-TRACE$_{ac-opt}$ receives the arguments s_3, t_5, $antichain^+$ and the updated $antichain^-$. Also s_3 is not weak trace included in t_5; procedure WEAK-TRACE$_{ac-opt}$ can short-circuit this check using information in

$antichain^-$, concluding that at some point it needs not further explore the pair $(s_1, \{t_5\})$ since it is already represented in this set. It therefore returns false and a new antichain $\{(s_1, \{t_5\}), (s_2, \{t_5\}), (s_3, \{t_5\})\}$, which is assigned to $antichain^-$. Since at this point all states in *spec* have been checked for weak trace inclusion against t_5, we bail out of the loop (lines 8–14) and the test in line 15 passes, resulting in the algorithm executing line 16 and returning false.

5 Experiments

The proposed algorithms have been implemented in C++ and are available in the `ltscompare` tool in the mCRL2 toolset [3]. This tool can be used to compare labelled transition systems with respect to various preorder relations, such as, *e.g.*, stable failures refinement and the failures-divergences refinement relations discussed in [8], and equivalence relations such as, *e.g.*, strong bisimilarity [10], branching bisimilarity [17] and weak bisimilarity [9].

Table 1. The number of states and transitions for all cases in our benchmark.

Model	Ref.	states $\mathcal{L}_2$	trans. $\mathcal{L}_2$	$\sqsubseteq_{if}$	states $\mathcal{L}_1$	trans. $\mathcal{L}_1$
Coarse Set	[4]	50 488	64 729	*true*	55 444	145 043
Finegrained Set	[4]	3 720	3 305	*true*	5 077	9 006
Industrial	-	24	45	*false*	24 551	45 447
Lazy Set	[4]	3 565	3 980	*true*	24 496	41 431
Optimistic Set	[4]	25 435	28 154	*true*	234 332	389 344
Non Blocking	[13]	1 248	1 473	*false*	3 030	5 799
Treiber stack	[14]	87 389	124 740	*true*	205 634	564 862

To gauge the differences in performance of the various algorithms and optimisations we proposed in this section, we have carried out experiments on a small set of LTSs, see Table 1. For the various optimisations, discussed in Sect. 4.2, we test their individual impact on the performance and their combined effect. Note that for reasons of confidentiality, the industrial model cannot be made available. All experiments have been carried out on a laptop with an i7-12800H CPU with 64GB of main memory, measuring the average of 5 runs. The benchmarks consist of combinations of implementation and specification combinations of concurrent data structures [11]. All results are depicted in Table 2.

Analysing the results of Table 2, we find that the naive algorithm for checking for weak impossible futures inclusion, *i.e.*, Algorithm 2 and its naive antichain optimisation, see Algorithm 4, are not very performant and lead to a timeout in several cases. The stability check on its own yields up-to a 50-fold performance improvement in some cases, and allows all cases to terminate within the set timeout bounds. Storing only the antichains computed in inner weak trace inclusion checks that result in a *true*-verdict also has a significant effect, but the

Table 2. The average time in seconds for the naive and optimised implementations, $\perp$ indicates a timeout after 10 min. Four versions of Algorithm 6 are run: *stable*, which calls the inner weak trace inclusion check only for state pairs that have no outgoing τ-transition; ac^+ which saves the antichain of the inner weak trace inclusion check with verdict *true*; ac^-, which stores the antichain of the inner weak trace inclusion check with verdict *false*; and their combination ac_{ac-opt}.

	Algorithm 2	Algorithm 4	Algorithm 6 (*stable*)	Algorithm 6 (ac^+)	Algorithm 6 (ac^-)	Algorithm 6 (ac_{ac-opt})
Coarse Set	410.2	354.1	17.3	28.4	329.4	4.3
Finegrained Set	5.1	3.8	0.4	1.1	3.7	0.2
Industrial	$\perp$	$\perp$	0.1	318.9	$\perp$	0.1
Lazy Set	151.6	105.1	1.8	11.6	105.1	0.9
Optimistic Set	$\perp$	$\perp$	63.4	170.9	$\perp$	15.6
Non Blocking	2.4	1.6	0.1	0.1	1.7	0.1
Treiber stack	$\perp$	$\perp$	511.5	$\perp$	$\perp$	203.7

effect is less pronounced than the stability check. Keeping track of a negative antichain has minimal effect. By combining all three optimisations, we obtain improvements of up-to a factor 100 over the naive antichain algorithm, and up-to a factor 4 over the best-performing individual optimisations.

6 Closing Remarks

In this paper we studied various algorithms for checking weak impossible futures inclusion between two labelled transition systems. We showed that a naive algorithm runs into timeouts, even for relatively small labelled transition systems, and a naive adoption of antichains does not really lead to improvements. By means of a tight integration of the antichains and by postponing expensive weak trace inclusion checks, a more practical algorithm is obtained.

There are several further optimisations that may have a positive effect on performance. For instance, before running the rather expensive weak failures inclusion check, one may wish to minimise the labelled transition systems modulo branching bisimilarity, which can be done efficiently, see [6]. Furthermore, one could use the (weak) simulation preorder to reduce the antichain, see [1]. Lastly, we remark that our heuristic, storing only the initial state pair for which the inner weak trace inclusion check is carried out in the negative antichain in case this check fails, can be generalised to all state pairs in *working*, provided the weak trace inclusion check is conducted in a depth-first manner. We have not experimented with this option, but we expect it to lead to further speed-ups.

Acknowledgments. Part of this work was supported by Cynergy4MIE (ChipsJU, No. 101140226).

Disclosure of Interests. The authors have no competing interests to declare that are relevant to the content of this article.

References

1. Abdulla, P.A., Chen, Y.-F., Holík, L., Mayr, R., Vojnar, T.: When simulation meets antichains. In: Esparza, J., Majumdar, R. (eds.) TACAS 2010. LNCS, vol. 6015, pp. 158–174. Springer, Heidelberg (2010). https://doi.org/10.1007/978-3-642-12002-2_14
2. Bergstra, J.A., Klop, J.W., Olderog, E.-R.: Failures without chaos: a new process semantics for fair abstract ion. In: IFIP TC 2/WG 2.2 1986, pp. 77–104 (1987)
3. Bunte, O., Groote, J.F., Keiren, J.J.A., Laveaux, M., Neele, T., de Vink, E.P., Wesselink, W., Wijs, A., Willemse, T.A.C.: The mCRL2 toolset for analysing concurrent systems. In: Vojnar, T., Zhang, L. (eds.) TACAS 2019. LNCS, vol. 11428, pp. 21–39. Springer, Cham (2019). https://doi.org/10.1007/978-3-030-17465-1_2
4. Herlihy, M., Shavit, N.: The art of multiprocessor programming. Morgan Kaufmann (2008)
5. Hoare, C.A.R.: Communicating Sequential Processes. Prentice-Hall (1985)
6. Jansen, D.N., Groote, J.F., Keiren, J.J.A., Wijs, A.: An o(m log n) algorithm for branching bisimilarity on labelled transition systems. In: TACAS (2), vol. 12079. LNCS, pp. 3–20. Springer (2020)
7. Laveaux, M., Groote, J.F., Willemse, T.A.C.: Correct and efficient antichain algorithms for refinement checking. In: Pérez, J.A., Yoshida, N. (eds.) FORTE 2019. LNCS, vol. 11535, pp. 185–203. Springer, Cham (2019). https://doi.org/10.1007/978-3-030-21759-4_11
8. Laveaux, M., Groote, J.F., T.A.C.: Willemse. Correct and efficient antichain algorithms for refinement checking. Log. Methods Comput. Sci. **17**(1) (2021)
9. Milner, R.: Calculi for synchrony and asynchrony. Theor. Comput. Sci. **25**, 267–310 (1983)
10. Park, D.: Concurrency and automata on infinite sequences. In: Deussen, P., (ed.) Theoretical Computer Science. number 104. LNCS, pp. 167–183. Springer (1981)
11. Paval, R.: Modeling and verifying concurrent data structures. Master's thesis, Eindhoven University of Technology (2018). https://research.tue.nl/files/93882157/Thesis_Roxana_Paval.pdf
12. Roscoe, A.W.: Understanding Concurrent Systems. Texts in Computer Science. Springer (2010)
13. Shann, C.-H., Huang, T.-L., Chen, C.: A practical nonblocking queue algorithm using compare-and-swap. In: ICPADS 2000, pp. 470–475 (2000)
14. Treiber, R.K.: Systems programming: Coping with parallelism. Thomas J. Watson Research, International Business Machines Incorporated (1986)
15. van Beusekom, R., Groote, J.F., Hoogendijk, P., Howe, R., Wesselink, W., Wieringa, R., Willemse, T.A.C.: Formalising the Dezyne Modelling Language in mCRL2. In: Petrucci, L., Seceleanu, C., Cavalcanti, A. (eds.) FMICS/AVoCS - 2017. LNCS, vol. 10471, pp. 217–233. Springer, Cham (2017). https://doi.org/10.1007/978-3-319-67113-0_14
16. van Glabbeek, R.J.: The linear time - branching time spectrum II. In: CONCUR 1993, pp. 66–81 (1993)
17. van Glabbeek, R.J., Weijland, W.P.: Branching time and abstraction in bisimulation semantics. J. ACM **43**(3), 555–600 (1996)

18. Voorhoeve, M., Mauw, S.: Impossible futures and determinism. Inf. Process. Lett. **80**(1), 51–58 (2001)
19. De Wulf, M., Doyen, L., Henzinger, T.A., Raskin, J.-F.: Antichains: a new algorithm for checking universality of finite automata. In: Ball, T., Jones, R.B. (eds.) CAV 2006. LNCS, vol. 4144, pp. 17–30. Springer, Heidelberg (2006). https://doi.org/10.1007/11817963_5

Unfairly Efficient Byzantine-Fault Tolerant Random Number Generation

Tim Muller$^{(\boxtimes)}$ ⓘ, Xavier Carpent ⓘ, and Chenming Xu ⓘ

School of Computer Science, University of Nottingham, Nottingham, UK
{tim.muller,xavier.carpent,chenming.xu}@nottingham.ac.uk

Abstract. Byzantine faults present a major obstacle to unbiased distributed random number generation, because it allows an adversary to abort the protocol if they can predict a random value they do not like. There are computationally/communication heavy mechanisms to recover from such faults. Our approach avoids this by accepting a limited bias in favour of an adversary; in exchange, our protocols can run many times in the time it takes the heavier mechanisms to recover. Our protocols assume the strongest Byzantine adversary, as opposed to assuming an honest majority. Both theoretical analysis and simulation have been used to confirm and further evaluate the protocols' viability. The application of the randomness used in the paper is creating private pseudonyms.

1 Introduction

In distributed systems, achieving consensus on random numbers that are both secure and unbiased is a challenging task, particularly in environments where nodes may be compromised or act maliciously. Byzantine Fault Tolerant Random Number Generation (BFT-RNG) addresses these challenges by ensuring that even in the presence of Byzantine faults – where nodes can behave arbitrarily and unpredictably – the system can still generate unbiased random numbers. BFT-RNG has applications in secure multi-party computations, blockchain technology, decentralized consensus mechanisms and mental poker protocols. For example, in blockchain networks, random numbers are often used in leader election processes and for creating fair and tamper-resistant protocols. The examples rely on heavy cryptography. In this paper, we investigate lightweight alternatives.

In BFT (Byzantine Fault Tolerant) systems, users may drop out. If the first user to be able to compute the result does not like the result, he could abort the protocol. Unless the other users can recover the result, this introduces a bias to the randomness. The recovery mechanisms used in BFT protocols are expensive in terms of communication and/or computation. We propose to introduce mechanisms to limit the bias, rather than eliminate it, resulting in a "unfairly" efficient protocol.

The effect that the bias has differs from application to application. In this paper, we study *mixing* protocols, where users mix up pseudonyms to gain privacy – similar to, e.g., Mix-nets or bitcoin tumblers. Our technique resembles bitcoin tumblers more closely, but is not intended for cryptocurrencies. The mixing protocol consists of a *matching* phase and a *progress* phase, where the goal of the matching phase is to create a random grouping of users, to allow the groups to progress (i.e. mix up pseudonyms).

The adversary attempts to subvert the randomness in the matching phase, to ensure they are in a user's mixing group. Our results demonstrate that lightweight protocols are a viable and efficient way to implement mixing protocols, despite a limited bias.

Note by Tim. The paper circumvents heavy cryptographic machinery, in favour of a playful solution grounded in a rigorous formal foundation. To me, this is the typical Sjouke approach, and this paper's topic immediately sprang to mind when asked to contribute. Sjouke was my PhD supervisor. His supervision enforced the idea that research should also bring joy, through solving interesting puzzles. I strive to bring the same joy to my students – and the same rigorous foundation.

2   Related Work

Allowing pseudonymous authentication is not a novel idea. Attribute-based authentication is defined to support this idea [18], but updating attributes is relatively expensive. Alternatively, a simple centralised mechanism could sign a large number of cryptographically unlinked certificates, to be used pseudonymously by a single user, e.g. like the Security Credential Management System [6]. Again, supporting dynamic properties is hard, and may require non-standard cryptography (e.g. pre-signatures to prove reputation [1] or updatable anonymous credentials [3]). The EU proposes development of "digital wallets" [2] that have the goal of allowing citizens to use pseudonyms that can prove such dynamic properties (e.g. age). The proposed architecture involves registering pseudonyms centrally, without loss of privacy through the use of Zero Knowledge Proofs – but details are unclear[1].

Rather than creating pseudonyms anonymously and using cryptography to create a hidden link to a person, we can create pseudonyms publicly and use mixing to hide them. Mixnets [7] are a well-known example of using mixing to hide the link between (network) entities, and inspired the popular hidden network TOR [9]. These rely on specific entities to mix, rather than users of the protocol. Bitcoin tumblers [5] are also types of mixing protocols, with protocols such as "Tornado Cash" relying on Ethereum [20] smart contracts and zero-knowledge proofs [4].

Randomness beacons [12] are trusted (public) entities that generate a pseudo-random stream, where it is hard to determine the state of the random number generation (RNG) from the stream. Verifiable Random Functions [14] can be

---

[1] https://eu-digital-identity-wallet.github.io/eudi-doc-architecture-and-reference-framework/2.4.0/discussion-topics/g-zero-knowledge-proof.

used to create a pseudo-random stream, where the generator of the stream can prove that random numbers were generated fairly. A core point of this paper is that even knowing a value ahead of time biases protocols. The randomness beacon must be trusted not to collude, and protocols using VFR must ensure that the entity committing to a random value is not subject to Byzantine Faults – or make the protocol BFT. Example applications using VFR in distributed settings are Algorand [8] and Dfinity [11].

BFT means ensuring uninterrupted operation despite potential node failures, network delays, or malicious behaviour [17]. The Byzantine Generals Problem, formulated by Lamport et al. [13], defines the difficulties of achieving agreement in adversarial conditions, laying the foundation for modern BFT consensus protocols. BFT consensus can be used for RNG. Fairness, unpredictability, and resistance to adversarial control are critical. In distributed networks, RNG-based consensus is widely used in scenarios where deterministic decision-making is infeasible or undesirable. A common applications is leadership election, where a random selection process determines which user will take on a privileged role, such as proposing new blocks in Proof-of-Stake (PoS) blockchains [15]. Typical BFT consensus for RNG relies on being able to recover the random value even upon faults. RandHound and RandHerd [19] is an example of this approach. An important insight they make is that it is possible to use secret sharing (e.g. Shamir's Secret Sharing) to allow honest users to recover the random value. However, honest users must outnumber malicious ones for this to work, and the protocol requires quadratic communication for recovery – times in order of magnitude of minutes. Another alternative is to use timed commitments based on time-lock puzzles [16] to recover random values. For a timed commitment, it is easy to verify the revealed value, but to open without a reveal requires a computation (believed to be) bottlenecked by CPU clock speed. All devices take roughly equally long to force it open, hiding the value for a set amount of time. An adversary can slow the process down by not revealing, slowing down run times to an order of minutes to hours.

3   Limited Bias in RNG

The biggest challenge for protocols for Byzantine-Fault Tolerant (BFT) Random Number Generation (RNG), is the notion of bias. Take the trivial protocol where every user commits to a (random) value in a domain, and once all commitments are in, all users reveal their commitment, and the random value is computed as the sum of the values modulo the domain. There are two conditions that are sufficient for this trivial protocol to work: first, at least one user must have used a uniformly random value; second, nobody drops out between the commit and reveal phase. A malicious user could introduce a bias favourable to themselves, by waiting for everyone else to reveal, computing the hypothetical result, and dropping out if they don't like the result.

Before starting, we introduce some general notation used throughout the paper. Let N be the set of users and $n = |N|$. Let $M \subseteq N$ be the set of malicious users and $m = |M|$. Let $H = N \setminus M$ M and m are not known to honest users.

For existing BFT-RNG protocols, typically the issue of drop-outs is dealt with by ensuring the protocol can recover the result, even if a number of users drop out. These protocols do not need a quantitative definition of bias, as they guarantee the lack of bias (under their assumptions). A typical assumption is that the number of malicious users m is strictly less than half the total number of users n; i.e. $m < \frac{n}{2}$. As discussed in Sect. 2, however, this comes at a cost, as these protocols require heavy cryptography and/or many rounds of communication. Allow randomness to be biased makes the random number less useful, but may reduce this cost substantially. How bias affects the (expected) benefit of running a protocol depends on the application at hand. In the remainder of the paper, we look at *mixing protocols*, and define the benefit of the various outcomes explicitly. In this section, however, we keep the notion abstract.

Consider I to be a protocol that computes and uses unbiased randomness. The outcomes of I are described by distribution Δ_I with support S. Let $B : S \to \mathbb{R}$ be the benefit function. That means that for $x \in S$, $B(x)$ represents how much this random outcome benefits the honest user, in the protocol(s) following random number generation. With unbiased randomness, the expected benefit of a single run to an honest user is $\mathbb{E}_B(\Delta_I) = \sum_{s \in S} \Delta_I(s) \cdot B(s)$.

Our goal is to gain a substantial efficiency advantage in exchange for a minor relaxation of the bias of the randomness. To capture this, we introduce the notion of opportunity cost. The opportunity cost is inversely proportional to how often the protocol can be run in a given time. The expected benefit of protocol I (with opportunity cost c_I) per unit of time is, therefore, $\frac{\mathbb{E}_B(\Delta_i(x))}{c_I}$.

A lightweight protocol L is designed to run more efficiently than a heavy protocol that involves a lot of communication or computation. So $c_L \ll c_I$. The downside of L is that an adversary can influence the probabilities to minimise the expected benefit per unit of time. Let Δ_L be the distribution that minimises $\mathbb{E}_{\Delta_L} \frac{B(x)}{c_L}$. The bias against an honest user is then $\mathbb{E}_{\Delta_I}(B(x)) - \mathbb{E}_{\Delta_L}(B(x))$.

We say a protocol L is *viable* if $\frac{\mathbb{E}_B(\Delta_L)}{c_L} \geq \epsilon$, for $\epsilon = o(\frac{n-m}{m})$, and *preferable* if $\frac{\mathbb{E}_B(\Delta_L)}{c_L} \geq \frac{\mathbb{E}_B(\Delta_I)}{c_I}$. The benefit function is *friendly* if $B(x) \geq 0$, for all x, and *simple* if $B(x) \in \{0, 1\}$ for all x. A friendly or simple protocol may be non-viable, if the adversary can force a non-beneficial outcome with high probability. No protocol is viable under a typical network attack model (e.g. Dolev-Yao [10]), since an adversary can simply block all communication, ensuring the protocol fails to deliver any functionality, delivering 0 benefit. Our adversarial model is in Sect. 4.2.

Example 1. Ten users $\mathcal{U} = \mathcal{H} \cup \mathcal{M}$ want to elect a leader amongst them. The 6 honest users $\mathcal{H}$ do not know who the other honest users are, and the 4 malicious users $\mathcal{M}$ collaborate. The vote is decided by plurality, and ties are broken by randomly selecting one of the tied candidates at random. In a heavy and fair voting protocol I, malicious users do not see the honest users' votes, nor can they affect the tally. In a hypothetical lightweight protocol L, voting is done

164   T. Muller et al.

publicly, and malicious users can see the honest users' votes.

The *opportunity cost* of both the protocols is the same, as voting multiple times has no additional benefit, so $c_I = c_L = c$.

The *benefit function* B can be defined on the elected leader ℓ as $B(\ell) = 1$ when $\ell \in \mathcal{H}$ and $B(\ell) = 0$ when $\ell \in \mathcal{M}$. This is a *simple* benefit function.

Honest voters collectively pick a user $x \in \mathcal{U}$, and vote for this user x with $p = 80\%$ probability (the remaining 20% represent casting a vote at random). Hence, there is a 40% chance the honest users attempt to unwittingly vote in an malicious user. To analyse Δ, honest users must have picked an honest user x (60%) and sufficiently few must have deviated so that malicious votes cannot muster a tie or win. In the case of I, deviating votes are likely to be irrelevant to the tally. Specifically:

$$\Delta_I(\ell \in \mathcal{H}) = 0.6 \cdot \left[\binom{6}{6} \cdot p^6 + \binom{6}{5} \cdot p^5 \cdot (1-p) \cdot \left(\frac{8}{9} + \frac{1}{2} \cdot \frac{1}{9} \right) \right.$$
$$\left. + \binom{6}{4} \cdot p^4 \cdot (1-p)^2 \cdot \left(\frac{8}{9} \right)^2 \cdot \frac{1}{2} \right] \approx 0.44.$$

But in L, malicious users can see the deviations, and select a malicious candidate that has received a deviation vote (if it exists), giving:

$$\Delta_L(\ell \in \mathcal{H}) = 0.6 \cdot \left[\binom{6}{6} \cdot p^6 + \binom{6}{5} \cdot p^5 \cdot (1-p) \cdot \left(\frac{5}{9} + \frac{4}{9} \cdot \frac{1}{2} \right) \right.$$
$$\left. + \binom{6}{4} \cdot p^4 \cdot (1-p)^2 \cdot \left(\frac{5}{9} \right)^2 \cdot \frac{1}{2} \right] \approx 0.36.$$

Therefore, L is not *preferable*, since $\frac{\mathbb{E}_B(\Delta_L)}{c_L} = \frac{0.36}{c} < \frac{0.44}{c} = \frac{\mathbb{E}_B(\Delta_I)}{c_I}$.
Neither protocol is *viable*, since in both cases when $|\mathcal{H}| < |\mathcal{M}|$, the malicious users always win, and so the expected benefit is 0; less than any ϵ. This matches one's expectation that the protocol is insecure when there are too many malicious users.

4   Matchmaking Protocols

A matchmaking protocol is a (sub)protocol that groups users together (somewhat) randomly. A typical reason for matchmaking, might be as part of another protocol (*mixing* protocol) aiming to gain some form of anonymity. If you are in a group of k honest users, then it is easy to gain k-anonymity through the group. This changes if some (or all) other users in your group are malicious.

4.1   Sybil-Free Pseudonyms

In this section, we introduce an example of a (sub)protocol that gains anonymity if all users are honest: the *public key regeneration protocol*.

The public key regeneration protocol is to allow for anonymity through the use of ephemeral pseudonyms, while ensuring that nobody controls more than one pseudonym at a time. A group of k users, identified by their public keys, can get together and publish a notice that their set of k public keys is replaced by a new set of k public keys, signed by the k private keys corresponding to the old public keys. No honest user would sign the notice, if it does not contain a new public key that they have generated. Any group of colluding users will not be able to gain control of a greater number of keys than they have started with.

A potential application of these privacy-friendly pseudonyms is voting, rating or reviewing, where it is important that people do not provide multiple votes, ratings or reviews. These pseudonyms can protect against whitewashing and Sybil attacks in trust and reputation systems without sacrificing privacy[2]. Similar mechanism are, e.g., Bitcoin tumblers, but here, users have exactly 1 token.

The benefit of running the public key regeneration protocol with only honest users can be defined through anonymity set size. After a successful run of the protocol, each user's anonymity set is now equal to the union of the original anonymity sets, since any of the possible identities of the pseudonyms going in could be associated with one of the new pseudonyms. However, if a malicious user participates in the public key regeneration protocol, then they can block progress by refusing to sign the new set of public keys (or putting multiple new public keys on the list, inducing an honest user to disagree and refuse to sign). The benefit function B for matchmaking is, therefore defined as the increase in anonymity set size for a given matching, and is 0 if the adversary can prevent successful run of the protocol.

The opportunity cost of the mixing protocol is the opportunity cost of the matchmaking protocol plus the opportunity cost of the public key regeneration protocol. Note that the latter involves at least 2 peer-to-peer messages per user, and 1 public broadcast, as well as 2 public key operations (key-gen and signing), and we aim for matchmaking to have at most a similar opportunity cost.

4.2 Problem Statement

The goal of matchmaking is to divide users into groups (somewhat) randomly. An honest user benefits from being grouped with only honest others, and not from being grouped with malicious users (per Sect. 4.1). The core challenge is the absence of fair RNG, so this needs to be done cooperatively, despite the presence of a strong adversary controlling many malicious users.

Take the strongest adversary that does not rule out the existence of a viable protocol. If all-but-one users of the protocol are malicious, then they can trivially prevent matchmaking through collusion, so we assume there are at least 2 honest users. Furthermore, as observed at the end of Sect. 3, viable protocols

---

[2] A whitewashing attack refers to the ability to create a new account once a malicious user has ruined their reputation on their old account. And a Sybil attack is when a malicious user has multiple colluding accounts.

(for matchmaking) can only exist if honest users can reliably deliver messages to each other. Hence our goal is Byzantine-Fault Tolerance with $m = n - 2$ malicious users; malicious users can leave, deviate from protocol, collude and masquerade as honest users, but not prevent honest users from communicating. As the malicious users are capable of collusion, we view them as being controlled by the adversary in our terminology.

The matchmaking protocol must be lightweight, a couple of communications per user and no heavy cryptography. Keeping the matchmaking protocol light allows it in settings with cheap IoT devices, allowing for privacy-friendly pseudonyms through the public key regeneration protocol.

Observe that if $n-2$ users are malicious, then any group of 3 or larger contains a malicious user. Hence, under this strong adversary, the only reasonable group size is 2. While in Sect. 7, we consider alternatives under weaker adversaries, recall that our goal is to make progress under the most adversarial setting. Thus, matchmaking reduces to pairing for formal analysis in our context.

4.3   Mixing Protocol Structure

There is an inherent information imbalance between the users that provide randomness first and those that provide randomness last. The issue is that an effective adversary can use non-determinism to their advantage and ensure that they always go last[3]. The general solution is to have users commit to their randomness, and then to reveal their randomness later on.

The general protocol design has three phases:

1. Commitment phase.
2. Reveal phase.
3. Progress phase.

The first two stages are the matchmaking (sub)protocols that we study in this paper, and the progress phase is instantiated with the public key regeneration protocol, for the reasons indicated in Sect. 4.1.

In the commitment phase, users pick a random value, and publish a commitment to their chosen value. The adversary can pick chosen non-random values, but they will not be able to see the values of the honest users at this stage. The commitment is tagged and authenticated with the (pseudonymous) public key of the users. Consensus on commitments is reached by having all users publish the list of (authenticated) commitments, and using any commitment on the list that is consistent (as differing signed commitments means the sender must have deviated from protocol).

In the matching phase, users reveal their random value (tagged and authenticated). The adversary can choose not to reveal certain malicious users values

---

[3] Unless there is a specific mechanism to prevent this, but if the application involves pseudonymity, then keeping track of whether a specific user has been last recently might be incompatible.

(or equivalently, to have them reveal incorrect values). A similar round for consensus is done here, so values are either revealed to all or to none. The revealed value must also be checked to be valid for the commitment. At the end of this round, groups are formed based on a rule defined in one of the next sections – this does not require additional communication.

We define an abstract representation of the protocol:

Definition 1. *Let V be the set of values users can commit to. The* commitment map $C : N \to V$ *defines the commitments of users. The* reveal map $R : N \to (V \cup \{\perp\})$ *defines the valid and invalid reveals of users. Either $R(z) = \perp$ or $R(z) = C(z)$, for invalid/no reveal and valid reveal, respectively. A* run *of a protocol is the pair (C, R). A* grouping $\mathcal{G}$ *is a subset of $\mathcal{P}(N)$, such that each $x \in N$ is in at most one $g \in \mathcal{G}$. Let $G : (N \to (V \cup \{\perp\})) \to \mathcal{P}(\mathcal{P}(N))$ be the* grouping function, *which takes the revealed values and outputs the grouping.*

The user behaviour can be defined similarly:

Definition 2. *The honest users pick values according to some distribution δ and always reveal their commitment. An adversarial strategy is a pair (c, r), with $c : M \to V$ defining malicious commitments and $r : C \to (M \to \{\top, \perp\})$ whether the adversary chooses to reveal commitments ($\top$) or not ($\perp$). The probability of a run (C, R) is $\prod_{h \in H} \delta(C(h))$ if: $C(h) = R(h)$ for $h \in H$, $C(m) = c(m)$ and $R(m) \in \{r(m), C(m)\}$ for $m \in M$, and otherwise 0. The probability of a grouping is $\Delta = G(\delta)$.*

The protocol determines δ, but in all protocols in this paper, δ is the uniform distribution, which we shall implicitly assume from now on. Our definition assumes that the adversary is not stochastic, because honest users are not strategic, so mixed strategies are not necessary.

Remark 1. The benefit function is not independent between runs of the protocol. In the case $m = n-2$, the benefit function can only be 1 once and if the expected benefit of one run is χ, then it is $1 - (1 - \chi)^{\kappa}$ for κ runs. For small χ and κ, $1 - (1 - \chi)^{\kappa} \approx \kappa \cdot \chi$ as χ^2 is negligible.

Each of the three phases has a set end-time, and the actions of the users (including malicious ones) does not affect the time it takes to run the protocol in question. Hence, in our analysis, we can ignore the opportunity cost, as this is constant. The opportunity cost becomes relevant when doing comparisons with protocols that are not in the form of the mixing protocol.

4.4   Naive Protocol

Naively, we can let each user commit to a random large integer, and let the grouping be decided by a random number generator with a seed determined by the sum of all revealed integers. In a fair scenario, the probability of the two honest users being grouped together without malicious users is at most 1 in $n-1$, if users are being paired up. However, if a (malicious) user does not reveal their value, then either we (1) abort and restart or (2) continue with the incomplete value. With option 1, the probability of a grouping with exactly the two honest users is 0 – the last malicious user can compute the outcome before revealing their value, and simply not reveal their value if it helps the honest users, forcing a restart. For option 2, the adversary can compute the outcome as soon as the two honest users reveal their values (through collusion of all malicious users), and select a subset of malicious users that ensures that the resulting value does not lead to a pairing of the two honest users. There are a lot of subsets to consider (2^m), and the resulting probability is:

$$\prod_{0 \leq i \leq m} \left(\frac{1}{i+1}\right)^{\binom{m}{i}} \approx \left(1 - \frac{1}{m+1}\right)^{2^m} \approx 0 \tag{1}$$

The naive protocol is not viable under our definition. The protocols proposed in the next sections work by proposing smarter ways to use randomness to group users, ensuring viability.

5   Bucketing Protocols

In this section, we introduce a class of matchmaking protocols based on the idea that users randomly select a bucket to get into, so that the adversary's behaviour has no impact on two honest users ending up in the same bucket. As we shall prove, the protocols in this section share the property that it is never advantageous to the adversary not to reveal their committed value. This ability is what gave the adversary a lot of power in the naive protocol, and these protocols neutralise that ability.

5.1   Bucket Protocol

The first protocol we introduce is the bucket protocol. In the bucket protocol, users commit to a large whole number value from V in the commitment phase. In the matching phase, users reveal their value. Every value is taken mod k, for some value k determined by the protocol, meaning that every value falls in one of k buckets. Every bucket defines a matching group, which is now publicly known, so users can proceed with the progress phase. Progress is made if both honest users y^* and y' are in the same bucket, and no malicious user z is in the same bucket. Formally:

Definition 3. *The k-bucket grouping function is*

$$G_{B,k}(R) = \{U \subseteq N \mid \forall_{a \in U, b \in U, c \notin U}(R(a) \equiv R(b) \not\equiv R(c) \pmod{k})\}.$$

The benefit function B_B for the bucket protocol is $B(G_{B,k}(R)) = 1$ if $\{y^*, y'\} \in G_{B,k}(R)$, and 0 otherwise.

A crucial advantage of the bucket protocol over the naive protocol is that there is no incentive for malicious users not to reveal their value. Observe that if x and y commit to the same value $(\mod k)$, then matching can only be prevented if a malicious user also commits and reveals their value, because the honest users always reveal. Formally:

Proposition 1. *For all runs (C, R): $B_B(G_{B,k}(R)) \geq B_B(G_{B,k}(C))$.*

Proof. If $B_B(G_{B,k}(C)) = 1$, then $\{y^*, y'\} \in G_{B,k}(C)$, meaning $C(y^*) = C(y') \neq C(z_i) \mod k$, and thus $R(y^*) = R(y') \neq R(z_i) \mod k$, hence $\{y^*, y'\} \in G_{B,k}(R)$, and thus $B_B(G_{B,k}(R)) = 1$.

The strategic edge of the adversary is to pick non-random values in the commit phase. Specifically, the adversary wants to put a malicious user in as many buckets as possible.

If there are more malicious users than buckets, then the adversary puts at least one malicious user in each bucket, resulting in a non-viable protocol.

Proposition 2. *If $k \leq m$, and $R(z_i) = i$ then $B_B(G_{B,k}(R)) = 0$.*

Proof. Say $i = R(y^*) \mod k$, then $R(y^*) = R(z_i)$, thus $\{y^*, y'\} \notin G_{B,k}(R)$.

If there are more buckets than malicious users, then the optimal adversarial strategy is to ensure every bucket has at most one malicious user:

Proposition 3. *If $k > m$, then selecting R s.t. $i \neq j \implies R(z_i) \neq R(z_j)$ minimises $\mathbb{E}_{B_B}(\Delta_B)$.*

Proof. Let $K_M = \{R(z_i) \mid z_i \in M\}$. The honest users select buckets independently randomly, and so $p(B_B(G_{B,k}(R)) = 1) = (p(R(y^*) = R(y')) \cdot p(R(y^*) \notin K_M))$. Since δ_B is uniform, that equals: $\frac{1}{k} \cdot \frac{k - |K_M|}{k}$, which is minimised if $|K_M|$ is maximal, so $|K_M| = m$.

The expected benefit as a function of k can trivially be derived from the proofs: If $k \leq m$, then it is 0 and otherwise $\frac{1}{k} \cdot \frac{k-m}{k} = \frac{k-m}{k^2}$.

Theorem 1. *The expected benefit of the bucket protocol can be $\frac{1}{4n-8}$.*

Proof. Basic algebra shows $\frac{k-m}{k^2}$ is maximised when $k = 2m = 2(n-2)$.

To ensure optimal operation, without introducing additional rounds of "sign-ups", the value of k is determined at the end of the commit phase to be $2n - 4$. The uniformly randomly chosen large value remains uniformly random when reduced $\mod k$, if the range of large values is sufficiently large. (Note that the computation breaks if $m = 0$ as it would suggest $k = 0$ buckets – we ignore $m = 0$ for simplicity).

The bucket protocol is, therefore, viable and has a reasonably good performance already. The ideal protocol's expected benefit is $\frac{1}{n-1}$, so the difference is a constant factor of 4. Four runs of the bucket protocol is roughly equivalent to the ideal protocol. However, we have room to bring the constant down. Making k large enough to reduce the odds of sharing a bucket with a malicious user also reduces the odds of the other honest user being in there. Instead, what if we keep k small ($k = 2$ buckets), and recursively reduce the group size to 2?

5.2   Bitstring Protocol

In the commitment phase of the bitstring protocol, users commit to a large value, which is interpreted as a bitstring. In the reveal phase, users reveal their bitstring. The least-significant bit determines the first bucket, the second lsb the second bucket, and so on until we identify a bucket with at most 2 users. If there are two users, then they match, otherwise the match fails. Of course, the match is only beneficial if both users are honest.

Formally:

Definition 4. *Let* $\mathbf{pre}(v, w)$ *be the size of the shared prefix of bitstrings* v *and* w*. The bitstring grouping function* $G_{BS}(R) = \{\{a, b\} \mid \forall_{c \in (N \setminus \{a,b\})}(\mathbf{pre}(R(a), R(b)) > \max(\mathbf{pre}(R(a), R(c)), \mathbf{pre}(R(b), R(c))))\}$*. The benefit function* B_{BS} *for the bitstring protocol is* $B_{BS}(G_{Bs}(R)) = 1$ *if* $\{y^*, y'\} \in G_{BS}(R)$*, and 0 otherwise.*

It remains true that the adversary has no incentive not to reveal their committed values:

Proposition 4. *For all runs* (C, R)*,* $B_{BS}(G_{BS}(R)) \geq B_{BS}(G_{BS}(C))$*.*

Proof.
If $B_{BS}(G_{BS}(C)) = 1$, then $\{y^*, y'\} \in G_{BS}(C)$, meaning $\mathbf{pre}(C(y^*), C(y')) > \max_{z_i \in M}(\mathbf{pre}(C(y^*), C(z_i)), \mathbf{pre}(C(y'), C(z_i)))$, and thus $\mathbf{pre}(R(y^*), R(y')) > \max_{z_i \in M}(\mathbf{pre}(R(y^*), R(z_i)), \mathbf{pre}(R(y'), R(z_i)))$, so $B_{BS}(G_{BS}(R)) = 1$.

The adversary wants every user to commit to a unique prefix of length $\lceil \log_2(m) \rceil$. This strategy is optimal:

Proposition 5. *Selecting* R *s.t.* $R(z_i) = i$ *minimises* $\mathbb{E}_{B_{BS}}(\Delta_{BS})$*.*

Proof. Let $t = \mathbf{pre}(R(y^*), R(y'))$, and let p be that prefix. If there is a $z_i \in M$ s.t. p is a prefix of $R(z_i)$, then either $\mathbf{pre}(R(y^*), R(z_i))$ or $\mathbf{pre}(R(y'), R(z_i))$ is larger than t, since the $(t+1)^{\text{th}}$ bit of $R(y^*)$ and $R(y')$ differs, so the $(t+1)^{\text{th}}$ bit of $R(z_i)$ must match one of them. Hence, if p is a prefix of $R(z_i)$ then $\{y^*, y'\} \notin G_{BS}(R)$. Let $c(R, s)$ count the number of distinct prefixes of length s of $R(z_i \in M)$, out of a total 2^s possible prefixes. The probability that $\{y^*, y'\} \notin G_{BS}(R)$ therefore equals $\frac{c(R,t)}{2^t}$. Our choice of R has a count $c(R, s) = 2^s$ for $s \leq \log_2(m)$ and $c(R, s) = m$ for $s \geq \log_2(m)$. Therefore R has maximal coverage for all s, maximising $\frac{c(R,t)}{2^t}$.

The expected benefit under such an adversary is $\frac{1}{3m}$ if $m = 2^\ell$, and even better if m is not a power of 2. To be precise:

Theorem 2. *The expected benefit of the bitstring protocol is* $\frac{1}{3n-6}$ *if* $n - 2$ *is a power of 2, and strictly larger otherwise.*

Proof. The probability that $t = \mathtt{pre}(R(y^*), R(y'))$ is $\frac{1}{2^{t+1}}$. The expected benefit is $\sum_{0 \leq t}(\frac{1}{2^{t+1}} \cdot \frac{2^t - d(R,t)}{2^t})$. Let $\ell = \lfloor \log_2(m) \rfloor$. As $\frac{d(R,t)}{2^t} = 1$ when $t \leq \ell$, and $d(R,t) = m$ when $t > \ell$ that equals: $1 - \sum_{0 \leq t \leq \ell}(\frac{1}{2^{t+1}}) - \sum_{\ell+1 \leq t}(\frac{1}{2^{t+1}} \cdot \frac{m}{2^t}) = \frac{1}{2^{\ell+1}} - \sum_{\ell+1 \leq t}(\frac{m}{2^{2t+1}}) = \frac{1}{2^{\ell+1}} - \sum_{0 \leq t}(\frac{m}{2^{2t+2\ell+3}})$. Call $2^\ell = [m]$, and it can be written $\frac{1}{2[m]} - \frac{1}{4 \cdot [m]^2} \sum_{0 \leq t} \cdot (\frac{m}{2^{2t+1}}) = \frac{3[m]}{6 \cdot [m]^2} - \frac{m}{6 \cdot [m]^2}$. If $m = 2^\ell$, then $[m] = m$, and the formula simplifies to $\frac{1}{3m} = \frac{1}{3n-6}$. If $m \neq 2^\ell$ then $[m] < m$, and $\frac{3[m]-m}{6 \cdot [m]^2} > \frac{3m-m}{6 \cdot m^2} = \frac{1}{3m}$.

An intuitive representation of the problem is a (balanced) binary tree, where the leaves are the shortest unique prefixes of the malicious users (See Fig. 1a). To win, the two honest users must end up in the same leaf, and if they do, they need to match with each other. The former has probability $\frac{1}{m}$ in a perfectly balanced tree, and the latter has probability $\frac{1}{3}$, for a total probability[4] of $\frac{1}{3m}$. For unbalanced trees, that probability is better than $\frac{1}{3m}$, due to Jensens' inequality. Can we purposely create unbalanced trees?

The formal treatment of the unbalanced tree protocol is in Appendix A. Informally, let $k = \frac{2m}{3}$ be the number of initial buckets, followed by $k = 2$ for subsequent buckets. Proposition 4 does not rely on k, and thus implies adversaries also always reveal in the unbalanced tree protocol. The adversary's optimal strategy is to ensure each of the k initial buckets has 1 or 2 malicious users, and in any bucket with 2, the next bucket must be different. Assuming k is even, the expected benefit of the unbalanced tree protocol is $\frac{3}{8m}$ (i.e. $\frac{3}{8n-16}$).

To derive this probability, observe that the probability that two honest users are in the same bucket is $\frac{1}{k} = \frac{3}{2m}$. There are 1 or 2 malicious users in that bucket too. Using Theorem 2, the probabilities are $\frac{1}{3}$ and $\frac{1}{6}$, respectively. Total probability is $\frac{3}{2m} \cdot (\frac{1}{2} \cdot \frac{1}{3} + \frac{1}{2} \cdot \frac{1}{6}) = \frac{3}{8m}$.

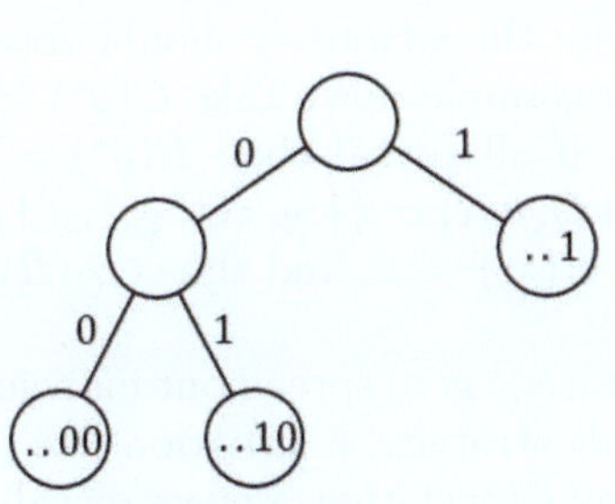

(a) Binary tree with $m = 3$

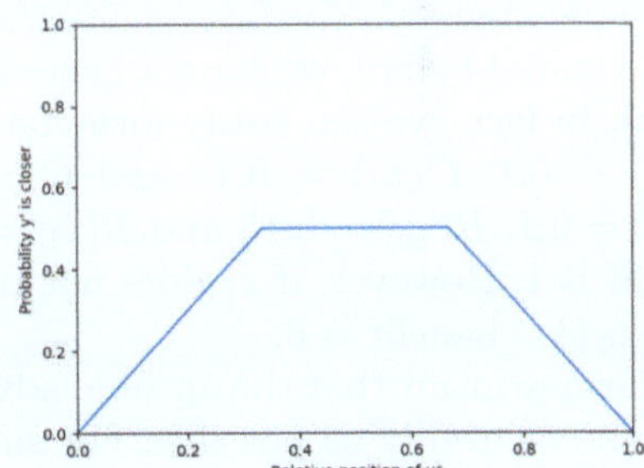

(b) Probability of matching honest user.

Fig. 1. Figures illustrating concepts in the bitstring and circle protocols

---

[4] Theorem 1 suggests $\frac{1}{4}$ to be in the same bucket without adversary, but there is also a $\frac{1}{4}$ probability all three are in the same bucket, so the probability is $\frac{1}{4} + \frac{1}{4} \cdot (\frac{1}{4} + \frac{1}{4} \cdot (\ldots)) = \frac{1}{3}$.

6   Proximity Pairing Protocols

The bucket protocols appear quite wasteful, as they leave many users in groups of 1. The alternative idea is that we should simply pair-up everyone (except one, if n is odd), based on randomness. The general idea is to match up users by some measure of closeness d of their random values, such that if the two honest users have committed to values that are closer to together than to any of the malicious users, then they are always paired up together. Contrary to bucket protocols, the proximity pairing protocols can have runs where not revealing helps the adversary.

In each of the following subsections, we rely on a different distance function d. The function d must at least be a semimetric (distances are positive, except $d(x, x) = 0$, and d is symmetric).

6.1   Circle Protocol

In the circle protocol, users commit to a value on a topological loop. The revealed values are used to compute a list of pairings of users. The first element is the pair of users closest on the circle; these two users are removed, and the next pair are the users that are now closest to each other. This continues until all (but one) are paired up.

Definition 5. *For $f : A \rightarrow B$, we may write $f - C$ to mean a function f', s.t. $f' : (A \setminus C) \rightarrow B$ and $\forall_{a \in (A \setminus C)}(f'(a) = f(a))$. The distance function $d_C : ((V \cup \{\bot\}) \times (V \cup \{\bot\})) \rightarrow (V \cup \{\infty\})$ is defined as $d_C(x, y) = \min(|x - y|, ||V| - x - y|)$ for $x, y \in V$ and ∞ otherwise. The circle grouping function G_C can be recursively defined $G_C(R) = \{\{a, b\} \mid \arg\min_{(a,b) \in N^2}(d_C(R(a), R(b)))\} \cup G_C(R - \{a, b\})$ if $|R| > 1$ and $\emptyset$ otherwise. The benefit function B_C for the circle protocol is $B_C(G_C(R)) = 1$ if $\{y^*, y'\} \in G_C(R)$, and 0 otherwise.*

As stated before, we cannot generally prove that the adversary should always reveal. In fact, we can easily formulate a counterexample now. Take $C(y^*) = 0$, $C(y') = 0.1$, $C(z_0) = 0.15$ and $C(z_1) = 0.16$, if all reveal then $R(y^*) = 0$, $R(y') = 0.1$, $R(z_0) = 0.15$ and $R(z_1) = 0.16$, and $G_C(R) = \{\{z_0, z_1\}, \{y^*, y'\}\}$ – benefit is 1. However, if z_1 does not reveal, then $R(z_1) = \bot$, and thus $G_C(R) = \{\{y', z_0\}\}$ – benefit is 0.

We may intuit that the optimal adversarial strategy is to spread out malicious commits as evenly as possible. For such a commit strategy, a situation like the counter example above cannot occur, and we may expect that always revealing is then optimal. Both intuitions are correct:

Proposition 6. *Selecting R s.t. $R(z_i) = \frac{|V|}{i}$ minimises $\mathbb{E}_{B_C}(\Delta_C)$.*

Proof. Let $z_i, z_j \in M^2$ be the pair s.t. the segment $[C(z_i), C(z_j)]$ is the shortest segment containing $C(y^*)$. Let σ be the length of the segment. If $C(y')$ is not in $[C(z_i), C(z_j)]$, there exists at least one z_h s.t. $d_C(C(y^*), C(y')) > d_C(C(y^*), C(z_h))$, and selecting $R(z_h) = C(z_h)$ and other $R(z_i) = \bot$ ensures

$\{y^*, y'\} \notin G_C(R)$. If $C(y')$ is in $[C(z_i), C(z_j)]$, then the probability that $\{y^*, y'\} \in G_C(C)$ reduces to the probability that (uniformly distributed) y^* and y' are closer together than either are to any endpoint. For given $C(y^*)$, we plot the relative size of the range of $C(y')$ values that meet that criterion in Fig. 1b. The probability is $2 \cdot \frac{1}{3} \cdot \frac{1}{4} + \frac{1}{3} \cdot \frac{1}{2} = \frac{1}{3}$.

The probability that $\{y^*, y'\} \in G_C(C)$ is a third of the probability that $C(y^*)$ and $C(y')$ are in the same segment. The bus paradox (a.k.a. inspection paradox) tells us that the probability is minimised if all segments are of equal size. This is achieved if $C(z_i) = \frac{|V|}{i}$.

The first pair of users added to G_C must contain an honest user, and thus $\{y^*, y'\} \in G_C(C)$ iff $\{y^*, y'\}$ are closest. If $\{y^*, y'\}$ are closest, then $\{y^*, y'\} \in G_C(R)$ regardless of R, and selecting $R = C$ ensures that it is the only case where $\{y^*, y'\} \in G_C(R)$.

The expected benefit follows rather straightforwardly:

Theorem 3. *The expected benefit of the unbalanced tree protocol is $\frac{1}{3n-6}$.*

Proof. If every segment is of equal size, then the probability of landing in the same segment is $\frac{1}{m}$ for uniformly distributed values. As proved for Proposition 6, the probability is $\frac{1}{3}$ if they do, for a total probability $\frac{1}{3m} = \frac{1}{3n-6}$.

The bitstring protocol could be recast as a proximity pairing protocol, by defining d_{BS} as the inverse of the length of the shared prefix. Similar to bitstring, it may be possible to create an imbalance – e.g. using a torus with Euclidian distances. However, through simulations, the practical impact is negligible (see Appendix B for the Torus model).

6.2   Hashed-Based Protocols

The advantage of the adversary in the Circle and Torus protocols comes from spreading out, and avoiding large open areas where pairs of honest users are likely to match. Dropping the triangle inequality eliminates that concern. I.e. the distance between a and b should have no bearing on the relationship between the distances (a, c) and (b, c).

Definition 6. *Let h be a hash function $h : (V \times V) \to [0, 1]$ in the random oracle model. In other words, the probability that $h(a, b) < t$ is t. Define $d_H :$ $((V \cup \{\perp\}) \times (V \cup \{\perp\})) \to [0, 1]$ as $d_H(a, a) = 0$, $d_H(a, b) = 1$ if $a = \perp$ or $b = \perp$, $d_H(a, b) = h(a, b)$ if $a < b$ and $d_H(a, b) = h(b, a)$ if $b < a$. The hash-based grouping function G_H can be recursively defined $G_H(R) = \{\{a, b\} \mid \mathrm{argmin}_{(a,b) \in N^2}(d_H(R(a), R(b)))\} \cup G_H(R - \{a, b\})$ if $|R| > 1$ and $\emptyset$ otherwise. The benefit function B_H for the circle protocol is $B_H(G_H(R)) = 1$ if $\{y^*, y'\} \in G_H(R)$, and 0 otherwise.*

By design, the function d_H is a semimetric, assigns maximum distance to non-revealed values, and is a random oracle (except in trivial cases where $a = b$, $a = \perp$ or $b = \perp$). Crucially, the probability that $d_H(a, b) < t$ is also t in the non-trivial cases. With this notion, we determine a lower bound on the expected benefit:

Theorem 4. *The expected benefit of the hash-based protocol is at least $\frac{1}{2n-3}$.*

Proof. If $d_H(C(y^*), C(y')) < \min_{z_i \in M}(d_H(C(y^*), C(z_i)), d_H(C(y'), C(z_i)))$, then $\{y^*, y'\} \in G_H(C)$ and since $d(a, C(z_i)) < d(a, \perp) = 1$, $\{y^*, y'\} \in G_H(R)$. Since $d_H(a, b)$ is a uniformly random value in $[0, 1]$, the probability that $d_H(C(y^*), C(y'))$ is smallest, is simply $\frac{1}{1+2m}$, since there are $2m$ other uniform random values that could be smallest. Hence the expected benefit is at least $\frac{1}{1+2m} = \frac{1}{2n-3}$.

Not all adversarial strategies obtain the lower bound, but there are two optimal strategies that are not mutually exclusive. Option one is for the adversary to commit to values that are far removed from each other, and revealing them indiscriminately:

Proposition 7. *Selecting C s.t. $\forall_{z_i, z_j \in M^2}(d_H(z_i, z_j) \geq 1 - \epsilon)$ and $R = C$ minimises $\mathbb{E}_{B_H}(\Delta_H)$.*

Proof. With probability $1 - \epsilon$, $d_H(C(y^*), C(y')) < 1 - \epsilon$. By taking $R = C$, $\{y^*, y'\}$ $\in$ $G_H(R)$ iff $d_H(C(y^*), C(y')) < \min_{z_i \in M}(d_H(C(y^*), C(z_i)), d_H(C(y'), C(z_i)))$.

Option two is for the adversary to commit to arbitrary values, but to only reveal the value closest to either honest user:

Proposition 8. *Selecting R s.t. for $z_i \in M$, $R(z_i) = \perp$, except for $\operatorname{argmin}_{z_j \in M}(d_H(C(y^*), C(z_j)), d_H(C(y'), C(z_j)))$ minimises $\mathbb{E}_{B_H}(\Delta_H)$.*

Proof. For this choice of R, if

$$d_H(C(y^*), C(y')) > \min_{z_i \in M}(d_H(C(y^*), C(z_i)), d_H(C(y'), C(z_i)))$$

then $\{R(y), R(z_i)\} \in G_H(R)$. So $\{y^*, y'\} \in G_H(R)$ iff $d_H(C(y^*), C(y')) < \min_{z_i \in M}(d_H(C(y^*), C(z_i)), d_H(C(y'), C(z_i)))$.

The practical problem with option one is that it is exponentially expensive (in m) to find a set of values to commit to. The add a malicious user z' to a collection of m users that have the property, the probability that their value works is $\prod_{z_i \in M} p(d_H(C(z'), C(z_i)) > 1 - \epsilon) = \epsilon^m$, requiring computing m hashes per try. For even moderately large ϵ, this becomes difficult.

The practical problem with option two is that it does not generalise nicely to a scenario where $m \ll n - 2$, as we want to match as many malicious users to honest users as possible, and relying on not revealing is counter-productive. Fortunately, the two options are not mutually exclusive. If the adversary commits to values that have larger than usual pairwise distances, then it can still strategically decide not to reveal.

In the next section, we look at these types of practical considerations, and more generally, no longer assume $m = n - 2$.

7   Analysis of BFT-RNG Matchmaking

We established that the theoretical results of the matching protocols are not far off from the ideal protocol, when there are only two honest users. In this section, we look at the performance of the protocols when there are more honest users. As we considered the strongest adversary, the results must be more favourable when there are more honest users. Our simulations support this.

Unless stated differently, protocols are run with the configuration viable for the strongest adversary. In reality, the honest users do not know which users are malicious or how many. The simulation measures the actual benefit to the honest user in the run – the value would not be known to a user in a real protocol run.

We first simulate single runs of the protocol under the strongest adversary. So the simulated malicious users follow the strategy that minimizes honest user's average benefit. Unless stated differently, the sample size is $10,000$ in all simulations. The x-axis denotes the number of users n, and $m = n - 2$. In Fig. 2a, the y-axis represents the average number of times the protocol successfully matched the two honest users. In Fig. 2b, the y-axis is normalised to the ideal protocol, showing the relative performance (1 meaning as good as ideal) – the sample-size was increased to $100,000$ as normalisation increased noise. Interestingly, the Bitstring and Unbalanced Tree graphs mostly overlap, but the Bitstring's dips around $n = 10$, $n = 18$ and $n = 34$ are not noise, here m is a power of 2, where the Bitstring's performance is $\frac{1}{3}$ (per Theorem 2)[5]. The results match our theoretical analysis.

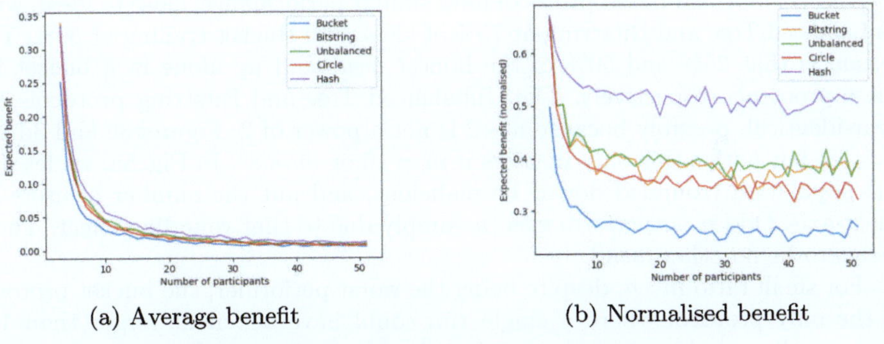

(a) Average benefit   (b) Normalised benefit

Fig. 2. Empirical evaluation of theoretical results

In Figs. 3a and 3b, we simulate single runs of the protocol, where the total number of users is 52, and the x-axis denotes the number of malicious users amongst the 52. Figure 3a has the raw average measured benefit on the y-axis, and Fig. 3b has the y-axis normalised to the ideal protocol. For smaller m values,

---

[5] To verify, the simulation was run $1,000,000$ times for $n = 32$ to give values within 0.3% of the predicted values.

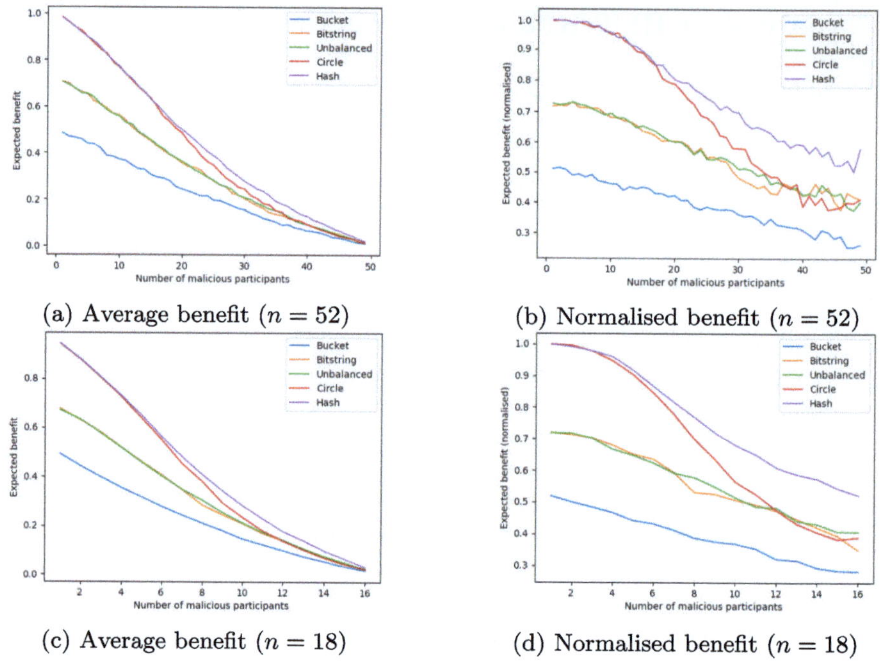

(a) Average benefit ($n = 52$)　　　　(b) Normalised benefit ($n = 52$)

(c) Average benefit ($n = 18$)　　　　(d) Normalised benefit ($n = 18$)

Fig. 3. Analysis of increasing adversarial power

the Circle and Hash-based protocol have similar performance, close to ideal, with Unbalanced Tree and Bitstring at 75% of ideal, and Bucket trailing at 50%. The reason is that 25% and 50% of the honest users end up alone in a bucket for these protocols respectively. The Unbalanced Tree and Bitstring protocols are near-identical, possibly because $n - 2$ is not a power of 2. Figures 3c and 3d use $n = 18$, but notice this only matters if $m = 16$ or $m = 8$[6]. In Fig. 5a, we let half the population (rounded down) be malicious, and put the number of users on the x-axis. Odd n outperform even n, simply due to that rounding effect. There seems to be no other trend.

For small ratio $m : n$, despite being the worst performer, the bucket protocol is the only protocol where a single run could have a benefit larger than 1 – theoretically capable of outperforming the ideal protocol. The parameter k is set based on n, not based on m, as m is not known to honest users. The reason $k = 2(n - 2)$, is that this is optimal when $m = n - 2$. What about more optimistic choices of k? In Figs. 4a and 4b, we show parameter choices $n = 50, k = \{2(n-2), n-2, \frac{n-2}{2}, \frac{n-2}{4}\}$, and the number of malicious users on the x-axis. The y-axis is the average benefit; as-is in Fig. 4a and normalised in Fig. 4b. Optimistic choices of k work better for very small m. The viability threshold gets pushed out for more conservative choices of k, with $k = n - 2$ being non-viable only for the strongest adversary.

---

[6] Again verified with 1,000,000 runs.

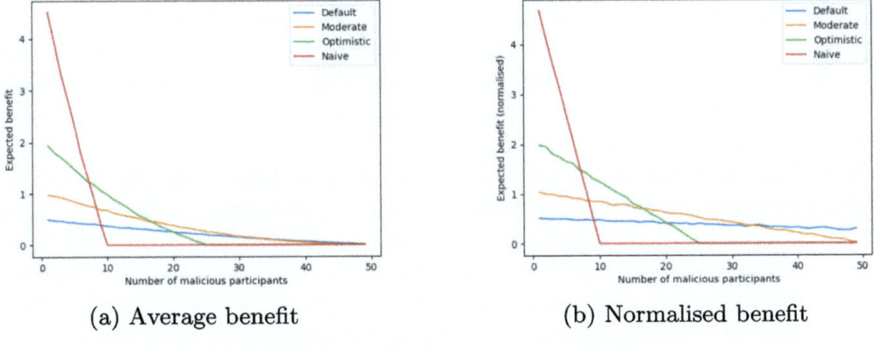

(a) Average benefit   (b) Normalised benefit

Fig. 4. Impact of bucket sizes

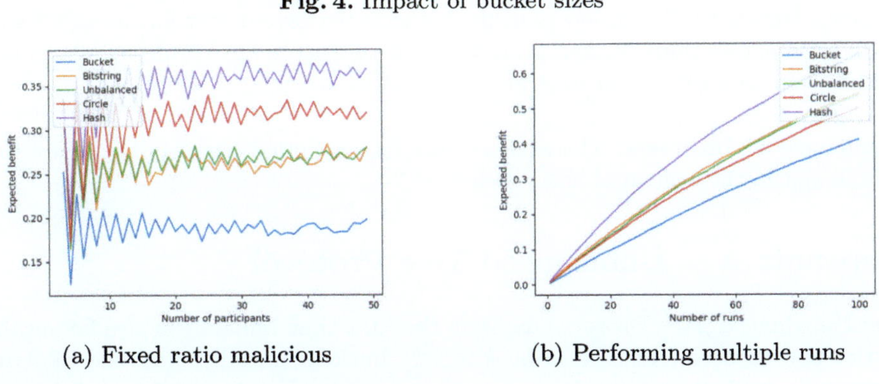

(a) Fixed ratio malicious   (b) Performing multiple runs

Fig. 5. Further analysis

Finally, we consider the notion that we can have multiple runs. In Fig. 5b, we measure benefit on the y-axis over the number of runs on the x-axis. The diminishing returns effect can be seen, but equally, it can be seen that the probability progresses quickly. After just 100 rounds, the probabilities are near 0.5. An ideal protocol with 100 times the opportunity cost would do 1 round and yield a benefit of just 0.02[7].

8   Conclusion

The paper set out to create "unfairly" efficient Byzantine-fault tolerant random number generation. The adversary has limited unfair advantage, but in exchange, the protocols are substantially more efficient. As a result, the biased protocols are less beneficial to honest users, but in exchange, they can be run multiple times in the time it takes to run the unbiased protocols once.

A variety of matching protocols are introduced, based on a variety of tricks to limit the bias. The simplest idea – the bucket protocol – needs to be run

---

[7] RandHerd has an opportunity cost of this order of magnitude, RandHound and Time-locked Commits have even larger costs.

a constant number of 4 times to be as beneficial as an unbiased protocol. The hash-based protocol has the best theoretical performance by being only a factor 2 out. Unbiased alternatives need expensive cryptography, such as time-locked commitments, or substantially more communication ($O(n)$ versus $O(1)$), hence they can be used in practice for speed-up.

A typical adversarial model in BFT requires at least half the users to be honest. Our model works for a powerful adversary controlling all but 2 users. And we only assume there are 2 honest users, because mixing is pointless if everyone else is colluding. We say a protocol is viable if there is some tangible benefit to running the protocol, with such a powerful adversary. Further investigation is required into alternative uses of biased randomness where viable protocols exist.

Finally, simulations show the relationships between the protocols under weaker adversaries. Proximity pairing protocols perform better for protocols with weak adversaries than bucket protocols. All protocols are viable in all circumstances, and running them several times is effective.

Disclosure of Interests. The authors have no competing interests to declare that are relevant to the content of this article.

Appendix A   Unbalanced Tree Protocol

The Unbalanced Tree Protocol exploits the idea that imbalances are favourable to the honest users. Let there be $k = \frac{2m}{3}$ buckets initially, and the bitstring protocol is applied to the group of users in each bucket. Formally:

Definition 7. *The unbalanced grouping function*

$$G_{UT}(R) = \{\{a, b\} \mid R(a) = R(b) \mod k$$
$$\wedge \forall_{c \in (N \setminus \{a,b\} \wedge R(a) = R(c) \mod k)}$$
$$(\mathtt{pre}(\lfloor \tfrac{R(a)}{k} \rfloor, \lfloor \tfrac{R(b)}{k} \rfloor) > \max(\mathtt{pre}(\lfloor \tfrac{R(a)}{k} \rfloor, \lfloor \tfrac{R(c)}{k} \rfloor),$$
$$\mathtt{pre}(\lfloor \tfrac{R(b)}{k} \rfloor, \lfloor \tfrac{R(c)}{k} \rfloor))))\}.$$

The benefit function B_{UT} for the bitstring protocol is $B_{UT}(G_{UT}(R)) = 1$ if $\{y^*, y'\} \in G_{UT}(R)$, and 0 otherwise.

We omit the proof that the adversary should always reveal, as this follows rather straightforwardly. The optimal approach for the adversary is to have half the buckets contain 1 malicious user, and the other half 2 malicious users with different first bits:

Proposition 9. *Selecting R s.t. $R(z_i) = i \mod k$ and $\lfloor \frac{R(z_i)}{k} \rfloor \mod 2 = [i \geq k]$ minimises $\mathbb{E}_{B_{UT}}(\Delta_{UT})$.*

Proof. Similar coverage argument as Proposition 5.

This is enough to prove the expected benefit, which just a bit better than the bitstring protocol at $\frac{3}{8m}$:

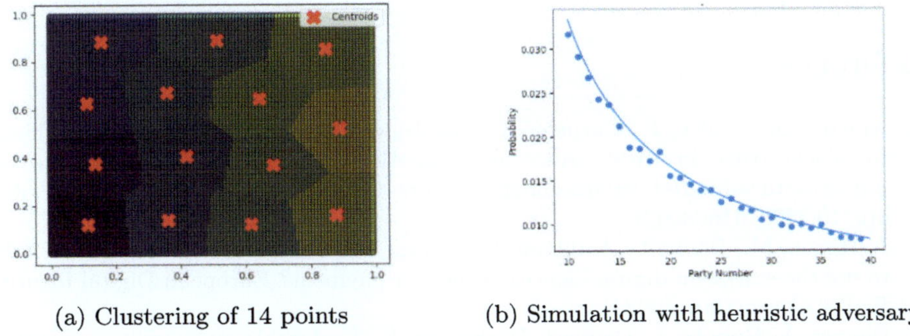

(a) Clustering of 14 points   (b) Simulation with heuristic adversary

Fig. 6. Illustrations of concepts for Torus protocol

Theorem 5. *The expected benefit of the unbalanced tree protocol is $\frac{3}{8n-16}$ if $n-2$ is divisible by 3.*

Proof. Using our proofs from before, probability for y^* and y' to end up in the same initial bucket is $\frac{1}{k} = \frac{3}{2m}$. The bitstring protocol is run with $n = 3$ and with $n = 4$ both with probability $\frac{1}{2}$, since k is even. Simple algebra: $\frac{3}{2m}(\frac{1}{2} \cdot \frac{1}{3} + \frac{1}{2} \cdot \frac{1}{6}) = \frac{3}{8m}$

Appendix B   Torus Protocol

The torus protocol uses Euclidean distance on a torus as distance measure. The protocol is interesting, because it is hard to find and prove optimal strategies for the adversary. If m is a perfect square, then we can take points on a grid, to ensure perfectly even spacing. Even then, it is not clear if this is optimal. Perhaps other tilings are superior.

We can formulate an adversary that uses optimisation techniques to find a set of points maximises the distances between nearest points. See Fig. 6a for an example with $m = 14$ points. Using the heuristic adversary, we can simulate the protocol. In Fig. 6b, we show the results. The solid line is the theoretical performance of the Circle protocol.

The Torus protocol raises some interesting questions. What is it that we are actually trying to maximise as adversary, in terms of distances between malicious values selected? We do not know if the grid is the optimal configuration for the malicious users (if they happen to have a suitable m), perhaps e.g. a hexagonal or triangular lay-out is better. We suspect that the performance in a grid is exactly $\frac{1}{3m}$. If this is the case, then there should be a geometric proof. Through experimentation, we realised that higher dimensional Toruses perform worse for the honest users, but it requires investigation into why. Finally, we have only conducted limited experimentation with alternative distance metrics, such as Manhattan or Chebychev distances. Our investigation into this halted when we found the Hash-based protocol, which we conjecture to be optimal.

References

1. Almani, D., Muller, T., Carpent, X., Yoshizawa, T., Furnell, S.: Enabling vehicle-to-vehicle trust in rural areas: an evaluation of a pre-signature scheme for infrastructure-limited environments. Future Internet **16**(3) (2024). https://doi.org/10.3390/fi16030077
2. Austenaa, M., Bailly, L., Kauhaus, S., Prasad, R., Vonno, J.V.: What does it take to use the european digital identity wallet for payment? European Digital Identity Wallet Consortium (2024)
3. Blömer, J., Bobolz, J., Diemert, D., Eidens, F.: Updatable anonymous credentials and applications to incentive systems. In: Proceedings of the 2019 ACM SIGSAC Conference on Computer and Communications Security, pp. 1671–1685 (2019). https://doi.org/10.1145/3319535.3354223
4. Blum, M., Feldman, P., Micali, S.: Non-interactive zero-knowledge and its applications. In: Proceedings of the Twentieth Annual ACM Symposium on Theory of Computing. STOC '88, New York, NY, USA, pp. 103–112. Association for Computing Machinery (1988). https://doi.org/10.1145/62212.62222
5. Bonneau, J., Narayanan, A., Miller, A., Clark, J., Kroll, J.A., Felten, E.W.: Mixcoin: anonymity for bitcoin with accountable mixes. In: Christin, N., Safavi-Naini, R. (eds.) FC 2014. LNCS, vol. 8437, pp. 486–504. Springer, Heidelberg (2014). https://doi.org/10.1007/978-3-662-45472-5_31
6. Brecht, B., Therriault, D., Weimerskirch, A., Whyte, W., Kumar, V., Hehn, T., Goudy, R.: A security credential management system for v2x communications. IEEE Trans. Intell. Transp. Syst. **19**(12), 3850–3871 (2018). https://doi.org/10.1109/TITS.2018.2797529
7. Chaum, D.L.: Untraceable electronic mail, return addresses, and digital pseudonyms. Commun. ACM **24**(2), 84–90 (1981). https://doi.org/10.1145/358549.358563
8. Chen, J., Micali, S.: Algorand. arXiv preprint arXiv:1607.01341 (2016)
9. Dingledine, R., Mathewson, N., Syverson, P.: Tor: the second-generation onion router. In: USENIX Security '04: Proceedings of the 13th USENIX Security Symposium (2004)
10. Dolev, D., Yao, A.: On the security of public key protocols. IEEE Trans. Inf. Theory **29**(2), 198–208 (1983). https://doi.org/10.1109/TIT.1983.1056650
11. Hanke, T., Movahedi, M., Williams, D.: Dfinity technology overview series, consensus system (2018). https://arxiv.org/abs/1805.04548
12. Kelsey, J., Brandão, L., Peralta, R., Booth, H.: A reference for randomness beacons. Technical report, NIST (2019). https://doi.org/10.6028/NIST.IR.8213-draft
13. Lamport, L., Shostak, R., Pease, M.: The byzantine generals problem. ACM Trans. Program. Lang. Syst. **4**(3), 382–401 (1982). https://doi.org/10.1145/357172.357176
14. Micali, S., Rabin, M., Vadhan, S.: Verifiable random functions. In: 40th Annual Symposium on Foundations of Computer Science (Cat. No.99CB37039), pp. 120–130 (1999). https://doi.org/10.1109/SFFCS.1999.814584

15. Nguyen, C.T., Hoang, D.T., Nguyen, D.N., Niyato, D., Nguyen, H.T., Dutkiewicz, E.: Proof-of-stake consensus mechanisms for future blockchain networks: fundamentals, applications and opportunities. IEEE access **7**, 85727–85745 (2019)
16. Rivest, R., Shamir, A., Wagner, D.: Time-lock puzzles and timed-release crypto (2001)
17. Senejohnny, D., Sundaram, S., De Persis, C., Tesi, P.: Resilience against misbehaving nodes in self-triggered coordination networks. In: 2018 IEEE conference on decision and control (CDC), pp. 2848–2853. IEEE (2018)
18. Shamir, A.: Identity-based cryptosystems and signature schemes. In: Blakley, G.R., Chaum, D. (eds.) CRYPTO 1984. LNCS, vol. 196, pp. 47–53. Springer, Heidelberg (1985). https://doi.org/10.1007/3-540-39568-7_5
19. Syta, E., et al.: Scalable bias-resistant distributed randomness. In: 2017 IEEE Symposium on Security and Privacy (SP), pp. 444–460 (2017). https://doi.org/10.1109/SP.2017.45
20. Wood, G., et al.: Ethereum: a secure decentralised generalised transaction ledger. Ethereum Project Yellow Paper **151**(2014), 1–32 (2014)

Improving Trust in Legal Automation: an Intelligible Approach for Consumer Complaints

Alessandro Parenti[1,2]([envelope]) [ID], Felix Stutz[2] [ID], and Tomer Libal[2] [ID]

[1] University of Bologna, Bologna, Italy
alessandro.parenti3@unibo.it
[2] University of Luxembourg, Esch-sur-Alzette, Luxembourg
felix.stutz@uni.lu, tomer@enidia.ai

Abstract. The recent advances in Artificial Intelligence (AI), among many other use cases, allows consumers to voice their concerns more easily. For instance, AI is used extensively for identifying infringements to consumer rights, preparing complaints and even submitting them to the authorities. However, these authorities are stripped from the ability to use similar Machine Learning-based tools due to concerns about correctness. Traditionally, one resorts to expert systems for providing robust and correct solutions. Such systems are not as wide-spread as desirable though. One key issue is that such systems are very powerful, making it often difficult for their users, i.e., jurists, to fully understand them without significant effort. Here, we consider one specific use case, consumer complaints, and propose an approach that puts *intelligibility* and *trust* first, which allows a jurist to partially automate the assessment of consumer complaints.

Keywords: Compliance Checking · AI and Law · Trust · Formal Methods · Binary Decision Diagrams

1 Introduction

Artificial Intelligence (AI) is significantly transforming our daily lives and people find more and more use cases for this powerful technology. Among these, AI has led to the proliferation of tools that automate and simplify the submission of legal complaints (e.g., airhelp.com), making it easier for citizens to voice their concerns. The present work is inspired by the challenges faced by governmental agencies in managing and elaborating the growing volume of requests and complaints they receive. This process, carried out by legal experts within these agencies, involves the following steps:

– A complaint is received, relating to a possible infringement of the law.
– The legal expert uses the facts provided in the complaint to navigate the relevant regulation.

© The Author(s), under exclusive license to Springer Nature Switzerland AG 2026
B. Fila et al. (Eds.): Sjouke Mauw Festschrift, LNCS 16365, pp. 182–200, 2026.
https://doi.org/10.1007/978-3-032-20684-8_11

– The legal expert reaches a conclusion for the validity or invalidity of the complaint, or is unable to make a decision due to missing information or legal interpretations.

While AI is increasingly used for the creation of such claims, tools for resolving legal issues are lagging behind, due to concerns regarding the reliability of machine learning applications [9]. Hence, those responsible for evaluating these submissions are often left without similar technological support and continue to rely on traditional manual methods – an observation based on discussions with the Directorate for Consumer Protection in Luxembourg. To provide support to the legal expert tasked with evaluating a complaint (henceforth, "user"), an automated reasoning tool should satisfy the following requirements:

(1) The user must be able to conclude whether the law is violated or not. In both cases, the user shall be given a formal proof towards the conclusion.
(2) The user shall be able to update and validate the legal knowledge underlying the tool, ensuring its accuracy with respect to the relevant statute.
(3) The user must be able to operate when information is incomplete.

Technological support to legal reasoning processes have historically been addressed by developing expert systems, which automatically apply legal rules to pre-defined scenarios and provide legal advice [8,20,23]. The advantage of such expert systems over their machine learning counterparts lies in their trustworthiness, as their results are grounded in codified expert knowledge that is applied deterministically.

Expert systems often struggle to satisfy all Requirements (1) to (3) at the same time [3]. In fact, a considerable effort is required in order to translate the legal language into the formal languages supported by these tools, as this normally requires the collaboration of two domain experts, a legal one and a technical one [28]. Moreover, increasing the expressiveness of the logic used for formalisation in order to capture finer details, such as vague terms or ambiguity, usually has an inverse relationship with both the efficiency of these tools as well as with their intelligibility for users [22,30]. For more details, we refer to Sect. 4. This paper explores the possibility to balance the expressiveness of the logic used for formalisation with both its computational properties and accessibility features to overcome these shortcomings.

We conducted this exploration during our time at the University of Luxembourg with Sjouke Mauw. While Sjouke might not have conducted research related to the legal field, our work has been strongly influenced by his ideas and approach to research. First of all, there is the theme of *trust*, which is so important to Sjouke that he put it equally next to security in the name of his research group: Security and Trust of Software Systems (SaToSS). Towards achieving trust, we also employed formal methods, as Sjouke did in many of his works. Here, we started from a clean slate and only added as much as needed for our particular use case, an approach that Sjouke also likes to consider in initial stages of projects. For our case study, this actually paved the way for intelligibility and understandability. Last but not least, this project was driven by sole curiosity of two researchers in his group who saw an opportunity to complement their expertise and learn something new. We all know that Sjouke loves to learn something new and we hope he will do so from this work. We have learned a lot from him and are incredibly thankful to have been part of this team.

In the remainder of this section, we outline our approach and introduce our case study. Afterwards, we present the formal foundations of the approach. We introduce a domain-specific logic for legislation together with guidelines for the formalisation process (Sect. 2) and explain how this logic can be made executable in the form of binary decision diagrams in a semi-automated manner (Sect. 3). Finally, we survey related work (Sect. 4).

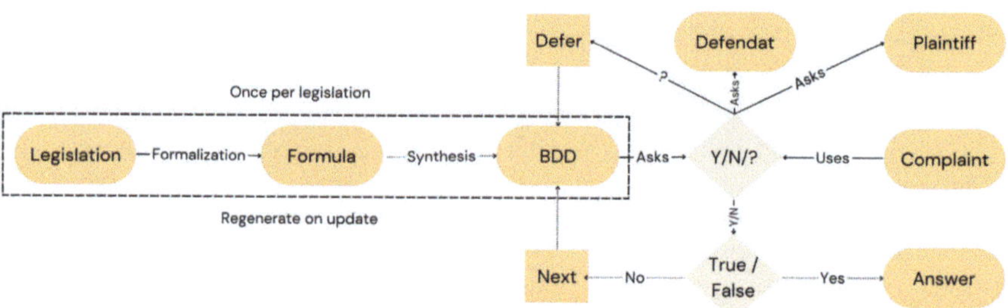

Fig. 1. Approach overview (solid line: manual steps; dotted line: automated steps).

1.1   Overview of the Approach

Our goal is to support jurists who verify consumer protection complaints by automating parts of the process as outlined at the beginning of the introduction. We visually represent the overall process in Fig. 1.

To start, jurists should be able to validate the representation of the legislation themselves. This involves translating the *legislation* from natural language into a *formula* of a domain-specific logic, a process we call *formalisation*. While done manually, we provide guidelines for this step, in order to maintain a high level of rigor, as detailed in Sect. 2.5. This step is only required once at the beginning and possibly to update when the legislation changes. The formula allows us to partially automate the complaint evaluation. We achieve this by translating the formula into a Binary Decision Diagram (BDD), a step we call *synthesis*. BDDs are data structures used to represent Boolean functions and are known for both their explainability and efficiency [7].

For each complaint, the BDD will guide the jurist in the analysis by asking questions about the specific case. The jurist will provide yes/no answers and will integrate legal interpretation if necessary. Ultimately, the BDD will return either a positive or negative answer about the validity of the complaint. To avoid disruptions and to save resources, this methodology can be augmented with the possibility to defer to the end questions that cannot be answered based on the complaint. In the future, one can also imagine to account for the resources required to answer individual questions and optimise the BDD accordingly.

Art. 5
1. In case of cancellation of a flight, the passengers concerned shall:
(a) be offered assistance by the operating air carrier in accordance with Article 8 [..] and;
(c) have the right to compensation by the operating air carrier in accordance with Article 7, unless:
(i) they are informed of the cancellation at least two weeks before the scheduled time of departure; or
(ii) they are informed of the cancellation between two weeks and seven days before the scheduled time of departure and are offered re-routing, allowing them to depart no more than two hours before the scheduled time of departure and to reach their final destination less than four hours after the scheduled time of arrival;
(iii) they are informed of the cancellation less than seven days before the scheduled time of departure and are offered re-routing, allowing them to depart no more than one hour before the scheduled time of departure and to reach their final destination less than two hours after the scheduled time of arrival.

Fig. 2. Case Study: legislation.

1.2   Case Study

To illustrate the application of our approach, we target the case of Air Passengers' rights compliance in Luxembourg, specifically under Regulation (EC) No 261/2004 [1] (henceforth 'Regulation'). This regulation establishes the rights of airline passengers in case of flight cancellations, delays, and other flight-related issues. It also mandates that member states appoint competent authorities to oversee the proper enforcement of these rights. In Luxembourg, the Directorate for Consumer Protection[1] serves as the designated authority responsible for ensuring compliance. If passengers are dissatisfied with the treatment they have received from an airline, they can file a complaint using a form provided by the Luxembourgish government.[2] This form includes all the necessary information for applying the relevant legislation. Currently, these complaints are manually reviewed and assessed by the authority's officers, leading to an inefficient and error-prone process.

With our approach, we demonstrate how simple complaints can be processed semi-automatically. We will focus on a specific portion of Art. 5 of the Regulation that deals with passengers' rights in case of flight cancellation, shown in Fig. 2. For conciseness, we will not consider the last provision, i.e., 5(c)(iii), in most of the examples to follow, as its treatment is identical to that of 5(c)(ii). Table 1 presents the relevant information provided by the passenger in the complaint form that will be used to evaluate the complaint from the complaint form.

---

[1] Directorate for Consumer Protection, the official website can be found at mpc.gouvernement.lu/en.html.
[2] Available at https://guichet.public.lu/dam-assets/catalogue-formulaires/loisirs/document/formulaire-plainte/formulaire-plainte-en.pdf.

Table 1. Case study: relevant information from the complaint form.

Form Question	Answer
When were you notified that the flight was cancelled?	One week before departure.
Were you informed of the reason for the cancellation?	Yes, the flight was canceled due to insufficient staffing levels.
Did you receive any financial compensation?	No.
Were you offered the choice between a refund or re-routing to your final destination?	Yes, I chose re-routing.

2   A Domain-Specific Logic for Legislation (DSLL)

In this section, we present a variant of a propositional logic with which such a legislation can be formalised. In its design, we strive for two traits: (a)intelligibility of the logical formula, in particular its relation to the legislation, and (b)opportunities for automation; ultimately satisfying Requirements (1) to (3) from the introduction.

For (a), our logic allows a representation that is close to the natural language text of the legislation: both from a structural point of view as well as in terms of word choice. While this is a noble goal, (b) requires a certain level of formality so that we can give (unambiguous) semantics to all formulas. In particular, we seek a specific kind of automation: the verification of compliance of the air carrier's behavior to the Regulation. For this reason, the DSLL is designed to express the relevant parts of the legislation as a formula.

For our setting, two components of a propositional logic are key: *propositions*, for which one should be able to say if they are true or false; and *logical connectives*.

2.1   Occurrence-Based Propositions: Actions, Conditions, and Normative Positions

Our approach is designed to perform a specific task: evaluating if a certain behavior (consisting of a sequence of actions) was compliant with the relevant legislation. This focus allows the formalisation to be streamlined, capturing only the essential information needed for this task, and keeping, for the rest, the language lighter and aligned with the original legal language. To this end, we use text propositions (i.e., subject-predicate clauses) as the starting point of our formalisation, and call them *occurrences*. We distinguish two kinds of occurrences.

- **Actions**: propositions describing an action featuring two agents: an active one and a passive one.
- **Conditions**: propositions describing a state-of-affairs, a property of another proposition, or an occurrence that is not produced by the agents involved in the compliance procedure.

These are the occurrences that will be either true or false according to the *complaint*, and determine the evaluation of the formula. Formally, we define them as follows.

Definition 1 (Actions and Conditions). *Let* Agents *be a finite set of agents. Let*

$$\text{Actions} := \{\texttt{act}(\text{agent}_1, \text{agent}_2, \text{descr}) \mid \text{agent}_1, \text{agent}_2 \in \text{Agents } and \text{ descr } is \text{ any text}\}$$

be the set of actions *and*

$$\text{Conds} := \{\texttt{cond}(\text{descr}) \mid \text{descr } is \text{ any text}\}$$

be the set of conditions. *We denote their union by* $\text{Occs} := \text{Actions} \cup \text{Conds}$ *as the set of* occurrences. *For actions, the first agent identifies the* active *agent, performing the action, while the second one is considered* passive, *e.g., the receiving end of an action.*

Example 2. Consider Art.5(1)(c)(ii) of the case study in Sect. 1.2. We can distinguish four different occurrences, two before and two after the comma. Using the constructs of Definition 1, they can be captured as follows:

- $\texttt{act}(\text{Aircarrier, Passengers, }$*"inform of the cancellation between two weeks and seven days*[..]*"*)
- $\texttt{act}(\text{Aircarrier, Passengers, }$*"offer rerouting"*)
- $\texttt{cond}($*"rerouting allow passengers to depart no more than two hours before*[..]*"*)
- $\texttt{cond}($*"rerouting allow passengers to reach their final destination less than four hours after*[..]*"*)

Each occurrence features a description (*descr*) as last argument which is used to report the content of actions or conditions as described in the original source. For the sake of space, here, and in the following examples, we abbreviate the representation using [..]; a full version of the formulas can be found at the end of Sect. 2.5.

For the evaluation of formulas, we use *assignments*.

Definition 3 (Assignment). *We assume a set of Booleans* $\mathbb{B} := \{\text{true}, \text{false}\}$. *An* assignment $\phi : \text{Occs} \rightarrow \mathbb{B}$ *is a function from occurences to Boolean constants.*

Legislations define normative positions such as *obligations, prohibitions,* or *rights*. The content of normative positions – what is obliged or prohibited – is constituted by acts [35], which are the actions in our DSLL. Since these are what will ultimately be evaluated as assignments, the DSLL design should provide the minimum features necessary to isolate them within the normative positions. For the purposes of this paper, we consider two normative positions: ***obligations*** [35] and (obligative) ***rights***[3].

Definition 4 (Obligations and rights). *We define the sets of* obligations *and* rights:

- Obls := $\{\mathtt{obl}(\mathrm{descr}, \alpha) \mid \alpha \in \mathrm{Actions}$ *and* descr *is any text*$\}$
- Rights := $\{\mathtt{right}(\mathrm{descr}_1, (\mathrm{agent}_1, \mathrm{agent}_2, \mathrm{descr}_2)) \mid$
  $\mathrm{agent}_1, \mathrm{agent}_2 \in \mathrm{Agents}$ *and* $\mathrm{descr}_1, \mathrm{descr}_2$ *are any text*$\}$

For rights, the first agent identifies subject entitled to the right, while the second the subject responsible for fulfilling the right.

Example 5. Let us consider Art. 5(1)(a) and 5(1)(c) from the regulation given in Fig. 2. The first article defines an obligation, while the second constitutes a right. We separate the normative identifier from the content of the right or obligation and translate the propositions as follows:

- $\mathtt{obl}$(*"shall"*, $\mathtt{act}$(Aircarrier, Passengers, *"offer assistance"*))
- $\mathtt{right}$(*"shall have the right"*, (Passenger, Aircarrier, *"to compensation"*))

Like in Example 2, the last argument (*descr*) is used to preserve adherence with the original source to report the normative identifier and the right's content.

Once correctly formalised, we exploit the formal definitions of legal concepts developed by legal theory in order to identify the actions underlying normative positions [31]. For obligations, e.g., *Aircarrier shall pay Passenger*, actions are usually expressed in an explicit form. Therefore, it is simple to isolate the action once the deontic identifier is separated: here, *shall* is the deontic identifier and *Aircarrier pays Passenger* is the action. Within rights, instead, actions are often expressed implicitly, e.g., *Passenger has the right to compensation by Aircarrier*. That is why their isolation will require an additional step that can be automated in the interpretation phase as shown in Sect. 2.2. Such rights are first transposed to their underlying obligation, here *Aircarrier shall pay Passenger*, which allows the user to easily identify the action as above.

Remark 6 (Propositions and predicates). The propositions in our DSLL are actions, conditions, obligations and rights. Syntactically, they resemble predicates, which are functions that take an input and return a truth value (*true* or *false*), except that most have multiple parameters, e.g., actions have three with their two agents and a description. For instance, in theory, one could imagine

---

[3] In this work, we focus on the concept of obligative rights [15]. They identify a kind of right instituted as protection of an interest of a specific subject through a corresponding duty on another subject [31]. This usually happens for legal relationships where one party is considerably stronger than the other, as is the case for consumer protection legislation. Hence, obligative rights also constitute the main object of the regulation discussed in this work, provided as a protection of passengers' interests from air carriers' practices.

defining an automatic evaluation function for actions that takes the input and returns the corresponding truth value. Note, though, that this would require precise semantics and seems infeasible in practice. This is why, for the time being, determining the assignment of occurrences will require a human in the loop, which also allows for manual inspection of the matters. For specific conditions, automation could be feasible though, e.g., checking if an offered rerouting satisfies its requirements could be automated.

2.2   Domain-Specific Logical Connectives

The second key component of our DSLL is the set of *connectives* describing the logical relations among *propositions*.

Definition 7 (Logic).

$$X, Y ::= \text{prop} \mid \texttt{not}(X) \mid X \,\text{AND}\, Y \mid X \,\texttt{or}\, Y$$
$$\mid X \,\text{IF}\, Y \mid \text{IF}\, X \,\texttt{then}\, Y \mid X \,\texttt{unless}\, Y$$
$$\text{IF} ::= \texttt{if} \mid \texttt{in case of} \mid \texttt{in the case of} \mid \texttt{when}$$
$$\text{AND} ::= \texttt{and} \mid \texttt{as well as}$$

where prop $\in$ Occs $\cup$ Obls $\cup$ Rights.

Formulas, denoted by $\mathcal{F}$, in our DSLL are constructed using this context-free grammar, which supports a variety of connectives. Some of those, e.g., the ones of IF and AND will have the same semantics. We provide different variants to allow the user to mirror the original legislation.

Example 8. Let us reconsider our case study from Sect. 1.2 and see how its propositions are represented in Examples 2 and 5. These can be combined through the connectives as follows:

```
in case of cond(flight cancellation) then
(
    (obl("shall", act(Aircarrier, Passengers, "offer assistance in accordance with art.8"))) and
    (
        right("shall have right", (Passengers, Aircarrier,
                        "to compensation in accordance with art.7")) unless
        (
            act(Aircarrier, Passengers,
                "inform of the cancellation between two weeks and seven days before[..]")
            and
            act(Aircarrier, Passengers, "offer-rerouting")
        )
    )
)
```

One specific complaint gives rise to an assignment of occurrences so we can evaluate the DSLL formula.

Table 2. Evaluation of formulas under assignment ϕ.

$\phi(\texttt{not}(X)) :=$	$\begin{cases} \textit{true} & \text{if } \phi(X) := \textit{false} \\ \textit{false} & \text{if } \phi(X) := \textit{true} \end{cases}$
$\phi(X \texttt{ and } Y) := \phi(X \texttt{ as well as } Y) :=$	$\begin{cases} \textit{true} & \text{if } \phi(X) := \textit{true} \text{ and } \phi(Y) := \textit{true} \\ \textit{false} & \text{otherwise} \end{cases}$
$\phi(X \texttt{ or } Y) :=$	$\begin{cases} \textit{true} & \text{if } \phi(X) := \textit{true} \text{ or } \phi(Y) := \textit{true} \\ \textit{false} & \text{otherwise} \end{cases}$
$\phi(Y \text{ IF } X) := \phi(\text{ IF } X \texttt{ then } Y) := \phi(\texttt{not}(Y) \texttt{ or } X)$ where $\text{IF} \in \{\, \texttt{in case of}\,,\ \texttt{in the case of}\,,\ \texttt{when}\, \}$	
$\phi(X \texttt{ unless } Y) := \phi(X \texttt{ if not}(Y))$	
$\phi(\texttt{obl}(\text{descr}, \alpha)) := \phi(\alpha)$	
$\phi(\texttt{right}(\text{descr}, (\text{agent}_1, \text{agent}_2, \text{descr}))) := \phi(\texttt{obl}(\text{descr}, \texttt{act}(\text{agent}_2, \text{agent}_1, \texttt{make\_active}(\text{descr}))))$ [a]	

[a] make_active is an abstract function: it takes a description and turns it to active form.

Definition 9 (Evaluating Formulas). *Given an* assignment $\phi : \text{Occs} \rightarrow \mathbb{B}$, *the evaluation of a formula is defined in Table 2.*

To reduce the need for excessive parentheses and increase readability, we define a precedence order for the logical connectives. Negation ($\texttt{not}$) has the highest precedence, then conjunctions ($\texttt{and}$ | $\texttt{as well as}$), disjunctions ($\texttt{or}$), conditionals ($\texttt{if}$ | $\texttt{in case of}$ | $\texttt{in the case of}$ | $\texttt{when}$) and, lastly, exception handling ($\texttt{unless}$).

The logical relations between propositions are interpreted by reduction to the fundamental connectives *not, and,* and *or* that are the ones supported by the semantics presented in Sect. 3.

Normative positions. As to normative positions, a clarification is required. The goal of our system is the *ex-post* evaluation of compliance of a sequence of facts to the regulation. A DSLL formula represents a rule for compliance with the regulation applicable to the air carrier. Therefore, a formula evaluated to true is equivalent to compliance. Using the terminology of [18], we can classify a DSLL formula as a constitutive rule and, as such, it falls within the category of rules that do not require reasoning with deontic concepts [6]. For example, the rule *If the flight is cancelled, Air carrier shall compensate* is complied with if, after the occurrence of "John breaks", the occurrence "John pays" occurs. A constitutive norm for compliance would be $\texttt{compliance} \leftarrow$ (*flight is cancelled* $\rightarrow$ *Air carrier compensate*) which then is interpreted as $\texttt{compliance} \leftarrow \neg$*flight is cancelled* $\vee$ *Air carrier compensate*. In fact, we could avoid stating normative positions in DSLL formulas and only report the relevant actions. In Sect. 2.3, we will come back to this aspect.

However, a syntax featuring normative positions is useful for two reasons: first, to preserve a close correlation to the legal text, increasing trust; second, to allow their manipulation, as it happens with rights. For these reasons, normative positions are represented syntactically in alignment with their legal sources, while at the semantic level they are mapped onto the actions they entail.

References. Legislations often provide crossreferences within their body. For example, the same obligation may be triggered by multiple events described in different parts of the legislation. Similarly, the content of an obligation could be defined in an article different from the one where it is introduced. For our approach, this means that the compliance to a certain provision can only be checked by integrating all the referenced provisions in the evaluation process. One way of doing this would be to inline such referenced provisions. However, this would negatively affect the correspondence between the formalisation and the legislation. For this reason, we aim at integrating our representation with a map identifying each article of the legislation. The map shall feature unique identifiers that can be used within any formula to link that provision to the formula of another article, while keeping a correspondence with the original text of the legislation. We demonstrate the use of references in the following example.

Example 10. Art. 5(1)(c) from Sect. 1.2 provides that passengers shall *"have the right to compensation by the operating air carrier in accordance with Article 7"*. The provision refers to Art. 7 of the Regulation to specify the content of the right to compensation. Consequently, the corresponding formula references Art. 7 as follows:

> `right_ref`(passengers, aircarrier, *"to compensation"*, Art. 7)

Art. 7 specifies different compensation amounts based on the distance of the original flight. For example, passengers are entitled to 250€ for flights of 1,500 km or less. In terms of compliance evaluation, this means that for Art. 5(1)(c) to be considered fulfilled, the system must first assess whether the original flight distance corresponds to the appropriate compensation amount.

2.3   The Use of Propositional Logic for Legal Knowledge Representation

The AI and Law research field has long focused on employing logic to model legal knowledge in a computable form [33]. In order to capture legal reasoning as faithfully as possible, different logics have been developed, varying with respect to expressiveness and complexity [14]. Our goal in this paper is to define a system which provides automated legal reasoning for consumer protection compliance and which can be integrated into the process already used by authorities. In order to achieve this, a balance needs to be struck between expressiveness, computability, and intelligibility. To meet these requirements and the objectives outlined in Sect. 1, we adopt classical propositional logic.

On the one hand, propositional logic is sufficiently expressive to support automation tasks such as checking whether airlines have complied with specific regulations. While deontic logic [35] formally captures normative concepts like obligations, prohibitions, and permissions, we argue that in our case study (consumer protection in airline regulation) these modalities can be adequately reduced to condition-action rules. In particular, we define compliance as follows: if the conditions for the application of an obligation are satisfied, then the action within this obligation must have been executed. We define non-compliance as having failed to execute the respective action. Formally, if an obligation is expressed as $C \Rightarrow Ob(A)$, where A is an action that an airline is obliged to and C is a set of conditions, we reduce this to $C \Rightarrow A$. To verify compliance, we simply check whether this implication holds.

On the other hand, compared to more complex logic formalisms [13], propositional logic features a simple enough structure to be clear and intelligible to legal experts and officers in charge of validating, maintaining and using these systems.

The presented approach is not intended to be generalised to all legal domains, but rather leverages the characteristics of consumer protection law, which often consists of concrete lists of actions and procedures. These can be represented using propositional logic without significant loss of faithfulness, while providing nice computational properties (such as the ability to be translated into binary decision diagrams).

2.4   Sanity Constraints

Sometimes, formalisations may correctly capture the semantics of a legal provision but still represent scenarios that are impossible or contradictory in the real world.

For example, Art. 5(1)(c) of the Regulation (Sect. 1.2) provides that compensation is due when either one of the conditions defined in (c)(i), (ii) or (iii) is satisfied. A straightforward formalisation such as

$$\textit{compensation}\,\texttt{if}\,(C_i\ \texttt{or}\ C_{ii}\ \texttt{or}\ C_{iii})$$

is correct. However, these provisions include mutually exclusive occurrences such as "they are informed of the cancellation at least two weeks before the scheduled time of departure", i.e., (c)(i), and "they are informed of the cancellation between two weeks and seven days before", i.e. (c)(ii). Note that this is an artifact of using propositional logic for our abstraction. In a more expressive logic, one could express this. There is a simple fix to mitigate this in our setting: *sanity constraints*. These impose restrictions on the assignments when evaluating a formula. Here, a sanity constraint on the assignment would impose that at most one of the two occurrences can be *true*.

Formally, we can introduce the concept of sanity constraints, which are sets of mutually exclusive occurrences, meaning that within any such set, at most one occurrence can be *true* at any given time.

Definition 11 (Sanity Constraints). *A sanity constraint is a finite set of occurrences. We say an assignment ϕ is* well-formed *with respect to a sanity constraint $\{o_1, \ldots, o_n\}$, if at most one of the occurrences $o_1, \ldots o_n$ is assigned* true, *i.e.,*

$$\textit{for all } i \neq j. \quad \textit{if } \phi(o_i) = \textit{true}, \textit{ then } \phi(o_j) = \textit{false} .$$

When evaluating formulas in the presence of sanity constraints, we assume all considered assignments are well-formed *with respect to all sanity constraints.*

Example 12. For the representation of our case study presented in Sect. 1.2, we can define the following sanity constraint:

{ act(Aircarrier, Passengers, *"inform of the cancellation is at least two weeks before [..]"*) ,
   act(Aircarrier, Passengers,
        "inform of the cancellation between two weeks and seven days before [..]") }

In Sect. 3, we will exploit sanity constraints to make the evaluation of formulas using BDDs more efficient.

2.5 Translating Legislation to DSLL Formulas

The DSLL aims to enhance trust in the representation of the legislation. The features are simple and minimal but shall be expressive enough to correspond with the original legislation as well as formal enough to support automation.

While these features should make the DSLL intelligible to legal experts, our goal extends further: to equip legal experts with the means to use approach on their own, i.e., without the help of a computer science expert, in contrast to other works [16,27]. In fact, since every formalisation of a piece of law always requires a certain degree of interpretation, legal professionals are best suited for the task, and should be able to do by themselves. Therefore, we propose guidelines for a rigorous treatment of such a translation and exemplify it with our case study.

The formalisation process is structured into five steps, each building upon the previous one. It leverages the expertise of legal professionals, particularly their legal interpretation skills, in that they are to be the ones involved in the compliance checking. In general, this yields a DSLL formula for the legislation. We present the five steps applied to our case study below.

Step 1: *Expand all pronouns and implicit terms to explicitly include subject, verb, and object in each sentence.*
In case of flight cancellation, the passengers concerned shall:
   (a) **passengers concerned shall** be offered assistance by the operating air carrier in accordance with Article 8; and
   (c) **passengers concerned shall** have the right to compensation by the operating air carrier in accordance with Article 7, unless
   (i) **passengers** are informed of the cancellation at least two weeks before the scheduled time of departure; or
   (ii) **passengers** are informed of the cancellation **by the operating air carrier** between two weeks and seven days before the scheduled time of departure and **passengers** are offered rerouting **by the operating air carrier, rerouting allows** to depart no more than two hours before the scheduled time of departure and **rerouting allows** to reach their final destination less than two hours after the scheduled time of arrival.

Step 2: *Reveal conjunctions hidden by punctuation.*
In case of flight cancellation **then** the passengers concerned shall:

(a) passengers concerned shall be offered assistance by the operating air carrier in accordance with Article 8; and

(c) passengers concerned shall have the right to compensation by the operating air carrier in accordance with Article 7, unless

(i) passengers are informed of the cancellation at least two weeks before the scheduled time of departure; or

(ii) passengers are informed of the cancellation by the operating air carrier between two weeks and seven days before the scheduled time of departure and passengers are offered rerouting by the operating air carrier **and** rerouting allows to depart no more than two hours before the scheduled time of departure and rerouting allows to reach their final destination less than two hours after the scheduled time of arrival. [..]

Step 3: *Turn passive into active voice.*

In case of flight cancellation then:

(a) the operating air carrier **shall offer** assistance to the passengers in accordance with Article 8; and

(c) passengers concerned shall have the right to compensation by the operating air carrier in accordance with Article 7, unless

(i) **operating air carrier informs passengers** of the cancellation at least two weeks before the scheduled time of departure; or

(ii) **operating air carrier informs passengers** of the cancellation between two weeks and seven days before the scheduled time of departure and **operating air carrier offers rerouting to passengers** and rerouting allows to depart no more than two hours before the scheduled time of departure and rerouting allows to depart no more than two hours before the scheduled time of departure and rerouting allows to reach their final destination less than two hours after the scheduled time of arrival; [..]

Step 4: *Place parentheses around sentences separated by full stops, and around subparagraphs, letters, or numbered items following the legislative structure.*

In case of flight cancellation **then**:

((a) the operating air carrier shall offer assistance to the passengers in accordance with Article 8;) **and**

((c) the passenger concerned shall have the right to compensation by the operating air carrier in accordance with Article 7, **unless**:

((i) **operating air carrier informs passengers** of the cancellation at least two weeks before the scheduled time of departure;) or

((ii) operating air carrier informs passengers of the cancellation between two weeks and seven days before the scheduled time of departure **and** operating air carrier offers rerouting to passengers **and** rerouting allows to depart no more than two hours before the scheduled time of departure **and** rerouting allows to reach their final destination less than two hours after the scheduled time of arrival; [..];))

Step 5: *Translate the natural language text into formal logic.*

in case of cond(*"flight cancellation"*) then
(
  (obl(*"shall"*, act(Aircarrier, Passengers, *"offer assistance in accordance with art. 8"*))) and
  (
    right(*"shall have right"*, (Passengers, Aircarrier, *"to compensation in accordance with art. 7"*)) unless
    (
      (act(Aircarrier, Passengers, *"inform of the cancellation at least two weeks before the scheduled time of departure"*)) or
      (
      act(Aircarrier, Passengers, *"inform of the cancellation between two weeks
                     and seven days before the scheduled time of departure"*)
      and act(Aircarrier, Passengers, *"offer-rerouting"*)
      and cond(*"rerouting allow passengers to depart no more than two hours before the scheduled time of departure"*)
      and cond(*"rerouting allow passengers to reach their final destination less than four hours
          after the scheduled time of arrival"*)
)
)
)
)

3 Evaluation of DSLL Formulas with Binary Decision Diagrams

This section shall answer the following question: how do we use DSLL formulas for complaint checking? Intuitively, every complaint (form) gives raise to an assignment of either *true* or *false* for every occurrence in the formula.[4] With this, we can simply evaluate the formula to check compliance. Practically, such an assignment is obtained by the jurist: from the complaint directly and possibly by reaching to the defendant and plaintiff if necessary (see Fig. 1). For efficiency, it would be beneficial to only require the truth value for as few occurrences in the formula as possible. For our case study, imagine the trivial example where the flight was neither cancelled nor delayed. Then, the respective formula will evaluate to *true* no matter which truth values are assigned to the other occurrences. Binary Decision Diagrams provide the means for such a treatment.

Binary Decision Diagrams (BDDs) are data structures used to represent Boolean functions in a compact and efficient way. They are directed acyclic graphs composed of decision nodes which represent occurrences and leaf nodes which represent the outcome [7]. BDDs are used in various applications such as digital circuit design, formal verification, and model checking where manipulation and evaluation of Boolean expressions are required. Here, we use them to evaluate DSLL formulas to check compliance with the regulation. We reach the leaf node representing *true* in case of *compliance* and the one representing *false* in case of *non-compliance*. We amend the definition of BDDs to our setting.

Definition 13. *A Binary Decision Diagram (BDD) is a rooted, directed acyclic graph with the following properties: (1) each internal node is labelled by an occurrence and has two outgoing edges, labelled as the false and true branches, representing the assignment of the occurrence to false and true, respectively; (2) each*

---

[4] Technically, we consider Boolean functions where assignments are possible parameters of this function but we use the term formula for simplicity.

leaf node is labelled by one of the Boolean constants false or true. A BDD is ordered, denoted by OBDD, if the occurrence appears in the same order along any path from the root to a leaf node. An ordered BDD is reduced if there are no two distinct nodes with isomorphic subgraphs.[5]

We want to use BDDs to represent DSLL formulas. For this, we need to translate our DSLL formula into a (classical) propositional formula, e.g., using solely negation as well as the logical operators *and*, *or*, and *if*. This is a rather trivial exercise, given that we define the semantics of DSLL formulas using these operators (see Table 2). For instance, the connective `unless` is translated to *if ...not*. Similarly to the evaluation of formulas, we strip off some information from the obligation and right propositions and keep only the action, preserving the semantics and reducing the number of propositions.

The BDD representations of a formula can be obtained via the Shannon decomposition [34]. An OBDD is created recursively as follows. We create a node for the first occurrence in the order. We consider the two scenarios where its assignment is either *true* and *false*. For each, we simplify the formula accordingly and recursively apply the same approach for the next occurrence according to the order until the simplified formula is either *true* or *false*. We can change this standard treatment slightly to use the efficiency benefits enabled by sanity constraints (see Sect. 2.4): whenever an occurrence from a sanity constraint is considered, we use the information from the sanity constraint to simplify the formula even further if possible.

Given the BDD representation, a jurist can start at the top (the only node without incoming edges) and determine the assignment for the given occurrence. Depending on the assignment, they follow either the true or false edge from the node. They repeat this process until they end up in a leaf node, determining the outcome of the compliance check. We argue that this is similar to a lawyer's work style, i.e., ask questions and adapt subsequent actions, potentially increasing trust at this stage as well.

Figure 3 shows the reduced OBDD, which is generated from the propositional formula of Example 8 via Shannon decomposition, as well as the path (solid black line) taken by the legal expert when evaluating the example complaint. The answer given by the tool is that the airline's actions are compliant with the law. One can also note that not all information given in the complaint was necessary to reach this conclusion.

Note that the use of reduced OBDDs instead of OBDDs is not strictly required for our use cases. Usually, this provides memory and efficiency benefits but due to the size of typical legislations, we strongly believe that this is not that relevant to the overall performance. What it can help with though is understandability, i.e., the reduced version of an OBDD, as depicted in Fig. 3, is easier to understand than the non-reduced version.

---

[5] We assume a standard textbook definition for isomorphic subgraphs.

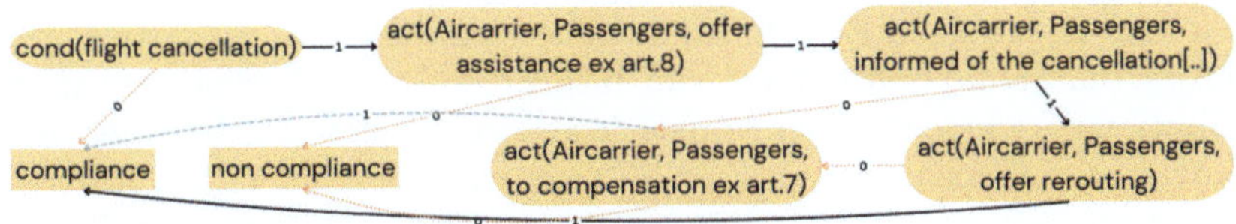

Fig. 3. Reduced OBDD of Example 8.

4   Related Work

Various tools for legal advice have been developed to enhance access to justice and legally relevant information for citizens and professionals in the legal domain.

Traditional approaches build on the symbolic AI paradigm: legal rules are codified into computational formalisms allowing for automated reasoning [33]. In these systems, usually, propositional logic is the default formalism used due to the rather simple tree based structure it provides (e.g., https://bryter. com/, [24]). There are two main drawbacks for such systems. First, the user interfaces often require logicians, whether through the use of Prolog for instance or to design the propositional processes directly. In our approach, we provide a language close to the legal one, and provide guidelines for the transformation into formulas systematically. The second drawback of these systems is their generality. Compliance has some specificities which are not easy to implement in general tools. The most obvious of them is the ability of checking compliance when some facts are absent. General tools would not support it easily and additional values and rules must be added. Using BDDs, one can make use of various BDDs algorithms to reorder the diagrams and push unknown parameters to the end, with the hope that compliance can be checked without them.

In order to capture semantic nuances absent from propositional logic, researchers have developed more expressive formalisms that could represent defeasibility [12,32], vagueness [2], dynamic rule updates [11] or elements specific to a particular law domain (e.g., [25,26], for tax law). Although these approaches excel to different extents to capture the semantic nuances of legal reasoning, they all remain hard for jurists to read or edit, so that both the creation and each statutory amendment force a hand-off to specialised knowledge engineers [10,25]. This slows updates and risks semantic drift when translating natural language obligations into code. But even more importantly, they usually do not pose an efficient computational model.

To address these issues, one line of work gives lawyers understanding of the code they cannot write. For example, by using validation pipelines to automatically paraphrase logical formulas back into controlled English, letting experts confirm accuracy without touching code [4,5,29]. Nevertheless, any correction still requires a programmer, so long-term maintenance costs persist, in addition to the added complexity of having multiple stakeholders.

A complementary strategy is to design rule languages that are readable by jurists. Controlled Natural Languages such as Logical English (LE) re-cast Prolog in a near-natural syntax [19]. LE sentences compile into predicates, yielding rule bases that non-programmers can inspect end-to-end. However, while LE formalisations are indeed easier to read, they are not necessarily easier to write. Developing an LE formalisation can be as cumbersome as writing Prolog, and at times even more challenging because of the rigidity of its syntax [17].

Within this context, the work presented in this paper aims to enable legal-domain experts to develop and maintain a knowledge-based system, without incurring additional costs for cross-domain expertise. Our approach combines three elements: (i) propositional logic, adopted as a simple yet sufficiently expressive formalism for the selected legal domains; (ii) Binary Decision Diagrams, used as an intuitive and transparent computational method which can support specificities of compliance checking, like ignoring missing parameters which might not be essential for obtaining an answer; and (iii) a detailed methodology for translating natural language into a domain-specific syntax.

5   Conclusion

In this work, we explored one possible way to help jurists partially automate their workflow when checking compliance according to consumer related regulation. Here, semi-automation can allow jurists to be more efficient in handling the ever-growing number of complaints they receive, which are often generated with the help of Artificial Intelligence nowadays. We employed lightweight formal methods for this purpose and put a particular focus on intelligibility so that jurists can build trust in the methodology. With a domain-specific logic for legislation, we allow the formal representation to be very close to the legislation. At the same time, being based on propositional logic, it admits automated evaluation of compliance using Boolean Decision Diagrams (BDDs) where the jurist provides the input from the respective complaint form.

The use of BDDs can not only evaluate under partial information but allows for interesting further improvements. First, by postponing occurrences for which the assignment cannot be determined at the given moment. Technically, this could be achieved in two ways: either by precomputing all possible orders, which should be feasible for the sizes of formulas in our case study or by dynamic changes to the BDD through a so-called sifting algorithm [21]. In both ways, the occurrences can be pushed to the end and either the remaining information is sufficient to evaluate the formula or the BDD could report the occurrences for which it still requires information. Second, one can observe that determining the assignment for different occurrences may take different resources. Hence, one could imagine adding weights to the occurrences and compute optimal BDDs with respect to these weights. To the best of our knowledge, such algorithms have not been considered yet, probably because assignments are usually given in the original application areas of BDDs and rather the evaluation itself with the BDD is the bottleneck for performance.

Disclosure of Interests. The authors have no competing interests to declare that are relevant to the content of this article.

References

1. Regulation (EC) No 261/2004 of the European Parliament and of the Council of 11 February 2004. http://data.europa.eu/eli/reg/2004/261/oj (2004). Accessed 24 Nov 2025
2. Arias, J., Moreno-Rebato, M., Rodriguez-García, J.A., Ossowski, S.: Automated legal reasoning with discretion to act using s (law). Artif. Intell. Law 1–24 (2023)
3. Ashley, K.D.: Artificial intelligence and legal analytics: new tools for law practice in the digital age. Cambridge University Press (2017)
4. Bartolini, C., Lenzini, G., Santos, C.: An interdisciplinary methodology to validate formal representations of legal text applied to the GDPR. In: Twelfth International Workshop on Juris-informatics (JURISIN 2018) (2018)
5. Bartolini, C., Lenzini, G., Santos, C.: An agile approach to validate a formal representation of the GDPR. In: New Frontiers in Artificial Intelligence: JSAI-isAI 2018 Workshops, JURISIN, AI-Biz, SKL, LENLS, IDAA, Yokohama, Japan, November 12–14, 2018, Revised Selected Papers, pp. 160–176. Springer (2019)
6. Bench-Capon, T.J.: Deep models, normative reasoning and legal expert systems. In: Proceedings of the 2nd International Conference on Artificial Intelligence and Law, pp. 37–45 (1989)
7. Bryant, R.E.: Binary decision diagrams. Handbook of Model Checking, pp. 191–217 (2018)
8. Contissa, G., Lasagni, G., Caianiello, M., Sartor, G.: Effective protection of the rights of the accused in the EU directives: a computable approach to criminal procedure law. Brill (2022)
9. Cooper, A.F., Moss, E., Laufer, B., Nissenbaum, H.: Accountability in an algorithmic society: relationality, responsibility, and robustness in machine learning. In: Proceedings of the 2022 ACM Conference on Fairness, Accountability, and Transparency, pp. 864–876 (2022)
10. Cummins, J., Clack, C.D.: Transforming commercial contracts through computable contracting. J. Strateg. Contract. Negot. **6**(1), 3–25 (2022)
11. Genesereth, M.: Dynamic logic programming. In: Prolog: The Next 50 Years, pp. 197–209. Springer (2023)
12. Governatori, G.: An asp implementation of defeasible deontic logic. KI-Künstliche Intelligenz **38**(1), 79–88 (2024)
13. Governatori, G., Rotolo, A.: Deontic ambiguities in legal reasoning. In: Proceedings of the Nineteenth International Conference on Artificial Intelligence and Law, pp. 91–100 (2023)
14. Governatori, G., et al.: Logic and the law: philosophical foundations, deontics, and defeasible reasoning. College Publications (2021)
15. Hohfeld, W.N.: Fundamental legal conceptions as applied in judicial reasoning. Yale Law J. **26**(8), 710–770 (1917)
16. Huttner, L., Merigoux, D.: Catala: moving towards the future of legal expert systems. Artif. Intell. Law 1–24 (2022)
17. Idelberger, F.: The uncanny valley of computable contracts: analysis of computable contract formalisms with a focus towards controlled natural languages. Ph.D. thesis, European University Institute (2022)
18. Jones, A.J., Sergot, M.: Deontic logic in the representation of law: towards a methodology. Artif. Intell. Law **1**, 45–64 (1992)
19. Kowalski, R., Datoo, A.: Logical English meets legal English for swaps and derivatives. Artif. Intell. Law **30**(2), 163–197 (2022)

20. Lauritsen, M., Steenhuis, Q.: Substantive legal software quality: a gathering storm? In: Proceedings of the Seventeenth International Conference on Artificial Intelligence and Law, pp. 52–62 (2019)
21. Layeb, A., Saidouni, D.E.: A new quantum evolutionary algorithm with sifting strategy for binary decision diagram ordering problem. Int. J. Cogn. Inform. Natural Intell. (IJCINI) **4**(4), 47–61 (2010)
22. Libal, T.: Legal linguistic templates and the tension between legal knowledge representation and reasoning. Front. Artif. Intell. **6**, 1136263 (2023)
23. Libal, T., Pascucci, M.: Automated reasoning in normative detachment structures with ideal conditions. In: Proceedings of the Seventeenth International Conference on Artificial Intelligence and Law, ICAIL 2019, Montreal, QC, Canada, June 17–21, 2019, pp. 63–72. ACM (2019). https://doi.org/10.1145/3322640.3326707
24. Listenmaa, I., Morris, J., Ang, A., Hanafiah, M., Cheong, R.: An nlg pipeline for a legal expert system: a work in progress. arXiv preprint arXiv:2107.02421 (2021)
25. Merigoux, D., Chataing, N., Protzenko, J.: Catala: a programming language for the law. In: Proceedings of the ACM on Programming Languages, vol. 5(ICFP), 1–29 (2021)
26. OpenFisca: Openfisca: The most widely adopted free and open-source engine to write rules as code. https://github.com/openfisca. Accessed 24 Jan 2025
27. Palmirani, M., Governatori, G., Rotolo, A., Tabet, S., Boley, H., Paschke, A.: Legalruleml: Xml-based rules and norms. In: Rule-Based Modeling and Computing on the Semantic Web: 5th International Symposium, RuleML 2011-America, Ft. Lauderdale, FL, Florida, USA, November 3–5, 2011. Proceedings, pp. 298–312. Springer (2011)
28. Palmirani, M., Martoni, M., Rossi, A., Bartolini, C., Robaldo, L.: Legal ontology for modelling GDPR concepts and norms. In: Legal Knowledge and Information Systems, pp. 91–100. IOS Press (2018)
29. Ramakrishna, S., Górski, Ł, Paschke, A.: A dialogue between a lawyer and computer scientist: the evaluation of knowledge transformation from legal text to computer-readable format. Appl. Artif. Intell. **30**(3), 216–232 (2016)
30. Routen, T., Bench-Capon, T.: Hierarchical formalizations. Int. J. Man Mach. Stud. **35**(1), 69–93 (1991)
31. Sartor, G.: Fundamental legal concepts: a formal and teleological characterisation. Artif. Intell. Law **14**, 101–142 (2006)
32. Satoh, K., et al.: Proleg: an implementation of the presupposed ultimate fact theory of japanese civil code by prolog technology. In: JSAI international symposium on artificial intelligence, pp. 153–164. Springer (2010)
33. Sergot, M.J., Sadri, F., Kowalski, R.A., Kriwaczek, F., Hammond, P., Cory, H.T.: The British nationality act as a logic program. Commun. ACM **29**(5), 370–386 (1986)
34. Shannon, C.E.: A symbolic analysis of relay and switching circuits. Electr. Eng. **57**(12), 713–723 (1938)
35. Von Wright, G.H.: Deontic logic. Mind **60**(237), 1–15 (1951)

Two Decades of Secure Software Development: Shifting Left, Right and down

Erik Poll[(✉)]

Digital Security group, ICIS, Radboud University, Nijmegen, Netherlands
`erikpoll@cs.ru.nl`

Abstract. In the early 2000s security began to receive serious attention in the IT community. This led to the birth of several methodologies for secure software development (notably Microsoft SDL) and many other forms of security advice: Top N lists of common vulnerabilities, secure coding guidelines, and many security frameworks and standards. Now that twenty years later the cry for more secure software has reached policy documents such as the US National Cybersecurity Strategy and the EU Cyber Resilience Act, this paper reflects on developments in the field of software security over these past two decades.

1 Introduction

In the early 2000s there was a growing recognition in the IT community that security was becoming a big problem and that the insecurity of software played a key role here. This led to increased attention to software security, also called application security (or AppSec for short), as field of study. It was also around this time that I got to know Sjouke Mauw, as we were both taking our first steps in the field of security coming from the field of formal methods.

In January 2002 Bill Gates wrote his by now famous email to all Microsoft employees announcing security as key priority for Microsoft in the years to come [16]. A year earlier, in 2001, OWASP had started as community initiative to improve security of web applications. A few years later SAFEcode [49] followed as a collaboration between several large corporations to improve software security.

Fast forward 20 years and the security of software has become an important focus of government policies. The US National Cybersecurity Strategy [39] from 2023 explicitly mentions secure software development; it even announced plans to introduce legislation for software liability but these never materialised. Also in 2023, the EU introduced the Cyber Resilience Act (CRA) [14] that sets cyber-security rules products containing software: it requires manufacturers to ensure that software in products is free from 'known exploitable security vulnerabili-ties'. The EU Radio Equipment Directive (RED) [13], which is narrower in scope than the CRA but came into effect sooner, also requires this.

With all this legislation more organisations will have to pay attention – or *more* attention – to the security of software they use or produce in the years to come, so this is good occasion to look back on developments in the field of software security over the past two decades. There is a *lot* of information around about how to make software more secure – so much so, that it can be confusing for newcomers to the field, even experienced software engineers and computer scientists who never had to deal with security before. This paper aims to provide an overview for such newcomers to the field of software security.

1.1   Process vs Product

Many guidelines, standards, frameworks and methodologies for software security have been published over the past decades. Some security guidelines focus on the *process* of developing software: they propose activities that can be done in the development process to produce more secure software. Some of these guidelines aim to provide comprehensive *methodology* for all security activities in the entire software development lifecycle. The best known of these methodologies is Microsoft's SDL (Secure Development Lifecycle) but there are many others, as we discuss in Sect. 2.

Other forms of security advice focus more on the *product*. There is a huge variety here, as we discuss in Sect. 4, incl. lists of common security vulnerabilities such as the OWASP Top 10, secure coding guidelines, and standards prescribing security requirements or security controls.

The distinction between *process* and *product* is useful to keep an overview of different kinds of security guidance, but the two perspectives are related. Security activities in the development process often require knowledge about the software product. For example, all methodologies propose the use of tools to detect common security vulnerabilities as part of the development process; such tools obviously need information about common problems in software products. The two perspectives can even be mutually dependent. For example, doing vulnerability management as part of the software engineering process (with activities for handling reported security flaws, triaging these, fixing important ones and rolling out security updates) may require features in the software product (such as having the possibility to update, automated checks for updates, or crash reporting to help with detecting flaws).

Many security standards mix advice for the process and the product. For example, the ISA/IEC 62443 standard [24] for operational technology (e.g. industrial control systems) defines a secure development process and also lists detailed security requirements to implement in systems. NIST's cybersecurity standard for smart grids [40] even includes a discussion of common classes of software vulnerabilities (so-called CWEs, discussed in Sect. 5).

Some security standards and frameworks, for instance ISA/IEC 62443 or NIST's Cybersecurity Framework [42], have a broader scope than just the (software) development process and also consider wider deployment and organisational issues. More generally, any secure software development process will have to interact with security practices at an organisational level, for which the ISO 27000 family of standards for information security is the most widely used.

2 Security Guidelines for the Software Engineering Process

The growing attention to software security in the early 2000s led to several proposals for software engineering methodologies that take security into account, also called secure SDLC (Software Development Life Cycle) frameworks.

Gary McGraw, one of the founding fathers of the field of software security, proposed the 'Building Security In' methodology [33], later known as Cigital Touchpoints. Microsoft came with its Secure Development Lifecycle (SDL) [22]. OWASP initially came with CLASP (Comprehensive Lightweight Application Security Process), which no longer exists, and then with SAMM (Software Assurance Maturity Model) [5], which still does.

All these methodologies propose activities (or practices) to be carried at various stages in the software development lifecycle to improve security. A basic tenet in all methodologies is that security should be considered *throughout* the development lifecycle. The activities are usually grouped by the stages of the development lifecycle, such as design, coding, testing and incidence response, alongside overarching activities for education and training and for governance of the entire process. Some of these activities are very specific to software and software engineering, for instance the use of static or dynamic analysis to check code for flaws, commonly referred to as *SAST (Static Application Security Testing)* and *DAST (Dynamic Application Security Testing)*. Other activities are generic security activities that are not specific to software or software engineering, for example threat modelling as initial step (using techniques such as attack trees [32]) or having a process to handle security incidents.

As several large IT organisations began to roll out software security initiatives, using one of these approaches or a home-grown variant, BSIMM (Building Security In Maturity Model) was introduced as a maturity model to measure and compare such initiatives. The first edition of BSIMM from 2009 compared software security initiatives at nine large organisations [35]. BSIMM still exists and is periodically updated[1]. OWASP SAMM is another maturity model. Unlike BSIMM, SAMM is not just meant for *measuring* maturity: SAMM can also be used as framework to introduce or improve a secure software development process; the checklist used by BSIMM is far too long and detailed to be used for that.

Many more secure software development methodologies have been proposed over the years. A survey from 2009 compared the three well-known methodologies at the time [10]: SDL, CLASP and Touchpoints. A more recent survey from 2023 found 28 secure software development methodologies to compare [28]. The key ingredients of all these methodologies are very similar but there are differences in emphasis, in level of detail, and in the way that activities are grouped.

---

[1] BSIMM is a commercial activity of Synopsys (formerly of Cigital, which was acquired by Synopsys). Detailed public information about the latest versions (e.g. BSIMM14 [56]) can be hard to find, but the BSIMM13 checklist is publicly available at https:// github.com/rtxsecurity/bsimm13-parsable.

For example, OWASP SAMM (version 2) lists 15 security activities grouped in 5 'business functions', while BSIMM (version 14) has 12 practices across 4 'domains', with a further breakdown of these 12 practices into 126 activities. Microsoft SDL has been reorganised several times: the initial version had 12 stages, each corresponding to a phase in the development lifecycle, plus 'Education and Awareness' as a special initial stage [22]. The 2012 version had 5 phases – Requirements, Design, Implementation, Verification, Release – with 3 practices per phase, plus 'Training' and 'Executing an incident response plan' as practices in the pre- and post-SDL phase [37]. In the latest edition of SDL this has been reorganised and trimmed down to 10 practices [44].

One of the more recent methodologies is NIST's Secure Software Development Framework (SSDF [41]). It lists 20 practices in four groups, with a further breakdown of these 20 practices into 43 actions. These practices and actions are taken from 25(!) earlier documents (incl. Microsoft SDL, BSIMM and OWASP SAMM). This large number shows how messy the landscape of security standards unfortunately is.

At least SSDF provides clear cross-references to these other standards. An interesting initiative to cope with the growing set of security standards is OWASP OpenCRE (Open Common Requirement Enumeration [15]): it aims to provide mappings between security requirements in different standards.

2.1 SAST and DAST Tools

All methodologies mention the use of SAST and DAST tools as practices to improve software security. Many such tools have appeared over the year.

A popular technique in DAST tools is *fuzzing* aka fuzz testing. The basic idea here is to send many (semi)automatically generated malformed inputs to an application and then see if it crashes due to bugs (notably memory corruption bugs). Fuzzing is a very old idea: it was used in the late 1980s to find memory corruption bugs in UNIX utilities [38]. Fuzzing techniques have improved significantly since then. Commercial fuzzing tools for specific protocols and file formats came on the market in the early 2000s (for instance Codenomicon [57]). These tools needed to be tailored to specific protocols or formats, but Microsoft's SAGE fuzzer avoided this by using symbolic execution to find inputs that trigger obscure code paths. SAGE successfully found many bugs in Microsoft Office and in Windows 7 and its successors [18]. The biggest breakthrough in fuzzing came with `afl` [63] in 2013 and its coverage-guided evolutionary approach (aka greybox fuzzing) to find interesting test cases. Fuzzing with afl could have prevented high-profile security problems such as the HeartBleed bug in OpenSSL; this observation led Google to launch the OSS-Fuzz initiative [53] to fuzz open source projects at scale: since 2016 this has discovered over 36,000 bugs in over 1,000 open source projects.

Most SAST tools use *data flow analysis* be to detect if user input can end up in dangerous places, as for instance happens in injection attacks (discussed in Sect. 5.5). This requires detailed information about the APIs involved. When there is a rapid evolution or turnover in platforms (as is the case with JavaScript frameworks for web applications) keeping tools up to date requires constant effort. Most SAST tools can be configured with rules (or queries) for specific bug patterns, but some of the newer so-called query-based SAST tools [30], notably CodeQL and Semgrep, just provide generic analysis capabilities and always need to be used in combination with some rule-set; sharing such rule-sets may be a way around the need to update tools. With ever more SAST and DAST tools choosing the right one can be tricky. Unfortunately is not much research into comparing tools: commercial tool vendors are not keen to participate and it is hard to decide on a good set of benchmarks to base any comparison on. Already in 2005 NIST started the SAMATE initiative to evaluate and compare tools [3], but unfortunately it never produced the clear insights into the relative performance of tools that were hoped for.

2.2   Shifting Left and Shifting Down

Adopting a secure software development methodology is not something that can be done overnight. Introducing and then improving it will take time and be an ongoing process. The way that most organisations evolve to a more mature security process is by gradually moving security activities and knowledge to earlier development stages, moving from a reactive to a more proactive stance. This is known as *shifting left*. For example, a typical first step to improve software security is to have applications pen-tested, but ideally security problems would be caught earlier by shifting left: e.g. by deploying DAST or SAST tools during development, by improved training for developers, or doing risk analyses when the software architecture is designed, prior to any code development.

The ultimate way to shift left is to *shift down* by addressing security risks in underlying technology stacks, e.g. with the safer APIs or safer programming languages. This can eliminate entire classes of vulnerabilities, a goal that is highlighted in CISA's security-by-design guidance [7]. It can be regarded as the ultimate form of security-by-design, discussed below, as security is then already considered in the design of technology stacks before the development of individual applications that run on these stacks even begins. One could argue that shifting down should be called shifting up, as the outcome is that developers can focus on issues higher up in the software stack. We discuss such structural solutions to some common classes of security vulnerabilities in Sect. 5.

2.3   Security by Design

All the methodologies mentioned in Sect. 2 stress the importance of taking security into account right from the start. The slogan *secure by design* has become popular to express this idea. Long before the slogan security-by-design became popular McGraw used the slogan 'building security in' as opposed to 'bolting security on' to express the idea that security should be considered in all stages of the development lifecycle [33].

Beware that people can interpret the term security-by-design differently, as pointed out by Del Real et al. [11]: some people use a narrow interpretation where it *only* refers to the initial design phase of a system, whereas others take a broad interpretation where it applies to all the stages of the software development lifecycle. The 'Secure by Design' white paper by CISA and other national cybersecurity agencies [7] clearly takes a broad interpretation of the term. For example, it mentions having a vulnerability management program as a secure-by-design practice. In fact, it mentions documented adherence to a secure software development methodology as a secure-by-design practice, which implies that security-by-design spans the entire development life cycle.

2.4 Shifting Right and Resilience

All the talk of shifting left should not overshadow the fact that shifting right can also be important. No matter how much we try to shift left, some security flaws may be missed and some security threats may be overlooked altogether. Processes to deal with incidents will always be necessary: ideally to mitigate the impact when incidents occur, but at least to investigate incidents after the fact and discover and address root causes. Indeed, many good security solutions, not just in software in general, rely more on detection and response than on prevention.

Here we can still benefit from shifting left by building in possibilities for monitoring and response from the start (as argued for by Etalle [12]), which could be considered an instance of security-by-design. An example of this is the use of RASP (Runtime Application Self-Protection) in mobile apps [21], where the software is instrumented to detect suspicious behaviour at runtime. Building in such monitoring is an example of shifting left, using it can be seen as an example of shifting right.

The term *resilience* has become more popular in recent years to refer to the ability of systems or organisations to cope with security incidents. While the term may be useful to stress the importance of detection and recovery, we would argue that good security always includes resilience.

3 Changes in Software Engineering

Software development has changed a lot over the past two decades. Some of these changes complicate the adoption of a more secure software development methodologies, others introduce new risks which then require special attention, as discussed below.

3.1 Agile and DevOps

The methodologies discussed in Sect. 2 all use the classical stages of the waterfall model as frame of reference to position security activities. But software engineering has moved away from this model in the past decades, with Agile and DevOps as popular trends. This has led to proposals on how to integrate security practices in Agile or DevOps approaches. For example, Microsoft published guidance on how to carry out SDL activities in an Agile setting [17] and the term DevSecOps was coined for ways to incorporate security practices into the DevOps process[2].

Adopting an Agile or DevOps way of working does not mean that the security activities proposed by the original secure development methodologies should no longer be used, or that different activities are needed. But incorporating these activities in the shorter and more frequent development and release cycle does pose an extra challenge. For example, when Agile or DevOps approaches lead to many incremental changes in a product it is hard to decide when to have it pen-tested: you cannot do a pen-test after every sprint or for every release. This means that shifting left becomes more important. It also means that automation of activities becomes more important, so that e.g. SAST or DAST can be integrated in CI/CD pipelines.

3.2   Supply-Chain Risks

Another big change in software development in the past decades has been the dramatic rise in the use of open source components, enabled by code repositories such as github, Sourceforge, PyPi for Python, NPM for JavaScript, or Maven for Java. Most proprietary software products nowadays contain large amounts of open source code.

Using such third-party, often open-source, components comes with security risks: risks of accidental security flaws (such as the Log4J vulnerability discovered in 2021 [9]) and risks of deliberate security flaws or backdoors (such as the SolarWinds incident in 2020 [59]). Sonatype reported a 742% increase in supply chain attacks on open source software in 2022 [54].

All this has led a new popular type of static analysis tool, namely *SCA (Software Composition Analysis) tools*, to analyse the dependencies of software projects.

Another measure to manage software supply chain risks is the *SBOM (Software Bill of Materials)*. An SBOM is a machine-readable listing of the software components of a product. CISA's website[3] provides extensive documentation about SBOMs. For a discussion of benefits of SBOMs and challenges in adopting them see Zahan et al. [62]. A report by Idaho National Lab from 2023 gives insight into current adoption [55].

Software supply chain concerns have also led to new standards. For instance, OWASP's Software Component Verification Standard (SCVS) [46] proposes measures to reduce software supply chain risks; some of these are included in NIST's SSDF. More recent is the P-SSCRM framework for managing supply chain risk [61]; it includes mappings to another 10 standards (incl. SCVS, SSDF and BSIMM). The latest version of Microsoft SDL also stresses the importance of securing the software supply chain by making this one of the ten SDL practices.

---

[2] DevSecOps was started by a group of security practitioners, see https://www.devsecops.org). Microsoft publishes information about it (at https://www.microsoft.com/en-us/securityengineering/devsecops), as does OWASP (at https://devsecops.owasp.org); here there is even also a proposal for a DevSecOps maturity model.

[3] https://www.cisa.gov/sbom.

3.3   Risks of Leaking Credentials

Several trends in software development have increased the risks of leaking credentials (or secrets). There are ever more credentials around, in the software development process or in the software itself. For instance, Service-Oriented Architectures (SOAs), which have become more popular, involve credentials: to use external services an application will often need API keys to authenticate. Source code repositories, cloud storage solutions, automated build and deployment processes in CI/CD pipelines, cloud services to support this such as Azure DevOps all come with logins and credentials – and with ways of leaking them [36], for instance in logs. Secrets can also be leaked via Jira, Slack, Confluence, Microsoft Teams, etc. The trend of 'process as code' also contributes to more code that needs to use credentials.

These risks have led to a new type of security tools, namely *secret scanning tools*; for a comparison of such tools see Basak et al. [2]. The popularity of SaaS, SOAs and micro-services has led to proposals for *SaaS Bill of Materials* or *SaaSBOMs* [23]. Just like an SBOM lists the software components used in an application, a SaaSBOM would list the SaaS services used by an application. After all, just like software components can pose security risks, so do software services.

An advantage of services over components is that it is not the responsibility of the application maker to do security updates of any services it uses. Downside is that it may involve credentials that can be leaked. Also, for all their problems, CVEs do provide insight in security issues in components, whereas for some services there may be less transparency about security issues.

4   Security Guidelines for the Software Product

The methodologies and tools discussed in Sect. 2 still need to be fed with more concrete information about common security problems and ways to avoid them. There is a broad range of such information, some of which is specific to a particular programming language, API, or type of application (e.g. web applications).

Top N list of standard security vulnerabilities, such as the OWASP Top 10 and CWE Top 25, are crucial for awareness and training and provide starting point for improved detection – or better still prevention.

Coding guidelines can help to reduce security problems or more generally improve software quality. Well-known examples are the SEI/CERT coding guidelines for C, C++, Java, Perl and Android [52].

Downside of Top N lists is that they tend to focus on flaws introduced in the coding phase so that design flaws may not get the attention they deserve. There are also lists of common mistakes in the design phase [1] which provide a starting point for design principles to avoid these. The seminal article by Saltzer and Schroeder [50] already provided general design principles for building secure systems back in the 1970s.

There are also documents that propose standard security requirements – or security controls to implement to meet such requirements. One of the oldest and more mature examples is the OWASP ASVS (Application Security Verification Standard) [47], currently in its 4th edition. The ASVS aims to provide a comprehensive list of security requirements to ensure and security controls to implement to achieve this. Simply put, whereas the OWASP Top 10 provides a list of dont's, the ASVS provides a list of dos. The ASVS can be used in different ways: as guidance during design, implementation and testing; as metric when assessing security; or as standard in procurement. The awkward acronym has probably not helped the ASVS in getting the attention it deserves.

Alongside the ASVS for web applications OWASP also published a similar MASVS standard for mobile apps [48] and, as already mentioned in Sect. 3.2, the SCVS standard [46] aimed at tackling supply chain security. More standards with security requirements will be produced for the latest EU cybersecurity regulation, i.e. the CRA and RED.

5   Common Vulnerabilities and Ways to Avoid Them

Most people will start to learn about software security through examples of common security vulnerabilities such as buffer overflows or SQL injection. Knowledge about such common problems is crucial; without it you do not stand any chance to produce secure software. The OWASP Top 10 and the CWE Top 25 are the best known lists of common classes of security vulnerabilities (aka 'bug categories')[4]. Changes in these Top N lists over the years can also shed light on progress in improving software security – or the lack thereof.

Any Top N list should be taken with a serious pinch of salt: it is hard to get accurate statistics about security vulnerabilities, hard to classify them into categories, and hard to weigh impacts to pick the most important ones. Moreover, any Top N list is only an incomplete list of potential problems, as it will not include application-specific risks[5] Indeed, there are already several OWASP Top 10s by now: in addition to the original Top Ten of Web Application Security Risks, there is also an Mobile Top Ten, an API Top Ten and most recently a Top Ten for Large Language Model Applications.

The full CWE classification[6] has ballooned to around a thousand categories of security flaws. This may be useful to record very detailed statistics (though the very fine-grained nature makes accurate classification hard: plenty of bug categories overlap) but it is clearly far too long for developers to use, say as a checklist.

---

[4] See https://owasp.org/Top10 and https://cwe.mitre.org/top25.

[5] These may be instances of broad and vague categories in the CWE classification (e.g. CWE-435, 'Improper Interaction Between Multiple Correctly-Behaving Entities') but such categories usually do not come with actionable advice on how to prevent them.

[6] https://cwe.mitre.org.

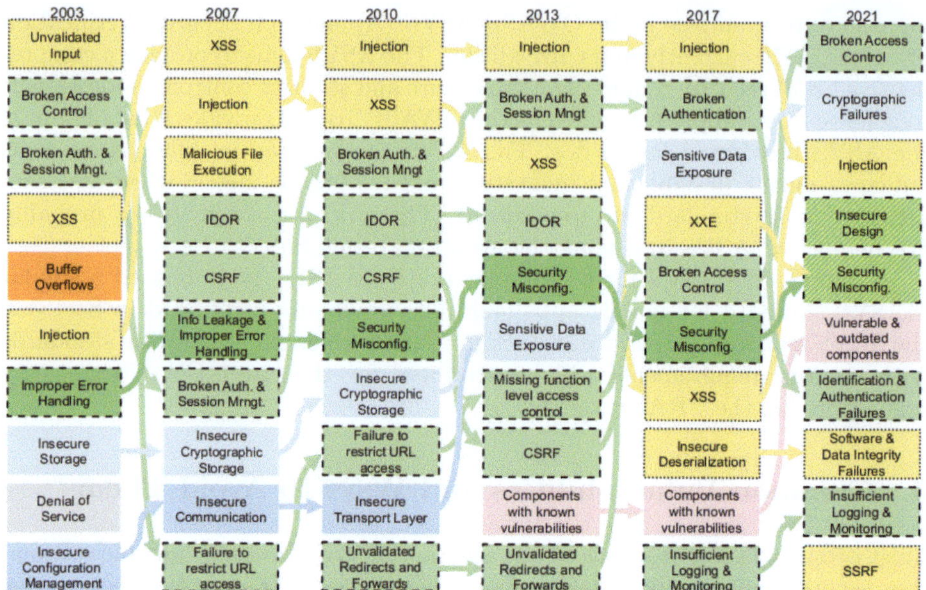

Fig. 1. Evolution of the OWASP Top 10 from 2003 to 2021 with access control problems in green (and dashed line) and input handling problems in yellow (and dotted line). These colours and the arrows indicating inclusions between categories are only approximate. E.g., 'Insecure Design' and 'Security Misconfiguration' mainly include access control issues, but also some that can be regarded as injection problems.

Some changes over time simply reflect the popularity of certain technologies: as XML became more popular XXE attacks became a bigger risk and entered the Top 10; SSRF made its appearance with the rising popularity of service-oriented architectures. Other changes are due to improved knowledge of attackers. For example, possibilities for insecure deserialisation had been around for decades but only entered the Top 10 in 2017 when attackers became aware of this.

There are some positive signs of improvements over the years. Buffer overflows disappeared after the first edition because web applications are mostly written in memory-safe languages. CSRF has dropped over the years because modern platforms for web applications provide good built-in session mechanisms. The authors of the 2021 edition conjecture that injection attacks dropped from the top spot due to improvements in platforms such as safer APIs. So these improvements are due to *shifting down* as discussed in Sect. 2.2.

Most changes in the OWASP Top 10 over the years are due to changes in the way that bug categories are organised. This highlights the difficulty in making a taxonomy of security vulnerabilities. As bug categories have been broadened, the OWASP Top 10 has become less specific to web applications: apart from the absence of memory corruption bugs, the 2021 edition of OWASP Top 10 is probably a good guide for just about any piece of software.

The 2021 edition saw a big shake-up in the categories: it is now a mixture of very broad categories, such as 'Insecure Design' (included to highlight the importance of shifting left) alongside very narrow ones, such as SSRF. Inclusion of 'Insecure Design' means it is encroaching on the territory of the methodologies discussed in Sect. 2. Indeed, the authors of the OWASP Top 10 suggest that organisations just beginning with efforts to improve software security could use the Top 10 as a starting point [45]. (Color figure online)

5.1   The Big Three

It is easy to be overwhelmed by long lists of common security flaws, especially when looking through the entire CWE list. Fortunately, there are only three important families of problems that make up the large majority of problems. In no specific order, these are:

1. access control flaws, incl. authentication problems;
2. memory corruption flaws; and
3. input handling flaws, notably injection attacks.

If you look at any of the OWASP Top 10s or CWE Top 25s from the past decades you will find that nearly all entries belong to one of these three families.

There are overlaps between these three families. Exploitable memory corruption flaws often arise in input handling, so these could also be regarded as input handling flaws. Injection attacks, where some user input ends up in an API or back-end service that then can be abused, can be seen as access control problems because they involve by-passing access control by tricking a privileged victim application into performing actions (aka the Confused Deputy problem) and tighter access control can mitigate the impact. CSRF and SSRF (client-side and server-side request forgeries) are usually regarded as access control problems, as weak or implicit authentication is to blame, but they can also be viewed as injection attacks.

5.2   Access Control

Access control in the broad sense involves not just authorisation but also authentication, as well as logging and monitoring[7]. Security problems commonly arise in all these aspects: authentication mechanisms can be too weak, authorisation can be misconfigured or may be missing, and there can be insufficient logging and monitoring.

Access control flaws are fundamentally different from the other two families because we deliberately introduce access control to provide security; in fact, it is the most important security control that there is. Whereas we can hope to get rid of memory corruption or injection problems by improved platforms, we will always need access control, so flaws in it – esp. misconfiguring or forgetting it – will always remain a risk. This is not to say that better platforms or better design cannot make a difference. For instance, having a robust mechanism for session management built into platforms can help in reducing CSRF flaws.

5.3   Memory Corruption

For software written in memory-unsafe programming languages it is hard to overstate the importance of memory corruption bugs. Both Microsoft and Google's

---

[7] A useful mnemonic for this is AAAA: Authentication, Authorisation, Auditing and Action. The AAAA quartet often provides more actionable guidance than the more widely known CIA triad (Confidentiality, Integrity and Availability).

Chrome team report that around 70% of all their security flaws are memory corruption bugs [20,58]. Of the 130 critical security flaws in Chrome up to 2019 only 5 were *not* clearly due to memory corruption [19].

Many countermeasures against memory corruption attacks have been introduced over the years. Most platforms now come with countermeasures to detect flaws (e.g. stack canaries, shadow stacks or more advanced forms of control flow integrity) or make exploitation harder (e.g. ASLR, non-executable stacks and pointer encryption). There are coding guidelines for C(++) [52], improved libraries that are less error-prone[8], and many SAST and DAST tools that look for memory corruption flaws.

While the measures above will catch some memory corruption bugs or make them hard to exploit, it is clear that they only offer limited protection. In fact, what is amazing about the statistics from Microsoft is that the percentage of memory corruption bugs has remained around 70% and not changed over the years (at least from 2006 to 2018 [58]) despite huge investments in training, coding guidelines, improved libraries, and SAST and DAST tools.

Structural Solutions: Memory-Safety and LangSec. The obvious structural solution against memory corruption is to switch to memory-safe programming languages. In 2023 CISA in the US, in collaboration with other national cybersecurity agencies, launched an initiative to push for a transition to memory safe programming languages[9]. With large industry players joining the Rust Foundation there is some real momentum building behind Rust as memory-safe programming language for low-level system programming.

The LangSec methodology [4,29,51] provides an interesting perspective on memory corruption problems in input-handling. It highlights underlying root causes and suggests structural ways to tackle these. LangSec stands for language-theoretic security. The languages it refers to are not programming languages but *input languages*, i.e. the data formats, file formats or protocol message formats that applications have to process. Key observation behind the methodology is that important factors contributing to input handling problems are: (i) the complexity of input languages, (ii) the large number of input languages, (iii) the sloppy definitions of these input languages, and (iv) the expressivity of input languages. Hand-written parser code written in a memory-unsafe programming language for a complex and poorly-specified input format is almost guaranteed to contain exploitable security flaws. Having clearly defined and ideally simpler input formats and using parser generators to produce parsers instead of hand-writing them can avoid all this.

---

[8] The notoriously insecure function `gets()` was removed in the 2011 edition of the ISO C standard.

[9] https://www.cisa.gov/case-memory-safe-roadmaps.

5.4   Injection Attacks

In injection attacks input supplied by an attacker ends up being parsed and processed by some back-end service or API which can be abused to trigger unwanted actions. There are many variants of injection attacks: the CWE classification includes over 30.

The category of injection attacks is larger than most people realise: XSS is also an injection attack, as are deserialisation attacks, XXE and SSRF. After all, in an SSRF attack malicious input to a server (often a URL) causes the server to make inappropriate requests to other systems; conceptually this is no different than a SQL injection or path traversal. Attacks with Word or Excel documents that contain malicious macros, a long-standing popular attack technique, are also examples of injection attacks.

Structural Solutions. An early initiative to provide structural help in making web applications more secure was the OWASP ESAPI project[10] to provide APIs for various forms of validation and encoding needed in web applications. Important root cause of security problems in web applications, notably XSS, is that web applications handle a set of complex languages, namely HTTP, URLs and HTML, with JavaScript and CSS as sub-languages, which can be nested and then require various encodings to prevent misinterpretation. Note that this involves some of the root causes signalled by the LangSec approach, namely the large number and complexity of input languages.

Safer APIs can reduce the risk of injection attacks. The classic example is the use of parameterised queries or prepared statements to prevent SQL injection. A generalisation of this idea is the use of 'safe builders' to ensure proper output encoding [26], where the type checker of the programming language will catch insecure use of APIs. The Trusted Types API, an improved version of the DOM API in web browsers, uses this idea to combat XSS; this approach has shown to be very effective at Google to root out XSS, incl. DOM-based XSS as the most complex variant of XSS [60].

5.5   Improper Use of 'improper Input Validation'

The notion of input validation has proved to be a persistent source of misunderstanding both in classifying and tackling input handling problems. It is telling that the first edition of the OWASP Top 10 had 'Unvalidated Input' as top entry but this category then disappeared in all subsequent editions (see Fig. 1). This is not because the problem was solved, but because bug classification was improved.

The classic example of lack of input validation is an application accepting a negative number when a positive number is expected. The *only* way to fix this is for the application to reject such invalid inputs. Input validation *can* be used to prevent injection attacks, but it is not the best solution and usually totally

---

[10] https://owasp.org/www-project-enterprise-security-api.

inappropriate. Using *output encoding* is better, ideally using the type system of the programming language to ensure proper encodings, as discussed above; using a safer API that is not injection-prone is best. Similarly, input validation *can* prevent memory corruption bugs from being exploited, by preventing malformed inputs from reaching vulnerable parser code, but again this is not the best solution: validating input before it is parsed means introducing yet another parser, for the validation process, which can again be a source of problems. Instead of validating data it is better to parse data into an appropriate data structure to avoid problems with possible malformed or misinterpreted data once and for all, as nicely expressed by the slogan *'parse, don't validate'* [27].

Sloppy use of terminology adds to the confusion about input validation. There is a fundamental difference between (i) *rejecting invalid data* (e.g., rejecting an email address that is not a valid email address) (ii) *normalising* data (e.g., removing trailing space characters in a username or changing all characters to lower case) and (iii) *encoding data* because special characters may cause problems in some back-end (e.g., HTML-encoding data to prevent XSS). Unfortunately the terms 'validation' or 'sanitisation' are commonly loosely used for any of these operations, or indeed any combination. The existence of many (near)synonyms – neutralising, quoting, escaping and filtering – adds to the confusion.

6   Conclusion

The good news is that we know a lot about software security, and a lot more than 20 years ago. There are many methodologies for secure software engineering that broadly agree in the steps to be taken. There are many SAST and DAST tools that can be used as part of these methodologies – with fuzzing as a big success story – and standards proposing lists of security requirements. We know what the common security vulnerabilities are, even though the business of classifying them remains very messy, and we have insights into root causes for many and some ways to structurally tackle these.

Secure-by-Design is a nice slogan for all this but, as discussed in Sect. 2.3, may mislead people into thinking that just sticking a 'security by design' phase in front of their usual development process will take care of security. That would be a mistake, as all secure software development methodologies stress that security requires attention *throughout* the development lifecycle.

The bad news is that the huge number of standards, frameworks and tools makes it hard to see the forest for the trees. In fact, there are several forests: there is a forest of secure development methodologies, a forest of tools, a forest of standards proposing security requirements and the forest of vulnerability categories provided by the CWE classification. A single methodology or standard by itself can already be a mini-forest with dozens of activities or requirements.

Many methodologies and standards make very similar, if not identical, recommendations, but differences in terminology or ways of grouping things can make that hard to spot. NIST even produced a report documenting their standard approach to map relations between security standards [43]. This is not a new phenomenon: already in 2009 BSIMM was started to provide a common frame of reference for the first secure software development methodologies that had emerged at the time.

A forest we have not even mentioned in this paper is the forest of known security vulnerabilities provided by the CVE catalogue. One initiative to cope with that forest is the KEV (Known Exploited Vulnerabilities) list, which was introduced by CISA in 2022 as a subset of the CVE list to help organisations prioritise certain patches. The EU CRA will force many software producers to improve their vulnerability management processes in years to come, as it requires produces to be free from known exploitable vulnerabilities. Here new scoring systems for the severity of vulnerabilities, for instance EPSS [25], have been proposed as alternative to CVSS [31] to help with prioritising patches.

Looking back over the past two decades it is actually surprising how little has changed: the basic ingredients of Microsoft's SDL or McGraw's Touchpoints are still the main ingredients of the newer methodologies. Looking at the kind of vulnerabilities that cause the bulk of security problems it is disappointing – not to say depressing – to see how little has changed, as vulnerabilities that were common two decades ago are still common today.

For memory corruption vulnerabilities it can be probably be excused that they still dominate the CWE Top 25. Getting rid of these bugs in memory-unsafe programming languages has proven to be very hard. The best hope to get rid of these bugs seems to be to move to memory-safe languages. Here it is good to see the momentum building behind Rust as an alternative.

For many of the common vulnerability types on the other hand, e.g. standard injection flaws such as SQL injection or path traversal, there is no excuse why these should still be so prevalent. These were already deemed to be 'unforgivable' back in 2007 [6]. It is embarrassing for the professional software engineering community that in 2024 government agencies still have to launch appeals to get rid of such vulnerabilities [8]. Their prevalence could be due to a lack of knowledge – i.e. security still not getting enough attention in training even though there is so much information about it – or a lack of incentives to put this into practice. It will be interesting to see if legislation such as the CRA will change that.

It is telling that in May 2024, 22 years after Bill Gates's original email to highlight security as a top priority, Microsoft was one of the companies to sign up to CISA's Secure-by-Design pledge[11]. Clearly the job to improve software security is never done. Looking ahead, one big unknown factor in the future is how AI will impact all this. AI can be a useful tool for both attackers and for defenders and it is not clear who has most to gain here. Moreover, the use of AI in software products will give rise to new risks [34].

Acknowledgement. Research funded by the Dutch Research Council NWO through the INTERSECT project (NWA.1160.18.301) and NCSRA III (ENCRY.2021.001). The author has no competing interests to declare that are relevant to the content of this article.

---

[11] https://www.cisa.gov/securebydesign/pledge.

References

1. Arce, I., et al.: Avoiding the top 10 software security design flaws. Tech. rep., IEEE Computer Society Center for Secure Design (CSD) (2014)
2. Basak, S.K., Cox, J., Reaves, B., Williams, L.: A comparative study of software secrets reporting by secret detection tools. In: Empirical Software Engineering and Measurement (ESEM). IEEE (2023)
3. Black, P.E.: Software assurance with SAMATE reference dataset, tool standards, and studies. In: Digital Avionics Systems Conference. IEEE (2007)
4. Bratus, S., Locasto, M.E., Patterson, M.L., Sassaman, L., Shubina, A.: Exploit programming: From buffer overflows to weird machines and theory of computation. USENIX ;login, pp. 13–21 (2011)
5. Chandra, P.: OWASP Software Assurance Maturity Model (SAMM), version 1.0. OWASP (2009)
6. Christey, S.: Unforgiveable vulnerabilities. Tech. rep, MITRE (2007)
7. Shifting the balance of cybersecurity risk: Principles and approaches for security-by-design and -default. Tech. rep, CISA, June 2023
8. Secure by design alert: Eliminating directory traversal vulnerabilities in software. Tech. rep, CISA, May 2024
9. Cyber Safety Review Board: Review of the December 2021 Log4J event. Tech. rep., U.S. Department of Homeland Security, July 2022
10. De Win, B., Scandariato, R., Buyens, K., Grégoire, J., Joosen, W.: On the secure software development process: CLASP, SDL, and Touchpoints compared. Inf. Softw. Technol. **51**(7), 1152–1171 (2009)
11. Del-Real, C., de Busser, E., van den Berg, B.: Shielding software systems: a comparison of security by design and privacy by design based on a systematic literature review. Comput. Law Secur. Rev. **52** (2024)
12. Etalle, S.: From intrusion detection to software design. In: Foley, S.N., Gollmann, D., Snekkenes, E. (eds.) ESORICS 2017. LNCS, vol. 10492, pp. 1–10. Springer, Cham (2017). https://doi.org/10.1007/978-3-319-66402-6_1
13. EU: Commission Delegated Regulation 2022/30 supplementing Directive 2014/53/EU (2022), aka Radio Equipment Directive (RED)
14. EU: Cyber Resilience Act: Regulation 2024/2847 on horizontal cybersecurity requirements for products with digital elements (2024)
15. Gasteratos, S., van der Veer, R.: Open Common Requirement Enumeration. https://www.opencre.org
16. Gates, B.: Trustworthy computing (January 15 2002), internal memo to all Microsoft employees
17. Gluck, D., Mazolli, R.: SDL-Agile requirements. Tech. rep, Microsoft (2012)
18. Godefroid, P.: Fuzzing: hack, art, and science. Commun. ACM **63**(2), 70–76 (2020)
19. The rule of 2. Google (2019). https://chromium.googlesource.com/chromium/src/+/master/docs/security/rule-of-2.md, documentation of the Chromium project
20. Chromium security - memory safety. Google (May 2020). https://www.chromium.org/Home/chromium-security/memory-safety
21. Haupert, V., Maier, D., Schneider, N., Kirsch, J., Müller, T.: Honey, I shrunk your app security: The state of Android app hardening. In: Detection of Intrusions and Malware, and Vulnerability Assessment, pp. 69–91. Springer (2018)
22. Howard, M., Lipner, S.: The Security Development Lifecycle. Microsoft (2006)
23. Hughes, C., Haydock, W.: The case for a SaaS bill of material. CSO online (2021). https://www.csoonline.com/article/571267/the-case-for-a-saas-bill-of-material.html

24. ISA/IEC 62443, Security for Industrial Automation and Control Systems, parts 1-4. International Society of Automation (ISA), 2007-2023
25. Jacobs, J., Romanosky, S., Edwards, B., Adjerid, I., Roytman, M.: Exploit Prediction Scoring System (EPSS). Digital Threats **2**(3) (2021)
26. Kern, C.: Preventing security bugs through software design (2015), invited talk at USENIX Security'15
27. King, A.: Parse, don't validate (2019). https://lexi-lambda.github.io/blog/2019/11/05/parse-don-t-validate, personal blog
28. Kudriavtseva, A., Gadyatskaya, O.: Secure software development methodologies: A multivocal literature review (2023)
29. LangSec: Recognition, validation, and compositional correctness for real world security (2013). http://langsec.org/bof-handout.pdf
30. Li, Z., Liu, Z., Wong, W.K., Ma, P., Wang, S.: Evaluating C/C++ vulnerability detectability of query-based static application security testing tools. IEEE Trans. Dependable Secure Comput. **21**(5), 4600–4618 (2024)
31. Liska, A.: CVSS scores are dead. Let's explore 4 alternatives (2021), presentation at RSA 2021 conference
32. Mauw, S., Oostdijk, M.: Foundations of attack trees. In: Information Security and Cryptology (ICISC 2005); revised selected papers, pp. 186–198. Springer (2006)
33. McGraw, G.: Software security: building security in. Addison-Wesley (2006)
34. McGraw, G., Bonett, R., Shepardson, V., Figueroa, H.: The top 10 risks of machine learning security. Computer **53**(6), 57–61 (2020)
35. McGraw, G., Chess, B.: The Building Security in Maturity Model (BSIMM). In: USENIX Security. USENIX (2009)
36. Meli, M., McNiece, M.R., Reaves, B.: How bad can it git? characterizing secret leakage in public github repositories. In: NDSS. The Internet Society (2019)
37. Microsoft Security Development Lifecycle (SDL) – version 5.2. Microsoft (2012). https://learn.microsoft.com/en-us/previous-versions/windows/desktop/cc307748(v=msdn.10)
38. Miller, B.P., Fredriksen, L., So, B.: An empirical study of the reliability of UNIX utilities. Commun. ACM **33**(12), 32–44 (1990)
39. National Cybersecurity Strategy. The White House, March 2023
40. NIST: IR 7628 (version 1), Guidelines for Smart Grid Cybersecurity, September 2014
41. NIST: Secure Software Development Framework (SSDF) version 1.1: Recommendations for mitigating the risk of software vulnerabilities, February 2022
42. Cybersecurity Framework (CSF 2.0). NIST, February 2024
43. NIST: IR 8477, Mapping relationships between documentary standards, regulations, frameworks, and guidelines: Developing cybersecurity and privacy concept mappings, February 2024
44. Ornstein, D., Rice, T.: Building the next generation of the Microsoft Security Development Lifecycle (SDL). Tech. rep, Microsoft (2024)
45. How to start an AppSec program with the OWASP Top 10. OWASP. https://owasp.org/Top10/A00_2021-How_to_start_an_AppSec_program_with_the_OWASP_Top_10/, date visited 4-Sept-2023
46. Software Component Verification Standard (SCVS), version 1.0. OWASP (2020)
47. Application Security Verification Standard (ASVS), version 4.0.3. OWASP (2021)
48. Mobile Application Security Verification Standard (MASVS), version 2.0.0. OWASP (2023)
49. SAFECode secure development practices. SAFECode. https://safecode.org/category/resource-secure-development-practices

50. Saltzer, J.H., Schroeder, M.D.: The protection of information in computer systems. Proc. IEEE **63**(9), 1278–1308 (1975)
51. Sassaman, L., Patterson, M.L., Bratus, S., Shubina, A.: The halting problems of network stack insecurity. USENIX; login **36**(6), 22–32 (2011)
52. SEI CERT coding standards. SEI (Software Engineering Institute), CMU. https://wiki.sei.cmu.edu
53. Serebryany, K.: OSS-Fuzz - Google's continuous fuzzing service for open source software (2017), invited talk at USENIX 2017
54. 8th annual state of the software supply chain. Tech. rep., Sonatype (2022)
55. Stoddard, J.T., Cutshaw, M.A., Williams, T., Friedman, A., Murphy, J.: Software Bill of Materials (SBOM) sharing lifecycle report. Tech. Rep. INL/RPT-23-71296-Rev000, Idaho National Laboratory (2023)
56. BSIMM 14 report. Tech. rep., Synopsys (2023)
57. Takanen, A.: Fuzzing: the past, the present and the future. In: Symposium sur la Sécurité des Technologies de l'Information et des Communications (SSTIC) (2009)
58. Thomas, G.: A proactive approach to more secure code (2019), Microsoft Security Response Center blog. https://msrc-blog.microsoft.com/2019/07/16/a-proactive-approach-to-more-secure-code
59. United States Government Accountability Office: Federal response to SolarWinds and Microsoft Exchange incidents. Tech. Rep. GOA-22-104746, U.S. Department of Homeland Security (2022)
60. Wang, P., Bangert, J., Kern, C.: If it's not secure, it should not compile: Preventing DOM-based XSS in large-scale web development with API hardening. In: ICSE'21, pp. 1360–1372. IEEE (2021)
61. Williams, L., Migues, S., Boote, J., Hutchison, B.: Proactive software supply chain risk management framework (P-SSCRM) version 1. arXiv preprint (arXiv:2404.12300) (2024)
62. Zahan, N., Lin, E., Tamanna, M., Enck, W., Williams, L.: Software bills of materials are required. are we there yet? IEEE Secur. Privacy **21**(2), 82–88 (2023)
63. Zalewski, M.: American fuzzy lop (afl) (2012). https://lcamtuf.coredump.cx/afl/

Getting Into a Jam with Attack Trees

Zach Smith[(✉)] [iD]

Esch-sur-Alzette, Luxembourg
`zach@almou.se`

Abstract. The "Lindy Hop" is a social partnered swing dance that originated from Harlem, New York, in the 1920s and 30 s. It is characterised by dynamic and lively movements, including solo jazz steps, drawing its roots from traditional African- and African-American- dance forms.

One artefact of these cultural roots is "Jam Circles" – a social configuration in which a group of dancers form a circle around a space for individual or partnered performances to take place. This can include solo improvisation, performances by couples, or even playful "stealing" of partners between dancers.

While Jam Circles are celebrated for their energy and communal spirit, they also bring several problems. Most notably, it can be intimidating for new dancers to participate – not only because of the difficulty of the dance itself, but also because of the addition of several unique social customs relating specifically to Jam circles.

In this paper, we investigate the use of formal modelling methods to support the analysis of Lindy Hop. We use Attack Trees to analyse the effectiveness of different strategies for participating in a Jam Circle. The attack tree is parameterised using expert insights from field research.

Keywords: Attack Trees · Lindy Hop · State Transition Systems

1 Introduction

In this section we introduce the two core components of this research: Attack Trees and Lindy Hop. We give some insight into their rich individual histories and briefly examine previous works on their intersection.

1.1 Attack Trees

Attack trees are a modelling tool for categorizing the ways a system can be attacked [25]. A root node of the tree represents the ultimate objective of the attacker, while child nodes represent the subgoals the attacker may have to overcome in order to reach this objective. These subgoals can be further *refined* until a set of "leaf" nodes have been found, which represent the atomic steps involved in an attack.

For example, suppose we are tasked with producing an attack tree for the task of "Listen to Jazz Music". An attacker may pursue several distinct strategies:

Z. Smith:—Independent Researcher

B. Fila et al. (Eds.): Sjouke Mauw Festschrift, LNCS 16365, pp. 219–236, 2026.
https://doi.org/10.1007/978-3-032-20684-8_13

- They could play the music themselves
- They could listen to a recording
- They could attend an event where Jazz music is being played

An example of such an attack tree is given in Fig. 1.

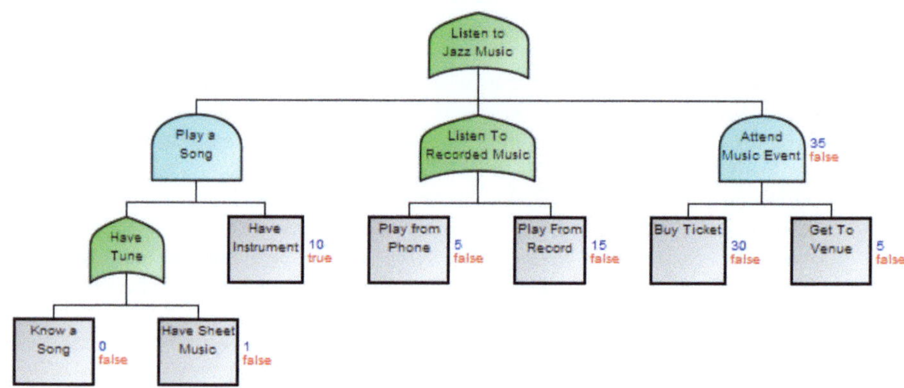

Fig. 1. Attack Tree for Listening to Jazz Music. Decorators indicate the cost and the need of special tools or knowledge (in this case, being able to play a musical instrument).

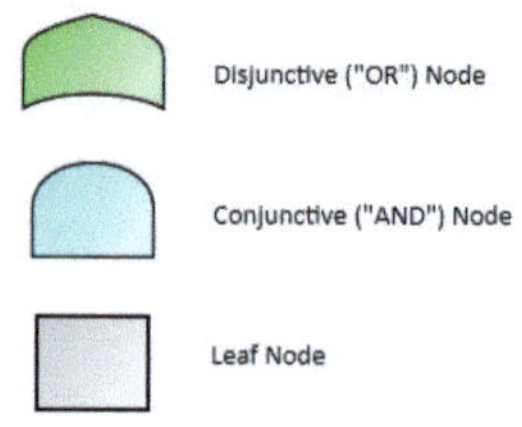

Fig. 2. Legend for attack trees.

A *refinement* of a node – the addition of sub-nodes – can be *conjunctive* or *disjunctive*, indicating whether all subtasks must be performed, or if just one is enough. For example, to 'Attend a Music Event', the attacker must both 'Buy Ticket' **and** 'Get to Venue'. By comparison, to "Have Tune", it is sufficient either to "Know a Song" or "Have Sheet Music". Some extensions [12] to Attack Trees propose "Sequential Conjunctions" ("SAND"), to indicate that a set of steps must be all done and in a specific order (Figs. 2, 4 and 5).

Decorated Trees. A key addition of attack trees is to use *decorators* (equivalently, attributes) on nodes. These decorators describe properties of a node – for example, its cost, difficulty, or required expertise. A set of *combinators* describe the interactions between these decorators. For example, the cost of 'Entering the Venue' is the combined cost of 'Buying a Ticket' and 'Getting to the Venue'. Meanwhile, the cost of the overall tree (assuming one wishes to minimise expenses) is the cost of its cheapest child node.

As well as the intuitive depictions of Attack Trees as visual aids, foundational analyses such as that of Mauw and Oostdijk [19] allow describing an Attack tree as a mathematical object. Such a framing is used to address the problem of decorating nodes using empirical data when concrete information is not available, by converting it into a constraint solving problem that can be processed by automated tools [5]. This provides an alternative to a "bottom-up" approach, which relies on the analyst being able to accurately evaluate any labels added to leaf nodes.

Analysing Attack Trees. Once an Attack Tree has been created and decorated with labels, automated tooling (or manual observation) can be used to identify the most viable attack paths – for example, those with the highest likelihood, lowest cost to the attacker, or requiring the least specialist skills. Tools such as ADTool [8] can be used for this purpose.

Figure 3 gives an example of the analysis of our working example, showing the relative costs of the different attack options and proposing an optimal attack.

Attack-Defense Trees. Suppose our attack tree modelled the related but fundamentally different task of "Listen to Blues Music". An analyst working on the tree may be interested in learning what countermeasures are available to minimise the risk of the proponent achieving their goal. Upon seeing that the cheapest attack involves listening from one's phone, the analyst may implement countermeasures to increase the cost of using phone streaming services. Alternatively, the analyst may be worried about the likelihood of these attacks rather than the cost – for example, by ensuring that people are not exposed to public music events.

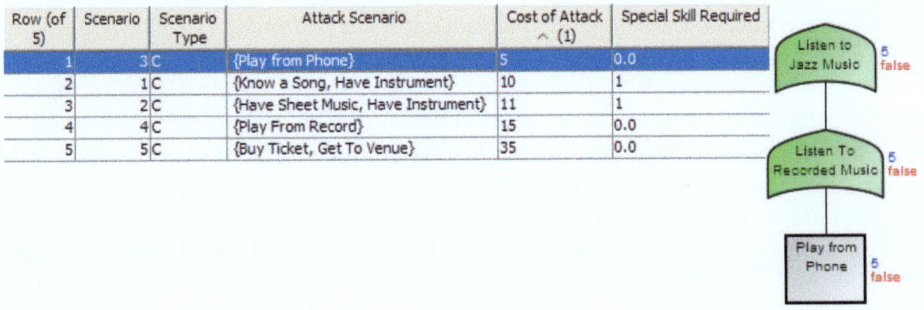

Row (of 5)	Scenario	Scenario Type	Attack Scenario	Cost of Attack ⌃ (1)	Special Skill Required
1	3	C	{Play from Phone}	5	0.0
2	1	C	{Know a Song, Have Instrument}	10	1
3	2	C	{Have Sheet Music, Have Instrument}	11	1
4	4	C	{Play From Record}	15	0.0
5	5	C	{Buy Ticket, Get To Venue}	35	0.0

Fig. 3. Analysis of the "Listen to Jazz Music" attack tree given the decorators shown earlier.

The modelling of countermeasures in the tree was originally suggested by Schneier [25], by re-labelling nodes. However, newer formalisms include adding "Defender-owned" nodes to the Tree, explicitly modelling action taken by the defender. This approach is referred to as an *Attack-Defense Tree* [15], enabling some of the constraint solving problems listed above to also be analysed under this new setting.

Some approaches also demonstrate the dynamic nature of Attack-Defense trees. Once a defender has refined the tree by adding a new security hardening step ("Increase the Cost of Phone Services"), the attacker might implement new attacks ("Borrow a friend's phone"). Kordy et al. [14] demonstrate that under this approach, Attack-Defense Trees are equivalent to Two-Player Binary Zero-Sum Extensive Form Games.

Coordinated Attack Graphs. Braynov and Jadliwala [3,4] introduced the concept of coordinated attacks. In this setting, multiple attackers cooperate in order to execute an attack. This is represented in the context of Attack Graphs, in which time costs are associated with tasks. Attackers can cooperate by working on multiple tasks simultaneously, or subdividing tasks. Attackers with individual capabilities can perform enabling tasks on behalf of attackers without such capabilities – for example, an insider can install a backdoor that will later be exploited by an outsider.

Similar approaches exist in other domains, such as using Petri Nets [6]. Here, attackers are represented as tokens moving through a series of states once certain transition conditions are met. For example, a transition may require an attacker with specific capabilities (represented by decorators or 'colours' associated to tokens), or multiple attackers to be present.

1.2   Lindy Hop

Lindy Hop is an energetic partnered social dance, which emerged from Harlem, New York, in the late 1920s [18]. Originating from primarily African-Americans in the ballrooms of Harlem such as the Savoy, it drew heavily from the other dances of the era, as well as from its African roots. The Lindy Hop was formed from a conglomeration of other dance styles from the time period – such as the Charleston and Breakaway. This led to unique elements from a variety of sources, such as call-and-response patterns, and breakaways in dancing to allow the partners to show their individual flair.

Swing music and Lindy Hop remained popular in the United States through the 1930s and early 1940s, but declined in visibility during the post-war decades. A revival began in the 1980s, when dancers —- many based in Europe —- sought to reconnect with the original form by studying archival footage and, in some cases, learning directly from original Lindy Hoppers such as Frankie Manning and Norma Miller. Since then, the dance has continued to evolve and expand globally.

Lindy Hop is structurally rich as a dance form. Unlike many partner dances that rely on a single canonical "basic step", Lindy Hop includes multiple basic rhythms, such as the six-count, eight-count, and Charleston variants—each of which can be smoothly interchanged during a dance. In addition to rhythmic variation, dancers may move between a series of positions – such as closed, open (facing), or side-by-side, as well. A wide vocabulary of swing moves exist to enable dancers to move between these different positions while respecting the different rhythms and timings presented by the music. The dance also emphasises a high level of agency on the dancer assuming the role of "follower". Unlike many ballroom dances, the follower in Lindy Hop has much more freedom to react to- and alter moves in a variety of ways in order to connect to the dance, rather than solely following instructions from the leader.

Showtime, Jam Circles. A longstanding tradition in Lindy Hop—and its precursor styles—is the practice of gathering in what is now commonly called a *Jam Circle*. In such an event, a group of dancers forms a circle, and one or more dancers enter the center to showcase their best moves.

This tradition predates the Lindy Hop dance itself. According to Frankie Manning [18], dancers would "show off" at informal house parties, even before the dance took hold in the ballrooms. At the Savoy Ballroom, dancers often gathered in a space known as the "Cats' Corner," where the most skilled dancers would jam, watch each other, and trade ideas [21]. In more formal settings, these circles were often introduced by a host announcing it was "showtime" [7], prompting a crowd to form and performers to step forward. The trend of Jam Circles continues to thrive even in modern Lindy Hop.

Birthday Jams, Stealing. In modern Lindy Hop – particularly since the Swing Revival – Jam Circles often follow established social formats. One popular example is the *Birthday Jam*, in which a dancer celebrating a birthday remains in the center of the circle, while others take turns dancing with them for short segments of a single song. Partner transitions can happen in many ways, but the most iconic is the *steal*: an incoming dancer separates the pair in order to replace one of them. This can involve intercepting momentum from a move, pulling the follow away, or inserting oneself between the two dancers mid-step.

Fig. 4. Photos of classic Lindy Hoppers Willa Mae Ricker and Leon James in Life Magazine [20].

Similar jams may occur to welcome newcomers or mark achievements. In this paper, we refer to all such circles as "Birthday Jams" for simplicity. We distinguish these from the "Standard Jam", where dancers can enter and exit the circle freely, without any designated central dancers. Such Jam circles often form in response to a particularly appreciated song played by a band, around a particularly energetic couple, or by a group of dancers wanting to share the experience with each other.

Academic Analysis of Jam Circles. There is some modern academic commentary on Jam Circles in Lindy Hop. Given [10] emphasizes that Jam Circles are a core part of the culture of Lindy Hop. He states that a disconnection from community participation in Jam Circles – transforming them into spectacles for audiences rather than collaborative and inclusive events – is a major factor in the dance becoming distanced from its origins.

Heinilä [11] performs a deep historical analysis on the progression of the Lindy Hop community, with a focus on on the dancers' struggle for recognition and integration. They mention Jam Circles were a positive factor in integrating new dancers into a communal experience. They write:

> *Although dancing in the middle of the Circle could be considered a performance, the Savoy dancers, however, were connected to each other via these Circles and the Circles happened during regular nights. Thus, they were part of the social dancing at the Savoy.*

Keevallik & Ekström [13] analyse Jam Circles in swing dance under the lens of "turn-taking" (as one would in conversation). They give details of several case studies marking precise details of a series of Jam Circles. This includes, for example, how each couple in a Jam entered the circle, and how long they danced for.

1.3   Related Work

We look at some of the other approaches that have been made in applying modelling techniques to dance.

Dancing as a State Transition System. There are a few examples of applying formal modelling techniques to dance. Gentry [9] presents Lindy Hop as a finite state machine. The states represent the relative position of the partners to each other, with transitions caused by dance moves. They use this FSM to construct a game in which the players are a set of dancers (on one side) against a judge who ranks their "choreography" based on their moves over the FSM. Models of hip-hop dancers have also considered using state machines [1]. We discuss this in more detail in Sect. 2.

Fig. 5. A Lindy Hop Jam Circle in progress [2].

Dancing as a Decision Tree. Lozano [17] models variations of the Lindy Hop basic step as a decision tree (represented in the form of a matrix). Branches refer to decisions made – which side the dancers pass each other on, which of the partners perform a turn – allowing them to describe different moves in a common language. Unlike the previous examples, which look at a corpus of many different movements and positions within the dance, Lozano focuses on enumerating the variations of a single movement.

Other Uses of Modelling in Dancing. There are some examples of the usage of (risk) modelling tools used to gain insights in the overall environment regarding dancing, rather than performing analysis of the dance itself.

- Liu et al. [16] performed risk modelling against factors that might cause a dancer to become injured as part of their training. They considered factors such as likelihood and severity to classify risks
- Websites such as *performingartsreadiness.org* [23] create disaster recovery plans for dance-related incidents, along with risk assessments

In contrast, the focus of this work is how we can formalise the specific activity of dancing in its various forms.

1.4   Contributions

In this work we primarily focus on the use of Attack Trees as a modelling tool. Within this, we model specifically the concept of Jam Circles, as introduced in

Subsect. 1.2. We apply this to provide dancers an optimal route to participating in Jam Circles – taking the "attacker" role in an Attack Tree:

> *1. What is the optimum attack path a dancer should take in order to participate in a Lindy Hop jam circle?*

We then perform an analysis from the perspective of the "defender". This represents the hypothetical gatekeeper who wishes to reduce participation in their local dance community.

> *2. What actions can be taken to hinder dancers from participating in Jam Circles?*

In order to answer these questions, we have performed an extensive case study on Jam Circles. From this study we have constructed an Attack Tree that defines the options available to an attacker to engineer and participate in a Jam Circle. This allows dancers to evaluate the most successful strategy to achieve their goal.

1.5   Structure

The rest of the paper is structured as follows: In Sect. 2 we demonstrate a simple approach for modelling Lindy Hop as a Labelled Transition System. We discuss the advantages and limitations of this form of modelling a dance form. Section 3 contains the discussion of the Attack Tree constructed from our analysis. We discuss the approach taken in generating the attack tree as well as performing quantitative analysis. We conclude in Sect. 4 by discussing the options for future work in modelling both Attack Trees and Lindy Hop as a whole.

2   Lindy Hop as a Labelled Transition System

In this section we consider the ability to model Lindy Hop with Labelled Transition Systems.

A Labelled Transition System (LTS) is a triple $(S, A, \rightarrow)$, where S is a set of states, A a set of actions and $\rightarrow$ a ternary relation on $S \rightarrow A \rightarrow S$. We write $S_1 \xrightarrow{a_1} S_2$ if $(S_1, a_1, S_2) \in \rightarrow$.

As an example, consider the dance of Lindy Hop. Over the course of a dance, dancers will transition between a series of positions (states, S) relative to each other. For example, in open position, two dancers stand at arm's length, whilst in closed position they stand adjacent in a V-shape.

Different dance moves (actions, A) allow the dancers to transition between these states. A simplified example of such a transition system is given in Fig. 6. Actions can be labelled intuitively (e.g. by the given name of a move), or with information-carrying tags (e.g. the time it takes for the move to complete, whether it is part of a larger category of moves).

Some related work uses Finite State Machines for modelling dancing [1,9]. In these cases, their FSMs are grounded upon labelled transition systems. Gentry's [9] ground transition system is much more intricate than the example we present here – with a corpus of a few hundred actions. They extend it with a choice function for selecting which series of transitions to take with the end goal of performing the best dance possible (in the context of "winning" a game played against a player in the role of "judge").

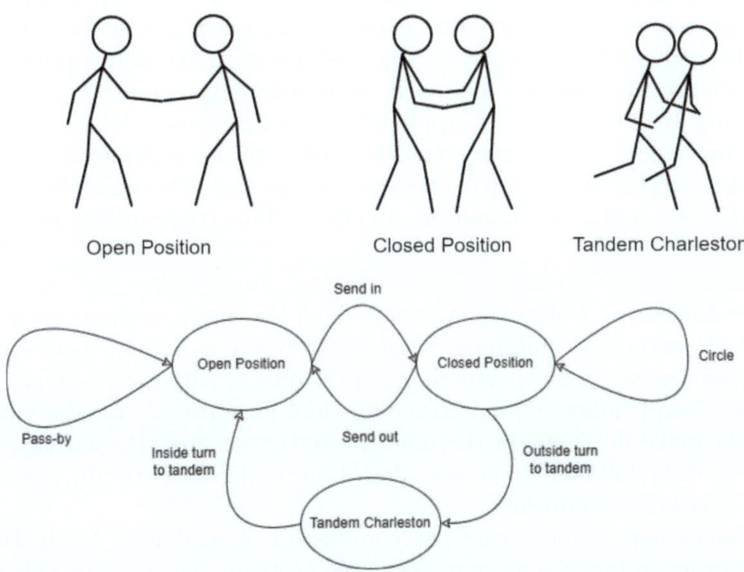

Fig. 6. Common Lindy Hop positions and a labelled transition diagram between them.

An advantage of modelling dancing in this way is that it allows for model verification. Linear Temporal Logic [22,24] is a language for reasoning about the incidence and order of transitions within a LTS (or other model). Through labelling subsets of states, it would allow us to formulate and answer key queries such as:

- Is it possible for dancers to enter the hand-to-hand position without first entering a Charleston position?
- From which starting positions can I guarantee that I can perform a "Break" action after exactly 4 actions?

For example, the latter query is useful to follow the general flow of many Swing music songs which are broken up into phrases of four bars.

2.1   Pitfalls

Although a framing of Lindy Hop in this way is often seen within the community as a useful tool, there are some pitfalls revealed after further analysis.

Granularity. As one extends the transition system, a common issue is where to determine if two actions (or indeed two states) should be defined equivalently.

For example, in a "pass-by" transition, the Follower of the dance may pass to the left or to the right of the Leader. This could be represented in our transition system as two separate actions ($S_{open} \xrightarrow{pass\text{-}by\text{-}left} S_{open}$ and $S_{open} \xrightarrow{pass\text{-}by\text{-}right} S_{open}$, or as a single action.

There are potential solutions in two directions:

- Allowing a large expansion of the state- and action- sets by permitting minor differences to be seen as separate entities. This allows for greater granularity, but the increased complexity of the model may make it less readily usable and increase the computational cost of model analysis tools.
- Following the "reductionist" approach to Swing Dance, which asserts that every movement in the dance can be broken into a series of 2-count moves (e.g. step-step or triple-step). The set of states and actions can be reduced to a single state and a small handful of actions. This trades utility for precision.

Representation of Follower Agency. The transition systems we have seen represent the actions as unilateral decisions. In truth, as Swing Dance is a couple dance, there are two active participants in the dance. Although they are labelled as a "leader" and "follower", it is common (and encouraged) for the follower to proactively make decisions in the dance, altering its flow. By not representing the choices of the follower in these models, their ability to faithfully model Swing Dancing is heavily diminished.

The issues here demonstrate the complexity of modelling Lindy Hop as a whole. In order to tackle a more manageable problem, we prioritise this work on the specialised domain of Jam Circles, which represent a unique situation within Lindy Hop to be analysed.

3   Attack Trees for Jam Circles

In this Section we discuss the model produced as the output of our case study. In Subsect. 3.1 we discuss the labelling of the nodes used for quantitative analysis. Subsection 3.2 provides an overview of the tree structure and key branches. Subsection 3.3 analyses optimal attack paths from the perspective of the attacker, while Subsect. 3.5 discusses the defensive actions.

Throughout this Section we use the phrases "Dancer" and "Attacker" interchangeably.

3.1   Tree Labelling

We apply the following four decorators to the leaf nodes of our tree:

- **Exploitability.** The probability that an attacker will successfully perform the step

- **Time Required.** The estimated duration of the task in minutes. This includes both in-the-moment execution and preparation time, but excludes long-term skill acquisition (as in the next two labels)
- **Technical Skill Requirement.** Indicates whether a step requires advanced technical capabilities—such as training in specialised dance techniques
- **Social Skill Requirement.** Represents the need for embedded social connections in the target community, enabling the attacker to perform insider attacks

3.2   Model Analysis

The attack tree produced from our analysis is presented in Fig. 7. Leaf nodes are decorated to indicate required attacker capabilities, as well as an expert estimate of success probability based on extensive empirical fieldwork.

Many of our observations line up with the previous work of Keevallik & Ekström [13]. For example, they mark three steps required for a successful entrance:

- Displaying "couplehood"
- Displaying imminent entrance
- Occupying the exclusive central space

Many of the observations from the cited work can be seen as branches on our tree, although we also include engineering the presence of the Jam Circle itself.

Tree Overview. In order to successfully participate in a Jam Circle, the attacker must meet three objectives in sequence. First, they must ensure that a circle is present for them to join. Second, they must set the groundwork for the attack by entering the proximity of the circle and having a partner available. Finally, must time and execute their entry into the Jam Circle.

Instigating Circle. The first main branch of the attack tree ensures that a Jam Circle exists. This can be achieved through one of three paths:

- The attacker may attend an event where there is a high chance of a Jam Circle forming organically – for example, one where a live band will perform, or a festival-style event.
- By compromising the event host the attacker can ensure that a Jam Circle will be a part of the event. This could consist of a social engineering attack in which an honest host is tricked into believing that there is a special event worth celebrating, or use of a malicious insider who can manipulate the event schedule
- The attacker may attempt to spontaneously trigger a Jam Circle themselves, for example by leveraging the enthusiasm of nearby dancers

Preparing for Entry. Once a Jam Circle has started, the attacker must prepare to enter, by selecting a partner and reaching a suitable position on the circle's boundary.

- When choosing who to dance with, the attacker has three options.
    - The attacker may ask a nearby dancer, regular partner, or someone across the room using a series of increasingly complex eye signals
    - The attacker may plan to "steal" an existing dancer in the circle to use as a partner
    - With specialist training, the attacker may enter alone via Solo Jazz, bypassing partner requirements entirely
- For navigating to an entry point:
    - Depending on the size of the audience, navigating to the centre may be time-consuming and the attacker might be blocked by other enthusiastic participants
    - In certain cultures, the presence of a queueing system of dancers simplifies this goal

Entering the Circle. In the final phase of the attack, the dancer must choose the timing and method of their entry.

- Regarding timing, several options are available:
    - The attacker can exploit a vulnerability in the standard structure of Swing music, (i.e. phrasese of four 8-count bars). A perceptive attacker can predict natural lulls in the music to time their entry – as long as noone else is attempting the same thing
    - The attacker may leverage social engineering to elicit an invitation from an insider, exploiting community friendliness
    - The attacker can wait for a moment where the circle is left empty and thus vulnerable – for example, once the majority of participants are too fatigued to continue
- The final objective is to seize control of the central dance area. Often this involves driving out the existing dancers in order to secure the circle's centre.

3.3   Attack Path Analysis

We now consider the most vulnerable paths for an attacker to exploit. We examine the options available to an unskilled attacker, and the advantages gained by highly capable adversaries such as nation-state actors or extroverts.

Calculating Exploitability and Time. We follow standard procedures for computing the value of decorators on higher-level nodes for a given attack path. Table 1 summarises these calculations.

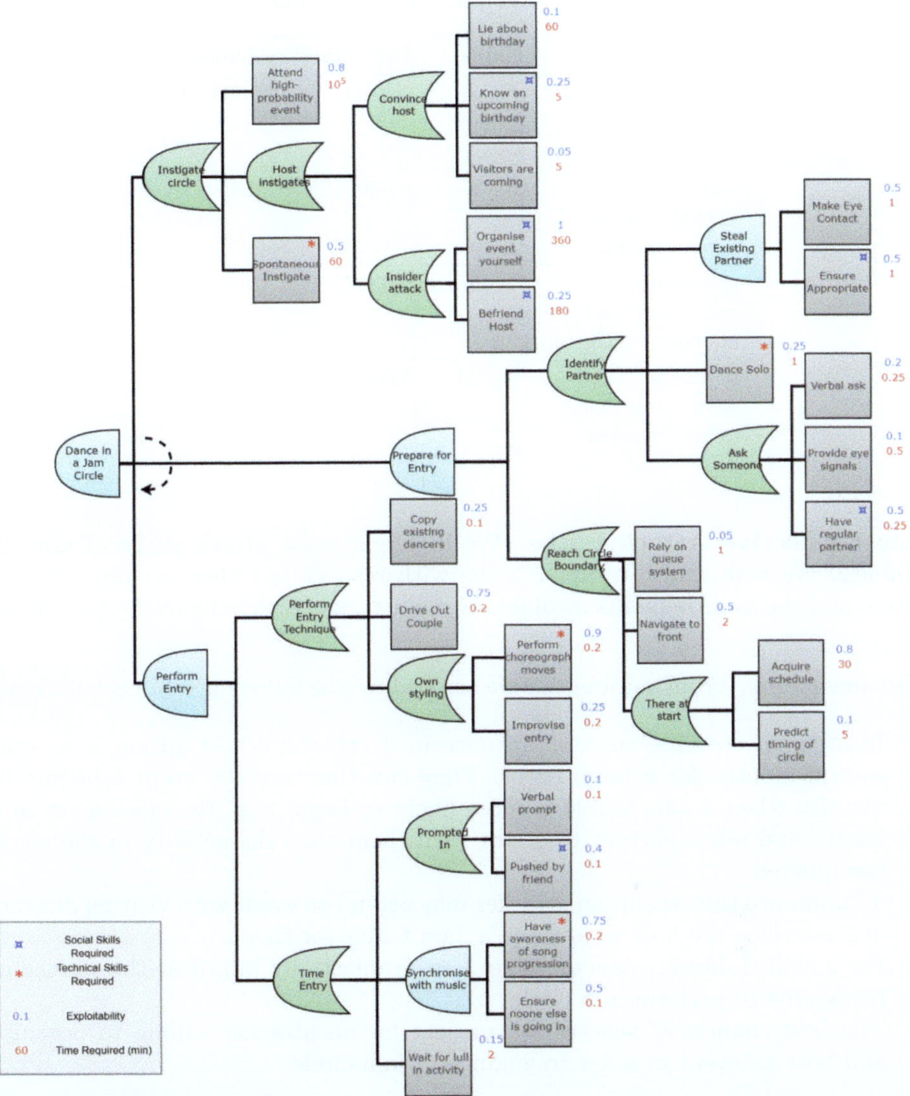

Fig. 7. Attack Tree for Entering a Jam Circle. Dotted line --→ indicates Sequential AND.

Table 1. Exploitability and Time Cost Calculations

Node Type	Exploitability	Time Cost
Disjunctive (OR)	Maximum of children: $E_{OR} = \max(E_1, E_2, ..., E_n)$	Minimum of children: $T_{OR} = \min(T_1, T_2, ..., T_n)$
Conjunctive (AND)	Product of children: $E_{AND} = E_1 \times E_2 \times \cdots \times E_n$	Sum of children: $T_{AND} = T_1 + T_2 + \cdots + T_n$

Table 2. Most Efficient Attack Paths

Attack Route	Skills	Exploitability	Time
highprob *verbal - schedule* *drive - wait*	None	0.0144	10032.45
visitors *verbal - queue* *copy - verbal*	None	0.0000125	6.45
spontaneous *solo - schedule* *choreo - synchronise*	Technical	0.03375	91.5
organize *steal - schedule* *drive - pushed*	Social	0.06	392.4

Most Effective Attack Paths. We highlight some attack paths of note in Table 2. We look at the optimal paths with respect to either exploitability or time, and the improvements available by an attacker with enhanced capabilities.

Observations. From our analysis we can deduce the following main conclusions:

- In order to optimise success, an untrained attacker's best option is to wait several months for a large event. They can then use the event schedule to identity when a Jam Circle is most likely to begin (e.g. the closing set of a band), and ask a partner to dance with them once the activity in the circle has quieted.
- To minimize time spent, an attacker may attend an event with visiting dancers and convince the host to arrange a Jam Circle for them.
- For a skilled dancer, dancing Solo Jazz dramatically improves the chance of being able to perform in a circle.
- The best chances of success are present for an attacker willing to organise and host an event in order to engineer a jam circle.

3.4   Multiple Attackers

Thusfar our model has assumed a single adversary, working in isolation to perform the attack. However, this is often not the case. In fact, it may well be the case that a collection of attackers work in combination to enact a Jam Circle. This might be intentional – in the case of a Birthday Jam, multiple attackers intentionally collude in order to ensure a single individual participates in the circle. It may also be that several attackers, each individually attempting to execute an attack, inadvertently assist each other.

Existing formalisms [3,4] address the topic of multiple attackers by subdividing multi-step tasks, and quantifying the complexity of a task by its number of dependencies. Instead, we propose parameterising the decorators (Time Cost, Likelihood) of leaf nodes, viewing them as functions over a (globally defined) parameter corresponding to the number of attackers. We identify three main families of parameterisations:

- **Synergistic steps**: Nodes that become easier with more attackers, such as *Organise Event* or *Acquire Schedule*
- **Antagonistic steps**: Nodes that become harder with more attackers, such as *Wait for lull* or *Navigate to front*
- **Non-monotonic steps**: Nodes where the difficulty fluctuates with the number of attackers (e.g. according to parity), such as *Have regular partner* or *Verbal ask*

Ultimately these are calculated from the Attacker's perspective of the costs required in order successfully execute the attack – the calculations will be different from the perspective of a defender, who must guard against every attacker simultaneously.

3.5   Countermeasures

Several options are available to Lindy Hop event organisers in order to mitigate the ability of an attacker to participate in Jam Circles:

- Limit event sizes in order to reduce the likelihood of celebrations (e.g. Birthdays) that might trigger a Jam Circle
- Increase social barriers by maintaining a separation between organisers and participants – for example, by running a group as a business instead of a community, and by restricting community discussion and event promotion
- Cultivate unapproachability of higher-level dancers to hinder attackers from building dance skills or forming the social connections required for insider access.

Lindy Hop communities interested in reducing the frequency and participation in Jam Circles should consider pursuing some or all of these options.

4   Conclusion

In this work we analysed threat modelling techniques when applied to the area of Swing Dance. We performed a case study analysing the capability of attackers to gain entrance to Jam Circles, and the measures defenders can take to prevent (or facilitate) such attacks. Quantitative analysis enables the identification of critical attack paths.

A common trend when applying mathematical modelling techniques is dealing with the explosion in complexity. For example, the state space can grow exponentially when attempting to refine the model, which can impact the ability to closely represent reality. Here, the model is made more complex by the presence of multiple attackers who could be working either in isolation or collaboratively.

4.1 Future Work

Despite the depth of our initial analysis, there is clearly much further research to be performed in this area. We highlight a few avenues for future work:

On Attack Trees

- The quantitative analysis of the attack tree presented was based on expert analysis of a small sample set of swing dance communities. However, different swing dance communities follow different social customs, which has the potential to dramatically modify the most critical attack paths. An intensive international collaboration will be necessary to continue these efforts
- As discussed in Subsect. 1.2, Jam Circles are often initiated due to special circumstances, such as celebrating birthdays or welcoming guests. By producing separate models for these distinct situations, a more precise analysis could be performed

On Other Modelling Techniques for Lindy Hop. Through extensive effort, the task of producing a high-fidelity Labelled Transition System for representing Lindy Hop should be attainable. However, it should consider several key components:

- Partitioning the State and Action sets to represent leader- and follower- led situations
- Modelling not only the roles (leader, follower) but the mapping from dancers to roles
    - This is required for modelling the concept of "switch" dancing, in which special moves reverse the allocation of roles between the two dancers

The scope of this task seems large, but there is at least one scenario for Swing Dance modelling where a LTS would provide an excellent solution.

Swing Rueda. A group dance, performed by multiple pairs of dancers performing together around a circle. It is derived from Rueda de Casino, a style of Cuban Salsa. Within this dance, one central leader calls out moves that each couple performs simultaneously. Unlike traditional social dancing, in which a dancer remains with their partner for the duration of a song, in a Rueda the dancers frequently swap partners through a series of special moves.

Like standard socially danced Swing, Swing Rueda has a series of states and a set of actions that link the states together. Unlike traditional swing, these states include a variety of interesting options. As well as many moves originating from Lindy Hop, Rueda takes inspiration from folk dances for a range of moves. For example, in the *amoeba* move, all dancers in the circle join hands and bounce together as a cell, whilst people turn inside the circle to represent a pulsing, swelling movement.

This means that the consideration for the state object is different:

- Although there are multiple sets of dancers, we can assume that they are dancing in-sync, and so only the overall state of the Rueda needs to be modelled
- Although there are multiple pairs of dancers participating, there is a single approved caller who decides how each step of the LTS will be carried out, which everyone follows, avoiding the initial leader/follow bipartite problem.
- The state now has to consider the set of positions that each couple will be in. This is more restrictive than in the "full" Lindy Hop, as the Rueda community will typically put forth a set of approved moves
- On the other hand, the state space is now grown to $S = (\mathcal{P} \times \mathcal{D})$, where $\mathcal{P}$ is the (set of) positions the dancers are in and $\mathcal{D}$ is the symmetry group on the dancer matchings.

The authors believe that vast improvements stand to be made in the field of Swing Rueda by performing more in-depth studies in order to produce one of these high-fidelity models to be studied for aspirational dancers to come.

Acknowledgments. When I first arrived in Luxembourg, I sent an email to the local Swing Dance society, asking if I could attend that night's "Balboa" night, as I had only ever danced the Lindy Hop. Of course, I got a reply saying that I would be welcome regardless. And of course, that reply was written by Prof. Sjouke Mauw, who was one of the people organising the society at the time.

I hope that I can make use of Prof. Mauw's (and others'!) excellent research across his prolific history in order to make progress on this – an as-yet unaddressed – issue in the Swing Dance community. During my PhD, Sjouke helped me to identify and solve problems in payment cards, passports and helped me grow as a person. It is the least I can do to finally formalise (and thus solve) Lindy Hop, once and for all.

Disclosure of Interests. The authors have no competing interests.

References

1. Anthologen: a finite state dance machine (2020). https://anthologen.com/2020/05/06/a-finite-state-dance-machine/, Accessed 01 June 2025
2. Bayman, T.: Poppy's birthday jam (2006). https://www.flickr.com/photos/doublebug/91080455/, photo licensed under CC BY-NC-SA 2.0
3. Braynov, S., Jadliwala, M.: Representation and analysis of coordinated attacks. In: Proceedings of the 2003 ACM workshop on Formal methods in security engineering, pp. 43–51 (2003)
4. Braynov, S., Jadliwala, M.: Detecting malicious groups of agents. In: IEEE First Symposium on Multi-Agent Security and Survivability, pp. 90–99. IEEE (2004)

5. Buldas, A., Gadyatskaya, O., Lenin, A., Mauw, S., Trujillo-Rasua, R.: Attribute evaluation on attack trees with incomplete information. Comput. Secur. **88**, 101630 (2020)
6. Chen, T.M., Sanchez-Aarnoutse, J.C., Buford, J.: Petri net modeling of cyber-physical attacks on smart grid. IEEE Trans. Smart Grid **2**(4), 741–749 (2011)
7. Engelbrecht, B.: Swinging at the savoy. Dance Res. J. **15**(2), 3–10 (1983)
8. Gadyatskaya, O., et al.: Attack trees for practical security assessment: ranking of attack scenarios with adtool 2.0. In: International Conference on Quantitative Evaluation of Systems, pp. 159–162. Springer (2016)
9. Gentry, S.E.: Dancing cheek to cheek: Haptic communication between partner dancers and swing as a finite state machine. Ph.D. thesis, Massachusetts Institute of Technology (2005)
10. Given, W.: Lindy hop, community, and the isolation of appropriation. In: George-Graves, N. (ed.) The Oxford Handbook of Dance and Theater. Oxford University Press (2015)
11. Heinilä, H.M.J.: An Endeavor by Harlem Dancers to Achieve Equality: The Recognition of the Harlem-Based African-American Jazz Dance Between 1921 and 1943. Ph.D. thesis, University of Helsinki (2016)
12. Jhawar, R., Kordy, B., Mauw, S., Radomirović, S., Trujillo-Rasua, R.: Attack trees with sequential conjunction. In: IFIP International Information Security and Privacy Conference, pp. 339–353. Springer (2015)
13. Keevallik, L., Ekström, A.: How to take the floor as a couple: turn-taking in lindy hop jam circles. Vis. Anthropol. **32**(5), 423–444 (2019)
14. Kordy, B., Mauw, S., Melissen, M., Schweitzer, P.: Attack-defense trees and two-player binary zero-sum extensive form games are equivalent. In: International Conference on Decision and Game Theory for Security, pp. 245–256. Springer (2010)
15. Kordy, B., Mauw, S., Radomirović, S., Schweitzer, P.: Attack-defense trees. J. Log. Comput. **24**(1), 55–87 (2014)
16. Liu, Y., Sun, H., Sun, W.: Risk assessment of hip-hop dance and cheerleading athlete's daily training based on fmea. In: 2013 International Workshop on Computer Science in Sports, pp. 17–20. Atlantis Press (2013)
17. Lozano, J.: Breakdown of the swing-out. https://www.fluidandformless.com/breakdown, Accessed 01 May 2025
18. Manning, F., Millman, C.: Frankie Manning: Ambassador of Lindy Hop. Temple University Press, U.S. (1999)
19. Mauw, S., Oostdijk, M.: Foundations of attack trees. In: International Conference on Information Security and Cryptology, pp. 186–198. Springer (2005)
20. Mili, G.: How to dance the lindy hop. Life **15**(8), 91–98 (1943). photo essay featuring Leon James and Willa Mae Ricker demonstrating Lindy Hop aerials
21. Miller, N., Jensen, E.: Swingin' at the Savoy: the Memoir of a Jazz Dancer. Temple University Press, U.S. (1996)
22. Pnueli, A.: The temporal logic of programs. In: 18th Annual Symposium on Foundations of Computer Science (sfcs 1977), pp. 46–57. IEEE (1977)
23. Readiness, P.A.: Risk assessment for dance and theatre (2024). https://performingartsreadiness.org/risk-assessment-theatre-dance, Accessed 01 Apr 2024
24. Rozier, K.Y.: Linear temporal logic symbolic model checking. Comput. Sci. Rev. **5**(2), 163–203 (2011)
25. Schneier, B.: Attack trees. Dr. Dobb's Journal **24**(12), 21–29 (1999)

Automated Symbolic Verification of Quantum Cryptographic Protocols

Rolando Trujillo-Rasua[1]([envelope]) [iD], Jesse Laeuchli[2] [iD], and Reynaldo Gil-Pons[3] [iD]

[1] Universitat Rovira i Virgili, Tarragona 43007, Spain
`rolando.trujillo@urv.cat`
[2] University of New South Wales, Sydney, NSW 2052, Australia
`j.laeuchli@unsw.edu.au`
[3] NearOne Organization, Kirchberg, Luxembourg
`Reynaldo.gilpons@nearone.org`

Abstract. Significant progress within the area of symbolic verification of cryptographic protocols has made it possible to formally analyze the security of several large-scale internet protocols, such as TLS 1.3, 5G-AKA, EMV, and Apple iMessage. Notably, these verification results can be reproduced and scrutinized by simply downloading the protocol specification and checking it with a fully-automated protocol verification tool, such as Tamarin. By contrast, the symbolic analysis of quantum security protocols remains a challenge even for relative simple quantum protocols like BB84. In this article, we introduce a symbolic model that quantum protocol designers can use to formally verify their protocols with the verification tool Tamarin. We provide symbolic interpretations of various quantum operations, such as entanglement and measurement, and communication protocols, such as teleportation and superdense coding. We illustrate the strengths and limitations of our symbolic model by specifying and formally verifying two prominent quantum protocols.

Keywords: Quantum Cryptographic Protocols · Symbolic Verification · BB84 · Tamarin

1   Introduction

Quantum protocols use the laws of quantum mechanics to provide information-theoretic security guarantees that are out of reach in classical computing. A prominent example is the *BB84 protocol* [2], introduced by Bennett and Brassard in 1984, which uses the no-cloning theorem to show that it is possible for two parties to agree on a fresh and secret random value without resorting into hardness computational assumptions. In this case, the no-cloning theorem prevents

---

R. Gil-Pons:—Independent Researcher.
Sjouke has been the most influential person in my research career, combining intellectual rigor with a great sense of openness and curiosity. He is a mentor, a guide, a role model, and a very good friend. One of his greatest lessons was the importance of playfulness in both work and life, a lesson that has shaped me more than he knows. Another was "family first", which needs no explanation. For that, and for his deep support, I will remain grateful to him forever.

an adversary from copying an arbitrary quantum state, making it unfeasible for the adversary to read/measure the quantum state communicated by Alice while simultaneously letting Bob completes the protocol.

Another cryptographic application where quantum computing has made advances is *bit commitment* [3]. Suppose that Alice and Bob are playing coin flipping, i.e. one party bets on the outcome of a random coin tossed by the other party. In this game, the party making the second move (either betting or tossing) can successfully cheat. If Bob communicates its bet to Alice, Alice can always claim that her coin flipped on the opposite side of the bet placed by Bob. A Quantum commitment protocol [3] (see Fig. 1) solves this problem by letting Alice creates a series of qubits $|\psi_1\rangle, \ldots, |\psi_n\rangle$ as follows: if $b = 0$ then $|\psi_i\rangle$ is randomly sampled from the set of rectilinear bases $\{|0\rangle, |1\rangle\}$, otherwise $|\psi_i\rangle$ is randomly sampled from the set of diagonal bases $\{|+\rangle, |-\rangle\}$. Alice then provides the qubits $|\psi_1\rangle, \ldots, |\psi_n\rangle$ to Bob, who measures each qubit on a random basis (rectilinear or diagonal). Lastly, Alice reveals b and the polarizations of the qubits. For each qubit $|\psi_i\rangle$ whose basis Bob guessed correctly, which amount to about half of them, he can check that the outcome of its measurement is exactly b, giving Alice only $1/2^{n/2}$ probability of changing b without being noticed by Bob.

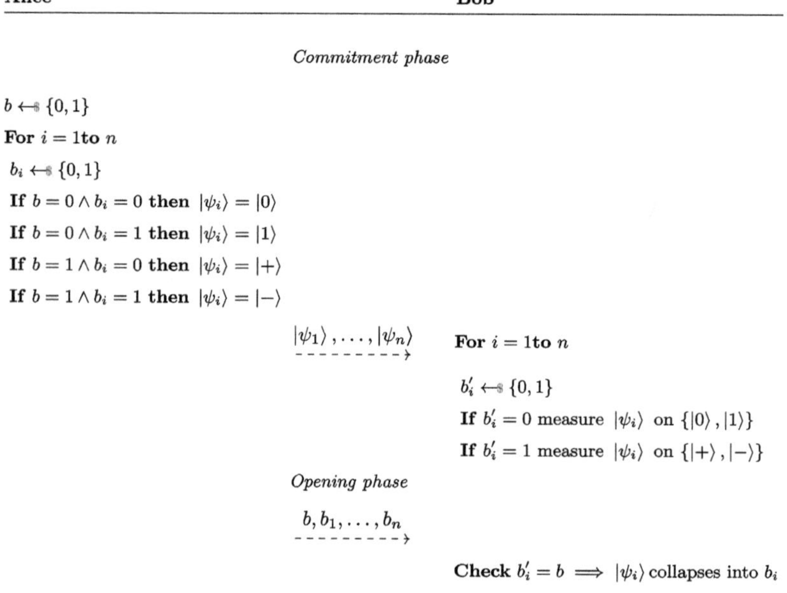

Fig. 1. Bit commitment scheme by Brassard et al. [3].

What makes the two protocols just described unique (from the perspective of classical information theory), is that the non-cloning theorem prevents an attacker from eavesdropping on the communication channel in a fully stealthy manner (like a Dolev-Yao attacker would). That may explain why, despite quantum computers being far from practical for everyday use, researchers are actively looking for clever uses of quantum effects to achieve advanced security goals, such as e-voting [7,19], private information retrieval [20], multi-party computation [1,21], cryptocurrencies [16] and memory attestation [9,12].

Contributions. This article is motivated by a series of design and security flaws we recently found in the quantum-based memory attestation protocol introduced in [9], which was reported in [11]. We observe that most of those flaws stem from counter-intuitive effects in quantum mechanics, such as entanglement, and the absence of formal specification and validation. Indeed, entanglement was used by Lo and Chau [14] to successfully attack the bit commitment protocol described earlier. In their attack, Alice *entangles* the qubits $|\psi_1\rangle, \ldots, |\psi_n\rangle$ with other qubits, allowing her to determine the outcome of Bob's measurement. Our goal, therefore, is to develop a simple symbolic security model, amenable for automatic verification, that can be used to formally check the correctness and security of quantum-based cryptographic protocols.

2   Related Work

The main approach used in the literature to symbolically verify quantum protocols is by modelling quantum processes as concurrent systems, which translates into introducing process algebras for their specification and verification [4,6,10,13,17]. These models, however, are limited in their capacity to automatically verify quantum processes against a network attacker. Xudong, Yuxin and Wenjie [17] use ground bisimulation in qCCS [5] to capture the resistance of protocols against a passive adversary. Their specification, however, is restricted to a single-qubit. Takahiro et al. [10] verify BB84 in a noisy quantum channel controlled by the adversary. They require the communication channel to be either public or private, while we show that an authentic channel is enough.

In this paper, we follow a different approach. Our goal is to test the strengths and limitations of standard protocol verification tools, such as TAMARIN and ProVerif, for the verification of quantum protocols. The preprint by Hirschi [8] has been the main source of inspiration for our security model. Like the works on bisimulation, however, Hirschi's theory is restricted to reasoning at the qubit level, making it cumbersome to use for relatively simple protocols. We deviate from his approach by reasoning at the level of quantum states rather than qubits.

3   Multiset Rewriting: A Background

We provide in this section a brief introduction to multiset rewriting, which is the underlying specification language employed by the TAMARIN verification tool [15], and the one we use in this paper. For a comprehensive overview on the specification and verification of protocols as multiset rewriting systems we refer the reader to the various resources available at https://tamarin-prover.com/.

3.1 Cryptographic Messages

Cryptographic messages are modelled as terms from an order-sorted term algebra $(\mathcal{S}, \leq, \mathcal{T}_{\Sigma}(\mathcal{V}))$ where $\mathcal{S}$ is a set of sorts, $\leq$ a partial order on $\mathcal{S}$, Σ is a signature, and $\mathcal{V}$ is a countably infinite set of variables. We consider three sorts: $msg, fresh, pub \in \mathcal{S}$, where msg denotes any message, $fresh \leq msg$ fresh names (a.k.a. nonces), and $pub \leq msg$ public names (often written in between quotations, e.g. 'hello'). That is, msg is the super sort of two incomparable sub-sorts $fresh$ and pub, denoting fresh and public names, respectively. We write $x \colon s$ to indicate that x is a term of sort s.

3.2 Multiset Rewriting Rules

In Tamarin, protocols are specified by a set of multiset rewriting rules. A multiset rewriting rule is a tuple (p, a, c), written as $[p] \xrightarrow{a} [c]$, where p, a and c are sequences of *facts* called the *premises*, the *actions*, and the *conclusions* of the rule, respectively. A fact is a term of the form $F(t_1, \ldots, t_n)$ where F is a symbol from an unsorted signature Γ and $t_1, \ldots, t_n$ are terms taken from a term algebra $\mathcal{T}_{\Sigma}(\mathcal{V})$. Tamarin reserves the facts $\mathsf{In}(m), \mathsf{Out}(m)$ and $\mathsf{Fr}(m)$ to express that: m is being received, m is being sent, and m is a nonce, respectively. These three facts are sufficient, for example, to define one rule for sending a nonce and another one for receiving it.

$$\mathtt{SendNonce} := \left[\mathsf{Fr}(b)\right] \xrightarrow{\mathsf{SendNonce(b)}} \left[\mathsf{Out}(b)\right]$$

$$\mathtt{RecvNonce} := \left[\mathsf{In}(b)\right] \xrightarrow{\mathsf{RecvNonce(b)}} []$$

Unless otherwise specified, terms in facts, such as b, are assumed to be variables.

3.3 Execution

The execution of a set of multiset rewriting rules (a.k.a. protocol) is modelled as a Labelled Transition System (LTS). A state in the system is a multiset of facts. The execution of a protocol starts with the empty multiset of facts, evolving through the application of multiset rewriting rules. A transition in the LTS is performed by applying a *ground* instance of a transition rule, which is obtained via substitution. Formally, the application of a rule requires substituting each variable in the rule with a ground term, where a ground term is any element of $\mathcal{T}_{\Sigma}$ and a *substitution* is a function $\sigma \colon \mathcal{V} \to \mathcal{T}_{\Sigma}(\mathcal{V})$ from variables to terms that is type-preserving, i.e. $(\sigma(x) = y \wedge x \colon s) \implies y \colon s$. For example, given a term

x: *fresh*, an instantiation of the **SendNonce** rule is the following, where $b1$: *fresh* and $b1 \in \mathcal{T}_\Sigma$:

$$[\mathsf{Fr}(b1)]\xrightarrow{\mathsf{SendNonce(b1)}}[\mathsf{Out}(b1)]$$

The rule is applicable if the current system state contains all facts in the premises of the rule. In the example above, the rule can only be applied if there exists a fact $\mathsf{Fr}(b1)$ in the current state. It is worth mentioning that, for fresh values, TAMARIN has a built-in rule that generates facts of the type $\mathsf{Fr}(x)$, which are treated as unguessable for an adversary. An example of an execution of the two rule examples above is as follows, where the first two steps consists of adding fresh values by using TAMARIN's built-in rule.

$$\emptyset^\sharp \rightarrow \{|\mathsf{Fr}(b1)|\} \rightarrow \{|\mathsf{Fr}(b1), \mathsf{Fr}(b2)|\} \xrightarrow{\mathsf{SendNonce(b2)}}$$

$$\{|\mathsf{Fr}(b1), \mathsf{Out}(b2)|\} \xrightarrow{\mathsf{SendNonce(b1)}} \{|\mathsf{Out}(b1), \mathsf{Out}(b2)|\}$$

Without formalising how the LTS transitions, we note that the application of a rule modifies the current state as follows. *Linear* facts in the premise are removed from the state, *persistent* facts are kept in the state, and facts in the conclusion of the rule are added to the state. The distinction between linear and persistent facts is defined syntactically by the operator !, which is added as a prefix to persistent facts. In general, linear facts model resources that change over time, such as the local state of an agent; persistent facts model resources that do not change, such as the long-term key of an agent. We will make use of persistent facts in our security model for quantum protocols in the next section.

Often we will reason about the sequence of actions executed in a protocol run, known as a *trace*. Formally, a trace is a sequence of actions $a_1 \cdots a_n$ such that there exists an LTS path $s_0 \xrightarrow{a_1} s_1 \cdots \xrightarrow{a_n} s_n$ with s_0 being the initial state.

4 A Symbolic Model for Quantum Cryptographic Protocols

This section introduces a symbolic model for the specification of quantum protocols as mutliset rewriting systems. This makes the model amenable for automated symbolic verification in TAMARIN. We argue it can be easily adapted to other modelling languages.

4.1 Quantum States

In contrast to classical cryptographic protocols, which rely on the manipulation of bitstrings, quantum protocols rely on the manipulation of quantum states.

The smallest quantum state is a qubit, which in its most basic form is either $|0\rangle$ or $|1\rangle$; each commonly referred to as a *computational basis*. Unlike classical bits, however, a qubit can exist in a linear superposition of both basis, denoted by $\alpha_0|0\rangle + \alpha_1|1\rangle$ where α_0 and α_1 are complex coefficients satisfying the normalization constraint $|\alpha_0|^2 + |\alpha_1|^2 = 1$.

It is useful to think about $|0\rangle$ and $|1\rangle$ as the matrices $\begin{bmatrix} 1 \\ 0 \end{bmatrix}$ and $\begin{bmatrix} 0 \\ 1 \end{bmatrix}$, respectively, which means that an arbitrary qubit has a matrix representation $\begin{bmatrix} \alpha_0 \\ \alpha_1 \end{bmatrix}$. We then obtain a two-qubit system by applying the tensor product $\otimes$ on two qubits. For example, the computational basis of a two-qubit system is $|00\rangle, |01\rangle, |10\rangle, |11\rangle$, where $|b_0 b_1\rangle$ is used as shorthand notation for $|b_0\rangle \otimes |b_1\rangle$. A multi-qubit state composed of n qubits is thus expressed as $|\psi\rangle = \sum_{i=0}^{2^n - 1} \alpha_i |i\rangle$, where $|i\rangle$ is the multi-qubit state $|b_1 \ldots b_n\rangle = |b_1\rangle \otimes \cdots \otimes |b_n\rangle$ with $b_1 \cdots b_n$ being i's binary representation.

Modelling choice. We will not model the amplitude of quantum states directly. Rather, we will model the encoding and decoding of classical information via quantum states. We thus define a quantum state as a pair (id, s) where id is a unique identifier, used to track the creation and destruction of quantum particles, and s the binary string the quantum state is encoding. To control the creation, use, and destruction of quantum states, we define the action facts $\mathsf{QSEnc}(a, id, s, \mathsf{E})$, $\mathsf{QSUsed}(a, id)$ and $\mathsf{QSDec}(a, id, s, \mathsf{E})$ to mark the execution steps where quantum states are created for the purpose of encoding classical information, use, and measured for the purpose of decoding classical information, respectively. The term a refers to the agent executing the action and E to the type of encoding used. How these facts are used will become clearer next, while we describe two popular encoding mechanisms in quantum cryptographic protocols.

Amplitude Encoding. An example of an encoding mechanism is *amplitude encoding* which, given a binary string $s = b_1 \cdots b_n$, produce the following quantum state.

$$|\psi\rangle = \frac{1}{\|s\|} \Big[b_1|0\rangle + \cdots + b_n|n-1\rangle \Big]$$

where $\|s\|$ is the Euclidean norm of the vector $(b_1, \ldots, b_n)$, often called the *normalizing factor* of the encoding. The normalizing factor is necessary to ensure that the sum of squares of the amplitudes of the quantum state equals 1.

Amplitudes of a quantum state can only be observed by *measuring*, which makes a quantum state collapse into one of its basis states. According to the Born rule, the probability of obtaining any basis state $|i\rangle$ on measurement on the computational basis is $|\alpha_i|^2$. This means that, given a quantum state $|\psi\rangle = \frac{1}{\|s\|} [b_1|0\rangle + \cdots + b_n|n-1\rangle]$, obtaining the binary string $b_1 \cdots b_n$ would require the measurement of many copies of $|\psi\rangle$. After measuring $|\psi\rangle$, the probability of collapsing into $|i\rangle$ is $\frac{b_i}{\|s\|^2}$. We would need several measurements to recover all bits of the sequence $b_1 \cdots b_n$ when measuring.

Modelling choice. The process above is known as quantum tomography, which we model as follows.

$$
\begin{bmatrix} \mathsf{QS}(id_1,s),\ldots,\mathsf{QS}(id_K,s), \\ \mathsf{Own}(a,id_1),\ldots,\mathsf{Own}(a,id_K) \end{bmatrix} \xrightarrow[\qquad\qquad\qquad]{\substack{\mathsf{QSDec}(a,id_1,s,\text{‘T’}),\\ \mathsf{QSUsed}(a,id_1),\\ \vdots\\ \mathsf{QSDec}(a,id_K,s,\text{‘T’}),\\ \mathsf{QSUsed}(a,id_K)}} [\mathsf{Dec}(a,id_1,\ldots,id_K,s)]
$$

Where the fact $\mathsf{QS}(id,s)$ denotes a quantum state with identifier id and (encoded) binary string s, K denotes the expected number of copies necessary to recover s, the fact $\mathsf{Dec}(a,id_1,\ldots,id_K,s)$ expresses that agent $a\colon pub$ has successfully decoded s from the corresponding quantum states, and the fact $\mathsf{Own}(a,id)$ is used to indicate that a has the (physical) capacity to measure the quantum state identified by id. In other words, $\mathsf{Own}(a,id)$ establishes who can observe/measure a given quantum state. Notice that both QS and Own facts are linear and, therefore, are consumed by this rule. This models the expectation that quantum states are consumed after measurement. For the moment action facts (those above the arrow) can be ignored; their role will be made clear further below, once we establish how quantum states are created, used and destroyed in a consistent manner.

Random Basis Encoding. A different way to encode classical information within a quantum state is by using Bennett and Brassard's idea in the BB84 protocol [2]. It consists of encoding a bit b in either a rectilinear or diagonal basis state based on the outcome of a random coin c. If $c = 0$ then b is encoded as $|b\rangle$ in the rectilinear basis, i.e. $|0\rangle$ or $|1\rangle$, otherwise as $|b\rangle$ in the diagonal basis, i.e. $|+\rangle$ or $|-\rangle$.

Modelling choice. Random basis encoding satisfies that, without knowing the random basis c, the adversary has $3/4$ probability of correctly guessing b. Hence, the property we wish to symbolically model is that b cannot be learned without knowing c[1].Cryptographically this can be achieved by letting the encoding be then encryption og b with key c. Then, for decoding, one would measure the quantum state on a basis c', which equals to decrypting the cipher text $enc(b,c)$ using key c'. This approach, however, fails to capture entanglement-based attacks [14], where the adversary can reason about the outcome of the measurement without the need to know c'. In other words, this modelling is too strong and risks missing attacks.

---

[1] If the adversary correctly guesses c, it learns b with probability 1, otherwise it learns b with probability $1/2$.

We model random basis encoding as a one-time pad instead. That is, the classical information held by a quantum state that encodes b via a random basis c is defined by $b \oplus c$. And, the outcome of decoding such classical state with a basis c' would give $b \oplus c \oplus c'$. This modelling choice is an over-approximation in the sense that it gives more information to an attacker than its quantum counterpart. Notably, because random basis encoding is neither commutative nor associative, it reveals nothing about c when b is revealed, in contrast to one-time pad where $b \oplus (b \oplus c) = c$. This means our modelling choice may lead to false attacks in the quantum world, which should be accounted for in the verification methodology.

The following rule models the decoding process of random basis encoding, where c' denotes the random basis used by honest agents to measure the quantum state.

$$\left[\mathsf{Fr}(c'), \mathsf{QS}(id, s), \mathsf{Own}(a, id)\right] \xrightarrow{\mathsf{QSDec}(a,id,s,\text{'R'}),\mathsf{QSUsed}(a,id)} \left[\mathsf{Dec}(a, id, s \oplus c')\right]$$

4.2 Collapse of Quantum States

Unlike bits, quantum particles collapse after being read/measured. We thus require every quantum state to be given a unique identifier and, once a quantum state is consumed, it cannot longer be used. This means that our model should keep track of the creation, usage and destruction of quantum states.

Modelling choice. We define the action facts $\mathsf{QSEnc}(a, id, s, \mathrm{E})$, $\mathsf{QSUsed}(a, id)$ and $\mathsf{QSDec}(a, id, s, \mathrm{E})$ to mark the execution steps where quantum states are created for the purpose of encoding classical information, used, and measured for the purpose of decoding classical information, respectively. The term id refers to the quantum state identifier, a to the agent executing the action, and E to the type of encoding used.

Of course, these action facts ought to be consistently used within a protocol specification. Hence, we assume each protocol rule complies with the following syntactical restriction.

Assumption 1. *Each rule R in a protocol specification satisfies that:*

- *if R adds a fact $\mathsf{QS}(id, s)$, R adds an action fact $\mathsf{QSEnc}(a, id, s, \mathrm{E})$ to the trace with E being the encoding type and a the agent creating the quantum state.*
- *if R contains a fact $\mathsf{QS}(id, s)$ either in its premise or conclusion, R adds an action fact $\mathsf{QSUsed}(a, id)$ to the trace.*
- *if R consumes a fact $\mathsf{QS}(id, s)$, R adds an action fact $\mathsf{QSDec}(a, id, s, \mathrm{E})$ to the trace.*

It is worth noting that, in our security model, we are restricting the creation and measurement of quantum states to be made solely for the purpose of encoding and decoding classical information. This makes the model simpler without preventing us from modelling the protocols we are interested in.

Definition 1 (Measurement-collapse property). *A trace $\tau_1 \cdots \tau_n$ is said to satisfy the measurement-collapse property if, for every $i \in \{1, \ldots, n\}$, all the following conditions hold.*

- $\mathsf{QSDec}(a, id, s, \mathrm{E}) \in \tau_i \implies \nexists j > i\colon \mathsf{QSUsed}(b, id) \in \tau_j$, *i.e. consumed quantum states cannot longer be used.*
- $\mathsf{QSEnc}(a, id, s, \mathrm{E}) \in \tau_i \implies \nexists j < i\colon \mathsf{QSUsed}(b, id) \in \tau_j$, *i.e. quantum states cannot be used before their creation.*

4.3   Quantum Communication

We model a quantum channel as the transfer of ownership of a quantum state. The fact $\mathsf{QSOut}(a, id)$ denotes the sending of a quantum state id owned by agent a. The change of ownership is established by the following rule.

$$\left[\mathsf{Own}(a, id), \mathsf{QSOut}(a, id)\right] \xrightarrow{\mathsf{QSUsed}(a,id),\mathsf{QSTransfer}(a,b,id),} \left[\mathsf{Own}(b, id), \mathsf{QSIn}(b, id)\right]$$

The rule allows for the recipient b to be any agent, letting the *network* decide where and when to route the message. Once the rule is executed, the fact $\mathsf{QSIn}(b, id)$ can be used by b to receive the identifier id.

4.4   Non-cloning Theorem

A key property of quantum particles is that they cannot be cloned. We model the non-cloning theorem by making the ownership relation injective. That is, at any point of an execution trace no two agents can simultaneously observe the same quantum state.

Definition 2 (Non-cloning restriction). *A trace $\tau_1 \cdots \tau_n$ is said to be correct with respect to the non-cloning restriction if, for every $i \in \{1, \ldots, n\}$,*

$$\mathsf{QSUsed}(b, id) \in \tau_i \implies$$
$$(\exists j < i\colon \mathsf{QSEnc}(b, id, s, \mathrm{E}) \in \tau_j \vee \mathsf{QSTransfer}(a, b, id) \in \tau_j)$$
$$\wedge\, \forall k \in \{j + 1, \ldots, i\}\colon \mathsf{QSUsed}(c, id) \in \tau_k \implies c = b$$

In words, a quantum state can exclusively be used by the agent who owns it.

4.5   Entanglement and the Bell Basis

One of the most striking features of quantum mechanics is *entanglement,* a phenomenon in which quantum states exhibit correlations that persist regardless of spatial separation. A quantum state is said to be *entangled* if it cannot be factored into a product of other quantum states. For two-qubit systems, an important set of entangled states is the *Bell basis,* which consists of the following four maximally entangled states:

$$|\Phi^+\rangle = \frac{1}{\sqrt{2}}(|00\rangle + |11\rangle)$$

$$|\Phi^-\rangle = \frac{1}{\sqrt{2}}(|00\rangle - |11\rangle)$$

$$|\Psi^+\rangle = \frac{1}{\sqrt{2}}(|01\rangle + |10\rangle)$$

$$|\Psi^-\rangle = \frac{1}{\sqrt{2}}(|01\rangle - |10\rangle).$$

These states exhibit perfect correlations: if two parties, Alice and Bob, each hold one qubit of a shared Bell state and one of them performs a measurement, the outcome immediately determines the result of the other party's measurement, even if they are separated by a large distance. This fundamental property is the basis for quantum communication protocols such as quantum teleportation.

Modelling choice. We let protocol participants, including the adversary, entangle qubits they own. In our model, we let the fact $\mathsf{Entangled}(id_1, id_2)$ establishes that two quantum states $\mathsf{QS}(id_1, s_1)$ and $\mathsf{QS}(id_2, s_2)$ are entangled. And, crucially, we require that if $\mathsf{Entangled}(id_1, id_2)$, then both quantum states decode the same information.

Definition 3 (Entanglement restriction).   *A trace $\tau_1 \cdots \tau_n$ is said to be correct with respect to entanglement if, for every $i, j, k \in \{1, \ldots, n\}$,*

$$\mathsf{QSDec}(a_1, id_1, s_1, \mathsf{E}_1) \in \tau_i, \mathsf{QSDec}(a_2, id_2, s_2, \mathsf{E}_2) \in \tau_j,$$
$$\mathsf{Entangled}(id_1, id_2) \in \tau_k \implies s_1 = s_2$$

In this way, we ensure perfect correlation between the measurement/decoding performed on both quantum states.

The following rule models the creation of entangled quantum states.

$$\left[\mathsf{QS}(id_1, s), \mathsf{Own}(a, id_1), \mathsf{Fr}(id2)\right] \xrightarrow{\begin{array}{c}\mathsf{Entangled}(id_1, id_2),\\ \mathsf{QSEnc}(a, id_2, s),\\ \mathsf{QSUsed}(a, id_1),\\ \mathsf{QSUsed}(a, id_2),\end{array}} \left[\begin{array}{l}\mathsf{QS}(id_1, s), \mathsf{QS}(id_2, s),\\ \mathsf{Own}(a, id_1), \mathsf{Own}(a, id_2),\\ !\mathsf{Entangled}(a, id_1, id_2),\end{array}\right]$$

4.6   The Threat Model

We consider an adversary in full control of the network, with the capacity to intercept, block, inject and modify messages. In the case of classical information, the adversary cannot decrypt messages without knowing the decryption key, nor can guess the random values generated by honest agents. In the case of quantum information, the adversary is restricted by the non-theorem cloning and can only decode information as established by the decoding rules.

To ensure the adversary is given the same power as the protocol participants to manipulate quantum states, we should ensure that, for each encoding/decoding rule, there exists an identical rule that can be used by the adversary. For example, to let the adversary decode quantum states that have been created via random basis encoding, we provide the adversary with the following rule.

$$\left[\mathsf{Dishonest}(a), \mathsf{QS}(id, s), \mathsf{Own}(a, id)\right] \xrightarrow{\substack{\mathsf{QSDec}(a,id,s,\text{`R'}),\\ \mathsf{QSUsed}(a,id),}} \left[!\mathsf{Dec}(a, id, s), \mathsf{Out}(s)\right]$$

Where $\mathsf{Dishonest}(a)$ indicates that a is an adversarial agent and $\mathsf{Out}(s)$ establishes that s is leaked. Notice that adversarial decoding does not use a random basis, but the zero basis instead. This simplifies the model, which speeds up verification, without restricting the adversary.

A word of caution. While most protocol verification tools have the adversary capabilities builtin, in our model we are making them explicit via protocol rules. The analyst, therefore, has to be careful on not giving protocol participants powers out of reach for the adversary, unless that is the intention. For example, to provide the adversary with the capacity to intercept quantum particles we use the following rule.

$$\mathtt{QAdvIntersect} := \begin{bmatrix} \mathsf{Dishonest}(c), \\ \mathsf{QSOut}(a, id), \\ \mathsf{Own}(a, id), \end{bmatrix} \xrightarrow{\substack{\mathsf{QSUsed}(id),\\ \mathsf{QSTransfer}(a,c,id),}} \begin{bmatrix} \mathsf{QSIn}(c, id), \\ \mathsf{Own}(c, id), \end{bmatrix}$$

Definition 4 (Security property). *A security property is a statement on the set of traces produced by a set of multiset rewriting rules, including the rules modelling the adversary. In our quantum security model, we restrict traces to satisfy the correctness properties established by Definitions 1, 2 and 3.*

5   Case Studies

Next, we specify three quantum-based protocols within the security model described previously and report on the verification results given by TAMARIN. The source code is available online at [18].

5.1 BB84

Our symbolic specification of BB84 consists of Alice encoding a nonce n within a random basis k. Alice sends the resulting quantum state to Bob. Upon reception, Bob measures the quantum state by using his own random basis r. Alice and Bob publicly compare which bases they used, which allows Bob to retrieve n after learning k. The goal of the protocol is for Bob to learn n while keeping it secret from the adversary. An MSC diagram of the protocol is depicted in Fig. 2.

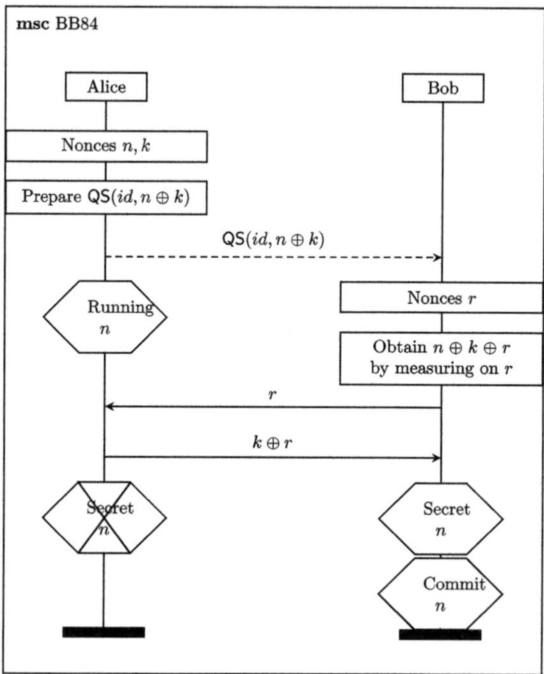

Fig. 2. MSC diagram of BB84.

We verified agreement on and secrecy of n, both of which are satisfied by the protocol. The secrecy claim is made by Bob. If Alice were to claim secrecy, TAMARIN finds an attack where the adversary measures the quantum state she sent while letting Alice and Bob complete the protocol. In this attack, the attacker exploits the fact that the channel is authentic yet not confidential. This means that the channel ensures messages come from the claimed sender, but does not ensure messages remain secret.

One of the strengths of using an automated verification tool is that one can easily verify modifications on a protocol. For example, by switching between non-authentic and authentic channels, we prove that BB84 needs both channels, namely the classical and quantum channel, to be authentic. Should either of these two channels be insecure, then the adversary can impersonate Bob. Another condition we found out for the protocol to be correct, which is not obvious from the literature, is that Alice should transmit to Bob the session identifier, otherwise the network can provide Bob a message from a different session, making Bob to incorrectly retrieve the nonce n.

5.2   Commitment Scheme by Brassard Et Al. [3]

Our symbolic abstraction of the bit commitment scheme displayed in Fig. 1 is as follows. Alice non-deterministically chooses one of the following paths:

1. Commit to $b = 0$ and use the rectilinear basis for encoding a random string $s_1 \ldots s_n$, resulting in $|s_1 \ldots s_n\rangle$. This quantum state satisfies that, when measured on the rectilinear basis, collapses into $s_1 \ldots s_n$. However, when measured on the diagonal basis, collapses into a random bitstring.
2. Commit to $b = 1$ and use the diagonal basis for encoding a random string s. This quantum state satisfies that, when measured on the diagonal basis, collapses into s. However, when measured on the rectilinear basis, collapses into a random bitstring.

Alice then sends the resulting quantum state to Bob, who also proceeds non-deterministically to measure on either the diagonal or rectilinear basis, obtaining a value s'. Lastly, Alice reveals b and s to Bob. Bob accepts the value committed by Alice if one of the following conditions hold:

1. $b = 0$, Bob measured on the rectilinear basis and $s = s'$
2. $b = 1$, Bob measured on the diagonal basis and $s = s'$

An MSC diagram of the protocol is depicted in Fig. 3. In the protocol, we model commitment as an agreement property, where Alice places a commit signal with her choice of b and Bob places a running signal with the value he sees once Alice opens b. To model an adversarial Alice, we introduce a rule that allows dishonest agents to place commit signals. We also allow dishonest agents to establish an authentic channel with Bob and execute the opening phase of the commitment protocol.

The attack Tamarin finds is as follows. Alice entangles the quantum state $QS(id_1, s)$ sent to Bob with another quantum state $QS(id_2, s)$. Then Alice waits for Bob to measure $QS(id_1, s)$. Regardless of Bob's choice with respect to the measurement basis, Alice can measure her side of the entangled pair to the same value obtained by Bob. On the one hand, if Bob measured on the wrong basis, say the rectilinear one, then he obtained a random value s' out of the measurement. In this case, Alice can claim having committed to $b = 0$ and send s' as a proof. A similar attack occurs if Bob wrongly measured on the diagonal basis. If, on the other hand, Bob measured on the right basis, then Alice can always claim he measured on the wrong basis. In that case, TAMARIN does not find an attack as Bob does not place the commit signal.

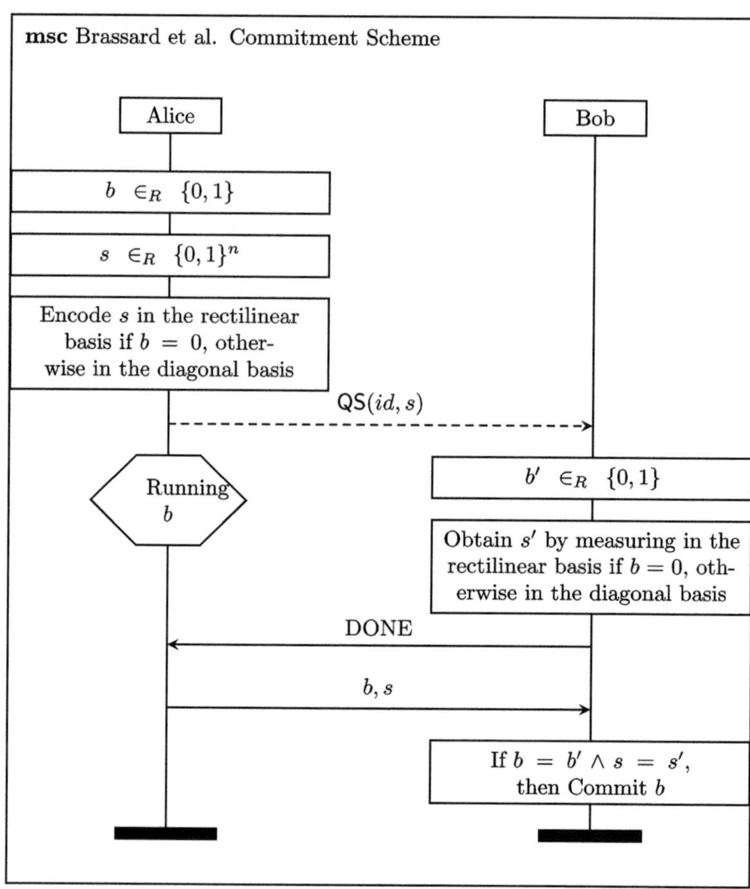

Fig. 3. MSC diagram of the commitment scheme by Brassard et al.

6   Conclusion

In this work, we have introduced and tested a security model for the symbolic verification of quantum protocols. By providing symbolic representations of core quantum operations, including entanglement and measurement, we have created a framework that allows protocol designers to model and analyze quantum protocols with a level of automation comparable to that of classical protocols. Our case studies demonstrate the feasibility of this approach. While challenges remain, particularly in proving soundness and completeness of our framework, we see this as a necessary step for a future in which quantum protocol verification is as accessible as that of classical cryptographic protocols.

Acknowledgements. Rolando Trujillo-Rasua was supported by a Ramón y Cajal grant (RYC2020-028954-I) from the Spanish Ministry of Science and Innovation and the EU, as well as by projects PROVTOPIA (PID2023-150098OB-I00), funded by

MICIU/AEI/10.13039/501100011033 and FEDER (EU), and HERMES, funded by INCIBE and the EU's NextGenerationEU/PRTR.

Disclosure of Interests. The authors have no competing interests to declare that are relevant to the content of this article.

References

1. Abulkasim, H., Mashatan, A., Ghose, S.: Security improvements for privacy-preserving quantum multiparty computation based on circular structure. Quantum Inf. Process. **21**(1), 25 (2022). https://doi.org/10.1007/s11128-021-03357-w
2. Bennett, C.H., Brassard, G.: Quantum cryptography: public key distribution and coin tossing. Theor. Comput. Sci. **560**, 7–11 (2014). https://doi.org/10.1016/j.tcs.2014.05.025, https://www.sciencedirect.com/science/article/pii/S0304397514004241
3. Brassard, G., Crepeau, C., Jozsa, R., Langlois, D.: A quantum bit commitment scheme provably unbreakable by both parties. In: Proceedings of 1993 IEEE 34th Annual Foundations of Computer Science. pp. 362–371 (1993). https://doi.org/10.1109/SFCS.1993.366851
4. Deng, Y., Feng, Y.: Open Bisimulation for Quantum Processes. In: Baeten, J.C.M., Ball, T., de Boer, F.S. (eds.) TCS 2012. LNCS, vol. 7604, pp. 119–133. Springer, Heidelberg (2012). https://doi.org/10.1007/978-3-642-33475-7_9
5. Feng, Y., Duan, R., Ji, Z., Ying, M.: Probabilistic bisimulations for quantum processes. Inf. Comput. **205**(11), 1608–1639 (2007). https://doi.org/10.1016/j.ic.2007.08.001, https://www.sciencedirect.com/science/article/pii/S0890540107000855
6. Gay, S.J., Nagarajan, R.: Techniques for formal modelling and analysis of quantum systems. In: Coecke, B., Ong, L., Panangaden, P. (eds.) Computation, Logic, Games, and Quantum Foundations. The Many Facets of Samson Abramsky: Essays Dedicated to Samson Abramsky on the Occasion of His 60th Birthday, pp. 264–276. Springer, Berlin, Heidelberg (2013). https://doi.org/10.1007/978-3-642-38164-5_18, https://doi.org/10.1007/978-3-642-38164-5_18
7. Hillery, M., Ziman, M., Bužek, V., Bieliková, M.: Towards quantum-based privacy and voting. Phys. Lett. A **349**(1), 75–81 (2006). https://doi.org/10.1016/j.physleta.2005.09.010, https://www.sciencedirect.com/science/article/pii/S0375960105014738
8. Hirschi, L.: Symbolic abstractions for quantum protocol verification (2019). https://doi.org/10.48550/arXiv.1904.04186, http://arxiv.org/abs/1904.04186, arXiv:1904.04186
9. Khan, M., Aman, M., Sikdar, B.: Soteria: A quantum-based device attestation technique for the internet of things. IEEE Internet Things J. **PP** (2023). https://doi.org/10.1109/JIOT.2023.3346397
10. Kubota, T., Kakutani, Y., Kato, G., Kawano, Y., Sakurada, H.: Semi-automated verification of security proofs of quantum cryptographic protocols. J. Symb. Comput. **73**, 192–220 (2016). https://doi.org/10.1016/j.jsc.2015.05.001, https://www.sciencedirect.com/science/article/pii/S0747717115000462
11. Laeuchli, J., Rasua, R.T.: Approaches to quantum remote memory attestation (2025). https://arxiv.org/abs/2503.04311
12. Laeuchli, J., Trujillo-Rasua, R.: Software-based remote memory attestation using quantum entanglement. Quantum Inf. Process. **23**(6), 208 (2024). https://doi.org/10.1007/s11128-024-04421-x

13. Lalire, M.: Relations among quantum processes: bisimilarity and congruence. Math. Struct. Comp. Sci. **16**(3), 407–428 (2006). https://doi.org/10.1017/S096012950600524X

14. Lo, H.K., Chau, H.F.: Is quantum bit commitment really possible? Phys. Rev. Lett. **78**, 3410–3413 (1997). https://doi.org/10.1103/PhysRevLett.78.3410, https://link.aps.org/doi/10.1103/PhysRevLett.78.3410

15. Meier, S., Schmidt, B., Cremers, C., Basin, D.A.: The TAMARIN prover for the symbolic analysis of security protocols. In: Computer Aided Verification - 25th International Conference, CAV 2013, Saint Petersburg, Russia, July 13-19, 2013. Proceedings, pp. 696–701 (2013).https://doi.org/10.1007/978-3-642-39799-8_48

16. Moulick, S.R., Panigrahi, P.K.: Quantum cheques. Quantum Inf. Process. **15**(6), 2475–2486 (2016). https://doi.org/10.1007/s11128-016-1273-4

17. Qin, X., Deng, Y., Du, W.: Verifying Quantum Communication Protocols with Ground Bisimulation. In: TCS 2012. LNCS, pp. 21–38. Springer, Cham (2020). https://doi.org/10.1007/978-3-030-45237-7_2

18. Rasua, R.T.: Tamarin theory for quantum protocols (2026). https://github.com/rolandotr/quantum-protocols-theory

19. Vaccaro, J.A., Spring, J., Chefles, A.: Quantum protocols for anonymous voting and surveying. Phys. Rev. A **75**, 012333 (2007). https://doi.org/10.1103/PhysRevA.75.012333

20. Yang, Y., Liu, B., Xu, G., Zhou, Y., Shi, W.: Practical quantum anonymous private information retrieval based on quantum key distribution. IEEE Trans. Inf. Forensics Secur. **18**, 4034–4045 (2023). https://doi.org/10.1109/TIFS.2023.3288989

21. Zhang, C., Long, Y., Li, Q.: Quantum summation using d-level entanglement swapping. Quantum Inf. Process. **20**(4), 137 (2021)

Author Index